HENRY AND MARY PONSONBY

...am M. Kuhn's previous book, *Democratic Royalism*, was an editor's
...e selection in *History Today*, and attracted favourable attention in *The
...ator*. His articles have appeared in *The Historical Journal*, *Victorian
...y*, and *The Journal of British Studies*. He is a contributor to the *New
...ionary of National Biography* and a member of the Society for Court
...es, founded by David Starkey, Philip Mansel and others. He is associate
...sor of history at Carthage College in the US and spends part of the year
...UK.

From the reviews:

...ordinarily accomplished ... This is a sophisticated and beautifully organised
...that still manages to read as easily as an historical novel. Kuhn manages
...o bring the Ponsonbys to sparkling life and to make serious and impor-
...oints about the way that government works'
Kathryn Hughes, *The Sunday Telegraph*

...cellent book, instructive as well as highly entertaining and deserves a
...y prize'
John Jolliffe, *The Spectator*

...ows a fascinating new light on the closing quarter-century of the
...'s reign.'
A.N. Wilson, *Critic's Choice, Daily Mail*

...imate picture of the inner workings of the monarchy at one of its less
...oments'
History Today

...grossing double biography'
Sunday Times

...e realities, eccentricities and foibles of the Victorian court this book is a
...highly recommend it.'
Historical Novels Review

...is a good story, excellently told; a combination of serious royal and
...titutional history and deft character painting.'
Country Life

Henry and Mary Ponsonby

Life at the Court of Queen Victoria

William M. Kuhn

Duckbacks

941.0810922

Published in 2003 by Duckbacks,
a paperback imprint of Duckworth Publishers

First published in 2002 by
Gerald Duckworth and Co. Ltd.
First Floor, East Wing
90-93 Cowcross Street
London EC1M 6BF
Tel: 020 7490 7800
Fax: 020 7490 0080
email: inquiries@duckworth-publishers.co.uk
www.ducknet.co.uk

A CIP catalogue record for this book is available
from the British Library

ISBN 0 7156 3230 2

All internal plates courtesy of Shulbrede Priory

Typeset by Derek Doyle & Associates, Liverpool
Printed in Great Britain by
BOOKMARQUE Ltd, Croydon, Surrey

For Lisa Jane Graham

CONTENTS

Abbreviations

AP	Arthur Ponsonby (Lord Ponsonby of Shulbrede), *Henry Ponsonby, Queen Victoria's Private Secretary: His Life from his Letters* (1942).
AVP	Colonel Arthur Valetta Ponsonby, Henry Ponsonby's brother (1827-68)
DNB	*Dictionary of National Biography*
Haile	Haile Hall, Egremont, Cumbria
HFP	General Sir Henry Frederick Ponsonby, PC, GCB (1825-95)
JP	General Sir John Ponsonby, KCB, *The Ponsonby Family* (1929).
LQV	*The Letters of Queen Victoria*. First series, 1837-61, edited by A.C. Benson and Viscount Esher, 3 vols. (1907). Second series, 1862-78, edited by G.E. Buckle, 3 vols. (1926-28). Third series, 1879-1901, edited by G.E. Buckle, 3 vols. (1930-2).
Longford	Elizabeth Longford, *Queen Victoria: Born to Succeed* (1964).
MEP	The Honourable Mary Elizabeth Ponsonby, *née* Bulteel (1832-1916)
MP	*Mary Ponsonby, A Memoir, Some Letters and A Journal*, ed. Magdalen Ponsonby (1927).
QV	Queen Victoria (1819-1901)
RA	The Royal Archives, Windsor Castle, Berkshire
SHL	Shulbrede Priory, Lynchmere, Haslemere, Surrey
SPF	The Rt Hon. Sir Spencer C.B. Ponsonby-Fane, GCB (1824-1915)

Acknowledgements

I would like to thank Her Majesty Queen Elizabeth II for permission to read, make quotations and reproduce photographs from materials in the Royal Archives. Those who look after the library, photograph collection and archives at Windsor, including Oliver Everett, Frances Dimond, Pamela Clark, Allison Derrett, Jill Kelsey and Helen Gray, made it a pleasure to work there as well as a privilege.

Members of the Ponsonby family have also given me much help and taken a kind interest in what I was doing. My thanks go to Lady Ponsonby for allowing me to look through papers at Haile left to her by her husband, Major General Sir John Ponsonby, the eldest son of Henry and Mary Ponsonby. I am grateful to Frederick Ponsonby of Shulbrede for referring me to his aunts, Laura Ponsonby and Catherine Russell, who look after the Ponsonby papers at Shulbrede Priory. They have done everything for this book besides write it. They picked me up from the train, guided me through the documents, gave me breakfast, coffee, lunch, tea, drinks and dinner, talked it over at the kitchen table, encouraged me tremendously and thought of diplomatic ways of criticising drafts, of which they read several. They have been at my side throughout and, though they do not agree with all the conclusions, they are the book's guiding spirits.

Librarians and archivists at Girton and Magdalene Colleges, Cambridge, as well as Bryn Mawr College in the USA, provided access to papers in their collections and gave me much of their time. This book was written in the London Library, the British Library, the University of London Library, the library of Carthage College in Kenosha and the library of Northwestern University in Evanston. I am grateful to the staff of all these institutions for their help and their welcome.

Martin Rynja, now of Gibson Square Books, commissioned this book. Sarah Such and Lucy Nicholson at Duckworth edited it. I am enormously grateful to all of them. It could not have been completed without the support of F. Gregory Campbell, the president of Carthage, who helped to arrange leave from teaching duties. Kurt Piepenburg, the dean at Carthage, as well as members of the Quality of Life Committee, were also instrumental in granting sabbaticals and travel funds. My generous father remains the book's most significant benefactor, as he was with the last one.

The book has taken me to wonderful places and I have had helpful guides in each of them. I would like to thank Douglas Watt-Carter for showing me Flete, Mary Ponsonby's childhood home in Devonshire; Stuart Cleaver, rector of St Mildred's Church, Whippingham, where Henry Ponsonby is buried; Air Chief Marshal Sir Richard Johns, Governor of Windsor Castle, for taking me and a family party around the Norman Tower; Jean-Paul Marix Evans, who now lives in the west wing of Fritz Ponsonby's house at Great Tangley Manor, for his hospitality there; and Mrs J.A. Pateman for her help in locating Ponsonby graves in Highgate Cemetery.

Academic colleagues and experts have helped me with specific questions. I would like to thank Walter Arnstein, Tabitha Barber, Stephen Butcher, Robert Bucholz, Robert Bud, Jonathan and Katherine Clark, Deirdre Godwin-Austen, Tracy Hargreaves, Hermione Hobhouse, Mark Kishlansky, Robert Lacey, Philip Mansel and other members of the Society for Court Studies, Tom Noer and fellow members of the history department at Carthage, Sarah Parker, David Parrott, Kim Reynolds, Ian Russell, James Sack, David and Eileen Spring, Peter Stansky, Mark Studer, Miles Taylor, Lynne Vallone and Yvonne Ward.

Several people did me the kindness of reading through an entire draft, pointing out errors and suggesting improvements. Sheila de Bellaigue, Lisa Jane Graham, Albert J. Kuhn, Marilyn Morris and Frank Prochaska made this a better book, though some of them are still uneasy with parts of it. None of them is responsible for the errors that remain, which are all mine.

Charles and Jessica Anderson, Thomas Lyttelton, as well as Richard and Gabrielle Fyjis-Walker all did a great deal more than putting a roof over my head.

Students in my classes at Carthage helped me more than they know. Some of them also worked on organising my notes and writing the bibliography. In particular I would like to thank Lori Gorton, Joy Hoffman, Rachael Randolph, Rebecca Russell and Caroline Towns. Jane Duchac and Tami Villup at Carthage gave me more adult help and were indispensable in every way.

My friends held the whole structure in place. I hope they know with what tenderness I write their names. Jane Bond, Bradford Brown, Caroline Clark, George Dickson, Gregory and Christina Gaymont, Marla Greenspan, Michael Holland, Nigel and Cressida Hubbard,

Sheila Markham, Marilyn Morris, Emma Riva, John Martin Robinson, Wyger Velema and Pauline Bieringa, Paul Wolfson.

My brother, Fritz, helped me imagine what Henry Ponsonby's feeling for his brother, Arthur, must have been.

My greatest debt is acknowledged in the dedication.

Illustrations

Preface

Henry Ponsonby was Queen Victoria's private secretary for a quarter of a century from 1870 to 1895. For seventeen of those years he was also keeper of the privy purse. He was one of the few people in modern times to have combined the two offices. Thus, he was one of the most important people in the queen's court; although his impulse was always to deprecate what he did and make light of his position. His description of a procession in 1889 is typical. He wrote to his cousin at the Lord Chamberlain's office to say that the queen's granddaughter had just returned to Balmoral with her new husband, the duke of Fife. 'Grand arrival of the Duke and Duchess of Fife today. 20 Highlanders in full Royal tartan, headed by Bigge [assistant private secretary] and me ... in old shooting jackets was very imposing.'[1]

Having been appointed a maid of honour to the queen in 1853, Mary Ponsonby was as familiar with the court as he was. She resigned her appointment on her marriage to Henry in 1861, but remained at the centre of the court's social life at Windsor for another thirty years. She was also active on committees where one does not expect to find Victorian ladies in waiting: she was among the early supporters of Girton, the first college for women at Cambridge, and she served on the managing committee of the Society for Promoting the Employment of Women in London. She was friends with literary figures such as George Eliot and Edmund Gosse. She invited republicans, radicals and high churchmen to her dinner table in the Norman Tower at Windsor. At the turn of the century she wrote or contributed to long articles for journals like *The Nineteenth Century* and *The Quarterly Review*.

As a couple Henry and Mary Ponsonby often collaborated in his work for the queen. He showed her drafts of difficult letters he had to write and she suggested revisions. Their letters to each other when apart are filled with exchanges on the topics that interested them both, politics and royalties, trade unions and duchesses, reform of the army and odd behaviour in church. Mary Ponsonby was friendly with both the queen and with her eldest daughter, the Princess Royal, who later became the Empress Frederick of Germany. This made her useful to both. The Ponsonbys' youngest son, Arthur, Lord Ponsonby of Shulbrede, remembered seeing his father and mother in action.

I noticed that my father would have long talks with her and seem to be consulting her and on one occasion when we were in the Carpenter's shop a messenger from the castle brought her a letter. On the bench with a carpenter's pencil she drafted a reply. The Queen had sent her a letter from the Princess Royal (afterward Empress Frederick) at a time of her constant quarrelling with her son (the Emperor William) and asked my mother how she should reply. As my mother had drafted the suggestion for the Princess Royal's letter she found no difficulty in drafting a suggestion for the reply.[2]

Doubtless this was an exceptional case, but Mary Ponsonby knew the minds of mother and daughter well enough to speak for them both.

The Ponsonbys were both familiar with the inner workings of the Victorian monarchy. Their lives and letters offer a perspective on how it operated in practice that is better-informed than Bagehot, whose *English Constitution* (1867) remains one of the foundation texts for understanding what the monarchy did in the nineteenth century and might do today. The story of their lives hints at a dimension of the Victorian monarchy's attractiveness and staying power that is absent from Bagehot's text.

Henry and Mary Ponsonby are interesting people, not only for the influence they exercised at court, but also for the records they left behind of a Victorian marriage and partnership. The refrain of Henry's letters to his wife is not only a wish to consult her but also a longing to be with her. Mary filled her diaries with reflections on a life in which she had loved intensely, but there was no one whom she admired more, or to whom she was more strongly attached than Henry. His position with the queen, however, meant that they were often separated for up to three months in the year. The ladies and gentlemen of the court moved when the queen moved, but their husbands and wives usually stayed behind. This was a source of distress to both Henry and Mary, though he perhaps felt it more than she did. Nevertheless, they survived these separations and their marriage endured for more than thirty years. Their joint lifetimes span nearly a century. Henry was born ten years after the battle of Waterloo, in which his father took part. Mary died during the First World War, in which two of their sons fought and against which a third made a pacifist protest.

Their children all published books and these are important sources for any account of Henry and Mary Ponsonby's lives together. Their daughter, Magdalen Ponsonby, published a selection from her mother's diaries and letters, together with an introductory memoir, in 1927.[3]

Their eldest son, Sir John Ponsonby, published a family history in 1929, from notes initially collected by his father.[4] Arthur Ponsonby published a full biography of his father, with many excerpts from his letters, in 1942.[5]

These books printed only a small portion of the manuscript sources left behind by their parents. Henry Ponsonby wrote to Mary daily, sometimes even twice a day, during the months of the year when they were apart. This was usually when he had followed the queen to Balmoral Castle next to the River Dee in Scotland or to Osborne House on the Isle of Wight. He was also away from home for several weeks in the spring when he travelled with the queen to Italy, or the south of France, or to visit her relatives in Germany. Except for the occasional letter here and there, Mary's replies to him have not survived. Arthur Ponsonby speculated that, while preserving his father's side of the correspondence, his mother had destroyed her own letters to him.[6] Henry's letters to Mary now occupy 33 boxes in the Royal Archives.[7] A series of his official papers also survive in the Royal Archives, given to the sovereign by Arthur Ponsonby after he completed his 1942 biography of his father.[8]

In addition to these papers, his descendants have preserved Henry Ponsonby's diaries and some of his unofficial letters. Important diaries of Mary Ponsonby survive, as do her letters to and from friends and family. She also left behind published articles, manuscripts for several articles that were not published, artwork and photograph albums. Neither historians nor biographers have much consulted these materials, except for the light they shed on specific problems. For example, Elizabeth Longford made good use of the Ponsonby letters for her 1964 biography of Queen Victoria.[9]

What this biography attempts is different. Its aim is to describe the quality of the Ponsonbys' lives together, the activities of their lives apart, and some of their typical attitudes to the monarchy. The queen paid their salary and lent them their houses; her court provided the atmosphere in which they lived their lives as well as all their best stories at dinner. Those curious about the monarchy's future now may be interested to know what these two insiders of several generations ago thought of the institution to which they devoted their lives.

The descendants of Queen Victoria have sometimes been uneasy about the Ponsonbys' irreverence. King Edward VII disapproved of what he guessed was Mary Ponsonby's participation in the writing of a 1901 article about his mother. King George V did not like one of their sons, Fritz Ponsonby, bringing out a book on his aunt and Fritz's godmother, the Empress Frederick.[10] King George VI and his mother, Queen Mary, were distressed by what Arthur Ponsonby proposed to publish in the 1942 biography of his father. The feeling one gets from reading through their papers today, however, is that the Ponsonbys' attitude to the throne, their particular combination of loyalty and laughter, suggests one way forward for understanding the appeal of the modern monarchy.

Chapter 1

Starting in the Middle

c. 1870-73

Windsor Castle is arranged along a steep slope above the River Thames. Seen from a distance it seems to be all on one massive level. Enter the lower ward of the castle through the Henry VIII gate, however, and it quickly becomes clear that there is quite a hill to climb before you reach the upper ward where the state and private apartments are to be found. The Norman Tower is high up on the hill at the entrance to the upper ward. It stands alongside the Round Tower, the highest point of the castle. Go through a gateway under the Norman Tower and its entrance is on the right. It is a large, self-contained house within the walls of the castle; its three principal rooms have windows that overlook the dry moat of the Round Tower, which serves as the garden of the Norman Tower. From the rooms over the gateway there is a commanding view over what was once countryside, but is now the suburban sprawl of Slough, though the chapel at Eton and the green riverbanks remain the same as they were more than a century ago. A warren of smaller rooms at the back of the Norman Tower look out on the central quadrangle of the castle and on to the windows of the apartments inhabited by the royal family. There are snug rooms for reading and writing, as well as big rooms for dining, sitting and talking. The different staircases and corridors ranging off in odd directions are enough to baffle weak-kneed guests, as well as to delight children.

Snapdragon on the Broken Parapet

This was the house the Ponsonbys moved into in the summer of 1870. It was a grace and favour residence that went with Henry Ponsonby's new appointment as private secretary to the queen and was to be their home for twenty-five years. It left a distinct impression on children and visiting friends alike: A.C. Benson, an Eton schoolmaster and writer who later became a close friend of Mary Ponsonby, never forgot her or the interior she created at Windsor. Benson was a lifelong bachelor, the son of an archbishop and the brother of E.F. Benson, who was the author of a series of novels celebrating their social-climbing heroine, 'Lucia'. A.C. Benson loved the Norman Tower because it was the vision and creation of someone who had herself a sort of towering social confidence. Employing the ornate prose that was his particular style, Benson remembered the approach to the Norman Tower from the drive leading up to it next to the Round Tower and overlooking the garden in the dry moat.[1] 'Little horizontal paths were being levelled along the slope, flowers bloomed engagingly among piled rockeries, trellises dripped with trailing roses ... the process went gradually on, producing the particular kind of surprising beauty which is evoked by a close contact of things young, delicate, and fanciful with things antique, massive, and rude – the snapdragon on the broken parapet ... '[2] It was almost as if the garden were a metaphor for Benson's surprise at what greeted him when he first entered Mary Ponsonby's drawing room. If one were young, delicate and fanciful, too apt to pay attention to dripping roses, one might enter into conversation with the lady of the Norman Tower and suddenly have one's parapet broken. Mary Ponsonby did not tolerate fools gladly and she liked her guests to have some conversational mettle.

Mary Ponsonby's eldest son, John Ponsonby, a soldier who served in both South Africa and the First World War, recalled his mother as a small lady with a starched cap that matched the queen's and well-made hands. Those beautiful hands were happiest when they were operating a blowtorch. She 'made many improvements in the moat garden which is attached to the Norman Tower, but her chief delight was her own workshop which she had erected in the garden. Here she could be found with her lathe, her carpenter's bench, woodcarving tools, blow tools, blow pipes and tools for *repoussé* work.'[3]

The interior of the Norman Tower Benson described as 'a modern civilised house inside an entirely uncompromising feudal fortress. It was approached by a steep stone stairway' and seemed to be 'a labyrinth delved and quarried out of a mass of craggy rocks. The deepset windows, the narrow winding passages ... were like the linked excavations of a mine; and the surprise was to find a cheerful interior, curtained and carpeted, full of books and pictures ... '[4] All the family were great readers; most of them were accomplished writers too. Once again Benson's 'uncompromising feudal fortress' hints at the exacting conversations entered into there, and the way in which entrance to the Ponsonby drawing room was barred to those who were not adept with words.

Another writer who came to love the Norman Tower as a refuge on

Sundays from Eton was Mary Ponsonby's nephew Maurice Baring. In his autobiography he remembered his aunt's rooms over the gateway. She

> had discovered and laid bare the stone walls of two octagonal rooms in the tower which had been prisons in the olden times for State prisoners, and she had left the walls bare. There were on them inscriptions carved by the prisoners. She had made these two rooms her sitting rooms, and they were full of books, and there was a carpenter's bench in one of these rooms, with a glass of water on it ready for painting.[5]

That Mary Ponsonby should choose these state prisons, with their inscriptions carved in the walls by royalists imprisoned during the Commonwealth, is further evidence of her slightly morbid and waspish sense of humour. They were in fact among the best rooms in the house. To call them 'the prisons' was a characteristic Ponsonby inversion of the truth designed to raise a smile.

The composer Ethel Smyth had a similar impression of Mary Ponsonby's decoration of the Norman Tower. A feminist, a political activist and a larger-than-life personality full of exaggerated remarks and unsinkable enthusiasms, Smyth developed a crush on Mary Ponsonby. Although her feeling was never quite reciprocated, she nevertheless had an important and affectionate place in Mary Ponsonby's later life.

> The Prisons [Smyth wrote] became Lady Ponsonby's sanctum and the extraordinarily characteristic furniture included a tool table with a glass of water on it ready for painting. In fact there were facilities for 'occupations', as the family used to call them, all over the house; in her bedroom window an easel at which she often painted, in another little room a table sacred to silver *repoussé* work, and books, books, books everywhere.[6]

The Norman Tower may have been a grace and favour residence, but its decorations and equipment were as unconventional as the couple who moved in during the summer of 1870. The lady of the house liked her carpentry bench as much as her watercolours. Her husband would have increasingly less time for leisure in the round reading room of the British Museum, a regular haunt when he was simply an equerry, but he could still make his home in book-lined rooms.

*

Henry Ponsonby was a quiet man with a disarming sense of humour quite different from his wife's. A nervous official who came to Windsor to meet the queen would find Ponsonby wearing a frayed tailcoat and elastic-sided boots. Ponsonby would give the man a warm welcome and then make some unexpected remark that would make him laugh and forget his nervousness as he was being ushered in to meet the sovereign. When he was at home, though, it was Ponsonby's turn to laugh. The centre of the Norman Tower was the dinner table. Arthur Ponsonby, the couple's youngest son, described his father's enjoyment of the family circle in *Henry Ponsonby*.

> He was not loquacious himself but while seemingly inattentive to much of the children's talk, punctuated as it was with special words and expressions invented by his daughters, he would quietly use the very words afterwards as if they were part of the English language. He would smile at the recital of events and a story or the imitation of someone by one of them might make his face redden and the tears flow … The children much preferred having their parents present to being left to themselves. So when, as frequently happened at Windsor, sometimes at almost the last moment, the announcement was made 'Papa and Mama are dining with the Queen,' there was a chorus of protest expressed with great volubility by the children and sympathetically shared by the parents. When they returned the children insisted on an account of all that happened. This was apt to go on late till their father put an end to it by saying 'I think we had better go and lie down for ten minutes.'[7]

The children's wanting to have their parents always with them and Henry Ponsonby's joke about going to bed at night for nothing more than a ten-minute nap is reflected in another of Arthur Ponsonby's works, although he never published this fragment of his autobiography. It dwells more on his relationship with his mother. Arthur was uninterested in her public persona; if anything he was intimidated by his mother's appearance when she was about to leave to attend a meeting or a party. The 'glimpses I caught of my mother when she was booted and spurred for public intercourse made me rather shy. I quite recognised how she could shine but it did not interest me. I was always longing for her to put on an old hat and come off with me to some occupation where I could have her all to myself.'[8] He conceded that he was jealous and that competing 'with amusingly loquacious sisters and brothers' resulted in his sometimes having 'recourse to lazy silence'.[9] None of the children, however, was allowed to mope about the house. Doing 'occupations' was something his mother

> always insisted upon. Whether it was drawing, music, carpentering, reading or cleaning out a cupboard or even any childish pursuit which we

might invent she was there to help. But wandering about doing nothing was strictly forbidden. This for all five of us ... We were each given a little table in various corners of the room for our 'occupations'. They were called offices. In one of these situated behind an upright piano on a small deal table covered with scarlet turkey twill I can remember really working at something.[10]

Sometimes Arthur worked together with his mother hammering away designs on metal or silver, what they called *repoussé* work. He remembered producing an 'inconsiderable' silver tray, but he learned at the same time 'endeavour was more important than accomplishment'.[11]

Word play, hobbies sent up as 'office' work, love between parents and children communicated through shared jokes, and the demands of Henry Ponsonby's other office with the queen often requiring one or both parents to slip away at dinner: these were the principal hallmarks of Ponsonby family life in the 1870s. The other characteristic of their lives together was a taste for discussion and argument. Magdalen Ponsonby said that her mother 'loved controversies and arguments, whether they were political, religious or scientific: a real battle of wits was to her like a breath of fresh air and satisfied her innate sporting instinct and love of adventure'.[12] Neither of the parents was much interested in the blood sports traditional among country families, but both enjoyed a spirited debate, which could be frightening to an outsider. A.C. Benson reported that Mary Ponsonby was the more forbidding partner in conversation, while her husband had a deft touch for putting people at their ease.

What she said was often critical, and could even be contemptuous; but it was always an impersonal contempt, and she was never either peevish or petulant. The truth was that she played the game with great zest, and with a real desire for getting at the truth of opinions; and just as in football a player may sometimes spill an opponent, no resentment is felt so long as the collision is incidental damage and not intentional injury. One was always conscious of her enjoyment and good-humour, and of a friendliness that was increased rather than diminished by honest disagreement.[13]

The children shared their parents' love of muscular debate. Their private family taste was at one with a great public tradition, for this was an era when parliamentary debate was at its prime. Politicians stood on their feet until two or three o'clock in the morning at Westminster and their speeches were reported word for word in the columns of *The*

Times. These same men came regularly to Windsor, walking under the gateway of the Norman Tower, seeing the queen and calling upon the Ponsonbys as well. It was a time when people were convinced that political debate mattered; and that confidence in parliamentary democracy was a small but significant underpinning of the debates at the family dinner table.

The correspondence between husband and wife carries on in much the same vein as the argumentative, jokey tone of the table. The difficulty in reconstructing their conversation is that many more of his letters and papers have survived than hers. Henry Ponsonby wrote his wife a daily letter when he was away with the queen at Balmoral or Osborne or on the continent. Often he was away for as many as three months in the year or even more. Usually Mary remained behind at Windsor, though in later years the queen lent them a house on the estate at Osborne during her stay there in January and in the summer months. More rarely they were given a place near Balmoral as well. With only a few exceptions, Mary Ponsonby's replies to her husband's letters have not survived. Whether she destroyed her side of the correspondence after his death, thinking it embarrassing or trivial or uninteresting, or whether it was lost in some other way, is unclear. Still, his letters are so regular and numerous, often making reference to arguments or ideas she has raised in her letters, that it is not hard to know the subjects that usually interested them both or to sense the deep affection between the correspondents.[14]

Being separated from his wife made Henry Ponsonby unhappy: his love for her is one constant theme of the correspondence. He was honoured to serve the queen, and nearly always had work nearby to keep him busy, but he felt deeply that time away from his wife was precious time lost. He wrote from Osborne in 1873, having just parted from her:

> Your letter with my things just arrived and I have a fit of emotions reading your dear dear words and don't know how to tell you how very very much I treasure them. Everything in my life is bound up so entirely with you that I can see and hear nothing but what is connected with you, and makes me think of you, which I do at every moment ... This makes it so severe to be dragged away from you so continually for I feel it is lost life. While as long as I am close to you all is happiness and joy to me.[15]

The letters give the impression that he was the more ardent, perhaps the more sentimental of the two. He told her in another letter that he had been reading an article about married life in *The Saturday Review* that claimed that wives could be too affectionate towards their husbands. Henry Ponsonby said that with them, it was the reverse. 'One thing is clear. You do not harass me by excess of petting. That you leave to me to do. But then there is this difference between me and the husband described in the *Saturday* that the fever of my passion has not subsided, quite the contrary, it has increased ...'[16] Mary Ponsonby certainly enjoyed her independence and perhaps sometimes rather liked the opportunities to develop her own friendships and interests that his absences provided.

Still, these physical absences produced the letters that make this biography possible. What comes across most clearly in them is exactly what the Ponsonbys' children and friends remembered about the Norman Tower. They were two people inhabiting an ancient and apparently unyielding building, who were nevertheless shaping it to suit their own intellectual tastes. They both loved the rough and tumble of political debate; they were both old hands in the reception rooms of the castle where debate was forbidden and a wry remark worked better than reference to that morning's leader in *The Times*. They both appreciated the absurdity of a life lived in castles and palaces, but neither of them for a minute underrated the opportunities that arose for contact with politicians that their position furnished.

Statesman and 'Lacquey'

The working routine of the royal year was highly predictable. The queen spent the autumn in Balmoral, arriving in late August. She enjoyed herself so much in the north that she sometimes did not go south again until it started snowing in November. Autumn in Scotland was followed by a month or so at Windsor until the queen de-camped to Osborne for Christmas and the first two months of the New Year. She came back to Windsor for a few months in the spring, often taking a holiday abroad in March, when she would go to Italy or the south of France, as well as calling on German relations. It was Balmoral again in May, back to Windsor for at least a part of June, Osborne in July and August. Except for a month's leave, which he usually took in September or October, Henry Ponsonby was in constant attendance on the queen, seven days a week. The office was not large. Until 1878 his senior and only colleague was Sir Thomas Biddulph, the keeper of the privy purse. Two clerks at Buckingham Palace and one additional clerk at Osborne assisted them, though the clerks rarely or never saw the queen. After

Biddulph's death, the queen asked Ponsonby to be both private secretary and keeper of the privy purse. Two young men were appointed to assist him and attend the queen, Arthur Bigge and Fleetwood Edwards.

When Ponsonby was promoted from equerry to the queen's private office in 1870, he found the contrast from his previous routine to be great. As an officer in the Grenadier Guards he had a good deal of leave, and whether inspecting men, attending a court martial, or participating in a field exercise, the duties were not time consuming. There was still plenty of time for the three months in the year that he attended the queen as one of her four equerries. Even the equerry's duty, which required accompanying the queen when she went out on a public engagement, or supervising the travel arrangements for one of her annual migrations, involved more time spent waiting to be called than real work. Hence, the term 'in waiting' was often literally true of the household. Equerries, maids of honour and ladies in waiting sat about in their rooms on the off-chance that the queen might ask to see them – which she seldom did, except when driving out or sitting down to dinner.

This gentle pace quickened considerably with the new office. For the first time in years of routine entries in his diary Henry reports himself 'very busy all day' in August 1870. This unusual activity typically combined attention to both serious issues and trivialities, for example, he wrote to his wife in June 1872:

> Today I have done a good bit. Two or three long letters to The Queen on the Yankee business and other things. Then a masterly letter to Lord Spencer on the state of Ireland written from the text of 'something should be said' when the statues were being blown up. A long and important disquisition to Bruce, Home Secretary, who sends a dollop of letters about the Thistle Order but which requires much more information, which I pointed out to him. They propose to make the Presbyterian St Giles like St George's, with stalls and banners. Then I wrote a history of the order of Victoria & Albert and sent it in. Another masterly paper on the employment of the Prince of Wales, rather long, so it won't be read for some days and sent it in and then no end of telegraphing and writing about a new gardener for Windsor, which has given more trouble than all the rest – and now the ball![17]

The 'Yankee business' is the arbitration of a long-running dispute between Britain and the US over damages incurred during the American Civil War. The 'something should be said' is clearly a passing remark of the queen's on civil disturbances in Ireland which she had asked

Ponsonby to pass on to the Irish lord lieutenant, Lord Spencer. Any letter prefaced by Ponsonby with the word 'important' means the opposite and this is his self-deprecating comment on correspondence about the Order of the Thistle. 'Masterly' has the same tone as 'important' to describe his ideas about some suitable work for the Prince of Wales, whom Gladstone was trying to persuade the queen to send to Ireland in an official capacity. 'The ball' is a ghillies' ball, a hunt servants' party, held regularly at Balmoral under Brown's tenure, at which the queen, household and servants danced Scottish reels until late, drunkenness among the servants increasing as the night wore on. Ponsonby hated these evenings, but was expected to attend.

This characteristic combination of letters to ministers and arranging for gardeners is reflected in the words of another private secretary, Michael Adeane, nearly a century later. According to Adeane, private secretary to the queen from 1953 to 1972, who was reacting to the suggestion that the sovereign's private secretary held an eminence similar to a permanent secretary of a Whitehall department in the Civil Service, 'it is no use thinking you are a mandarin. You must also be a nanny. One moment you may be writing to the Prime Minister. The next you are carrying a small boy's mac'.[18] Or in the words of the political scientist Harold Laski, the private secretary to the sovereign must be both 'statesman' and 'lacquey'.[19] This was as true of Ponsonby's day as it was of Adeane's, nearly a hundred years later.

Humbleness came naturally to Ponsonby and he would seize the opportunity to describe himself as a 'lacquey' both because he habitually underplayed his own importance and for its value as a joke. He also hated dressing up and would avoid it if possible. A writer in the *Edinburgh Review*, quoting Alexis de Tocqueville on how dress distinguished Lords from Commons, captured Ponsonby's attitude as well. The *Edinburgh* reviewer, he wrote to Mary in 1867,

> declares all excess of dress is out of place now and quotes a story of De Tocqueville who went to see The Queen open Parliament where the Peers were in their robes, the officials in their uniforms and all the court in the most gorgeous attire. 'When he beheld the Commons rushing in in plain clothes he exclaimed "*Voila le Maître*. The servants appear in livery, the master is above formalities." '[20]

Ponsonby preferred plain dress himself, but playfully acknowledged that his job was nothing more than that of a liveried upper servant, even if it did bring him into regular contact with the prime minister. It is typical of him also to be immersed in the relatively demanding *Edinburgh Review*, the equivalent today of the *TLS* or the *New York Review of Books*, while the other equerries read mainly the daily papers and sporting news.

Henry Ponsonby enjoyed the historical associations of British kingship. He liked, however, to deflate anything that sounded inflated or grandiose. In April 1873 he was working on a short speech for the queen to make in presenting new colours to a Scottish regiment. He told Mary:

> The Queen is going to present new colors to the 79th Highlanders on Thursday next and I am racking my brain for a few brilliant words for her to say. It does not in these days do to say too much about victory, the glorie of our arms, or anything of the Henry V at Agincourt sort of style – and yet a simple statement 'Here are new colors' is too bare and wants a little warmth to give it effect.[21]

He aimed at finding a ceremonial style for the queen that was in keeping with the modesty and lack of display she favoured in her everyday life. The triumphalism and grandeur of her later years, in the jubilees of 1887 and 1897 for example, were developments that Ponsonby disliked and resisted. One of the themes of his work for the queen was his powerlessness over attitudes to the monarchy that seemed to spring up from below.

Having withdrawn from public life following the death of her husband in 1861, the queen was still in retirement during the early years of Ponsonby's private secretariat. Speeches were not much required. Indeed, he even found that correspondence with ministers tailed off, as, during this stage of her life, the queen preferred not to be bothered with political news. To Ponsonby's distress, she was even willing to forgo the convention whereby, when she was away from London, a cabinet minister should be in constant attendance to give advice should occasion arise. The queen did not want to see ministers or entertain them in her house. Most ministers in turn found it irksome to be a day's journey away from London, whether in Scotland or on the Isle of Wight. Some of the old Whigs, grandees who were friendly to reform, allied with the radicals but insistent on gradual, orderly change, were quite content with the fiction that the queen governed. It allowed them to get on with business uninterrupted while the queen was out of the way. Ponsonby was impatient with this. 'The public are not fools enough to suppose that the Queen living up here [Balmoral] alone without

Ministers can be governing.'[22] Ponsonby called himself a Whig, but he was modern enough to dislike their cynicism about popular intelligence and to worry about the future of the monarchy when criticisms of the queen's retirement were being aired on all sides. These criticisms seemed to be given extra strength by the resurgence of republicanism in Britain, fed by the foundation of a new republic in France after the Franco-Prussian War of 1870.

*

Republican agitation in Britain was a short-lived phenomenon of the early 1870s. It tended to focus on criticism of the cost of the monarchy and to argue that a republic would be less expensive. This school of thought worried the upper classes, because it came at a time when the queen was unpopular and the working classes seemed ready for the first time to flex their muscles. The Ponsonbys' curiosity about the republican movement, their keeping in touch with it, indeed their open-mindedness about it, is among their most attractive features. This may have derived partly from a year they spent in Canada in 1862-3 and their travels around America. When they returned to Windsor Henry Ponsonby wrote to his younger brother, Arthur:

> Courtiers are arriving here in readiness for The Queen's coming tomorrow and we are being welcomed home again, but I rather prefer the peace of the last week to it. I am afraid one picks up some very free ideas in the republic, and though we neither of us admit it for a moment one cannot help thinking a little of the smallness of troubling oneself with what this Prince does, or that Princess thinks and yet one does trouble one's mind very much about it.[23]

In the wet Scottish weather, while the other men shot deer, or fished, or sat and smoked, Henry Ponsonby spent the early 1870s in his chintz and tartan-covered bedroom reading radical and republican newspapers such as *Reynolds News* and *The Bee Hive*. He sent the latter paper off to his wife pointing out that one of its letter writers was very close to her own view, which was clearly not unsympathetic to republicanism. Of another printed letter, he said he did not agree, but thought it well written.[24] Edward Cardwell, the Liberal war minister in Gladstone's 1868-74 government, with whom Ponsonby often did agree, told him that he did not 'think much of any republican spirit in this country. The best republicans think that our form of government is a republic.' This was Walter Bagehot's view too: that the sovereign was responsible for so little that a republic had already been concealed beneath the folds of monarchical drapery. Cardwell went on to say, however, that 'all this is well as long as there is a virtuous sovereign. If not there would be short work made of one part of our institutions.'[25] Ponsonby feared that the queen's staying so long away from London, and taking so little interest in performing public functions, were marks against her reputation for virtue. Nor was he the only one. Even his colleague in the household, Lord Bridport, a bluff old soldier with rigidly Tory views, heard that the fairly mainstream *Fraser's Magazine* was running a favourable article on republicanism, covertly critical of the queen. Ponsonby conveyed his distress with the state of things at Balmoral and the separation from his wife by writing to Mary:

> Your letters are the real great pleasure of my life here as I am bored with everything else. And as far as business goes The Queen seems to be gradually dropping out of the very little that She had to do before. Brid[port] even raised his eyes: 'It won't do will it? I hear there is an attack on her in Fraser, eh?'[26]

Mary Ponsonby was usually more to the left of centre in politics than her husband. She was enraged when *The Saturday Review* refused to pay one of the republican leaders proper respect, referring to him as 'Odger' rather than 'Mr Odger'.[27] Henry Ponsonby was prepared to countenance republican and even communist views. Following the short-lived success of the Paris Commune, he took note of the increased prominence of the Communist Internationale in the summer of 1871 and of its leaders, among whom were George Odger and Karl Marx. He deplored extremism, however, and thought that to declare war on capital was really too much.[28] This did not stop him from inviting Frederic Harrison, the author of a republican reply to Walter Bagehot's *English Constitution*, to dinner in the Norman Tower. Harrison had been involved with Mary Ponsonby in a newspaper debate about women's right to work in 1867. Now Harrison and his wife came to dine and do what the Ponsonbys enjoyed most, have some political debate. Ponsonby wrote to his mother: 'We had a dinner last night of the Lyulph Stanleys, Mr. and Mrs. Frederic Harrison (an extreme radical) and Charley Wood, who though liberal in politics is very high in church views and the arguments were fierce and frequent.'[29] The fact that people of all political complexions came to dine at the Norman Tower meant that Windsor was less a bastion of conservatism than of free speech; at the Ponsonbys' very free indeed. Their willingness to entertain and even to espouse radical ideas made them unusual in court circles. Their adeptness at dinner table conversation as well as their keen sense of humour made their unconventionality acceptable to the queen and her court, even when their political views were anathema. Perhaps the Ponsonbys' left-of-centre attitudes also helped to make queen and court acceptable to the representatives of the political left whom the Ponsonbys met both socially and at work. The monarchy's ability to survive depended on the social skills of prominent courtiers like the Ponsonbys: their charm and ability to deal frankly with persons of radically different political views proved that the crown could tolerate dissent as well as contemplate changes in the social and constitutional landscape without alarm. The Ponsonbys came into contact with a much wider social world than the queen could. The people they met in this wider world found these high servants of the queen neither forbidding nor distant, but attractive and approachable. It is hard to sustain an attack on the court when courtiers put themselves out to be friendly and invite you to dinner.

*

The Ponsonbys loved political talk; the queen hated it. Partly because of her temperament, partly because of her position, she avoided conversational conflict of all kinds. Prince Albert and his German adviser, Baron Stockmar, had been among the first to insist that the royal family must be perfectly neutral or impartial. They believed that, unlike her uncles, George IV and William IV, who had generally favoured conservative politicians over reformers, the queen needed to be free of political ties. If she were to serve as an arbiter among contending politicians and attract the support of persons of different, often bitterly opposed views, she could not be seen as an adherent of any particular party. It was also difficult for her to lose any sort of argument without feeling some threat to the dignity of her position. Ponsonby thought she took the ban on political talk a little too far; he reported from Balmoral in June 1871 on a dinner that it was not 'an unlively dinner except that I am quite at the end of my subjects. The only subjects are politics and they are tabooed so that it is most difficult to talk much.'[30] With the household cooped up together for weeks at a time in the Highlands, and politics off the agenda, it was hard to think of something to say at dinner. Even the queen's dogs could be an unsafe subject.

The Queen has bought a new dog and called Bids' [Sir Thomas Biddulph's] attention to it. 'Oh Mum, I thought that was the old dog.' 'Which old dog Sir Thomas?' A question that stumped up Bids who (like me) can never remember the names of the dogs. After much difficulty it was ascertained he meant Corrie, Prince Alfred's dog which always barks after dinner.[31]

While the household studiously avoided controversy, the dogs who came into the dining room with the queen could not always be stopped.

At dinner, or rather at dessert, the two old dogs who are horribly jealous of Rock the new dog fell savagely on him under The Queen's chair. Made the most appalling row. She jumped up, so did Jane [Churchill, a lady in waiting] on which we all rose and Brid[port] and I advanced to the scene with knotted napkins, but the appearance of Maslin [a page] seemed to calm the combatants and after they were severally carried off we sat down again.[32]

Argument was not, however, proscribed among the household when the queen was absent. Here Ponsonby was often on his own. He was the only persistent Liberal, Gladstonian advocate among all the ladies and gentlemen attending the queen. He was in favour, for example, of Gladstone's proposal to disestablish or withdraw the official endowment from the Church of Ireland, which served only a tiny Protestant portion of the immense, mainly Catholic population, and to redistribute the proceeds. In April 1869, he was on duty as equerry at Osborne and had a discussion on the Irish Church with Charles Grey, who was his predecessor as private secretary as well as Mary's uncle. The others were William Jenner, the queen's doctor, John Cowell, master of the household, and Robert Collins, tutor to Prince Leopold. Henry's account of the argument shows how much he liked a good debate, and is couched in his usual tones of ironic self-congratulation.

I do get so bored here when compelled to be in converse. Last night I had an Irish Church row, in which I flatter myself that my tactics gave me a victory. Uncle C[harles] condemned the bill neck and crop, ditto Jenner, ditto Cowell, Collins silent. What they ought to have done said Uncle Charles was to have endowed all religions ditto Jenner, ditto Cowell. I tried to say a word in defence but was crushed by the triumvirate. But I knew them. I knew that though they might agree in the desire to level up it was from quite different reasons. So I put in my knife. What religions would you endow? Uncle Charles said three. Cowell also, but extended it to all Presbyterians. Jenner said all. Very good and would you make rules how the money was to be spent say for religious purposes, or would you leave that to those who received it.

'Mind you' said Cowell 'it must go to support their churches.'

'Stuff and nonsense,' said Uncle Charles, 'let them do what they like with it.'

'Provided,' said Jenner, 'they acknowledge our control, that is to say that no R.C. bishop should be appointed without The Queen that is the government's permission.'

'But' said Cowell 'that would be acknowledging the R.C. religion.'

'Pooh,' said Uncle Charles, 'they won't stand the Queen's veto.'

'Then I won't give it 'em,' said Jenner.

'But you have' said Uncle Charles, 'you give them a lump [sum] and when they have got it they snap their fingers at you.'

'I don't given 'em a lump,' roared Jenner, 'I pay them yearly as long as they behave themselves.'

Ponsonby concluded his story, 'General row and triumph of HP.'[33] He was quite capable of more serious talk on Ireland. He had long experience serving in the viceregal court. Further, he always insisted that the Ponsonbys were Irish because of their connection with the Bessborough estate near Kilkenny, although in fact they were all brought up and generally lived in England. He was nettled by a conversation with Gladstone's home secretary, Henry Bruce, who was 'very bitter against the Irish' and said Ireland was 'unfit for the same government as England'. Ponsonby's reply to Bruce was in a benign, tolerant, Whiggish vein. His perspective was informed by Enlightenment views about the equality of men as well as the new mid-Victorian 'science' of man, elaborated by men like Darwin and Huxley. 'I said [to Bruce] you talk as if they were different men whereas Huxley says they are the same.' Then he undercut the seriousness of his point with a typical light touch in which he has Bruce reply: 'Ah Huxley goes rather far and not quite correctly too I think.'[34]

Ponsonby did not follow Huxley all the way, but he and his wife read him carefully. Ponsonby even sent a note to the *Pall Mall Gazette* pointing out one or two of what he thought were flaws in Huxley's case, probably inspired by the recent publication of Huxley's *Lay Sermons, Addresses & Reviews*.[35] These tastes for higher, drier literature made the Ponsonbys as out of the ordinary among courtiers as their preference for Gladstone's policies over Disraeli's. The couple was split, though, in their favourites among the two men. Henry loved Gladstone's forthrightness, his energy and his willingness to have political conversation, something that his Whig ministerial colleagues sometimes shunned when they came to court. Mary, as her daughter pointed out, 'held strong Liberal views, but was, on the whole, bored with Gladstone's strenuousness and lack of humour, and much preferred sitting at dinner near Disraeli, whose light but histrionic touch amused her intensely'.[36] She had a taste for the gossip and seasoned anecdotes of writer-bachelors such as A.C. Benson and Lord Ronald Gower, a style that Disraeli too had cultivated to a high degree. Henry Ponsonby was a little uncomfortable with Disraeli (and if the truth be known, with his wife's bachelor friends as well). He found it difficult to tell the difference between Disraeli's serious and satirical sides. Nothing could be further from Henry Ponsonby's taste than Disraeli's liking for show, costume and jewellery. When Disraeli came into office in 1874 Ponsonby wrote to his wife:

> I so fully believe that Disraeli really has an admiration for splendour, for Duchesses with ropes of pearls, for richness and gorgeousness, mixed I also think with a cynical sneer and a burlesque thought about them. When he formed the Government he spoke in the highest delight of the great names he had selected for the household offices and the minor offices – 'sons of great Dukes'. His speech here on the Palatial Grandeur, the Royal Physician who attended on him, the Royal footmen who answered his beck and nod, the rich plate, etc. – all was worked up half really, half comically into an expression of admiration for Royalty and the Queen. Yet there might also have been a sarcasm under it all.[37]

Ponsonby was not sure if Disraeli genuinely respected the queen or if he was merely using her for his own purposes. He remained suspicious of Disraeli throughout his premiership. Henry may also have disliked Disraeli because they had one trait in common. A duchess in pearls seldom turned Ponsonby's head – he liked a spirited woman who could hold her own, or indeed trump him in conversation; but he was not unlike Disraeli in enjoying the satirical or burlesque side of the royal family. All his favourite stories revolved around the faintly comic elements of life with the queen. His stories were never disloyal, but he infinitely preferred a joke about princes to a sermon on their virtues.

Disagreement about personalities did not prevent husband and wife from collaborating. For example, in the summer of 1871 the House of Lords rejected the government's legislation to reform the Army. One important provision of this legislation had been to introduce promotion by merit in place of the old system whereby promotion occurred through officers purchasing their commissions. Thwarted by the Lords,

Gladstone's cabinet took the unusual step of asking the queen to abolish purchase in a different way: to revoke the eighteenth-century warrant whereby purchase had first been established. Lord Halifax, another of Mary Ponsonby's uncles, came to Osborne on behalf of the cabinet asking for the queen to take this dramatic step at a time when Ponsonby was on his own. Biddulph was away, and more importantly, so was Mary. Ponsonby wrote to his wife saying how much he regretted her absence as he wanted to consult her about it.[38] Eventually Biddulph sent a telegraph saying that if the queen were asked to abolish purchase in this extraordinary way, there should be 'a clear written minute of the cabinet' or some other 'document calling on The Queen to do so'.[39] This would become one of the cardinal rules of Ponsonby's private secretariat. He insisted that official advice to the queen on important matters should be written down, to serve as a precedent for the future as well as to show how far the queen could act on her own and how far she must rely on responsible ministers. A written document could be produced to show that she had acted on official advice if any subsequent controversy should threaten to bring the monarchy into a political dispute.

Getting advice to the queen in writing, and taking time to consult his wife for a second opinion were two principles that guided Ponsonby's work throughout his career. He wrote to Mary in 1875 when the controversy of the moment was the Prince of Wales's proposed Indian visit, that being in Balmoral was trying, as he wished he were able 'to consult you more closely'.[40] When in 1878 Biddulph died and the search was on for some younger hands to assist Ponsonby, he wrote:

> You are more use to me than a thousand secretaries. You tell me everything. You are my eyes which see the outer world and know what is going on, your advice is worth more than anyone's … To be separated is the unhappiness of my life and makes me often long to give up everything.[41]

His misery at being away from her was real, but it was an advantage to his work as well. Writing to her was a joy and a consolation, and it also clarified cloudy issues in his head, provided a written record of what was happening and enabled him to write more clearly on behalf of the queen. Indeed, one reason why the queen chose him to be her private secretary was for his ability as a writer.[42]

Mary Ponsonby was modest about her contribution to her husband's work. After his death she reflected on the help she had given him as private secretary in an autobiographical note.

Of my share in helping him to come to the decisions which were almost
without exception wise and just, I must speak, lest I should be given
credit for more influence than I really possessed. A great deal of his daily
work was quietly got through every day without much comment.
Anything trifling that happened in the usual Court life, if it was amusing,
he of course told us all of it, and I think sometime how intolerable Court
life would have appeared if the extraordinary sense of humour which he
possessed had been absent. To go on to more important affairs on which
he had to make up his mind as to what advice he would give, he was by
way of keeping these entirely to himself.[43]

Henry was never tempted to titillate a dinner table by retailing a bit of
court gossip. Rarely did he share his knowledge of great events in the
political world, no matter how deeply they interested him. Even his
sisters complained about how little he told them. Mary Ponsonby's
account continues:

If a letter came requiring much thought and care in the answering
H[enry] would write a rough copy and bring it over from his office, and
if he had to pass its contents on with comments and advice to the
Q[ueen], he would show it to me and in nine cases out of ten there was
nothing to talk over ... Then in the tenth instance I might perhaps look
doubtful and ask if this or that was open to misconstruction, and might
not such a word be changed or cut out. He then considered it, was never
annoyed, and if he agreed, tore the letter up and wrote another. This was
the whole extent of my influence. I never remember a single instance of
disagreement or dispute on such matters. It never occurred to me to
meddle or inquire about any business on which he felt obliged to be
silent. He knew this, he knew also that I was not curious, and that until
the moment came when he felt inclined to discuss these private matters I
should be content to wait.[44]

Something about this restrained appraisal of her contribution to her
husband's work does not ring altogether true. She was as deeply interested in public affairs as he was. One can tell sometimes from his
replies to her letters that she was more impulsive, more inclined to a
'forward' policy than he was; at the same time, she could be shyer about
her own abilities. Her friends sometimes noticed the contrast between
her bold attack in an argument followed by an equally abrupt retreat
into silence. It was characteristic of women of her class and generation
to be modest about their talents, but Mary Ponsonby's modesty was
deeper than that and quite possibly a reflection of an inner insecurity. It
may also be a survival of her early Anglo-Catholic phase in which she

repeatedly criticised herself for an unbecoming and un-Christian sense of her own importance.

Although she was usually as discreet a courtier as he was, occasionally she gloried in and capitalised on court connections in a way her husband never did. Had their situations been reversed, Henry would scarcely have been as quick to help in an unauthorised memoir of Queen Victoria after her death, as Mary did Edmund Gosse with an essay in the *Quarterly Review* in April 1901.[45] Mary claimed that Queen Victoria's worry that Mary would sometimes meddle in Henry's affairs was groundless. The very fact of Mary's having written it down suggests perhaps she did wonder sometimes, after Henry's death, whether she had interfered too much.[46]

'This was the whole extent of my influence'

Had she not interfered, Mary Ponsonby would have been a less interesting character. This would have been a book about Henry alone had her public activities and ideas not themselves been noteworthy. The trouble is that much of the information that has survived about her is fragmentary, or comes second-hand, either via the letters of her husband or the recollections of her children and friends. It is clear, however, that labour, and especially opportunities for working women, were of special interest to her. Magdalen Ponsonby remembered that in the 1860s and 1870s

> about the time when the first Trade Union for women was formed, a society for the better employment of women was inaugurated by some keen social reformers of the day. Mrs Ponsonby was one of the most active members of the committee and regularly went up to London for its meetings.[47]

The Ponsonbys also took an interest in labour unrest. The year of the Paris Commune was also a year of many strikes in Britain. In September 1871 they were both closely following a large strike by engineers in Newcastle.[48] While he thought a fair compromise could be struck between the masters and the men, she was wholly on the side of the workers. They had a good-natured dispute about it, though it is clear that she was more sympathetic to the potential of labour to disrupt the capitalist system than he was.[49] She applauded the eventual victory of the engineers, who were to be paid for a nine-hour day what they had previously been paid for ten.

Mary Ponsonby was even more consistently interested in education and particularly in expanding opportunities for women's education. She and her sister organised a school near their childhood home in Devonshire, and she also helped to set up classes for school-age girls in Windsor taught by Eton masters. She sat on the committee founded by Emily Davies to oversee and organise the first college for women at Cambridge, Girton. All this arose partly from a desire to serve: according to Magdalen Ponsonby she had once, in her youthful high-church phase, dreamt of making 'her life really useful by joining some Anglican religious community'.[50] There may have been a connection between her wish to join a women's religious order as a young woman and her long association with Girton as an adult. She liked the company of other women. She enjoyed reading Enlightenment literature on child development and undertaking the education of her daughters. The idea of a sisterhood working together towards intellectual improvement was an idea that had enduring appeal for her.

She was also sympathetic to those who were considered radical in the 1870s for pointing out injustices and inequalities in the civil rights of Victorian women. One such was John Stuart Mill, who published *On the Subjection of Women* in 1869. Mill used an analogy bound to appeal to mid-Victorian liberals who were convinced of the necessity of a free market. He argued that to prevent women from competing for the same jobs as men was to impede the natural operation of the marketplace. If women were allowed to compete, fresh talent and greater abilities would be brought to bear. Better goods and services would result. Mill's book also shed fresh light on the injustice of women who were prevented from owning or managing their own property, which after marriage automatically belonged to husbands. Mary Ponsonby studied Mill closely and even tried (unsuccessfully) to get him to come for tea in the Norman Tower. The Ponsonbys discussed Mill's book, as can be seen in a letter from Osborne in January 1870 in which Henry Ponsonby gives an account of having teased one of his colleagues about it. Francis Seymour, known as Franco, was an old friend of the Ponsonbys. Henry reported:

> Violent row with Franco about Mill's book 'On the Supremacy of Women'. 'No' I said [referring to Seymour's misquote of title].
>
> 'Well it means that at any rate and every sentence in it is irreligious and shown to be at variance with the Bible.'
>
> 'But surely the Bible says nothing of the laws about women's property etc.'

'Ah well, yes it does, and the tone altogether. I haven't read it through but I have read enough.'[51]

Both Ponsonbys felt affection for their opponents in argument and Franco Seymour remained a good friend.

The other great women's issue of the early 1870s was Josephine Butler's ultimately successful agitation for the repeal of the Contagious Diseases Acts. Parliament had enacted the legislation to prevent the spread of venereal disease among soldiers and sailors in port and garrison towns. Any women suspected by the police to be prostitutes could under the law be stopped and subjected to searches to determine whether they were carriers of disease. Not only did this lead to innocent women being stopped, but it also targeted women as responsible for a disease that took two people to spread. Mary Ponsonby followed Josephine Butler's campaign with interest. Henry Ponsonby watched with amusement as the queen's reactionary doctor, William Jenner, spluttered and hissed with rage against the campaign, even going so far as to challenge Butler on medical points and seeing himself, as a result, denounced at one of her large public meetings. Henry Ponsonby's only concern was that Butler and her allies might get into trouble by stirring up big crowds.[52] The Ponsonbys retained Whiggish elements with their radicalism. They preferred enlightened ladies and gentlemen to settle matters by negotiation behind the scenes rather than pressure being put on politicians by popular demonstrations.

A.C. Benson confided to his diary that Mary Ponsonby was 'somehow the best specimen of the *great lady* I know'.[53] Perhaps it was the security that came from an upbringing among the English upper classes that gave her the confidence to be such an unconventional woman. She may have been modest about her own abilities, but she had a vast social confidence. Part of her unconventionality came from her delight in pastimes usually favoured by men. She had a carpentry shop in the Norman Tower, carpentry being a hobby she had learned from her father. Alongside these were other more traditional female occupations. She sang, she danced, she acted in charades and she painted in watercolours. But the masculine element keeps occurring. In Canada she went with her husband into the woods and took target practice with a rifle. She was also a keen pool player: in 1871 when Henry Ponsonby was away at Sandringham with the queen, attending the sickbed of the Prince of Wales, one of the equerries, Dudley de Ros, reported to him with mildly arched eyebrows 'Mrs Ponsonby has been distinguishing herself in the Billiard Room during your absence'.[54]

A faint element of ambiguity about Mary Ponsonby is one of her most intriguing traits. She was great friends, especially in later life, with Ethel Smyth and Violet Paget (better known by her male pen name, Vernon Lee), both of whom would be regarded as lesbians or bisexuals today. Both her son and A.C. Benson particularly noticed her friendships with other women. Benson says in his elliptical but emphatic way that the Ponsonbys were hospitable people 'and many interesting people came and went; but my impression is rather that Lady Ponsonby's intimate friends, at all events in her later years, were more often women than men'. Similarly, Arthur Ponsonby remembered that his mother

> inspired tremendous devotion in women. This seems to have been the case all through her life. The instances I came across I regarded from my infantile angle with unanalised [*sic*] disapproval partly I suppose because I received little attention but chiefly because they took up the time which I might be spending with her.[55]

Mary Ponsonby's having broken off an early engagement to marry W.V. Harcourt in the 1850s because she hoped to found a religious sister-hood adds to the pleasing sense of mystery about her. It certainly completes the image of a daring and bold woman who moved in a cautious world, but who was not afraid to rattle the gold-rimmed teacups.

CHAPTER 2

Henry Ponsonby from Birth to Marriage

1825-61

Henry Ponsonby was born on Corfu, one of the Ionian Islands, on 10 December 1825. His father, Frederick Ponsonby, a younger son of the earl of Bessborough and a veteran of Waterloo, commanded the British garrison there. His mother, Lady Emily Ponsonby, was a daughter of Earl Bathurst, who held cabinet office nearly continuously from the turn of the century until the fall of the Tories from office just before the passage of the first reform bill in 1832. Henry was her first child. His parents lived simple and unluxurious lives: they thought of their public office and its attendant income as a right and a duty rather than as a reward or recognition of merit. Frederick Ponsonby died young, having never properly recovered from war wounds. Emily Ponsonby lived to old age supported by a moderate pension in large apartments at Hampton Court Palace.

Courage, the worthiness of service to the state and a horror of admitting to one's achievements; an assumption that office, income and privileged apartments would follow in due course: these were the principal ideas inherited by Henry Ponsonby from his parents. His father grew up among aristocratic Whig cousins like the Cavendishes and Spencers, reached the rank of major general in the army and was repeatedly decorated for gallantry. He went by the name 'Fred'. He regularly dismissed his part in battle, however significant, as 'of no consequence'.[1] When he got a musket shot in the thigh that just missed hitting the bone during the Peninsular War against Napoleon, he wrote to his sister-in-law hoping his parents would 'not be in a great fuss about this scratch of mine'.[2]

The year after he was born, Henry's parents moved to Malta where his father became governor. A visitor from England remarked that

> The house in which the General lives is extremely small. He and Lady Emily received me very kindly. They are living in great retirement and have carried with them none of the luxuries and very few of the comforts

of life. They have only one servant, a Greek. The dinner was very unpretending and simple.[3]

Emily Ponsonby long outlived her husband, but simplicity and lack of pretension is also a feature of her surviving letters to her son. Never querulous, demanding or overly ambitious for his promotion, she inspired his conscientious, undemonstrative devotion over the whole of her life.

'For King, Read People'

Underneath this love of simplicity and lack of showiness lay a real pride in the family background. Almost every Ponsonby who has put pen to paper has written something about the family history.[4] The tone is often jokey, satirical or irreverent, but a sense of pleasure derived from the family's achievements is there too. Henry Ponsonby's younger brother Arthur kept a diary in which he outlined some of the history of his father's side of the family. The first Ponsonby had come to England with William the Conqueror as chief barber; hence the combs in the family coat of arms. Arthur has fun at the expense of medieval kings when he says that 'majesty' became nervous at the large numbers of people, including the Ponsonbys, putting coronets on their family crests. He mentions the family motto, '*Pro rege, lege, grege*' ('For the king, the law and the people'), but also puts in an aside, 'I dare say the ancestral barber did not care much for law or people, although he probably was obliged to respect the king, or else he might have lost his place.'[5] If Arthur was decidedly offhand in referring to the king, he was equally dismissive of the place-hunting in the family background.

The first Ponsonbys in reliable records were yeoman farmers settled in Cumberland. In the seventeenth century Sir John Ponsonby of Haile Hall followed Cromwell to Ireland, and was rewarded for military service with a landed estate near Kilkenny. In the eighteenth century Sir John's descendants resisted attempts by the Stuarts to mobilise Irish Catholics and return to the throne. They also farmed, acquired more property and sent MPs to Dublin who supported the Protestant Ascendancy and, as a result, were ennobled.[6] In the nineteenth century they were part of a large Whig cousinage who lived mainly in England, producing army officers, members of Parliament, ambassadors and clergymen. Another Arthur Ponsonby, Henry Ponsonby's youngest son, who held office under Labour in the twentieth century, described 'wit' as the Ponsonbys' distinguishing feature, 'a peculiar, apt, racy humour, a twinkle and, sometimes, a thrust which is extremely amusing'. The Bathursts, by contrast, Arthur dismissed as 'one of the dreariest families in the world ... snobbish aristocrats, pretentious and punctilious, honest enough, but without a spark of originality which the Ponsonbys certainly had'.[7] There may be a political element in his rejection of the Bathursts, who were Tories. Henry Ponsonby himself never showed the same *animus* towards his mother's family.

All the Ponsonbys took politics seriously. There is a distinct continuity between the Regency Ponsonbys who were alive at the time Henry was born and their descendants in the twentieth century. The reform-minded Whigs among them supported the great constitutional changes after 1828: for example, the admission of dissenters and Roman Catholics to political privileges formerly held only by members of the Church of England, as well as the expansion of the electoral franchise. This set them apart from many of the landowning aristocracy who resisted such changes. The mid-nineteenth-century Ponsonbys sided with Gladstone and supported his army and Irish reforms. (Many of the old families from the same milieu chose to view Gladstone as a lunatic.) Likewise, Henry Ponsonby's youngest son was a pacifist during the First World War and a leader of the Labour party when such positions were deeply unpopular. Even Loelia Ponsonby, Henry Ponsonby's grand-daughter, who served time as a not particularly Labourite duchess of Westminster in the 1930s and 1940s, liked to point out that the family motto might be translated 'For king, read people'.[8] Scepticism about royal authority and friendliness to sweeping political reforms played a part in the stories the Ponsonbys told one another, and the world, about their family background.

In the era of Henry Ponsonby's birth his family were not unimportant in governing circles. Peter Mandler, an authority on the constitution and high politics of the first half of the nineteenth century, has described the Ponsonbys as part of a 'revived high Whig aristocratic tradition', which was 'cosmopolitan and bent on governing' especially in the 1830s and 1840s. In the years following the first reform bill, they enjoyed an 'unexpected renaissance' and returned 'Whig family dominance' to Westminster. Their power base was Holland House, where Henry Ponsonby was launched as a young man. He remembered making adolescent gaffes at the dinner table among his cousins and celebrities of the day, including T.B. Macaulay, Charles Dickens and Lord John Russell, whose conversational swordplay could be swift and sharp. The Ponsonbys generally had broad church views and subscribed to an old Whig variety of religion: 'inclusive, non-dogmatic, tolerant, spiritu-ally egalitarian'.[9] They may have been quietly aware of their family standing, apart from and above the crowd, but at least they were, in an age of increasing religious earnestness, easy about the creed and circum-stances of those with whom they worshipped. For them the eighteenth-century monopoly on office of their ancestors, the court Whigs who indulged and patronised the Hanoverian royal family, giving them the illusion that they were in control while all important political business was really settled in their own country houses, was very recent. A sense of the right to rule was in their blood. It was tempered only by an upbringing that rewarded individual modesty and punished children for calling attention to themselves.

When the Army ordered Henry Ponsonby's younger brother to Corfu in the 1860s, he found that his parents were still remembered there forty years after their tenure had ended. They were also popular in Malta where their second son, Arthur Valetta Ponsonby, and three daughters, Melita, Julia and Barbara, were born. It was here that Henry and Arthur became best friends as well as brothers. They shot quail and rabbit with their father at a palace in San Antonio, some miles outside Valetta. They stole food from the dinner as it was taken in to their parents and their guests. They adopted Paolo, a boy not much older than themselves who had been chosen to be their servant, as sidekick and companion. They watched the goings-on at their parents' parties where, at one fancy dress ball, Captain Roberts, their father's aide-de-camp, came 'dressed as an old fruit woman with a wheel barrow full of fruit'.[10]

Another young man who paid Henry's parents a visit in fancy dress and who was to play a large part in Henry's later life as the queen's private secretary was Benjamin Disraeli. Disraeli was a camp and charming show-off. He wanted to pay court to the governor who was the brother of the notorious Lady Caroline Lamb; and he arrived wearing a striking jacket, white trousers and a rainbow-coloured sash. Caroline Ponsonby had married William Lamb before he became Lord Melbourne, prime minister and tutor of Queen Victoria. Society knew her as a wild woman who had an affair with Byron and snipped off some of her pubic hair to send him in a letter. Disraeli the social climber regarded the Ponsonbys as a sort of social Mount Olympus, because Frederick's mother was the legendary beauty Henrietta Spencer, hence his aunt was Henrietta's sister, the glamorous, gambling Georgiana, duchess of Devonshire. Disraeli's friend and travelling companion takes up the story where Disraeli in his wonderful costume ... paraded all round Valetta, followed by one half the population of the place, and as he said putting a complete stop to all business. He of course included the Governor and Lady Emily in his round to their no small astonishment. The Governor, a brother of Lady Caroline Lamb, was reputed a very nonchalant personage and exceedingly exclusive in his conduct to his subjects. Disraeli, however, was not dismayed and wrote to his father as follows:

> August 25th, 1830.
> Yesterday I called on Ponsonby. He was fortunately at home. I flatter myself that he passed through the most extraordinary quarter of an hour of his existence – I gave him no quarter, and at last made our nonchalant Governor roll on the sofa from his risible convulsions. Then I jumped up, remembered that I must be sadly breaking into his morning and was off: making it a rule always to leave with a good impression. He pressed me not to go ... [11]

Disraeli delighted Henry Ponsonby's parents because they loved style and talent, no matter what the social background of the performer. Disraeli, who had the words 'Jew boy' whispered behind his back all his life, was determined to have these high-born Englishmen accept him on his own terms. Rather than hiding his difference he made the most of it and the Ponsonbys applauded delightedly. Although their eldest son would have much to do with Disraeli in later life, he never saw the joke as clearly as his parents did. He was never quite sure when Disraeli was making fun of him and when Disraeli was making fun of himself. The brave and serious Henry revisited Malta on his way to the Crimean War in 1855. He saw Paolo and was taken over his boyhood home by the new governor. He would indulge in no melodramatic nostalgia on the eve of going off to a war where many of his friends and acquaintances had already died, however. Instead he wrote quietly in his diary 'I knew most of it again'.[12]

The key to Henry Ponsonby's gravity and conscientiousness as a young man was the unexpected death of his father when he was only eleven years old. In January 1837 the family had been visiting Henry's Uncle William de Mauley at Canford in Dorset. Arthur remembered stopping at an inn in Hampshire as the family was returning home.

> Henry, I and Lilly were the children and were just going to tea in a room up stairs, my Father and Mother being in a room down stairs and just going to dinner, when we heard a scream and down stairs we ran. I remember it as if it was yesterday. Somebody stopped us at the door of

the dining room not before I remember looking in and seeing my Father leaning back in a chair close to the fire. We were taken away and told our Father was dead. I believe he died of heart complaint, at any rate, it was awfully sudden. A messenger was dispatched to Canford and Lord de Mauley arrived next day to help my Mother in her troubles. The body was taken to Canford and my Mother and us left next day for London, posting. We were too young to feel the great loss we had ... I remember our governess a Miss Edwards telling us not to observe or ask my Mother questions when we saw her with a Widow's Cap on.[13]

Henry now became the man of the family, a considerable burden for a boy not yet in his teens. His mother 'was in a dreadful state and also found herself badly off'.[14] She had to give up their house in London, which she could no longer afford. She moved first to Brighton and then to Hampton Court Green where she hoped for grace and favour apartments in the palace nearby that were often assigned to widows of senior officers. The move paid off and in 1838, probably through the intercession of her friend the duchess of Cambridge, Queen Victoria's aunt, Emily Ponsonby was given leave to occupy the largest apartment in the palace for her lifetime.[15] Although Henry's mother was thus established in some splendour, she had to stretch her income to pay for the raising of a large family, for a sixth child, Frederick, was born after her husband's death.

Henry and Arthur briefly studied with a tutor in Switzerland, but ended up after their father's death at a school in Coombe Wood, near Kingston-on-Thames. The school was in a house rented from the duke of Cambridge. Dr Biber, a man who spoke good English but who broke into German when excited, was the headmaster. Arthur described the school, which housed about forty students, as being 'for on the whole gentlemanlike boys, but not good for education, too much was attempted'. When Arthur left, Dr Biber pronounced him 'idle but well conducted'.[16] All his life Arthur was less conscientious and less industrious than his brother, but there does seem an element of truth in his assessment of the school. It was typical of the reckless and chaotic places where the English upper classes sent their boys to be raised in the first half of the century. How young men with polished manners emerged from such violent academies is less clear: there were regular riots at Eton and Harrow before the reforms brought in by Dr Arnold of Rugby began to take general hold.

Though Coombe Wood was a preparatory school, rather than one of the public schools, Arthur's recollections suggest cheerful disorder and the same sort of mayhem that was characteristic of the great schools for older boys. This began at the top. Arthur suspected that Dr Biber 'thrashed' Mrs Biber 'in private'. The French master, a former French officer in Algeria told the boys 'tales of a decidedly immoral tendency'. There was a 'drawing master [who] was quite ignorant of the art, not only could not teach but unable to draw. He had a row with our Macay, a big boy who nearly licked him and he left soon after.' The boys enjoyed playing with fire. They set alight hay ricks belonging to a neighbouring farmer, and on Guy Fawkes' Night, they bought fireworks and built a bonfire. While they were throwing lighted fireworks at one another, one boy who had his pockets crammed with small incendiaries was set alight and had his suit burnt before the fire could be put out. His 'groans all night were fearful'. There were five or six boys to a bedroom and Arthur's greatest friend there was Charlie Wemyss. 'Wemyss was made Page to the Queen, a wonderfully pretty boy he was, got his commission' in the Grenadier Guards, then 'got into money difficulties, had to leave the Guards under a cloud and went into the 17th Regiment. Poor fellow he is now ruined and constantly in debtors' prison and I don't know what he does, as he has no money ... '[17] Life was far from certain for boys from noble families who were not particularly well off.

Henry was considered delicate at a young age. He was not allowed to accompany Arthur to an earlier day school he had attended at Brighton. At Coombe Wood he established that he was not soft, but he did not go in for the crashes that his brother and his friends suffered so gaily. He was older and more solemn than his years, without being censorious of his fellows; this inspired the respect even of young brutes in short trousers. At Coombe Wood Henry had to decide on which of the armed forces he would train for afterwards. There was no question of his going on to one of the public schools or to prepare for university. His father had been a soldier and he would be one too. Emily Ponsonby sent him a letter in 1839 advocating the Royal Military College at Sandhurst. If he did well there, he might get one of the commissions reserved for able cadets and that would save purchase money for later promotions. Henry's mother told him frankly that if he were in a regiment of the line, rather than in the artillery, which he was also considering, 'you may get promotion by interest. Which you are likely to have from many.'[18] In other words, his father had been a distinguished soldier, a friend of the duke of Wellington, and so Henry would be looked after, his advancement assured, if he went into the line.

The early nineteenth-century Army was led mostly by officers who had purchased their commissions. A small portion of commissions, perhaps a quarter, were free. They were set aside for the sons of prominent officers, or of widows and clergymen, or for qualified cadets. Luckily for Henry, he fell into more than one of these categories. Ordinarily commissions were expensive and were more expensive the more exclusive and prestigious the regiment involved. There were regulation prices for each of the ranks. For example, the entering rank, a cornetcy, in a cavalry regiment cost £840 in the 1820s, a very large sum of money in those days. A substantial landowner with an estate of 1,000 acres, putting him somewhere near the top of the landed gentry, might expect an income near £1,000 in a good year. The top rank that could be purchased was a lieutenant colonelcy, which cost literally a fortune at £6,175: rich officers could pay over the regulation prices if they wanted quicker promotions. The future Lord Cardigan was said to have paid more than five times that amount for his lieutenant colonelcy in the 1830s.[19] Only generals were named on the basis of merit. The Guards regiments that formed a sort of bodyguard of the sovereign were the most expensive of all. Here it took family connections as well as money to get one's initial commission. The rationale was that suitable fighting officers were those who had the biggest financial stake in the country and hence the greatest interest in defending it, as well as the family training that only generations of fighters could have. Today, the system seems indefensible and even at the time contemporaries were aware that rich young officers who had purchased their promotions were not always the best to lead men in battle. Corelli Barnett, whose work surveys the whole history of the British Army, is particularly critical of the officer class in the generation between Waterloo and the Crimean War.

> Between 1815 and 1854 the officer corps (a convenient misnomer, because in Britain there was no officer corps, but instead the tight little exclusive circle of each regimental mess) became even more stiff-necked and haughty, rigid in social etiquette and distinctions, and dominated by a hierarchy of birth, wealth, kinship, connexion and fashion. In colonial battles such officers displayed physical courage and iron self-control; 'character' rather than intelligence and professional education.

Henry Ponsonby did not fit this type, though he moved easily among those who did. He himself was not particularly indignant, as most of his fellow officers were, to see the purchase of officers' commissions abolished in the reforms of Gladstone's secretary for war, Edward Cardwell, in the 1870s. Indeed, he was to play a significant role in moderating court opposition to these changes. It is important to see, however, the sort of institution he was entering and the way it would shape his personality.

Henry took his mother's advice and went to Sandhurst from 1839 to 1841. It was his first separation from his brother, Arthur, whom his mother reported as 'looking very lost'.[20] Arthur himself confessed that when his brother left, he wept. The two boys were close; the absence of a father made them more reliant on each other and more concerned to look after each other's future. Henry was a faultless cadet at Sandhurst, winning praise 'for his uniformly good conduct, gentlemanlike manners and general attention to his studies' at the age of fifteen.[21] Did he somehow blame himself for his father's death and was all this scrupulously good behaviour an attempt to punish himself for a calamity with whose cause he had nothing to do? Arthur, by contrast, who followed Henry to Sandhurst, studied less and got into trouble more. He beat up one of the other cadets whom he accused of stealing bread, and it was only by the intercession of his Aunt Georgiana Bathurst that he was not expelled. As it was, the authorities at the Horse Guards prevented him taking his commission for a year as punishment. Henry was so responsible, so correct, so popular among his fellows that he set a nearly impossible standard for his brother to achieve. The only chance for Arthur to survive was to become something quite different.

Henry was a success at Sandhurst, but money was an ever-present concern. His mother told him near the end of his time there that she could not afford the sort of allowance he would require if he were to become a cavalry officer as his father had been. She also thought the Guards would be too expensive and did not like the thought of him 'idling in London', which that service would entail. So she recommended 'a good Regiment in the line. And I am enquiring which is best. I should like you to have a good Colonel ... '[22] Never forgetting the absence of a father for her eldest boy, she wanted him to have a good commanding officer instead. Intensely loyal son that he was, Henry took her advice. In 1842 he was commissioned as an ensign in the 49th Regiment. After two years the duke of Wellington offered him a commission in the Grenadier Guards. He and his mother had both expected it, but it was a high honour nonetheless, conferred chiefly because of Frederick Ponsonby's place close to the duke in the Peninsula. Henry was hugely pleased and determined to live up to the accolade.

Henry Ponsonby revered the duke of Wellington and marked the anniversary of the battle of Waterloo in his diary and his letters all his life. His father had fought in Wellington's campaigns on the Iberian Peninsula and had been seriously wounded at Waterloo. Knocked from his horse by a blow and lying on the ground, a French lancer approached him and asked '*Tu n'es pas mort coquin?*' He then thrust a pike through Ponsonby's chest. Somehow he survived an entire night on the battlefield, and afterwards he made a slow and miraculous recovery; but his health was shattered. His early death on the road from Canford was the legacy of a career in arms and wounds at the most celebrated battle of the nineteenth century. Henry Ponsonby remembered being taken by his Aunt Georgiana to Apsley House in about 1841 to see the room laid out for the annual Waterloo Banquet. 'The Duke spoke a few words to me about his recollections of my father and walked round to where his bust was. My father had always been a great friend of the Duke's.'[23] When the duke died in 1852, the Prince Consort organised the duke's funeral procession. Henry got special permission to march in it.

His Wellington fixation was entirely typical of the age, but it also shows an important facet of his personality. He was a soldier and identified with a soldierly ethic: obedient and honourable, he had a liking for regimentation and unhesitating loyalty to higher-ups. That he was later able to combine this with friendliness to reform, and a willingness to entertain radical measures to abolish traditional elements of church and state is an indication of his flexibility and trust in democratic institutions. He was the furthest thing in the world away from a red-faced Tory of reactionary principles or a clanking Prussian officer with chest full of medals, although he certainly got along with such types in later life. Henry Ponsonby knew when to concede the privileges of rank, family and profession. This knowledge was built on the confidence that came from the great Wellington having regarded his dead father as a friend. Generations of aristocratic office holders in his family background also played their part in telling him that he too must defend the public service. He was not particularly ambitious for public office himself; he only thought that given his birth it was not unlikely that office should fall to him too. He determined to uphold the honour of the public, of Wellington and of the Ponsonbys in equal measure. He was quite serious about this as a young man. It would take marriage and maturity to regard such convictions with a more satirical eye.

Henry Ponsonby came of age in December 1846. He had been two years in the Guards and now inherited nearly £3,000 on his twenty-first birthday as well as £1,200 on the death of his aunt, Susan Bathurst. These were princely sums, but all of the money had to be saved to buy his promotions in the Guards. At the age of twenty-one he had a more potent means to purchase his place: family connection. The new Whig government of Lord John Russell sent out Henry's uncle, Lord Bessborough, to Ireland to serve as lord lieutenant. Bessborough took his nephew along as an aide-de-camp. In those days nepotism was not thought of as an abuse, and if politics had been often discussed at the family dinner table this was considered a qualification rather than a disqualification for office. The appointment to the suite of the Irish lord lieutenant was Henry's first step on the ladder.

Appointment to the Staff of the Lord Lieutenant

Henry Ponsonby's arrival in Ireland coincided with a famine that had begun with the failure of the potato crop in 1845. The crisis continued for more than four years. During this period over a million people either emigrated or died. In 1847, for example, 250,000 died of hunger or disease; 200,000 left Ireland for America. Even after the worst of the famine was over, Ireland continued to experience a significant decline in population from 6.5 million in 1851 to 5.5 million in 1871.[24] The government imposed martial law and suspended civil liberties in 1848 to keep the peace among a hungry people inclined to rebel.

None of this appears in Henry Ponsonby's surviving diaries or letters. He was continuously on the staff of successive lords lieutenant for nine years from 1846 to 1855 at a time of unparalleled distress in the countryside. He recorded very little of it. It would even be possible to form the impression that it was not happening if his letters and diaries alone were relied upon. Instead, Henry made lists of his friends on the staff of the lord lieutenant or in Dublin with whom he talked, danced or had dinner. He lived with the lord lieutenant in the Viceregal Lodge, an elegant, low-slung Georgian house surrounded by trees in Phoenix Park just outside Dublin. Queen Victoria, who visited in 1849 and also stayed in the house, remarked on its view of the Wicklow hills. Henry Ponsonby walked almost every day to Dublin Castle to have luncheon and see acquaintances. He attended balls, levees and drawing rooms. His life consisted of going to parties, arranging transport or copying letters for the lord lieutenant. Meanwhile, a cholera epidemic raged. The sick died faster than they could be buried. Activists inspired by the 1848 revolutions on the continent spoke in muddy towns about expelling the British and organising armed bands to put rebellion into action. Landlords and their agents were murdered in broad daylight. Why did Henry Ponsonby fail to record this? And what impact did the episode have on one who was later to have so much influence on the most prominent symbol of British rule at home and abroad, the monarchy?

The lord lieutenant, or viceroy, was the representative of the sovereign in Ireland. He was nominally in charge of the armed forces, just as lords lieutenant are in the English counties to which they are still appointed by the queen today. In the name of the queen he dispensed hospitality, received Dublin society in huge levees in hot rooms at Dublin Castle and sustained the morale of English office-holders sent out to keep the peace amongst an unhappy population. Although this state of affairs varied depending on the ability and initiative of different lords lieutenant, ordinarily the chief secretary, who sat in the cabinet in London, carried out the real business of ruling Ireland. Henry's uncle died after only a year in office and was succeeded by Lord Clarendon, who re-appointed Henry to his suite. During the crisis of the 1840s Clarendon was an unusually active lord lieutenant. He personally recommended and drafted the legislation he thought necessary to restore order in a country that swung between anarchy and rebellion. The lord lieutenant was always a grandee, whose birth, charm and deep pockets were meant to persuade the Protestant landowners, or Ascendancy, that Ireland was better ruled from London than by returning a parliament to Dublin. This was expensive, and the lord lieutenant was expected to spend his own money entertaining. Clarendon told his brother-in-law that each Dublin season cost him £3,000 a month out of his own pocket.[25] The nickname 'lord loot' referred to the buckets of personal cash required to do the job.

During Henry Ponsonby's time in Ireland attitudes towards government were undergoing a fundamental change. Few politicians thought of the state as merely a commanding display that assured order. Nor did everyone believe, as a radical minority did, that government was something that might improve people's lives while at the same time assuring value for money. In the seventeenth century one of the tasks of the state had been to exhibit splendour.[26] This was part of a world view that earthly governors ought to have divine authority as well as live up to the high standards of rectitude and behaviour laid down in the Bible. In the early nineteenth century the Benthamites and utilitarians had developed a new measure for evaluating governing institutions. Everything should be judged by its results, namely whether it was useful in promoting the greatest happiness of the greatest number of people. On the one hand, this advanced the helpful idea that government should and could improve the lives of the majority by sweeping away corrupt and special interests. On the other, utilitarianism could be a dreary science of government with a dismal aesthetic. Its baleful trajectory leads straight from Jeremy Bentham to the high-rise tower blocks that line the suburbs of Warsaw, Moscow and Bucharest today.

The early nineteenth-century Whigs, from whom Ponsonby descended, took up and befriended these radical utilitarians. The Whigs saw the radicals as having new ideas likely to help them in their struggle to rein in executive tyranny, to protect individual liberty and to get themselves back into office. They wanted to dish the Tories by portraying them as ridiculously attached to outmoded institutions. The Whigs and radicals of the early nineteenth century had already measured parliamentary representation and the poor law by the standard of utility and found them in need of reform. They also had their eyes set on the viceroyalty in Ireland. Under Henry's uncle, Lord Bessborough, and his successor, Lord Clarendon, abolition of the position was under discussion. Lord Althorp, who had steered the first reform bill through the Commons, thought that 'the viceregal office should be abolished since it gave Ireland all the trappings and none of the advantages of monarchical government'.[27] The word 'trappings' is significant here. It has negative connotations suggesting that viceregal ceremonies were merely ornamental, essentially useless. It shows how completely the Whigs had taken on utilitarian functionalism.

The views of another prominent Whig, Lord John Russell, on the viceroyalty are also telling. As prime minister in 1847 he told Clarendon before sending him out to replace the dying Bessborough:

> A separate government – a separate court – and an administration of mixed nature, partly English and partly Irish, is not of itself a convenient arrangement. The separate government within fifteen hours of London appears unnecessary – the separate court a mockery – the mixed administration the cause of confusion and delay.

His criticism of the viceregal court as being unnecessary, laughable and a source of time-consuming delay, when added to other critiques from those in his party of the viceroy being 'expensive and useless',[28] resembles the attacks by republicans on the monarchy itself. The Irish viceroyalty and the royal family in England were conceived to have parallel functions and similar faults.

Henry Ponsonby would have absorbed these views from the Whig chiefs and his relations as well as from attending parties at Holland House in the 1840s. Thus, the man who would ultimately be responsible for advising the sovereign on her state and ceremonial role spent his first paid position in an atmosphere saturated with a suspicion of stateliness. He heard critiques of the viceregal court as a theatrical farce. This deeply-inbred scepticism about ceremonial and the uses of hospitality meant that he approached courts certainly without awe, but perhaps also with a bit more detachment than others did.

The sense that the viceroyalty was under threat of abolition, that his own hereditary party opposed it and that the opulence of his daily life might soon come to an end was the backdrop to Henry Ponsonby's stay in Ireland. He did not seem to mind. He attended country dances, some of which were rowdy enough for the dancers to break their legs. He played raquets with fellow officers from smart regiments sent out, in the words of that era, to 'coerce' the Irish. It meant compelling tenants to pay rent for houses that were really mud huts and jailing men so poor that they could not afford guns, but killed policemen with pikes instead. Henry may have been sanguine about the ultimate abolition of the viceroyalty, but he enjoyed the panoply and parties while they lasted, sketching the Viceregal Lodge and grand receptions of the lord lieutenant at hunt balls in the country houses of neighbouring landowners.

Over the nine years of his Irish service, Henry acted as aide-de-camp or private secretary to five lords lieutenant: Bessborough, Clarendon, Eglinton, St Germans and Carlisle. Of these Lord Clarendon was the most important because he took Henry's education in hand as well as recommending him for a series of high-flying positions in the years that followed. The most famous Lord Clarendon was a seventeenth-century statesman who served both Charles I and Charles II, wrote a definitive account of the civil wars and was devoted both to the rule of law and to constitutional government. That peerage had died out. Ponsonby's patron was from a second creation which was only distantly related to the first Clarendons. Nevertheless, the Clarendon who took on Ponsonby as his private secretary was, like the first, an active statesman, for more than a generation at the heart of power in both Whitehall and abroad. Clarendon's Whiggism ensured that he thought of political power almost as a family inheritance; but he also felt that power imposed a responsibility to foster and protect English liberties. For Clarendon princes were a sort of necessary evil; he approached the cynical view that royal parade kept the masses amused while intelligent men of business transacted affairs behind the scenes. He honoured Prince Albert and Queen Victoria, to whom he was unfailingly and mischievously polite. They trusted and relied on him. Behind their backs, like many of the other Whig nobles, he called them 'Joseph' and

'Eliza', the patronising nineteenth-century equivalents of 'Keith' and 'Brenda' today. He set Henry to read Macaulay's *History of England*. Published between 1848 and 1862, the *History of England* set out to vindicate the 'Glorious Revolution' of 1688. Macaulay attempted to show how Whig lords had won a victory for English liberties by defeating Stuart designs to impose French absolutism in Britain. Macaulay's book, which came to be the pattern of Whig history, showed that England's monarchy was different from continental monarchies because it was a parliamentary or constitutional monarchy. In England the king only governed because of an invitation to do so by Parliament and a guarantee to protect civil liberties agreed to by William and Mary in the bill of rights in 1689. Thus Clarendon taught his young protégé to be sceptical of any royal claims to authority outside those ratified by Parliament. Through Macaulay, Clarendon was teaching Ponsonby to see that the integrity of the British government lay in the crown's subjection to Parliament.

It may also have been Clarendon who set Ponsonby to examine Lamartine's *History of the Girondins*, which he was reading at about the same time. The Girondins were the moderate leaders of the French Revolution who were superseded by more radical politicians responsible for the Terror. The Girondins were the French equivalents, in English eyes, of the parliamentary lords of a century earlier who had successfully stood up against royal despotism and in favour of liberty, without wholly destroying the order that the monarchy guaranteed. Lamartine had also been a leader of the revolutionaries in France in 1848 who had dismissed King Louis Philippe. For a short time Lamartine and his fellow revolutionaries formed a government that broke the monopoly of the rich and recognised the rights of the working classes. In the long afternoons of his not-very-demanding job in the Viceregal Lodge, Henry sketched copies of the Girondin leaders from Lamartine's book. A book over which he took such trouble clearly had an influence on him. At neither Coombe Wood nor Sandhurst had anyone taken the trouble to teach him the details of constitutional history or political theory: under Clarendon, he began to appreciate the attractions of a government under which the sovereign was subject to the will of ministers – who were themselves answerable to representative bodies.

Henry continued to benefit from Clarendon's influence even after Clarendon had left Ireland to become foreign secretary. When at the beginning of the Crimean War, an anti-Albert campaign spread rumours that the prince was interfering at the Horse Guards and in the Foreign

Office, Henry wrote to his brother scoffing at the notion. This was unreliable gossip, he said. He could not for a moment imagine that Clarendon would allow an ounce of interference by the prince in his department.[29] When the war finally came and Henry Ponsonby was serving in the Crimea, Clarendon sent him additional volumes of Macaulay as they were published. These he dutifully read amidst the stirrings of a muddy Crimean spring.[30]

Ireland was a blind spot, even for those in the governing classes who prided themselves on their love of liberty. The scale of distress there took English politicians by surprise: some of them even thought callously that they would rather wait until disease and emigration had reduced Irish rebelliousness than intervene with food or legislation.[31] Ponsonby's failure to notice the desperation that was right under his nose was not atypical, but it *was* different from the experience and reaction of his own brother. The contrast between the two brothers' reactions was partly due to their different duties there. Arthur was serving with a regiment of foot soldiers and it was he who was actually on the firing line between the government and the local population, unlike Henry who was more insulated in the Viceregal Lodge. In 1848 successful revolutions on the continent led the government to reinforce troops in Ireland against the possibility of an uprising there. Arthur briefly visited his brother in Dublin before being sent to Tipperary, a great contrast with Dublin's Georgian elegance. 'Never shall I forget our disgust when we arrived [at] … a large barrack with a small mud town all round and bog in every direction. Such a dismal place I have seldom seen' he wrote in a retrospective diary.[32] Arthur downplayed the threat of rebellion, but he was not shy of committing to print some of the horrors of English rule in Ireland. When he was quartered with his regiment at Cashel, he was ordered to take soldiers to support the police in evicting tenants who refused to pay their rent.

> One morning I was told off to this with 20 men. We marched some distance and arrived at a lot of cottages. There [were] the police and the agent of the property. The agent went into the different cottages or rather hovels and warned them they would be immediately turned out, after a short time the working men employed set to work to batter the house down. No difficult matter being made of mud only, and then one by one would the wretched people come out howling and running to me for help. Of course I could do nothing. There they were old and young in their rags turned out into the road on a cold day and the house pulled

down. In one house there was great difficulty about getting an old woman nearly 80 out ... On we went to other cottages ... leaving the poor people in the road. The soldiers did not like the duty at all, however it could not be helped ...[33]

To Henry he wrote that it was 'a most beastly duty' and that the families who had been literally turfed out of their houses were 'in a most dreadful state'.[34]

On another occasion Arthur had to go and escort a rebel agitator into custody. 'He was in a covered car' he remembered in his diary. 'People assembled in the streets, yelled at us and threw stones ... ' Twelve soldiers were then ordered 'to fix bayonets and charge but not to touch anybody. The moment the mob saw the men turn on them, they all booed as hard as they could and we continued onward unmolested.'[35] The following year when quartered in Kilkenny, Arthur participated in an exercise that he thought of as a waste of time and described as 'a horrid bore'. The commanding officer ordered the whole regiment to go on a long march through the town and country 'to inspire the people with awe'.[36]

Arthur's disgust shows that it was possible to notice the distress of the local population and to deplore the devices of the governors intended more often to keep order than to feed the hungry or improve agricultural conditions. At this stage, however, Henry identified thoroughly with the executive who were trying to keep order; he had too little first-hand experience of the distress to notice the injustices his brother recorded.

A further contrast between the two brothers' personalities arose when Arthur was forced to enter his brother's world, which made him uncomfortable. In 1849 he was asked by the lord lieutenant to attend his levee, a mass reception for anyone in Dublin society who had the right clothes and wished to attend, as well as to join the private luncheon party afterwards. Formal occasions made Arthur nervous. His comment was 'had to go. Very alarming.'[37] Even worse was the occasion later that year when he had to attend the special levee held by the queen in honour of her first visit to Ireland. In his diary he wrote that he was 'in a horrid funk as I have got to be presented'. He also gives some idea of what an ordeal these levees could be, thousands of people lined up in crowded rooms in Dublin Castle waiting to file by and be presented, ordinarily to the lord lieutenant but in this case to the queen. 'The people began to assemble at 12 [noon]. I went up at half past 2 through a tremendous crowd. It was two hours going through and one room very hot. At length I came to the queen, made my bow and kissed hands. Not at all a pretty thing. It was not over till 5. Upwards of 4,000 people at the levee, the largest ever known.'[38] Henry, on the other hand, was never fazed by a large levee. He did well in managing the expeditions arranged for the queen's visit; it was the first time he came to the notice of the royal couple. Future entries in his diary make it clear that they had begun to recognise him and regard him as a promising young officer who, unlike his brother, did not get into a 'funk' when kissing hands in gilded rooms.

Attending big receptions was business as usual for Henry in Ireland. The large levee for the queen in 1849 was exceptional, but the numbers attending the lord lieutenant's levees and more informal drawing rooms were routinely more than a thousand.[39] Further, Henry saw the humour in these receptions when Arthur did not. Some of the ladies attending the queen's levee, unfamiliar with the protocol for kissing the queen's hand as they were presented, instead 'kissed their own [hands] in a cheerful manner to Her as they passed'.[40] He confessed in a fragment of a memoir of his time in Ireland that 'The Private Secretary's office at the Lodge was not one of the strict hard working places but occasionally cheerful … ' They did have to work hard occasionally when there were many 'loyal addresses' that had each to be given a different answer in reply. 'The "museum" or chimney piece was receptacle of all odd letters which were exhibited there to be laughed at.'[41] His friends sometimes teased him about the private secretary's work, which he combined with acting in theatrical productions for the staff and the men of the garrison. One friend implied that he gave as much 'general satisfaction in his character of Desdemona the other day at the Garrison Theatricals' as he did in his work for the lord lieutenant.[42] In fact the private secretary's job, as defined by Henry, involved something of the role of jester. It required the ability to produce every once in a while an amusing story, for example it was advisable to reduce the stiffness or pomposity of a state occasion by uttering a *sotto voce* joke to those in attendance.

Henry began a lifelong habit in Ireland of collecting 'queer' stories with which he amused his partners at dinner parties. One of the characters in Dublin in those days was the Anglican archbishop of Ireland, Richard Whately. He was an intellectual, the author of influential work on logic and a former professor of political economy at Oxford. He was also a man with broad church principles who collaborated with Catholics in devising a school curriculum for Ireland that could be studied by children of different denominations. All this would have been congenial to Henry, who read more books than his fellow army officers, whose party was in favour of religious liberty and who liked a good story. He wrote in a diary of recollections:

> Whately, Archbishop of Dublin was an eccentric man, tall, thin, with a loud voice talking at everyone and throwing his legs about in extraordinary positions. He dined once or twice with Lord Bessborough when Archbishop Murray the R.C. was there, and sometimes chaffed him. Such as one night: 'No thank Heaven those times are past. I don't wish to burn you. I should feel no pleasure in seeing it. I daresay you don't want to burn me.'

Whately's wry comments on ladies attending the lord lieutenant's receptions at the castle Henry also thought worth writing down. 'A lady with a very low gown was at the Drawing Room. Some one asked him "Did you ever see anything like that?" He answered "Never since I was weaned." '

Whately also had a healthy scepticism, which Henry was growing to share, for empty forms or ceremony.

> Being sent to be sworn in as Lord Justice he [Whately] tried to get off the ceremony as it was inconvenient to come on the day fixed, by saying he had been Lord Justice 20 times and saw no reason for being sworn in *de novo* each time. 'Still you have' said Chief Secretary Cardwell 'by law it is necessary that you be sworn in each time you are Lord Justice.' 'By law,' he replied 'stuff and nonsense. You might as well tell me it is necessary for you to have the marriage service performed every time you sleep with Mrs Cardwell.'[43]

Henry Ponsonby would acquire a keener, or at least a more articulate belief in the possibility of legislative reform effecting social improvement later in life. It is possible at this stage, however, that he thought of Irish troubles and hatreds as so intractable, Irish grievances so impossible of redress, that he sought not only to diminish the formality of state occasions but also to lighten the mood with harmless asides. Seriousness and solemnity are not the only responses to a particularly awful set of problems.

His own island in the midst of a sea of Irish troubles was a place in 1854 it soon became clear he would have to leave. The beginning of the Crimean War brought the recall of all officers to their regiments. Henry Ponsonby was not a young man of reckless bravado. Young officers who wanted to see fighting and prove their worth often schemed to get sent to small colonial wars abroad. Not Henry: he was a careful young man, who knew the financial value and political interest of a position on the viceregal staff. He was in no hurry to resign his position and rush out to the Crimea only to find the war had been settled before he arrived. The lord lieutenant, Lord St Germans, who had succeeded Lords Clarendon and Eglinton in office and like them found Henry to be a useful member of his suite, offered to apply to the Horse Guards to keep Henry as his private secretary at a time when his departure seemed imminent. Henry accepted the offer, which involved appealing to Prince Albert for his assistance as well, and was eventually allowed to stay at his post in Ireland.[44] As his brother wrote, it would have been 'very tiresome'[45] to give it up, especially if the war proved only a temporary emergency.

A series of reverses at the beginning of the war showed that it was not going to be over in a few weeks' time. Soon the papers were full of the news of the deaths of friends. Indeed, it was Henry who had to tell Lord St Germans, to whom he was still acting as private secretary in the autumn of 1854, of the death of his son, Granville Eliot, at the battle of Inkerman. Henry's expressive one-word comment in his diary on this task was simply 'fearful'. Lord and Lady St Germans, he recorded the next day, were 'in deep grief for poor Granville'.[46] During his time in Ireland he had had training in the sceptical ethos of his Whig mentor, Lord Clarendon, but he had had little or no experience of personal suffering and hardship. Perhaps the lack of commentary in his diary and letters on the distress reflects his mentor's hardened cynicism about Irish problems ever having a hope of being solved. The death of the St Germans's boy was the adult Henry's first brush with a deep personal tragedy. When he was himself called up a few months later, what must have been the thoughts that went through his head as he packed up his things in Ireland, returned to England, saw his mother, and as a last gesture before embarking, had himself photographed? The photograph itself has not survived, but the act suggests that he knew there was a chance that he might not come back.

The Crimea

The Crimean War of 1853-6 was the relic of diplomatic attempts to restore the balance of power that had been upset by Napoleon's empire building in the first decade of the nineteenth century. It also prefigured the break-up of the Ottoman empire, which was centred on Turkey, but extended its reach throughout the Balkans in the north and over much of the modern Middle East to the south. As Turkish influence dwindled, other powers, often championing Christian or Orthodox principles, tried to move in to take the place of the Muslim Turks. This problem was to flare up again in the Eastern Question of the 1870s, and even more catastrophically, instability in territory formerly controlled by the Ottoman Turks was one of the primary causes of the 1914-18 war.

In the 1850s the Russians claimed to have an interest in protecting the Orthodox subjects of the Turkish sultan. The British and the French were concerned that the Russians might extend their territory too far westwards into central Europe and establish a Mediterranean stronghold at Constantinople, so they supported the Turks in resisting Russian claims. This led to war, which took place in and around the Russian-held Crimean peninsula in the north of the Black Sea. Much of the fighting focused on the Russian fortress at Sevastopol, to which the British and French laid siege in September 1854. It was for the Crimean peninsula, and specifically to join British and French forces intending to conquer Sevastopol, that Henry Ponsonby embarked in the summer of 1855. Before he left, he ventured the first political opinion that occurs in his early diaries and letters. The British and French together, on the anniversary of Waterloo on 18 June – the one saint's day in Henry's calendar – had been defeated by the Russians in an attempt to take Sevastopol. News filtered back that the Russians had killed some prisoners of war. Henry wrote to his brother Arthur that, 'The Russians have always been anxious to prove themselves civilized, but this will show Europe they are regular barbarians.'[47] He was steeling himself to face bloodshed, to hate an enemy he had never seen, to live up to the reputation of his regiment, to match the heroism of his father. But this first definite view was also a young man's departure, his first step towards becoming something quite different from what he had been in the well-proportioned rooms of the Viceregal Lodge. Aged nearly thirty, he was no longer an inexperienced youth. Still, he had led an unusually sheltered life up to now. His first real contact with brutality would activate political interests and a social conscience that had been absent before. Nor was the brutality all on the Russian side.

Henry himself knew that great events were in the offing for him. His diary suddenly ceases to be a bare record of women he danced with and houses where he had dinner. It becomes more detailed and descriptive. He went on board the ship in which he was to sail, the *Orinoco*, on 21 July 1855.[48] He was sailing with some cavalry regiments and there were horses as well as men on board. A fanfare-filled departure from Southampton, 'the men cheering' was accompanied by a letdown when the *Orinoco* had to anchor just two miles down the Solent to wait for orders. Chaos, waiting and disorganisation accompany all wars. It must have been particularly frustrating, however, to have made one's goodbye to an emotional but stony-faced family and then to have to wait for several days in the Solent opposite Netley Abbey while the authorities dispatched more horses before they could actually leave. When the horses finally arrived and the *Orinoco* sailed down the channel into the Bay of Biscay, the weather became rough and the horses frantic. Their whinnying screams were the sounds to which the men listened in their first nights at sea as they set off for a war that was already becoming legendary in the British press for ineptitude on the part of the authorities and unnecessary bloodshed.

On 29 July 1855 the *Orinoco* arrived in Gibraltar. Henry's comments were those of a dispassionate tourist. Of Gibraltar he wrote simply: 'curious town full of Jews, Moors, Spaniards and English soldiers.' The *Orinoco* next sailed to Malta where they took on coal. Henry went ashore and revisited the haunts of his youth in the governor's palace.

On 9 August he got up early and found a marvellous sight: 'the minarets and domes of Constantinople appearing in the sun above the morning mist.' The next day the *Orinoco* 'passed along the Bosphorus which is beautiful' and by entering the Black Sea came into the immediate vicinity of the east and the war. Two days later Henry first 'saw the cliffs of the Crimea' as the *Orinoco* arrived off Balaklava. The next day they sailed into the 'harbour which is a wonderful basin crowded with ships of all nations and surrounded by heights covered with tents. Very hot indeed, did not go on shore.' Instead, Henry's brother, who had preceded him to the Crimea as aide-de-camp to one of the generals, came on board. More ominously, in the same diary entry, Henry recorded another first: 'Heard the firing at Sevastopol.'

The army of the Crimean War was in many ways unchanged from the time of the wars against Napoleon. It has been described by one prominent historian of the British Army, Corelli Barnett, as identical to Wellington's Peninsular Army 'brought out of its cupboard and dusted down' for renewed use. The one great difference was the press. As a result of the telegraph the newspapers in London learned rapidly about the misadventures of the war. Although these mistakes and difficulties were entirely typical of previous wars, the new factor was a reading public who rejected such problems as unacceptable.[49] The papers reported on the failure of supplies and unsanitary conditions that bred disease. W.H. Russell of *The Times*, who went out to the Crimea with the Army, sent back graphic reports of the lapses of the authorities in prosecuting the war. At the same time, new developments in photography allowed Roger Fenton's pictures of battle scenes to be cheaply reproduced, giving a very fair idea of the tent cities in which the army was housed. Critical media coverage of warfare is familiar to recent generations used to reporting on the Vietnam, Falklands and Persian Gulf Wars. In fact this sort of 'loyal opposition' conducted by the media in their commentary on a war effort is an older phenomenon; perhaps the only difference is that more recent reporters are a bit more self-important.

Reports on the war in *The Times* ensured that Henry Ponsonby knew what he was getting into when he left for the Crimea. On the first day he came off the *Orinoco* he attended the funeral of a fellow officer, 'poor Drummond'.[50] Two days later the Russians made an attempt to relieve the siege of Sevastopol by crossing the River Tchernaya. British forces were not involved, but the French, and Sardinians who had joined them, suffered losses in successfully repelling the enemy. As a result Henry recorded in his diary that 'Prisoners and wounded passed by our tent all afternoon'. The next day shells were launched from the batteries nearby and a soldier he had spoken to the day before was killed.[51] He was already in the thick of the action.

On the night of 24 August Henry experienced his first command in the trenches. The event was significant because it was the first long memorandum he kept of any episode in his life. He was becoming more self-aware, more articulate about his own place at the centre of historical events. He was in charge of a working party instructed to extend and deepen trenches that were in front of a Russian fortification defending Sevastopol known as the Redan. He assembled his men at seven in the evening when it began to grow dark. The soldiers set to work, everyone speaking in whispers, as the Russians were less than 200 yards away. Then, 'Suddenly the moon came out'.[52] The Russians saw Henry's working party and opened fire. One of his men was killed and several more were wounded. After they had retired a little and taken cover, a round shot hit the parapet behind which Henry and several others had taken cover. 'I was knocked in a hole. 3 or 4 men fell upon me and a heap of stone and rubbish.' At the bottom of the hole, with others on top of him, Henry struggled to breathe. Someone pulled him out covered in chalk dust. One of his fellow officers said that in the moonlight 'I looked like the ghost of the Commendatore in *Don Giovanni*'. The peculiar tone of a Guards regiment under fire required one to lighten the atmosphere produced by people dying and being maimed: a reference to the last opera one had seen at Covent Garden would do. It was an upper-class style that mixed ruthlessness with something near foppishness. Odder still was the fact that these sophisticates commanded troops described by Corelli Barnett as largely made up of 'desperate Irishmen escaping from famine'. These were men not so different from those whom Wellington had described as the 'scum of the earth', men who were serving long twenty-one-year terms in the Army, often 'worn out by age and drink' and living even when on home service in barracks 'less luxurious than jails'.[53] The wonder is that class tensions within the British ranks were not more marked. Perhaps the soldiers were less egalitarian than we assume, and rather liked being led by young men with tailored uniforms and strange accents.

Henry's night in the trenches did not end until six o'clock the next morning, as the men supposed to relieve him had been sent elsewhere. In the course of the evening the commanding officer in the trenches was wounded and for a short while Henry replaced him without having a distinct idea of what to tell subordinates who approached him for orders. The heat and thirst were overwhelming. The noise was frightening. 'One soon gets accustomed to the sounds of the shot and shell – but the horrible noise of the rockets always startles one.' After it was all over, unusually for him, he noticed the dawn. He saw the world around him afresh. 'It was the most lovely morning.' Henry concluded his memo by noting that on each of the three following nights three officers in charge of working parties on the same spot where he had been with his men were all killed.

It was not always gun and cannon fire that killed men. A few days after his first command in the trenches Henry 'Attended the funeral of … [his] sergeant R. Russell who died of cholera'.[54] The uncertainty of the water supply, primitive sanitation facilities, the terrible condition of the hospitals that Florence Nightingale would make famous – all these contributed to large losses of life.

The most significant conflict of the war was an enormously frustrating experience for Henry. On 8 September, the French and the British were to attack the Malakoff and the Redan, the two forts on which the Russian defence of Sevastopol relied. The plan was to let the French go first and await their success against the Malakoff before the British attack on the Redan began. Henry and his men were not in the first line of attack. They waited to support and follow the British advance. The French succeeded against the Malakoff, but the British only briefly entered the Redan before the Russians drove them out again. The rumour spread that the 'men refused to follow their officers over the parapet', an outrage to the officers. Ponsonby noted that everyone was 'disgusted' by the British failure to take the objective. The success of their old enemies, the French, must have made their own defeat particularly galling. Still, the Russians now abandoned Sevastopol, sank their ships, and like the Muscovites retreating before Napoleon, set the town on fire. In retreating they also abandoned 1,500 sick and wounded.[55] This brutality shocked Ponsonby; he was also horrified by the unexpected reverse against the Redan. Both made a deep impression on Ponsonby, whose Wellington mania had heretofore led him to believe that only victory attended British arms.

The relief of the siege of Sevastopol was the last major engagement of the war. An ambiguous and inconclusive peace was signed after six months' waiting; Ponsonby remained stationed in the Crimea the whole time. To him the era of Wellington's glorious victories over Napoleon, in which his own father had played a part, was now over. The failures of the Crimea showed that it was so. In another memo he wrote at the end of 1856, the first notes of irony and mild cynicism enter into his summary account of the war. He wrote a dry account of his own country's attitude at the peace negotiation in Paris. 'England was dissatisfied; her last action was the failure at the Redan. She wanted more glory.' This was impossible; and in reaction, the English turned on their own generals: 'The friends of one general cried down another till at length, if all was true, our generals must have been cowards and traitors … '[56] The futility of such carping merely added to Henry's sense of worthlessness and defeat. He wrote another memorandum on the leadership of the British forces in which even he, who had ever been unquestioningly loyal to those in command, conceded that General Simpson, on whom the command devolved after the death of Lord Raglan, 'was utterly unfitted for it'. There is an element of absurdity too in his account of the loss of life in attempting to take the Redan, the refusal to try it again after the initial repulse, and some Scottish soldiers creeping over a little while later to find the fortress, to their surprise, empty: the Russians had left. This last story, with its suggestion of the pointlessness of war, was one that Henry's youngest son Arthur, who was a courageous and committed pacifist during the First World War, could not resist quoting in full in his biography of his father.[57]

The period between the fall of Sevastopol and the peace six months later was one of uncomfortable anti-climax. Ponsonby had the gruesome task of removing 400 corpses from storehouses near the harbour, which the Russians had left behind, mixing the living with the dead, in their flight.[58] He was able to purchase a promotion to lieutenant colonel, which pleased him very much, except that his pleasure was diluted by his going over the heads of some of his friends who were senior to him – and it also destroyed much of his savings.[59] The Russian winter arrived and the British camp became a sea of mud. Henry played football, built snow forts for snowball fights, and helped to construct a temporary theatre. In February 1856 work was far enough advanced for the actors to rehearse 'in dresses before the men'.[60] This combination of burlesque and bravery, extraordinary brushes with mortality and long days filled with nothing better to do than getting into costume or reading in a tent insulated by newspaper was a feature of Henry's Crimean experience. What he concluded from it is best summed up in correspondence with his Aunt Georgy Bathurst. Only her response to his letter has survived, but it indicates that Russell, the *Times* reporter, had lately been abused by Henry's fellow officers for his articles critical of the military authorities in the field. As a punishment they were refusing to sit down to dinner with him. Henry on the other hand defended Russell on the grounds that he had to write something, and that it was clear that the last British engagement of the war had not been a success. His Aunt Georgy, a Tory, took violent exception to this.

> I think your officers [she wrote to Henry in his Crimean tent] quite right to refuse having Russell to dinner. It is all very well to say he must write something, but that need not be such big lies. He reported that General Codrington was bewildered and lost his head at the Redan which was quite believed by all the middle classes ... I should like to give him a good thrashing when he [Russell] takes army officers' characters in that manner.[61]

The Army's ambiguous record in the Crimea was to bring it very much to public attention. The officer class could not be the exclusive preserve of the upper classes for much longer, and a young officer on the spot with his eyes wide open must have seen this more clearly than his ageing aunt. Perhaps Henry was also more sympathetic than she was to press reporting opening the way for the reform of abuses and inefficiency in the Army. The Army was still his chosen profession and an institution of which he wished to be justly proud.

He was to witness one last significant example of brutality – this time on his own side – before he made his seaward journey home in the summer of 1856. In April one of the men was flogged. Henry does not record the offence, but there was a variety of quite minor infractions that could be punished with flogging: one of the most celebrated officers of the Crimean War, Lord Cardigan, once had an old soldier with decades of service behind him and about ready to return to England from a peacetime posting in India, flogged for being drunk while on guard duty.[62] It was a harsh punishment. The man was stripped to the waist, tied down to three pikes bound together in the shape of a triangle and beaten before an audience of his fellows, thus inflicting humiliation as well as pain. The man whom Henry saw beaten went the next day to prison and shot himself.[63] This was after the peace had been signed and preparations were underway to bring all those who had served their country abroad home; it was a display of excessive punishment by military authorities whose own conduct of the war had been regularly criticised in London. It made Henry so committed to the abolition of flogging that he would later raise the issue with the commander-in-chief. It also taught him to treat the powers-that-be with a sceptical eye; this was one of the foundations of his mature political philosophy.

*

By this time the news was out among influential ministers that Henry Ponsonby was a bright and capable young man with a pleasing manner. Before his return to England, there was talk that he would be appointed private secretary to the viceroy of India, Lord Canning. A tentative offer was extended but withdrawn when the first man to whom the job was offered accepted it. Henry was tempted, but would have hated to leave his military career at so young an age. He wrote in his diary after hearing that he would not go to India, 'I am glad.'[64] Nevertheless he was returning to England only to ordinary regimental duties. The lord lieutenant of Ireland, Lord Carlisle, had already written to him making clear that he had not room to re-appoint him to his staff.[65] So when he sailed back to England in July 1856 Henry was sailing back rather at a loss. He had grown an enormous beard in the Crimea and sketched himself wearing it before he had it shaved off on his return (see Plates).

He could not so easily remove the deep impressions warfare had made upon him, however. He was changed from the non-committal young man who had lived at the Viceregal Lodge. He was now compelled to view some of the glorious traditions of his regiment less naïvely: the galling incompetence in the Crimean chalk and mud changed his attitude. He had an increased tendency to be critical of his superiors and a new inclination to commit his own views to paper, rather than simply to copy out the views of others.

Equerry to Prince Albert

Henry was not at a loose end for long. In January 1857 Prince Albert appointed him as an equerry, an honour and a welcome addition to his pay, for he now became richer by £500 a year. It was a large sum for a young man with no wife or family to support, especially one who had grown up without a large allowance. The appointment resulted from his having impressed the prince and his German doctor-adviser, Baron Stockmar, when the royal couple had visited Ireland in 1849 and 1853. Henry also had vocal admirers in two of his former lords lieutenant, Clarendon and St Germans, as well as friends among the equerries already serving.[66] Theodore Martin, whom the queen later commissioned to write her late husband's biography, told Ponsonby he had been a 'favourite' of Stockmar's. This Ponsonby confirmed.[67]

The post-Crimean Ponsonby could be sceptical about both Stockmar and Prince Albert. Stockmar was a physician who became private secretary to Prince Leopold of Coburg at about the time of Leopold's marriage to George IV's daughter and heir, Princess Charlotte. After Charlotte's death in childbirth, Stockmar conducted the negotiations which took Leopold to the throne of Belgium in 1831. He then acted as Leopold's agent in England. When Queen Victoria came to the throne in 1837, he helped to bring about her marriage to Leopold's nephew, Albert. He stayed with the queen and Albert after their marriage as an unofficial adviser until 1857 when he retired and returned to Germany. Stockmar's ideas about separating the throne from partisanship and raising its moral character had a positive effect on the development of constitutional monarchy in Britain, but he was a schemer. This Ponsonby recognised and in later life he enjoyed the indignant recollections of Karoline Bauer who had been brought over by Stockmar and wed in a sham marriage to Leopold in order, she claimed, to keep Leopold amused after the death of Charlotte. He thought many of Bauer's recollections were probably lies, but the descriptions of old Leopold and his wig 'brought him to my mind again very clearly'.[68]

Ponsonby's attitude to Albert was more complex. The prince was legendary in the Ponsonby family as someone who was completely humourless (a serious failing in their view). They thought he resembled the mock hero of Lewis Carroll's nonsense poem, *The Hunting of the Snark*. The Snark was remarkable for

... its slowness in taking a jest.
Should you happen to venture on one
It will sigh like a thing that is deeply distressed
And it always looks grave at a pun.[69]

On the other hand, Henry was deeply affected, perhaps unconsciously, by the prince's high intellectual seriousness. As equerry he accompanied the prince to lectures, exhibitions and meetings of the Fine Arts Commission. He began a sort of further education, a broader and less vocational training than he had received as a boy at Sandhurst, and more scientific and technological in emphasis than the reading he had been assigned by Lord Clarendon. Albert was enormously active in promoting wider knowledge of science and industry during the 1850s. Receipts from his brainchild, the Great Exhibition of 1851, made the complex of museums, university and concert hall stretching today from Hyde Park to South Kensington financially possible. The very first month that Henry was in waiting on the prince, February 1857, he saw the new round reading room at the British Museum. He accompanied the prince to a meeting intended to found a new school in memory of the duke of Wellington. He listened to a lecture by the genius of chemistry and physics, Michael Faraday. A few months later he and the prince attended a lecture on glaciers given by John Tyndall, another prominent pioneer of Victorian science.[70] Thus, the prince harnessed the prestige of the monarchy to the fostering of technology and science, both increasing the reputation of the throne and lending the *imprimatur* of royal respectability to disciplines that Oxford and Cambridge still looked down upon, as inferior to the classics.

All this rubbed off on Henry Ponsonby, whose diary now begins to show evidence of regular visits to the British Museum in his own time. He also used the long periods of doing nothing that serving as equerry entailed to go and read in the Royal Library at Windsor. Under the prince's influence, he became a bookish young man, decidedly different from the other soldiers and sportsmen at court. Further, his researches bore fruit. He gave a lecture to the men in his regiment on Frederick the Great. He was proud enough of his paper to read it to his family the next week at Hampton Court.[71]

The prince and the queen thought of Henry as a suitable young man to help conduct their own eldest child's education. They had begun to realise how little effect their relentless regime of book-learning was having on the Prince of Wales and decided to send him on some instructive travels with specially selected boys of his own age. With Henry as one of the adult chaperons the party went to stay at Königswinter on the Rhine near Bonn. Henry genuinely liked the prince, but the boy certainly tested the adults' patience during the journey. He would ride his pony in a way that frightened the other boys, until he fell off while galloping down a hill and the bruises persuaded him not to do it again. He also teased the other boys, who felt no compunction about teasing him back, even beating him. Henry heartily approved of this egalitarianism, but he noted too how irritating spoilt young princes could be.[72]

Having returned from his journey with the Prince of Wales Henry resumed his regular waitings of three months in the year. He also served with his regiment in London and in Windsor. The work as equerry was still new and interesting to him. Members of the royal household, then as now, were in an odd position. An equerry was commonly an army officer, a gentleman whose duties were mainly social. Ben Pimlott, the most authoritative biographer of Queen Elizabeth II to date, explains it: the responsibility of an equerry is to be 'available, agreeable and inconspicuous'. Equerries swell a procession or two. They receive visitors and round out a dinner table. They are companions who are supposed to fade into the background the moment the queen or the prince is on display.

The equerries sometimes had hard work to do in arranging the details of trains, tips and accommodation when the royal family travelled; but the royal family travelled less then than it does now. They felt less troubled about justifying their own existence. Then as now, equerries were the social equals of princes and yet, as one of the current queen's former private secretaries has said, it must never be forgotten that 'you are their servant'.[73] Sir Thomas Biddulph, Henry Ponsonby's long-time colleague as keeper of the privy purse, used to refer to the queen as 'upstairs' and to everyone else, ladies in waiting and bottle washers included, as 'downstairs'. Some of the ladies and gentlemen of the court found this insulting. Ponsonby's response to his strange situation was to make gentle fun of princes behind their backs. This may have been partly a form of retaliation for the nonsense he sometimes had to endure, but it was also the reflex of someone whose natural enjoyment of life expressed itself in seeing the funny side of things. In January 1858 he had to go down to Dover to meet Leopold, king of the Belgians, who was arriving to attend the wedding of the Princess Royal. He was slightly annoyed at all the work arising from members of the royal family not knowing in advance when they might like to travel up to London. He told his brother, 'as one has to order all the carriages and Guards [of honour] etc. and cannot of course tell when these Royalties like to come up, one has to wait till their minds are made up and then telegraph away like fun ... '[74] It was as well that he enjoyed making a joke out of it, because such petty annoyances were to become a regular feature of his life for more than thirty years.

Why did he put up with it? He left no definite statement about why he took a position in the household and stayed there. It was possibly such 'common sense' to him that he never thought of writing down why he did it. The offer of such a position to a serving officer was a very high honour, something one could not easily refuse. His family had served before him. His father had served as aide-de-camp to the Prince Regent; his mother had sometimes been in waiting on the duchess of Cambridge. The addition to his income was welcome. It might lead to promotion in the Army. Further, after the Crimea, he was distinctly more interested in politics than before. Joining the court meant proximity to the leading political men of the day and while the prince was alive, though he tried to steer clear of partisanship, there was no ban on dispassionate conversation about political affairs. Being an equerry could have its attractions as well as its irritations.

*

One of the things Henry did enjoy about the job was the friends with whom he served. Often they were from titled families, whose parents and grandparents had known his parents and grandparents. Franco Seymour was one. Alfred Paget was another. Ponsonby was disposed to like anyone who could make him laugh: Paget made everyone laugh by raising racy topics in an innocent manner.

> He [Paget] asked one day in the Equerries' room whether we thought it wrong to kiss one's children, boys. 'Some fellows you know don't kiss their little boys and says it makes 'em effeminate. I always kiss my little boys.' Then after a pause, very seriously: 'but if they have any of their nonsense with me I whip their little bottoms too.'[75]

A similar instance occurred when two of the gentlemen in attendance on Prince Albert assembled as usual to wait for orders in the corridor at Windsor where some of the most valuable pictures were hung.

> The Prince usually came to us at 11 for orders and talked away. One day Lord Waterpark a very shy and quiet man stood some distance off. When the Prince came in he asked where he was. Lord Rivers looking back saw that Lord Waterpark was standing by a picture called the Artist's Gallery I think (a collection of pictures with Titian's Venus very prominent in the foreground). Lord Rivers said 'He's standing by that naked Venus Your Royal Highness he never can tear himself away from it.'[76]

Ponsonby's life in the 1850s had its odd contrasts and juxtapositions. Bloodshed and mud in the Crimea at one moment, he was acting as a sort of medieval manservant to a German prince the next. The absurdity of it lodged in his mind. To cultivate the art of describing the absurd was for him a mark of his growing maturity. Respect the sovereign, certainly, but don't for heaven's sake take it all too seriously. This view was coming to be the foundation of his personal philosophy.

Henry was most amused of all by excessive dressing up, or pomposity, or overblown formality of any sort. He dreaded accompanying the royal family to the German ducal and princely courts because he found them 'stiff'. They were fussier and more insistent upon artificial forms than was usual in England. There were too many bowings and scrapings and turnings out of ceremonial guards. He liked the relatively simple manners of Victoria and Albert's court. He had most fun with Englishmen whom he thought should have known better than to exaggerate the importance of their offices through their dress. Travelling north with the queen and prince in September 1858, he noticed the mayor of Leeds, 'who having a white beard and flowing grey locks and being dressed in crimson velvet and ermine looked the same as King Lear, or the Doge of Venice, or King Duncan or any other great theatrical Royalty'.[77] The wisdom in this joke is that the secret to emphasising one's dignity, whether as a prince or provincial official, is self-effacement, to underplay one's importance, to deprecate fanfares and showing off. The complaint of the tyrannical Stuart kings during the early seventeenth century was that Parliament was attempting to reduce them to the state of the doge of Venice, a ceremonial official notorious for seeming to be grand, yet being in fact the creature of a powerful merchant oligarchy. Henry Ponsonby was descended from Whig upholders of parliamentary precedence over mere kings, of parliamentary lords who were quite happy to keep English sovereigns in a state approaching that of a humble doge. His making fun of excessive pomp was thus edged with political suspicion of unchecked royal authority.

The phrase 'theatrical Royalty' is also interesting from another angle. Henry's implication is that princes should be as little histrionic and behave with manners as near to those of 'offstage', ordinary people as was consistent with their dignity. Perhaps more importantly, though less self-evident to Ponsonby, was the monarchy's longtime connection with the stage. From the eighteenth until fairly late in the twentieth century a prominent court official, the lord chamberlain, licensed all plays performed in London. He served as a censor; his authority was necessary for all performances. Further, the court itself was one place where significant productions were performed. Shakespeare's company was called the queen's men and sometimes performed before the sovereign. Critics have examined the intimate alliance between court and theatre in the sixteenth and seventeenth centuries. They have shown how royal masques and plays intended to represent and influence both desirable and undesirable qualities of Tudor and Stuart sovereigns.[78]

In the nineteenth century the court often staged amateur theatricals, charades and skits – usually performed by the household rather than professional actors. Indeed, Henry first came to royal attention when he helped perform two charades before the queen and her husband in Ireland in 1853.[79] Could it not be that Henry Ponsonby's continuous desire to amuse, especially at the expense of overly formal royalty, was in fact related to the light-hearted, comic style then prevalent in the sort of after-dinner performances regularly put on to amuse the royal family and their guests? Though comic, it may have been no less serious a lesson than those that were played before Stuart monarchs about the necessity for princes to be ordinary, self-deprecating and able to laugh at themselves.

Moreover, Henry's impulse to amuse, and the court's adoption of a parlour-game style of theatre, ran parallel to a change in the attitude of the press. As Richard Altick points out in his authoritative study of the first decade of *Punch*, mildly critical jokes at the royal family's expense were a staple of this popular journal in the 1840s and 1850s. No longer did members of the royal family appear as the object of ribald or scathing attacks as they had at the end of the eighteenth century and during the Regency. 'Scurrility was out; light satire was in.' Henry's instinct that too much showiness detracted from the dignity of the throne was echoed by William Thackeray, who argued in *Punch*: 'The hold of the great upon us now is by beneficence, not by claptraps and ceremonies ... Wisdom, simplicity, affection must be the guardians of the English throne.'[80] Although still several years in the future, Henry's private secretariat was marked in its efforts to achieve precisely this sort of simplicity, both in style and in substance.

His family background, Ireland, the Crimea, and his service as equerry to the Prince Consort all had an important effect in shaping Henry Ponsonby's personality. More important than any of these, however, was the woman whom he married in the spring of 1861. The story of who she was, how they met and how her upbringing had formed her into a decided young woman who turned Henry's head is taken up in the next chapter.

CHAPTER 3

Mary Bulteel from Birth to Marriage

1832-61

Mary Elizabeth Bulteel was born on 21 September 1832, the year of the great reform bill. Her grandfather, Lord Grey, was prime minister and the bill expanding the electorate was his greatest achievement. He was an ancestor of whom Mary was justly proud and she passed the feeling on to her children. Her youngest son, Arthur Ponsonby, described Charles Grey as 'an advanced, almost revolutionary aristocrat with a great love of domesticity – very charming and attractive, and wonderfully persistent, with a high sense of public duty'.[1] The family legend was that the Greys also had 'inflexible tenacity of purpose' and a liking for argument, or 'contradictiousness', which they handed down through the generations.[2] This may be a myth, but it was typical of the stories that the Greys, Bulteels, Bathursts and Ponsonbys told to themselves about themselves. They believed in nothing so firmly as the durability, continuity and heritability of personality traits such as tenacity, love of debate, and even left-of-centre political views. They traced these qualities through the branches of their family trees. Some of them even had the most *recherché* indexes of Burke's *Peerage and Baronetage* down by heart.

Arthur Ponsonby thought the Bulteels less distinguished than the Greys: 'a Devonshire county family, sporting and quite unintellectual' was his verdict.[3] He did not quite do them justice. They were a family that had been among the most prominent in the county for generations, who traced their descent from the Crockers, another family already well established in Devon at the time of William the Conqueror. They were not intellectuals, but there were artists among them. John Crocker Bulteel, Mary's father, was certainly a sportsman who travelled up and down the country with his own dogs for hunting, but he was also interested in drawing, decorating, architecture and woodwork. He married Lady Elizabeth Grey in 1826 and brought her to live at one of his family's houses, Lyneham, which is west of Plymouth. Built about 1700,

Nikolaus Pevsner's *Buildings of England* series on Devon describes it as a 'classic example of the compact gentleman's house, beautifully sited by a lake'.[4] Here four of the five Bulteel children were born. One of the great Whig hostesses, Lady Granville, visited them and found them very happy, 'devoted to each other, fond of all the same things, their children and place, drawing like artists, singing like Nightingales'.[5]

Father, Mother and Self Examination

Mary's father inherited from his father a much bigger house, Flete, together with an estate of about 3,000 acres in 1837. This had an annual income estimated at between £3,000 and £4,000 in 1801,[6] a tremendous sum in the days when a skilled workman might expect to live very well in London on his pay of about £1 a week. It emboldened John Crocker Bulteel to embark on an ambitious rebuilding of the house. Flete had a Tudor core, but had been rebuilt during the eighteenth century in a neo-classical style. Mary's father now extended it and entirely altered the façade, so that it resembled an enormous castle. It had, and still has, a commanding position on a hill overlooking the river valley. Anyone who grew up there could not have been shy, or at least not for long, on a first approach to a house the size of Balmoral or Osborne. Mary's father acted as his own architect and did much of the decorative design work himself. He added a completely new wing to serve as a riding school on the ground floor with new bedrooms above.[7] This was a work of extravagance as well as taste, and it bankrupted the Bulteels. John Crocker Bulteel became ill, possibly of heart disease, in 1843. The doctor told him not to travel. Instead, in a grand gesture, like Lord Marchmain climbing into his state bed to die, Bulteel drove up to Hampton Court to look one last time at the Raphael drawings. He died in London aged only 50 and was buried at Kensal Green.

It was a terrible year for the family. Mary lost not only her father, but also her brother Charles, who had gone to sea as a midshipman – he died of an outbreak of measles on board his ship. Bulteels knew when they were about to die. Charles Bulteel's commanding officer wrote to convey the boy's last words: 'Tell my mother I know I am on my deathbed, that I die loving her and my brother and sisters.'[8]

Soon after her husband's death Elizabeth Bulteel discovered the terrible condition of the estate finances, the income from which was now reduced to between a third and a quarter of what it had been 40 years earlier. Possibly the estate was also encumbered with large debts left over from the re-building.[9] She stayed on for a while at Flete, then shut it up and later sold it. She bought a largish farmhouse nearby, Pamflete, and put it in the name of her eldest son, also John Crocker Bulteel but known as 'Johnnie'. She also salvaged enough money to purchase the lease of a small London townhouse in Eaton Place West, where she took Mary as well as her two younger daughters, Georgiana (or 'Georgy') born in 1834 and Emily born in 1839, to be educated.

In 1843 Mary Bulteel was between ten and eleven years old. She had grown up till then in the country, and in a county where her family was among the principal residents. The Bulteels all had prominent memorials on the wall of the church in the neighbouring village of Holbeton, where her uncle, Courtenay Bulteel, was the rector. All at once, her family came steeply down in the world, an experience she shared with Henry Ponsonby, whose father had also died when he was young leaving his mother in straitened circumstances. Also like the Ponsonbys, who came within the orbit of London by moving into grace and favour apartments at Hampton Court, Mary Bulteel now had her first sustained experience of the metropolis, with all its concerts, parties and political hum. Like Henry she developed a taste for it she never lost. Both the Ponsonbys and the Bulteels had their roots in the country, but they were cosmopolitan at heart and their deepest love was for London.

Her father having died when she was young, the most important figure in Mary's early life was her mother. The family later remembered Elizabeth Bulteel as the ideal type of great lady – dignified, impeccably dressed and awe-inspiring. One of her granddaughters recalled her coming to visit in the 1870s.

> I can see her now, coming down from her room in the morning in a moiré dress with a full crinoline skirt ... She took off her gloves and went to her drawing table in a small room next to the drawing room, and there painted her lovely water-coloured sketches. She was tall and slim, although between 70 and 80 ... and was indeed a great lady. We were all rather frightened of her, and knew that '*tenue*' [decorum] was necessary, and nothing sloppy should be allowed, in dress or speech.[10]

Mary Bulteel developed the same habit in later life of going regularly to a drawing table to paint watercolours. She was also a little conscious of social distinctions, an *aficionado* of the 'great lady' or '*grand seigneur*' – at least she enjoyed making wry observations about the habits of dukes and duchesses. Where this minor kink in her make-up came from it is difficult to say. It may have come from her family's fortunes declining so rapidly when she was a child. It may have come from her mother setting so high a standard. Wherever it came from, it made her immensely attractive, especially in later life, to men like A.C. Benson, Ronald Gower and her nephew Maurice Baring, who tended to have the same small kink themselves. She picked up the habit from an influential French tutor, after her mother had brought her to London, of peppering her speech with French phrases.

Mary came to be a connoisseur of manners, rank and taste while at the same time a committed egalitarian, especially ahead of her time in demanding equality between men and women when it was a question of educational or employment opportunities. This was one of the animating contradictions in her personality: a liking for upper-class, understated style together with a fierce attachment to equality as a principle of politics and justice. After her husband's death she wrote two articles on the subject for a highbrow periodical, *The Nineteenth Century*. Both articles shed some light on her own childhood. She wrote of her regret that young women on the eve of the twentieth century, some of whom had benefited from the educational reforms she championed, had lost the distinction of the women of her mother's and grandmother's generation in the first half of the nineteenth century.[11] She remembered the Whig hostesses of her grandmother and mother's era carrying on a tradition that died out just as she herself was coming to adulthood.

The great Whig Houses had much to say in the training of the smart world of those days. The traditions of perfect manners, lax morality, political shrewdness, excellence of taste, unrivalled skills in holding a *salon*, were handed down from mother to daughter, till the ebb of the tide set in during the fifties [1850s]; then it is curious to observe the decline of each of these traditions. Who does not remember, if he is old enough, the courtesy without patronage, the gentleness to inferiors, the rigorous but perfectly natural bearing, which never failed, however morality or religion might fare in the days of his grandmothers? When I was a child it appeared to me impossible to believe that there could be any other way of getting old ... [12]

This nostalgic catalogue of the way women from earlier generations behaved gives some hint of how a stylish lady from a political house, ought, in Mary Ponsonby's view, to act. She ought to play the role of hostess with huge and effortless charm; she ought to have political opinions that might have a direct impact on active politicians of the day. It gives some idea of the salon entertaining that was just beginning to die away as her mother brought Mary and her sisters to live in London. Lady Elizabeth Bulteel hosted a sort of modified salon, a series of musical evenings at which there was singing and the playing of short chamber pieces. Young men of marriageable age came to meet her three eligible daughters. Radical political views are not always born among the underprivileged. Mary Bulteel's later views about the necessity of increasing the opportunities available for women's education had as their foundation this musical salon, and those of her mother's contemporaries, in Eaton Square.

In 1847, when she was fifteen, Mary Bulteel was preparing for confirmation. On the day before she was to be formally received into the church for the first time as an adult, she stayed at a rectory where also the bishop of Oxford, Samuel Wilberforce, was staying. He said evening prayers 'in sonorous tones' and for the first time, according to her eldest daughter Betty, she 'received an impression of ecclesiastical authority which had never reached her from the village parsonage at home'.[13] This was the beginning of an intense attachment to high church forms and doctrine in the Church of England. The Oxford Movement was then at its height, and the teenage Mary Bulteel enthusiastically took up its insistence on greater historical fidelity to Catholic forms in worship alongside a more serious and austere attention to doctrine. The revival of Anglican sisterhoods in the 1840s and 1850s that accompanied the Oxford Movement also influenced her.[14] She began to have dreams of self-sacrifice, of a life of service to the church, of founding an all-female religious order. Such religious phases were common among upper-middle and upper-class women of her generation,[15] and Mary Bulteel at this stage was not unlike Dorothea Brooke, the heroine of George Eliot's *Middlemarch*. Dorothea wanted only to give up her jewels and everything pleasant, to design better cottages for the poor and to lead an ascetic life inspired by the martyred reformer of a monastic order, St Teresa of Avila.

A few years later, aged twenty, Mary began to keep a diary 'intended to contain a solemn confession of sin in thought, word or deed, written every evening after self examination'. She wrote on the first page that she hoped 'with God's help, to write *truly* and without *comment* or *excuse* of any sort the faults I have committed, that I may see where and how I most often err and so keep a more jealous watch over myself ...'[16] The Victorian era was a great age of diary keeping. Religious feeling compelled diarists to render an account before God of all the time spent in the day, as if he were a great banker who disapproved of squandered minutes. The object was to eliminate sloth and evil, to encourage industry and conscientiousness. It is probably not a coincidence, however, that Mary Bulteel's diary started from about the time that William Harcourt came on her horizon as a suitor. There were other young men whom she noticed and then instantly reproved herself for noticing. Harcourt appears in the diary with greater regularity. He came from a prominent aristocratic family, not unlike the Greys. Like her he was articulate and enjoyed a debate. He was destined for high office and would serve as chancellor of the Exchequer under Gladstone in the 1880s, and he might well have replaced him as prime minister in the 1890s had the queen not opted for Rosebery instead. Less than two weeks after she had begun the diary Mary accused herself of having spoken 'for effect to Mr. W. Harcourt'.[17] A few days later she was ashamed of herself for having fished 'for compliments with Mr. W. Harcourt'. She had 'looked sometimes too interested while talking to W. Harcourt and wished, scarcely that, but thought that he admired me'.[18] Evidently she enjoyed repeating his name – as what twenty-year-old does not when first in love? She adored exchanging ideas with him in conversation, but worried that these conversations were somehow sinful because she enjoyed them and put herself forward too much. 'Once or twice while talking to W. Harcourt,' she wrote on the first of April 1852, he had asked her

> earnestly not to keep everything I thought upon every subject except those of the most trivial description to myself. I entirely forgot it was very easy, at least not easy but I might do as much good by explaining my opinions without in any way alluding to myself. Conversation of this kind [is] full of danger for one's own sense of the necessity of real humility.[19]

She was torn. She thought she had a duty to win him over to her own version of religious orthodoxy, but she also condemned herself for the pleasurable *frissons* she clearly experienced when talking to him.

William Harcourt was equally smitten with her. He wrote to his family:

> Lady E. Bulteel who, as I think I told you, is a very charming person, has a regular reception on Mondays which I attended last night. The little Bertha [one of Mary's younger sisters] is a great pet of mine, and the eldest daughter Mary something more.[20]

Their flirtation lasted for nearly two years, and finally in October 1854 Mary accepted Harcourt's proposal of marriage. But she was miserable.

'Engaged to be married to William Harcourt,' she confided to her diary. 'More earnestness and devotion required for fear of being led away. Still uncertain in my own mind whether this act is to bring a curse or a blessing on us both. Worn out by anxiety and doubts.'[21] This is not a very happy entry for a young woman to be writing who has just accepted a proposal of marriage. Considering how much she had enjoyed seeing and talking with him in the previous months, she seems awfully worried. It prepares the reader to learn that less than a year later, in the summer of 1855, much to the surprise of her mother and sisters, she broke off the engagement.[22] She later told her family that his religious heterodoxy and Whiggish scepticism were ill-matched to her religious earnestness at that stage of her life.[23] A much later entry she made in the diary, when she was in her fifties, shows that nevertheless Harcourt had had, and still had, a great hold on her.

> I cannot describe or discuss the man I engaged myself to marry, October 3 1854. His intelligence, his recklessness, his devotion ... [allowed him] to get such a hold over me that it required all the strength of the opposite passion of religious fanaticism to prevent my becoming an absolute slave.

She blamed herself for having been too passionate, although she also thought he was to blame for 'very unfair misrepresenting of his thoughts and opinions'. She confessed that even from the distance of 1884 and fully equipped with hindsight that her engagement to him in 1854-55 and subsequent separation 'was the most exciting, the most disappointing, the happiest and the most miserable year of my life'. After she broke off the engagement she thought he would be 'wretched but not angry. He never understood the matter in the least and behaved very cruelly but that is enough'.[24] Clearly the matter still rankled and aroused her feelings long after it was all over. Though she thought she had banished him for good, he was to make more than one agitating reappearance in her life.

Mary kept her diary regularly for seven years, and although Harcourt plays a large part in it, he is not the only person who had an influence on her in those years. The harsh self-criticism of her self-examination journal is related to another long-time love, that of the seventeenth-century theologian, Blaise Pascal and his *Pensées*. She described Pascal's book as 'magnificent' because it showed her the vanity and frivolity of worldly aspirations.[25] Pascal taught her how a life sternly devoted to loving God might destroy self-love. It was from this era that Mary's ambition to found a women's religious order grew. She yearned for a higher order of existence, more spiritually perfect than was possible in an everyday world in which her mother and sisters and other annoyances intruded. Unfortunately the temptations of the world often succeeded with her, if we are to believe some of the self-flagellation of the diary. She scolded herself for wanting to appear better than other people, to seem on good terms with the duke and duchess of Bedford, who were Devonshire neighbours of the Bulteels. She was critical of herself for having shown off the fact that she had been invited to stay at Windsor. She appears to have taken at this stage a resolution not to marry and devote herself to a life of service and contemplation. She enjoyed the self-denial in the prospect of not marrying, but there may also have been something in the resolution that suited her temper and natural inclinations.

It may be a little unfair to take too much advantage of a young woman's listing of her own faults. But Mary Bulteel showed a perceptive self-knowledge when she pointed to a weakness for being familiar with 'fine' people. For example, she found fault with herself on 18 March 1852 because she had been 'Glad that Colonel Estcourt should see on what terms we are with the Duke of Bedford and exaggerated about the opera saying he had asked me to go often in his box with the Duchess when I believe he only meant me to go next Tuesday'.[26] A few months later she chastised herself because she was 'Too fond of being intimate with fine people and anxious to make their acquaintance'.[27] In later life she could be witheringly contemptuous of anyone who had a fascination with princes. She labelled this 'royal *culte*', and taught her children to think of it as vulgar and utterly beneath them. There was also an element of good-natured teasing and enjoyment in finding that anyone was a shade too curious about the doings of the royal family. Yet, when she was first appointed maid of honour in 1853, at the age of twenty-one, she herself was riveted by how the court lived and what the queen did all day. She brought up opportunities to share what she knew with others who were less fortunate than she in seeing royal goings-on. She was almost certainly vigilant about ridiculing 'royal *culte*' in later life because she knew that as a young woman, and possibly sometimes even as an adult, she was liable to give in to it herself.

In fact a little royal *culte* was necessary in order to sustain oneself in the interminable weeks of royal service. To be a maid of honour involved three month-long waitings in the year. Generally two maids of honour were in attendance on the queen in the years before she was widowed. They were both unmarried women from good families, a relic of the extended households of medieval kings who had noble and knightly families living under the same roof with them. Queen

Victoria's maids of honour were companions rather than servants. There was a certain ambiguity about their social status that involved raised eyebrows and sniggering behind the arras, when girls from grand families believed they were being treated like housemaids. In the royal household the maids of honour were junior only to the ladies in waiting; they wore small brooches or badges when they were on duty. They did very little except to provide company on a walk, to run back to fetch a forgotten shawl, to chat amiably to the queen's guests at dinner, and to sing prettily afterwards. The pay was £300 a year, a welcome addition to the income of a young woman who came, as Mary Bulteel did, from a gentle family that was financially strapped. In fact, the queen often used household appointments as a way of coming to the assistance of highborn families who had fallen on hard times.[28]

When she was appointed Mary made an intriguing contribution to her diary. It shows that she felt the appointment was on the lines of a religious or providential opportunity. She thought it might give her the chance to influence the queen to take high church views more seriously; and through the queen, to influence people at large in favour of the otherworldly asceticism that she had acquired from Pascal.

> Sometimes I think it may be intended I should serve in an important [place] the cause of our Holy Church and religion. There is an intense power in earnestness and conviction. Were the Queen to have a great affection and love for the Church and her ordinances the effect I am convinced would be very great in the country, without its being necessary to do anything very active that might offend people, the very knowledge that she had a feeling for it, would insensibly work.[29]

This may appear overly optimistic to us today. We need to be careful, though, to see how much we ourselves have been schooled by Bloomsbury to scoff at Victorian moral enthusiasms. We instinctively jeer at the possibility of any moral superiority in princes. In later life, in a more agnostic phase and more familiar with the habits of the royal family, Mary Ponsonby would too. But in the 1850s the queen and the prince were in fact assiduous in their loyalty to each other and to their children: they were in many ways a morally admirable couple. Hannah More's evangelical tracts of the late eighteenth century, which warned the nobility to act with greater propriety because of their influence over classes beneath them, seemed entirely relevant to Mary Bulteel in the 1850s. The young William Gladstone had also read Hannah More and applied her doctrines to the court of Queen Victoria.[30] So we should not regard it as ridiculous that Mary Bulteel was thinking along these lines when she was first appointed maid of honour.

With hindsight, Mary's appointment appears exactly what might have been expected. She already had an aunt and uncle serving in the royal household. One of her Grey aunts, Caroline Barrington, was a lady in waiting; her uncle Charles Grey had been equerry to the queen almost since her accession, and private secretary to the prince since 1849. The queen recorded that she had filled a vacancy among the maids of honour by appointing 'Miss Bulteel, Lady Caroline Barrington's niece, a very nice girl'.[31] In later life Mary Ponsonby told Ethel Smyth that having family at court had led in part to her appointment. She emphatically denied, however, that the Greys were courtiers, a word that conveyed connotations both of servility and financial corruption. Its overtones were not unlike the word 'lobbyist' today. Instead, she claimed her appointment was, as Ethel Smyth remembered, 'partly because she had the reputation of being a first-rate actress, and chiefly because she was of a different type from the generality of courtiers'.[32]

Mary *was* different from the other men and women in the household. Elizabeth Longford, still the definitive biographer of Queen Victoria more than forty years after the publication of her book, delivers an enormously positive judgement on the young woman who would become Mary Ponsonby when estimating her place among the other members of the royal household serving in the mid-1860s.

> Mary Ponsonby soared through the Victorian age untrammelled by any of its inhibitions. From working-class rights to higher education for women, no Radical cause left her cold. Her diminutive size coupled with almost regal dignity reminded people of the Queen and though the two were as unlike as possible in ideas and intellect, they remained close friends.[33]

It is unlikely that the queen would have consciously chosen to bring such an odd bird in amongst her ladies, because she was not an adventurous woman when it came to choosing her household. Moral respectability, a good family background and coming from among people she already knew counted far more with her than wit or originality, both of which Mary Bulteel certainly had in quantity.

Acting Naturally

The comment about Mary Bulteel's acting ability is more plausible and more interesting. The royal family liked to be entertained after supper.

A young woman who could sing or play a spirited part in a game of charades was definitely a plus. The emphasis was on amusement, harmless high jinks, moderate hilarity. Seen from another angle the private amusements of the court were not unlike the public amusements the Victorian court itself provided for the state. The monarchy's essential purpose was less to oversee politics than to lend colour and a little light comedy to the otherwise dull business of legislation. St Augustine's correction to Cicero was that a state is held together not only by abstract principles of justice, but by 'things loved in common'.[34] Garry Wills, the American historian, makes this point in his biography of St Augustine when he suggests that things we laugh at together are another variety of social glue. Just as the dominant key in Victorian royal family theatricals was light comedy, so too had the monarchy reached a phase whereby what it did was less to generate order or to choose ministries than to put on a cheerful show. It may well have been that Victorian people were as often amused by the monarchy as they were reverent or obedient or inspired to deference. The post-reform-act monarchy was turning into a species of serious fun.[35]

This explanation would have seemed odd both to Queen Victoria and to her new maid of honour. For them the words 'show' or 'showy' were negatives that connoted superficiality or hollowness; they were used to describe empty gestures that lacked moral purpose or seriousness. The queen, especially in the period of her husband's prime, felt that her most important purpose in life was to sustain and supervise the government of the day as well as to assure an orderly transition between governments. In the uncertain state of parties characteristic of the post-Peelite breakup of the Tories and the fading away of the Whigs in the 1840s and 1850s, there was some truth in this. Ministers with small or unstable majorities relied on her selecting them from among competitors to attract supporters and form governments. Still, the importance Victoria and Albert attached to their political role can be misleading. The majority of politicians of all parties were happiest when the royal couple did not interfere in their departments. Most of them thought of royal intervention as a nuisance.

Mary Bulteel placed more weight on the queen's moral, social and religious influence in a society that looked to the royal family to set an example than on her political expertise. She was close enough to her Grey relations to have imbibed their Whiggish principles. Like them she would have pointed to the queen's traditional role as head of state. In their view this was one of the main objects of the monarchy. Someone had to observe historical niceties and proprieties, such as opening

Parliament, receiving dignitaries and presenting new flags to regiments. Better, they thought, that the queen should bother with this sort of protocol while public men got on with governing the country, protecting property and relieving, insofar as possible, the distress of the poor. Yet the significance of theatre in the promotion of both Mary Bulteel and Henry Ponsonby to court employment should not be over-looked. Both were aware of being able to get on with ladies and gentlemen of the household not only because they were cousins, acquaintances and friends, but also because they were literally as well as figuratively performers. When she looked back in the 1870s and recol-lected her first months in waiting in 1853 Mary kept coming back to the acting which had brought her there and used stage metaphors to describe what she found.

> Of course a first arrival at Osborne could not be dull work for a girl of twenty-two, but I am surprised to think how little frightened I was. It was natural that the *mise en scène* amused me more at first than afterwards, when I thought the dinners insufferably dull.[36]

She was embarrassed to remember how, on her first arrival, she had shown off. She had performed at house parties in the houses of Whig magnates like the dukes of Bedford and Sutherland, as well as reading all the most difficult books, as well as devoting herself to more religious self-denial than anyone else. She makes these points in connection with the impression made on her, and she on them, by the other members of the household:

> I must try and remember what impressions my colleagues made on me. I was rather odious in two opposite ways; coming straight as I did from Woburn, Wrest and Ampthill, where we acted, danced, flirted, and enjoyed ourselves, I found the Court atmosphere exceedingly dull, and on the other hand I am sure I was rather pompous. I advised my new friends to read Carlyle's *French Revolution*, and Ruskin's *Stones of Venice*, etc. Besides this priggishness, I made strenuous efforts to keep up a high standard of religious practice.[37]

The young Mary Bulteel, as remembered later by her older and wiser self, was making desperate efforts to compensate for her natural sense of inferiority by underlining her various excellences. She was saved from making too harsh an impression on the other ladies and gentlemen by 'having a decided turn for mimicry'. The only problem with that was that it nearly landed her a part she did not want: 'I nearly fell into the opposite snare of being a Court buffoon.'[38] The interest of the court *mise en scène*, its dullness compared to theatricals with the Sutherlands at Wrest, the hazards of becoming a jester – all these receive attention in Mary Ponsonby's recollections of her first moments in waiting as maid of honour. For her, service at court was simply like a new script that she acted before a more famous audience. When referred to in these terms by someone who knew it intimately, the monarchy's internal working sounds more like an exclusive little chamber piece meant for the mutual entertainment of the sovereign and her suite than an adjunct of policy or an engine of morality.

The usual arrangement in the 1850s was that one lady in waiting and two maids of honour served together for a month's time. The ladies in waiting were older and married or widowed, while the maids of honour were generally younger and always unmarried. Indeed maids of honour were expected to resign their appointments if they married. The ladies and maids all belonged to or were related to the nobility, though the queen and prince avoided choosing from the richest families or the oldest titles, generally preferring instead people from the outer edges of the aristocracy. They intended to give no encouragement to the smart society in which the Prince Regent had moved. By not inviting the most prominent noblemen to court, they also had fewer rivals.

While serving at court Mary Bulteel came to know three older women. All three were to become friends, mentors and admired elders on whom she came to have something like a schoolgirl's crush. 'I often feel very grateful that the fact of being in waiting,' she wrote, 'caused me to have such wonderful, beautiful, and clever friends as Lady Jocelyn, Lady Canning, and later Lady Macdonald.'[39] They made such an impression on her that even her daughter Magdalen described two of them, Charlotte Canning and Frances Jocelyn, as 'Perhaps her two greatest friends'.[40] She also told Ethel Smyth how much all three had affected her. Smyth was inclined to see the court as a place dominated by petty jealousies, squabbles and intrigues, a place detrimental to the character of those who spent much time there. In her sixties, Mary Ponsonby looked back on her first years at court and disagreed. What the three women she so admired had taught her was a sense of how unimportant one was during one's period in waiting. They taught her how necessary it was to be absorbed in one's work during the long spells of having nothing much to do: in drawing, or in books and literature, or in using one's wit to amuse others. Being in waiting on princes, she thought, imposed humbleness on courtiers and this produced a good effect on their characters, her own included.[41]

Charlotte Canning had married the son of George Canning, the early nineteenth-century prime minister. She served as a lady of the bedchamber from 1842 until 1855, when she resigned her post in order to accompany her husband to India. The queen's ladies in waiting were all officially either 'ladies' or 'women' of the bedchamber, depending on whether they had titles, either by birth or by marriage. The Cannings served at an extremely testing time in India. He was governor general during the mutiny against English rule in 1857; she would eventually grow ill there, unused as many English people were to the climate. Charlotte Canning had high church views and this was the first point of contact between her and the young Mary Bulteel. Lady Canning taught her that the court was a different sort of discipline; and 'what wonderful training' it was 'to give up for two or three months in the year, all *authority*, to give no orders, and to realize one was just a number and didn't count'. Lady Canning was the first to point out how solemn the court was about truly silly things, for example how everyone nodded with approval at mealtimes when the Prince Consort said that eating was a waste of time. This was precisely what Mary would later enjoy sharing with Henry. Mary remembered Lady Canning's 'pleasure in talking over the absurdities of the place', as well as 'her delight in the library and quiet look of amusement at what she called *my audacities*!'[42] Here was an older woman whom Mary respected deeply. It also pleased her that she could make Charlotte Canning laugh sometimes.

Frances Jocelyn, Mary remembered, was 'quite another type. Oh her fearlessness, her inexhaustible wit!' She had been among the twelve unmarried young women who carried the queen's train at her wedding. She married the son of an Irish peer and was appointed a lady of the bedchamber in 1841. She served for more than twenty years until 1867. Lady Jocelyn used to tell Mary in arch tones, ' "I have no husband or children ... from the day I come into waiting to the last in the month. I forget what they are like; the sound of the clock in the quadrangle fills me with a sense of duty, of bore, and of worth." Equally she forgot it all as soon as the front door was out of sight.'[43]

Lady Macdonald, who was a lady of the bedchamber in succession to Lady Canning, from 1855 to 1863, had somewhat less influence on Mary than the other two. Nevertheless, she had a 'passion for literature' and this impressed Mary who found another bookish lady rather *simpatico*, as there were not many of them around, especially at the court of Queen Victoria. Lady Macdonald may have been the first to introduce Mary to the novels of George Eliot, which would later have enormous weight with her.

From all three of these women Mary believed she had learned cold indifference to court favour. From them she learned 'the worthlessness of some of the distinctions which the outer and ex-courtier world seems to value so much more than do the initiated'.[44] Having seen what it was like at the top, she learned not to care so much about being there. At the same time she preserved all her life a faint pleasure at having been 'in', one of the few members of a pretty exclusive club, even if the club was not all that the world imagined it was.

For if there were Ladies Canning, Jocelyn and Macdonald with their perfect manners and attractive occupations, there were also members of the household whose manners Mary thought dismally inadequate. Jane Ely, though a good-hearted woman, came to be a figure of fun for both Ponsonbys. Her husband was the third marquess of Ely, but for most of her long service with the queen she was a widow, which later made a strong bond between the two. Though loyal to the queen, she was not particularly discerning. She was always whispering about trivialities at the dinner table as if they were state secrets. When Mary accompanied the queen on a state visit to France in 1855 she wrote to her mother:

> Lady E. is more utterly the reverse from what she ought to be on this occasion than anybody can possibly conceive. I mean, I see she is preparing to be foolishly cringing to all the little miseries of etiquette, as if they required so much thought; I quite long for somebody as the queen's first lady with more natural dignity – being quite sure of never being in fault about manners, etc. Uncle Charles [Grey] and I howled over it last night, and tried to impress upon her the necessity of representing properly what we were, and still being perfectly natural and easy – but it was in vain, quite.[45]

This letter touches on some of the themes that were to be important to Mary all her life. She placed great emphasis on natural manners. Anything overly formal, or savouring of a guide to good behaviour, was likely to divide people. Acting naturally meant being on equal terms, or at least finding some shared common bond, with everyone, from the maid who looked after your clothes to the queen, whose cap Mary sometimes helped to straighten, or whose wrap she helped to adjust. On the other hand, the letter shows a huge sense of superiority in so young a woman. Our personalities are all made up of contradictions even though we may aim for consistency. The central paradox in Mary Bulteel's character was that she valued an Enlightenment egalitarianism that she had acquired from reading Rousseau, and at the same time she never let anyone forget that she was the granddaughter of the second Lord Grey. A.C. Benson captures this tension in her character nicely in a diary entry written after a visit to her in 1904. In the old Lady Ponsonby he found definite traces of the young maid of honour who had so cuttingly lampooned Lady Ely's failings. He drove out to see her, accompanied by another bachelor writer friend of his, Howard Sturgis, one July afternoon when she was widowed and living in the country near Ascot.

> She is really a specimen of that almost extinct species, the old *Whig*. She is almost a Radical in many ways, had a high idea of freedom and equality, combined with an immense sense of superiority and a firm but unexpressed belief in the value of birth. Lady P. was talking about Katy [duchess of] Leeds and Milly [Countess] Grey etc. saying apologetically in each case 'a cousin of mine' half the afternoon. It was all quite natural and she expressed a *deep* contempt for people who wanted rank or cared for social considerations ...
>
> And yet I can't in my heart believe that if Lady P. were to discover that she was not a 'Grey' after all; but had been changed at birth, and was the child of a housemaid and a footman, we will say – well, I think she would be a good deal ruffled.[46]

Perhaps Mary Bulteel was aware of this. She certainly condemned herself in her youthful self-examination diary for trying to impress people by mentioning the names of her high-ranking friends. She may have remembered how Ladies Canning and Jocelyn had taught her the value of the court in lowering one's sense of self-importance because she realised that this was the very failing she most needed to guard against herself.

As a young woman she also observed minutely and was sometimes critical of the manners of the royal family. She seldom found the queen wanting in behaviour. Of her eight years as maid of honour she later wrote that 'there grew up in my mind a steady and deep affection for her which time only increased'.[47] Her verdict on Prince Albert was more mixed. She admired his just, resolute and philosophical way of looking at a question. She felt it was possible 'to rely upon him as upon a strong rock'. But

> His manner was the least pleasing thing about him unless he was perfectly at his ease, and this rarely happened. There was a complete absence of that frankness which was such a charm in the Queen's manner, and there was also a self consciousness which completely prevented one's recognition of being in the presence of a '*Grand Seigneur*'.[48]

All her life Mary loved coming across magnates who had the polished *insouciance* of what she thought of as easy or 'natural' manners, who could establish a human connection without trying too hard. Her disappointment at not finding this manner in the queen's husband suggests the disdain of grandees for a prince whom they laughingly described behind their hands as the 'foreign professor'. It also shows how she was more earnest than her blasé cousins in that she actually believed in the court as a school of good conduct for ladies and gentlemen. The influence of the court – as a model of religious devotion as well as of gentle behaviour – could not well raise the tone of society if low standards obtained there.

It also dismayed her that in the 1850s the royal family 'were on more natural terms with the servants' than with the ladies in waiting.[49] They liked jokes that involved pretending to slam the door on your finger. The queen wore outfits to Paris that included lavender cravats and looked like something her dressers might have chosen. This passed into family lore, as is clear when her youngest son, Arthur, made a similar point when he was reading some of the queen's letters just after the turn of the century. He noted how the royal family were themselves more like servants than members of either the middle or upper classes. 'It comes from their being shut off from natural intercourse with ordinary human beings. They use old fashioned rather ungrammatical language and have the same love of funerals and diseases and are touching and fussy.'[50] This sense of superiority to the royal family, to Prince Albert and to Lady Ely, shows that Mary Bulteel had a confidence in her own judgement and a willingness to be different. She would speak her mind. On occasion this would bring her into collision with the queen, who sought to ignore or silence her. Often, however, she found that the queen just shut her out. 'I became accustomed to see the door leading to the Queen's rooms shut silently behind the page who came backwards and forwards for orders.' She had anticipated that friendship with the queen would come naturally and easily. Instead she found the queen did not deviate from her rule of friendliness to all, friendship with none, even for a maid of honour who put herself out to be charming. Over time the queen and Mary did at last develop greater trust and intimacy. Even then, Mary always felt the queen's snubs when she wished to reprimand her for being too forward in her suggestions or too radical in her politics. As late as the 1880s, when she looked back on entries of twenty years earlier, she confided to her self-examination diary that she had been 'Sometimes angry with the Queen for treating me like a charwoman'.[51]

Self Mortification and Revelation

As for the young Mary Bulteel, still deep in her high church phase, she spent much more time in the 1850s mortifying herself rather than suffering mortification at the hands of the queen. The young Gladstone, who was similarly in earnest about his religion and punishing himself, had done the same with a whip when tempted by prostitutes. Mary lacerated herself with observations in her journal, which she resorted to whenever she had slept late, or been cross with her mother, or tried to impress people with who and how much she knew. She taxed herself with not saying grace before meals and with paying insufficient attention to her youngest sister, Emily's, lessons. She thought the world of her mother and sisters as insufferable as most late adolescents do. She longed to escape their world, to devote herself to a life of service, to join or better to found a women's religious order.

Lady Canning inspired in Mary a pinnacle of respect and devotion. She persuaded Mary not to enter a religious order; the scandal would be too great and the hurt she would cause her family would tarnish the good she hoped to achieve.[52] Better to devote herself to some good work that was nearer at hand. Mary reluctantly took this advice and, for the time being, gave up her dream. Instead, she and her younger sister, Georgiana, founded a school in Holbeton, the village nearest Flete. The dream, however, was not entirely abandoned.

In the late 1850s Mary met a young woman whom she began to worship. She was certainly moved by the flirtation, engagement and subsequent break-up with Harcourt, but there is also a certain urgency in her relationship with Mrs Wellesley. She speaks in a new register. In her lock-up book she wrote 'She was my first very great friend and I had unlimited faith in her'. 'The comfort and peace' derived from this new friend, Mary went on, 'were indescribable'.[53] Magdalen Wellesley, or 'Lily' as Mary called her, was the wife of Gerald Wellesley, dean of Windsor and nephew of the great duke of Wellington. Mary began to see her when she was in waiting, as the deanery at Windsor was one of the social axes on which the court turned. 'Her quiet sad look fascinated me and the quiet ready sympathy, the devotion to the routine of her charities and duties gave her an interest all absorbing in my eyes.'[54] Lily showed her what it was like to live a deeply Christian life without shutting oneself away in a cloister. Further, because she was close to Mary's age, she felt she had for the first time found an equal. 'Certainly Lady Canning was on a still higher pedestal, but she was older and the personal sympathy was not so strong. Lady Jocelyn amused me more', but in Lily Wellesley she found someone with equal religious seriousness and equally devoted to doing some measurable good in the world.

Another big event in Mary's world came in the shape of new authors and new books. In the later 1850s these books began to make her doubt the severity of her religious rule. George Eliot and John Stuart Mill revolutionised her view of the world. Mill's *On Liberty* (1859) sent her in the direction of a more determined radicalism and a more militant belief in fighting against the tyranny of social convention. As a result of reading Mill she came to believe more fiercely in the necessity of education and organisation if women and working men were ever to be freed from their political subordination. Eliot's *Scenes of Clerical Life* (1858) and *Adam Bede* (1859), on the other hand, weakened her love of the church. Reading these novels, she began to be alert to some of the hypocrisy involved in Christian morality. She wrote an article on George Eliot just after the turn of the century in which she clearly recalled the impression Eliot had made on her in the late 1850s. Perhaps she exaggerated the dullness of her surroundings as a young woman of 26 or 27 in order to show what a contrast Eliot provided. Nevertheless, she remembered that she and her generation had 'welcomed George Eliot as a prophet and a seer' because they

Had been brought up in a hopeless atmosphere of conventional morality, of early Victorian theology, of dull Whig politics and ingeniously stupid Tory beliefs. The denseness of the atmosphere was never relieved by any trace of scientific training or by any perception, artistic or aesthetic.

So she was struck as if by a thunderbolt when she saw that it was possible for this woman, who was not only a writer, but also a social commentator, to work out a morality for herself independent of the church. George Eliot was asserting her right to discuss ideas on the same intellectual plane and in the same arena as men. The excellences of the author of *Adam Bede* appealed to Mary's imagination as a young woman. In particular

The merciless showing up of artificial shams which did duty as morality and religion; the fierce denunciations of selfishness, money-grubbing and pharisaism met the needs of the moment; the glimpses of happiness which her delight in pure thought and moral elevation seemed to open out were a revelation.

It was as if all at once, by reading George Eliot, Mary had for the first time been touched by something bigger than the world of her

Devonshire parish or her mother's Eaton Square drawing room, something grander than the court and more spiritually elevating than the church. George Eliot was at once 'the modern spirit' and the model for an unconventional existence.[55] Mill and Eliot loosened Mary's ties to the religious discipline that had gripped her for much of the 1850s, but the breaking away from the church came only slowly.

*

In the autumn of 1860 Mary Bulteel accompanied the queen and the Prince Consort to Coburg. The purpose was to visit Stockmar, see their first grandchild, Prince William of Prussia, and also to attend the funeral of Prince Albert's stepmother.[56] Mary's opinion of the German court was exactly the same as one of the equerries who had come along in the party. She and Henry Ponsonby agreed that the Germans were far stuffier in paying obeisance to their petty princelings than was the custom in England. They found the manners absurdly 'stiff'. Sharing a joke about this may well have struck the spark that brought them together.

They were probably also thrown together on the trip to Coburg because of a crisis. Prince Albert was in a bad carriage accident when travelling with a coachman and the horses became frightened. Neither the prince nor the coachman, though they both pulled together on the reins, could stop them. Just before they smashed into a wagon waiting at a railway crossing, the prince jumped out. Henry, who saw one of the horses loose and suspected that something had happened, went to collect the doctors who were with the party. He wrote his mother that he and the doctors found a crowd gathered 'round a little house where the man sleeps who keeps the [railway] gate. We ran to it and The Prince opened the door. His face covered in blood and mud. But he comforted us at once with "I am not much hurt but I fear the poor coachman is," and I saw the man lying on the bed motionless.' The prince then said to Henry '"How can we prevent The Queen being alarmed?" '[57] Henry volunteered to go back and tell her. Although the prince was badly bruised, he recovered. Nevertheless, the equerry and maid of honour on duty would have been knit more closely together by this near miss than they would have been by the usual round of starchy dinners.

Henry and Mary had been acquaintances for a long time. She and her sisters appear frequently as dancing partners in Henry's diary from the 1850s, when they were often invited to the same parties in London.

Their waitings at court had sometimes coincided before the trip to Coburg. Though they were agreed about the laughable customs of the Coburg court, their two diaries were very different. Hers was a meticulous record of her faults; his was composed of careful lists of young women he had danced with or taken in to dinner. The two diarists had met before in Ireland too: Mary was in waiting when the queen and the prince went to Ireland in 1853, when Ponsonby was attending the lord lieutenant. He claimed later they had actually first met at a ball at Woburn, where she was staying in the house party and had barely deigned to notice him.

In the autumn of 1860 both Henry and Mary were a bit beyond the age when most of their class and generation married. She had turned down, some thought perversely, one eligible match. He had been too poor to marry until his appointment as equerry to the Prince Consort brought him more money. She was 28. He was nearly 35. Both had Whig connections. Her grandfather, Lord Grey, and his uncle, Lord Bessborough, had worked together on the passage of the first reform bill. Indeed, Mary's Grey grandmother was before her marriage a Ponsonby and a distant relation of his. Both were bookish people who had a shared knowledge and experience of the rarefied court world. Both had grown up among rich people, though neither was particularly well off. Both had lost their fathers at an early age.

So they had things in common. They made a mature decision to get married and they did it relatively quickly. Having been to Coburg together in October, in February they went to be introduced to each other's mother. Henry confessed to his brother, Arthur, that they were impatient to be married. 'The worst is that she has to do another waiting and then my waiting comes again, so the event cannot come off till the end of April at the earliest. We are now undergoing the introductions to each other's families which is rather nervous.'[58] Neither mentions being in love, though she does begin to appear in his diary oddly as 'her', suggesting some suppressed emotion on his part.[59] His mother noticed the difference in him, writing to her younger son, Arthur, 'I don't make out what sort of letters Henry manages to write to you for he is (to quote as Shakespeare says of true lovers) very "unstaid".'[60] For her part it is difficult to tell. I suspect that she only really came to love him after some years of marriage. Certainly in later life he claimed, with the playfulness that covers a deeply-felt emotion, that he was the more passionate of the two. She grew to admire him tremendously, though sometimes with an air of detachment that is nearly always absent from his fonder assessments of her.

They were married on 30 April 1861 at St Paul's Knightsbridge, the society church near the barracks where Henry often did duty as a lieutenant colonel in the Grenadier Guards. They were showered with gifts: the duke of Wellington's canteen of plate from his mother, a locket and Irish lace shawl from the queen, jewels from her uncle, the earl of Durham. Members of the household subscribed £140 for a silver kettle, tea and coffee pots. Friends and family gave them different sets of plates for breakfast, tea, dinner and dessert. From Henry's younger brother Frederick they received a table and from his Aunt Georgiana a sofa. Someone gave them a whip and a former colleague from the Viceregal Lodge gave them a case for spirits.[61] Mary had to resign her appointment as maid of honour on marrying, but he retained his pay as equerry. As Mary brought with her a £1,000 dowry from the queen and he had cash gifts from various rich relations, they were pretty well started on their way. Within the first months of their marriage, they had to make two journeys. One they chose to make: with the other, they had no choice.

CHAPTER 4

A Married Couple

1861-63

During the first decade or so of their married lives, Henry and Mary Ponsonby used a code, what they called a 'cipher' in writing to one another. Usually only the last part of the letter is in code. Nobody so far has been able to break it, although archivists, software experts and descendants have tried. The context suggests that the code was used for secrets about the royal family or for terms of endearment between the correspondents. Perhaps they thought a servant or one of the children might see a stray letter. Or perhaps it was the sort of secret language that lovers often use to say their love is unique. They stopped using it in the 1870s when Henry's duties as private secretary and Mary's as the mother of five young children became too time-consuming. Or perhaps their love had moved into a more mature stage where they felt it was less necessary and less exciting to exchange laboriously ciphered intimacies. The code illustrates some of the difficulties of trying to understand a marriage. It is hard, especially from this distance, to break the code of what was to become a lasting and loving relationship.

In 1861 they were both just embarking on the most important relationship of their adult lives. Although they had seen each other often during the month-long waitings when they were both at court, they had never kept house together, almost certainly they had never slept together, quite certainly they had never cooked together. By modern standards they hardly knew each other at all. After their wedding they set out on a seven-week pleasure trip through France and Italy. Travel is the test of any relationship, between friends and colleagues as much as between husband and wife. To recapture the quality of their first trip together as man and wife, it is worth remembering how much strain such a journey puts on two people as well as how much patience and forbearance are required to survive it.

A Wedding Trip and Return to Windsor

The Ponsonbys left London two weeks after the wedding, taking Mary's maid, Ayling, along with them. They travelled slowly, making several stops along the way, via Paris, Strasbourg, Basel, the Italian lakes, Milan and Vicenza to Venice. They stayed in Venice for nearly a week in mid-June, doing all the things tourists do. They went to San Marco, taking Ayling along with them to see both the cathedral and the square. They visited churches and museums. They took long walks, made sketches and went to the Lido. While they were there Mary Ponsonby's sister, who had married into a great banking family, the Barings, and her husband arrived. The two couples had dinner together and 'after a turn in the gondola on the Grand Canale sat in the Piazza and had ices at Florian's'.[1] The gondoliers sang rehearsed songs. The couples were overcharged to sit outside at one of the tables with pink tablecloths. They returned via Padua and Verona, Munich, Heidelberg and Cologne. In Cologne perhaps the former Mary Bulteel put her foot down. The journey so far had been too entirely predictable. It bears the marks of having been planned according to the expected outlines of a honeymoon on the Continent, a short version of a grand tour that might have lasted seven months in the previous generation and stuck to the same itinerary. Mary did not particularly like doing what everyone else did, and had done for generations. She was more musical and more high church than her husband. In his diaries he had never noticed a piece of music before and rarely mentioned a church service. So it was unusual for him to write 'attended Mass (Mozart) in the Cathedral' before returning via Brussels, Calais and Dover to London.[2] Here was the first hint that a responsible and pleasant, though perhaps slightly shapeless, young man had married a woman with determined ideas of her own.

Henry made light of the differences they had discovered in each other on their honeymoon. It was his family's tradition to keep a logbook, or a collection of drawings and diary entries, on any significant journey away from home. In the logbook from their honeymoon, Henry drew a picture of himself and Mary at teatime in Vicenza (see Plates). Mary is looking at an intricate window with the teapot in her hand; he has drawn himself ignoring the window and concentrating on a plate of food. His caption reads: 'Beautiful window at Vicenza. Some people like fine art better than tea. Some like tea better than fine art.'

Henry's brother Arthur met them at London Bridge on 1 July. It was Arthur's first chance to meet Mary as he had been away serving with his regiment when they had been married three months earlier. Two brothers who have been close naturally look upon the new wife of the other with wariness and apprehension. In Arthur's case, Henry had been father and friend to him as well as elder brother. He had looked after him all his life. It would have been only human to have mixed feelings about this new wife of his brother's standing before him on the railway platform. If he thought of any of this, Arthur repressed it. He chose to see Mary through Henry's eyes and wrote gallantly, if cryptically, in his diary 'She very nice and rather pretty'.[3]

Henry and Mary Ponsonby thought of living in London and considered a house in Eccleston Square, but eventually chose to live in Windsor after they were married. As Henry's mother, Lady Emily Ponsonby, told Arthur, 'They both fancy Windsor as less expensive than London and as being the locality [where] their friends and interests lay.'[4] They were not rich and had married on the strength of his pay as equerry of £500 per annum, to which he added his smaller pay as colonel in the Grenadier Guards. Officers in the army were expected to have independent incomes as their expenses, including uniforms, mess bills and accommodation charges, exceeded their pay.[5] Both Lady Emily and Arthur worried that they would not have enough. (It is difficult to say precisely how much £500 was worth then. A distressed Victorian gentlewoman could scrape by on £100 a year and the hospitality of her friends and relations. A country squire with an agricultural estate of 800 to 1,000 acres and an annual rental income of about £1 per acre would have lived like a prince in the country, but looked with horror on the expense of London, though in fact he could have well afforded it. The first lord of the Treasury, or prime minister, had pay of £5,000 per year, but was also expected to have resources of his own. A highly skilled workman would have been able to support his family respectably on £1 per week. A rich barrister at the top of his profession, for example one of the queen's counsels might have had something like £3,000 a year, while successful junior barristers earned between £500 and £1,200 a year.[6] The salaries of the keepers of departments at the British Museum, for example the keeper of Printed Books and the keeper of Manuscripts, were between £500 and £600 a year. So Henry Ponsonby's pay as colonel and equerry put him on a par with those in the upper reaches of the professional classes, although he moved in the more expensive world of the court, the county and London society.) Added to his pay were the cash gifts the pair received on the occasion of their marriage, the most substantial of which, apart from the queen's £1,000 to Mary, was £200 from one of Henry's uncles. So Henry and Mary Ponsonby were comfortably well off after their marriage, but by no means as relaxed about money as their Baring relations or even most of his brother officers.

Lady Emily's phrase about Windsor being a place where not only their friends but also their 'interests' lay has an old regime ring to it. She meant there might be some chance of either a promotion at court for Henry, or Mary being taken on as a woman of the bedchamber, that would increase their income. She thought that they would have enough money 'for the present and Court favour gives hopes for the future'.[7] There was thus an element of career calculation in their move to Windsor as well as wanting to be near their friends from the household and to his work in the barracks there. There is also the survival of a faint taste of the eighteenth-century world where Whig families schemed to augment their income through court places. Still, the house at number six The Cloisters was not a grace and favour residence. The Ponsonbys had to pay for their lease and redecoration of the interior. It would have been impossible, however, to move to such a desirable location within the Castle precincts without court connections. They had trouble with the builders, who were slow to get started. Henry was repeatedly going down to Windsor 'to see how the house was not getting on'.[8] Eventually, things were put right and Ponsonbys were able to take over their new home.

Death of the Prince Consort

Henry and Mary soon received a visit from the queen and Prince Albert. The visit pleased them both, though Henry Ponsonby immediately made fun of it all by telling Mary's mother, Lady Elizabeth Bulteel, that 'Our noses have been slightly turned up since this visit, and we are only just beginning to associate with other folk'.[9] Within months Mary was pregnant with their first child; but unforeseen events upset their plans and changed their view of the immediate future. In December 1861 they heard that there was a possibility that Henry's regiment might be ordered to Canada. Tensions between the USA and Britain had heightened as a result of the American Civil War, and the British government decided to strengthen the garrison at Montreal with a detachment of the Grenadier Guards.[10] On top of the news that Henry might shortly have to take his men abroad to North America, came more serious news still. The Prince Consort fell ill with a fever. At first his condition was not considered serious. Henry Ponsonby wrote his mother, 'I find here that the Prince is very low and weak though none of the doctors think badly about him.'[11] Like all the old political families who had historical memories of the madness of George III and the sometimes hysterical instability of George IV, Ponsonby paid attention to the effect of the prince's illness on the queen's mental health. So far it too did not worry him much. 'The Queen is only a little fussed and Princess Alice the same.'[12]

The next day the situation was worse, however. Henry merely confided to his brother: 'If he shouldn't recover, his loss will be a fearful thing. He was everything to The Queen and I can't imagine how she could get on at all without him and I am frightened to think of what the loss will be.'[13] On 14 December, there still seemed to be some hope for the prince. Henry wrote to his mother:

> The last account of The Prince this morning is that he is better having slept, and the oppression of his breathing gone but the doctors are not at all easy about him yet as he is so very weak and a return of the collapse would be more than he could bear. He was pretty well yesterday morning though wandering occasionally and unable always to recognize those about him but Ruland his German secretary said he liked being read to and that he seemed always to recognize him. He also would talk about the pictures to Jenner [the doctor] and kept perpetually talking about the beautiful expression of a Madonna by Raphael that is in his room. But yesterday afternoon a collapse suddenly came on and Jenner thought he could scarcely live many hours, he was so very weak. However in the evening he rallied and the feeling of oppression is gone. The Queen was most miserable yesterday but this morning She says The Prince is much better and talks as though all danger was over.[14]

The queen's denial of the prince's real danger left her unprepared for what was to happen. He died at about eleven that very night. Ponsonby told his mother

> It is really a most terrible event and the quick way it has come upon all of us who a week ago scarcely thought the illness anything is awful. The account in The Times today is very good in all particulars. [...] Franco [Seymour] came to my house [at 11:30] and told me all was over. It was a very peaceful ending. The Queen cried most bitterly till they moved Her from the room when She became calmer. The Prince of Wales ran in to Her and threw himself in Her arms and said 'Indeed Mama I will be all I can to you,' and She kissed him very much as She said this 'Sure my dear boy you will.'
>
> I am very glad of this as it will be a good thing for both to think of in future times. They tell me that opiates were given Her last night and that She slept very well and is calm today.[15]

Although Ponsonby assured his mother that the queen was quieter than she had been, her doctors and members of the household thought she had been unhinged by the event. This was only natural in such a crisis, but it gave rise to more fears for someone whose family background had episodes of mental imbalance.

Ponsonby relied on his income as equerry to the prince to support himself and his new wife. This salary ended with the prince's death, and it was not at all a sure thing that he would be given new employment under the queen. One of his fellow equerries, Dudley de Ros, wrote him two days after the prince's death:

> I have such confidence in the Queen's kindness that I have no fear of either DuPlat, you or myself being unprovided for in some way, but after having enjoyed his society and having benefited so much by his knowledge, which he always was too happy to impart to us, what a difference any other employment about Court will be, provided we have it.[16]

Now Henry Ponsonby had a pregnant wife, the lease on a new house and the possibility of going abroad, all to be paid for out of his exiguous salary as colonel in the Grenadiers.

A few days later some of the uncertainty lifted. Sir Charles Phipps, the keeper of the privy purse, told de Ros, who passed the news to Ponsonby, that the Prince Consort's four equerries were to be appointed extra equerries to the queen. They were to have a reduction in salary from £500 to £300 per year, but still with some expectation of taking occasional waitings of a month at a time. This appointment, Phipps pointed out, 'does not give them [the four extra equerries] *a claim* to be appointed Queen's Equerry upon the occurrence of a vacancy, though of course it does not exclude them'.[17] Arthur Ponsonby who heard this news wrote in his diary 'I'm glad of this for Henry, for he married on the strength of his being equerry and the loss of pay now would leave [them] very poor indeed, but the 300 will enable him to live with a little comfort'.[18]

As if all this were not enough turbulence in career and family life, suddenly a new opportunity presented itself. The day before the funeral of the Prince Consort in St George's Chapel, Ponsonby learned that Lord Elgin, the governor general of India, would be offering him a post as his military secretary at the enormous sum of £1,200 a year. Arthur takes up the story in his diary:

> Of course he can not take it now as his Regt. is on foreign service [Canada] and he is liable to be ordered out, though if he was not, is it wise leaving the Queen's staff which must end in something good, altho' his pay is not

large? I advised him to remain where he was, but he is much tempted and Mary likes the idea, she is Lady Elgin's cousin. Henry had the offer of Private Secretary, a better thing, to Lord Canning, when he was in the Crimea and refused it[19] and it turned out all for the best, as he was appointed to Prince Albert when he came home. But it is not so much as that. I am afraid his health would not stand a very hot climate. Although by no means delicate, I think heat would touch him up. I am afraid he thinks he ought to go, for the sake of his money, *but* I hope he won't.[20]

A question of honour may have been involved. Perhaps a serving Grenadier officer could not well leave his regiment in the lurch, as it might shortly see action, in order to take a lucrative staff position elsewhere. There is in addition a sad irony in Arthur's fear that the Indian climate would affect his brother Henry's health. It was disease born of the Indian climate and sanitary conditions that was to lead to Arthur's own downfall before very long.

Henry noted in his diary on New Year's Eve of 1861 that he and Mary had been to Hampton Court where they 'saw the eclipse of the sun ... This ends the year 1861 in which I married and Barby [his sister] is going to be married. I have lost a kind chief in the Prince. America has dragged us into a quarrel. I have refused the Military Secretaryship of the Governor General of India and am now an Extra Equerry to The Queen.'[21] These short declarative statements conceal the uncertainty that still hung over the young couple. They expected a new baby in May, orders to go abroad were still pending and all this had to be managed on a £200 reduction in pay. Their marriage was off to an anxious start.

Still, they both worked at it. They spent a good deal of January staying at Hampton Court. Mary went out of her way to learn about the things that counted with Henry and his family. She read a history in French of Napoleon's campaign in 1815 and confided to her diary, 'Never knew so much about Waterloo before'. She also studied Canadian geography and listened while Henry read out Dean Stanley's *Lectures on the History of the Eastern Church*. It was self-improvement and the cultivation of their marriage at the same time.[22]

Rumours about Canada were the backdrop to Mary's first pregnancy. This was a worry. 'Canada seems dreadfully certain,' she wrote in April. 'So much to do and think of will get accumulated while I am ill with such a journey before us.'[23] Mary was told she had to give up going to church in late April and reluctantly agreed. Perhaps it was the kneeling to pray the doctor considered dangerous, but she was still devout and disliked anything that got in the way of her religious duties. On 5 May the handwriting in her diary shifts to Henry's hand. On the sixth he recorded for her, 'Taken ill this morning at 2.30. A little girl born at 10.15. Very well and happy though rather bad at the time'. It's hard to tell whether she was breastfeeding, except that a short entry on 9 May suggests she may have been, like many new mothers, having trouble with it. 'My daughter a good deal with me. Rather a struggle'.[24] They named the baby Alberta Victoria. According to Henry this was 'by The Queen's wish, who sent her a locket and £20 to Mrs. Fleming the nurse'.[25] The queen eased her grief by compelling her children and many of her courtiers to pay tribute to her husband. Hence the eldest child of the Prince and Princess of Wales, born two years later, was 'Albert Victor'. Henry felt that the Prince Consort had been kind to him; they both liked and looked up to the queen so they probably did not mind her telling them what to name their first child. Indeed, they probably regarded it as an honour.

Canada during the American Civil War

Before Alberta was two weeks old, Henry Ponsonby heard that he was expected to be in Montreal in less than two months' time. The information about preparations to go abroad comes from the bare factual account Henry Ponsonby put into one of his diaries, so there is little about the difficult decisions they had to make. The most important of these was that Mary Ponsonby decided to accompany him rather than stay behind with her newborn daughter. Perhaps the majority of army and navy wives, especially those with newborn first children, would have chosen to stay at home. Instead, Mary sent Alberta off to stay with her mother. The move hints at her brisk, self-denying efficiency; perhaps she enjoyed playing the Christian martyr just a bit. She also had a fatalistic streak that led her to accept separations and even carriage accidents with cold equanimity. English upper-class women of her generation were often like that: a passionate core disguised by icy imperturbability. At nine in the evening on 9 July 1862 the Ponsonbys set off by rail from London for Liverpool and from there by sea to Montreal.

Their ship was the *North American*. They sailed on 10 July and after a brief call at Lough Foyle for the Irish mails they did not see land again for eight days. Victorian transatlantic vessels, powered by a combination of steam and sails, were not large. By comparison to the big ocean liners of a generation later, they were slow and flimsy – not much separated the crew and passengers from the great grey waves heaving back and forth in mid-Atlantic. The passage even in mid-summer was rough. It rained and the wind blew. Two days out Mary wrote that it was a 'Nasty cold day blowing hard. Had dinner or rather a little broth on deck'. She felt quite suddenly sick and 'was obliged to disappear early in the evening'. For two days they were both so seasick that they did not leave their berths. 'Couldn't stir. Wretched.' As she rolled back and forth in her cabin, feeling miserable, Mary would not give up on her determination to teach herself something about the place she was going to be living. She read Trollope's *North America*.[26]

The next day Henry Ponsonby reported the sea was 'Rather quieter. So we went on deck. And courage increasing, dined. Played chess'.[27] Mary's seasickness improved after a strange American took her in the cabin where he made her drink a glass of pale ale.[28] Two days later Henry reported with pre-Titanic innocence 'Saw an iceberg. Another and another. Passed within a couple of miles of a large one'.[29] Mary's entry for the same day mentions the icebergs, but also 'Played at chess and beat Henry 3 games'. They did not reach Montreal until 23 July, twelve days after they had set out.

They quickly found a house to rent at number one, Union Place, Montreal. They moved in on 1 August and Henry began to serve with his men. He wrote to his brother Arthur making light of Canadian customs. 'There is a difficulty in understanding the language here. If you speak in English you get answered in French. If you speak in French you get a reply "Be gorra I dun no." ' He found horses and houses both significantly more affordable than in Britain, but the Canadian habit of renting all houses from the first of May with the assumption that next May everyone might change their living quarters preposterous.[30] In Britain you lived and died where you were born. For North Americans life was a moveable feast. It was not the first shock to his sense of what was right that he would receive from living abroad.

Henry Ponsonby's duties included attending church with his men and observing them go though exercises on open-air field days. Mary Ponsonby oversaw domestic arrangements: she interviewed fifteen women in search of a cook and housemaid.[31] She gave cooking instructions to the woman she eventually hired, all from cookbooks and theory, never having prepared a meal in her life, although one suspects that she had the same unshakeable confidence about cooking as about politics and religion. She went to teach at a local school and was shocked to find the lack of discipline in North Americans. The girls were 'very different from English [girls] but got them in better order'.[32]

Henry must have smiled at this, for he drew a picture of Mary in her hat and coat addressing the children with the caption, 'Mrs P. at her school' (see Plates).

Mary quickly involved herself in the life of the cathedral in Montreal and sang in its choir. She was always at home in the life of an ecclesiastical chapter, whether at St George's or Montreal, with its giggling, scholarly clergymen. She found it less pleasant to go and visit the wives of the soldiers under Henry's command. Some had made their rooms clean and comfortable. Others had not bothered. Many of the children caught measles and one woman was suffering from consumption.[33]

The couple were not too busy to take time off and see the sights. In mid-August they took a two-week trip to see Toronto and Niagara Falls. At Toronto they were impressed by the university and wide streets, but less so by the custom of spitting on steamboats or by the sofas on the front porches of the hotels where men sat smoking and spitting until the doorsteps looked as if they were wet with rain. Mary Ponsonby, regarding herself as pioneer among the savages, simply picked up her skirts and, choosing her path, climbed up the steps.[34] As in Venice they did the touristy rounds at Niagara, but for the first time a note of dissatisfaction creeps in, perhaps because Mary Ponsonby was beginning to have an effect on her more conventional husband. Henry Ponsonby told his brother, 'We didn't go behind the falls as some do because you have to dress in oilskin, get wet through, struggle in the dark over rock ... and see nothing ... There are all sorts of pagodas, museums, and camera obscuras about that rather disgust one'.[35] The marriage was slowly joining together his sense of the ridiculous and her impatience with the ordinary ways of the conventional world. It might have been his idea to visit the falls, and they both enjoyed the spectacle of water rushing over rock, but she would have nothing to do with the cheap tricks for the crowd.

The Canadian winter came early. Already in October the Ponsonbys were struggling through slush and snow on muddy, unpaved streets. They bought all the things they needed for a more arctic winter than they had ever experienced in Britain: snow shoes, a fur cap, a fur robe and a sleigh. They were very pleased with the sleigh. Henry drew a picture of it to which Mary added watercolours, and sent the finished result home to his mother, Lady Emily. He also did a sketch of them both being dumped out of the sleigh, entitled 'An Upset' (see Plates).

There was more than one accident. Once the horse ran away with the sleigh and crashed through a fence. The owner of the fence, thinking a

British officer could well afford to pay for the repair and more, involved the Ponsonbys in a protracted dispute over the damages. The Guards were not exactly an army of occupation in Canada, but the Canadian legislature was not anxious to pay for them, seeing them as an instrument of British rather than of Canadian foreign policy. The sleigh dispute may have reflected on a small scale some of the Canadian ambivalence toward the English troops. Certainly the francophone Québecois would have been even less enthusiastic about uniformed Englishmen and their wives. Buying a sleigh abroad may have been relatively inexpensive for the Ponsonbys, but it was not all smooth running.

In the spring they went out to explore more of the continent. They spent three weeks touring Boston and New York. Americans surprised them very much. More direct and confrontational than the Canadians, they were also more fashionable and intellectual than the Ponsonbys had expected. Although they were more liberal-minded than many Englishmen, both of them began with a typically English *hauteur* in their attitude toward Americans. Henry Ponsonby told his mother that in Boston

> the crowds and smartness of the people struck me very much ... [Boston is supposed] to be the headquarters of knowledge and literature. Even the women in society are very learned I believe and the expression of the 'cold intellectualist of Boston' is used in talking of society here. All the public libraries of the town have reading rooms for ladies, and Mary has considerable thoughts of turning Bostonian, but unfortunately they are almost all Unitarians which she doesn't approve of.[36]

Here he permitted himself a slightly disloyal sending up of his wife's bookish feminism and her Established Church disdain for dissenters. The letters shows that she was interested in women's intellectual qualifications long before her association with Girton. In fact they were both rather bookish and at home in libraries. A few days later his diary shows them visiting two different libraries in a single day.[37]

They had a letter of introduction to a Mr Fay in Boston who showed them the sights. In a different diary entry Henry Ponsonby describes Fay as 'a gentleman (very like Lord Raglan) and a "Democrat" [who] would not allow me to say a word against the country'.[38] Like Alexis de Tocqueville, an acute and liberal-minded aristocrat who had written up his impressions of America several decades earlier, Ponsonby found that Americans were more egalitarian, more decisive about the fruits of self-government than Europeans, but strangely sensitive to criticism.

In New York Henry Ponsonby found that 'there is no shyness here of speaking on all subjects' and that Americans were 'very bitter against' Englishmen, whom they accused of helping the Confederacy in the Civil War in order to bolster British trade. Although President Lincoln opposed war with Britain, 'the people here ... [would] gladly go to war with us'.[39] Ponsonby was impressed by Americans' energy, by their willingness to argue, by a parade of soldiers up a fine avenue called Broadway that he watched from the drawing room window of some new American acquaintances. Americans slowly began to gain his respect.

Mary Ponsonby had been deeply interested by the Boston libraries with ladies' reading rooms. Now in New York she found, even better, women's political meetings. Henry's account does not do justice to the depth of her passion about women's civil rights. His sense of humour sometimes took him a little too far in the wrong direction and his account to his mother of a meeting Mary wanted to attend, but missed, underrates the strength of his wife's commitment to expanding women's role in political and intellectual discussion.

> Mary wanted to go last night to a women's meeting about the war but it poured with rain so we didn't. I see the report today shows it to have been a very nonsensical meeting and they branched off entirely upon the question of the rights of women instead of the question they came together to decide on.[40]

Mary Ponsonby would have been just as interested in the question of the rights of women, if not more so, than in their attitude to the Civil War. Probably Henry Ponsonby had not had the benefit of his wife's reaction to the newspaper report of the meeting, and a few sharp dissenting words from her for his light treatment of the subject, before he wrote to his mother.

They returned to Canada via a Hudson River steamer with a stop at West Point to satisfy Henry's professional curiosity about the American Army. He drew a picture of them on the steamer, captioned 'Rather windy on the Hudson'. The wind blows his beard and Mary's bonnet; at right a man holds his hat, while at left a small boy appears to fall overboard (see Plates).

Back in Canada the Ponsonbys were obliged to move out of Union Place in May and take another house in the countryside near Montreal for the summer. Strip malls and ugly tract housing today surround Chambly, about 30 kilometres from Montreal, but in the 1860s it was in the middle of the countryside. They took up country pursuits. Mary Ponsonby had a strong masculine and competitive streak. Earlier she had insisted on going as the only woman on an all-male expedition to visit the Hudson Bay Company.[41] She enjoyed shooting the rapids on a raft – 'most exciting' – and was not at all fussy about sleeping with the logging men in a rough wooden hut.[42] At Chambly she practised with her husband's rifle. She aimed at a kerchief and birds when they went out fishing.[43] She also went over to practise at one of the firing ranges used by the soldiers.[44] What the soldiers thought of Mrs Ponsonby being such a crack shot her husband does not say. Her great work was the garden. Henry Ponsonby told his brother:

> Mary has a cow and chickens, besides vegetables and flowers and sells me the produce. Gill [a soldier servant] was overheard saying he thought the Colonel [HFP] got the worst of the bargain, but Mary is indignant as she sells cheaper than markets. She plays the organ at our military service and has a very good choir.[45]

The only thing she could not abide was the visiting that went on in Canada, which she thought 'tiresome'.[46] She especially disliked Canadian ladies who came to visit her in the country. Henry described her in the garden walking about

> with an enormous knife as if she was going to stick us if we didn't work, and with sticks and paper and seeds in her red bag and in excellent working costume, full of orders and directions, with an occasional eye on Gill planting the tomatoes and a look at the poultry in the back yard. In the midst of this voices are heard and visitors announced in the drawing room, so she goes in in her grubby dress which is far better than Mme. Levilly's moiré antique piqué de mousseline de laine, and there receives the visitors who are dressed as duchesses. After which she returns furious at the follies of visiting in the country and ... I catch it accordingly.[47]

He was beginning to learn just how emphatic his wife could be and how intolerant of people she regarded as fools. She had less time for North Americans than he did, less patience with Canadian ladies who were perhaps over-polite to her in order to impress upon her that they were her equals. She knew duchesses. She liked duchesses. She was not for a second going to put up with pretend duchesses. Her snobbery was sometimes as marked as the Canadians' *naïveté*. Henry, shoulder to shoulder with his soldiers in the garden, was more indulgent of social affectation and contented himself with amusing letters in which he sent up the whole situation. He also drew a picture of Mary with a shovel superintending him and three others in the garden (see Plates).

After a year the authorities decided that the crisis had passed and that Henry was no longer needed in Canada. They sailed home on 5 September and were reunited with their baby daughter, Betty, eleven days after having set out. They had been gone for a little over a year. What effect had Canada had on them? Their son, Arthur, believed that it had consolidated their marriage.

> It afforded them an opportunity, surrounded as they were for the most part by strangers, of falling back on one another's company, learning to adjust their dispositions to one another and so laying the foundations of the sympathetic and enduring companionship, based on deep mutual affection, which lasted without a break through all the vicissitudes of thirty-four years of married life.[48]

This is certainly true, though it may just as easily be a description of his own happy partnership with Dorothea Parry at Shulbrede Priory.

For both Henry and Mary, the year in Canada represented a significant development in their characters. For Mary, Canada showed that it was possible to have independence inside a marriage. It is a mistake to think of Victorian wives as necessarily content with supervising domestic arrangements and deferring to their husbands on everything else. Mary Ponsonby was not the sort to stay at home or mope over children left behind. This insistence on pursuits of her own, out of the house and separate from her husband's, would later make her judgement, sharpened by a different, more thorough familiarity with the world outside the barracks and beyond the castle walls, of much use to him when he became private secretary. Canada also may have made her more of a woman of the English upper classes rather than less. She scorned local society in favour of raising hens and growing vegetables. Ideally she would have liked to sell at a profit, but had to settle for her husband as the only market. This is the keen commercial farmer who lies just below the surface of many a daughter brought up in an English country house. She was not much taken or tempted by North America. Canada was a minor martyrdom, imposing a separation from her newborn that an early religious training and marriage to a serving army officer had taught her to expect, to suffer and to enjoy.

For Henry the experience was positive in a different way. It led him to start a book on the history of North America from a military angle.

Although it was never finished, possibly because court duties became too pressing, possibly because he was unable to find a publisher, the manuscript indicates a fascination with the land and its people, joined to an expert knowledge of his own profession.[49] He relished arguments with Americans over the Civil War. Experience of both Canadians and Americans also made him re-think his position on Britain's colonial empire. A discussion with his brother Arthur on the empire, shortly after his return from Canada, shows how much he was poised to accept the anti-imperialism of the Liberals and to reject the enthusiasms of the Tories. He felt no particular attachment to the empire. He thought most of the colonies could be released with no harm to Britain and only benefit to themselves. Gibraltar he thought useful from a military point of view. Nor was he for giving up India, though he thought it a mistake to rule the sub-continent despotically: the governor general ought to undergo some form of control from an elected government in Britain. However, if New Zealand, the West Indies and Canada could all rule themselves, it would save Britain the expense of sending out troops. Further, he compared what he saw of Canadian lassitude to American dynamism and hinted this might be a result of Canada's lingering link to Britain. 'Certainly at present,' he wrote to his brother, 'to cross the boundary is a remarkable sight.'

> On the Canadian side there is a look of want of energy, old huts, clean it is true, and neat but no life. Go two or three miles [and] you will see Yankee enterprise, buildings, towns, railways, etc. All life and work. If their spirit could be instilled into the Canucks it would be a good thing for them … [50]

America opened his eyes to the possibility that freed colonies were more alive and purposeful than tied dependencies. It also made him see some of the smallness of attending to the whims of princes and princesses. It polished his manners by broadening his horizon, bringing him into contact with people of previously inconceivable points of view. This was the eighteenth-century Whig's view of the beneficial social byproduct of foreign trade and commerce. It fostered understanding of different sorts of people, cultivated a superior grade of person by extending his range and polishing the rough edges off a purely provincial, homogenous society. It made people cosmopolitan. It rendered them polite. This is just what had happened to Henry Ponsonby abroad. He became more tolerant. He grew more sceptical of the imperial enthusiasm in Britain that celebrated domination rather than getting to know the customs abroad as a way of refining manners at home. He grew more attached to his wife. Though he did not yet know it, he had returned to Windsor to begin an apprenticeship to the most important office in the queen's household.

CHAPTER 5

Henry Ponsonby in Waiting

1863-70

While the Ponsonbys were away in Canada, the Prince of Wales came of age and for the first time had his own household appointed. Arthur wrote that he was sorry Henry was not in England while this was happening, as he was sure Henry's prior connection with the prince would be worth an appointment in his new household. Henry replied that everyone expected him to get something with the Prince of Wales, but in fact he wanted nothing.

> As to my being in the way while he is filling up his household, it would be of no advantage to me, for I don't know that he has any appointment he could give me. As equerry to the Queen I can get away more than I should as his equerry and I know of no other place he would be likely to give me, unless it were some more busy place which I could not very well take. He would require a man in the Army, which I am, but then I couldn't hold my present rank and do the duty, and I should have to go on half pay and so become a yellow general thus losing considerably. I am therefore not at all anxious at present for any place about him. I say all this because here everyone from General Williams downwards winks at me when his name is mentioned and seem to think I am waiting to hear of some appointment which I most certainly am not.[1]

If he were to take a position looking after the prince's money, or as his private secretary, he could not still hold the rank of colonel without retiring to the reserves. A 'yellow general' was essentially a retired general with little chance of being called up for active duty; Henry Ponsonby thought he was too young to retire from his chosen profession. He had been promoted from 'extra' equerry following the death of the Prince Consort to be one of the queen's equerries. He could combine his rank with this equerryship to the queen because it required only three months in the year. The other jobs would be full time. He did not like being winked at, though even his mother expected that familiarity with the court would lead to valuable promotion.

There are indeed hints that he expected it himself. His eldest son, in his history of the Bulteels, writes as if his father's appointment as one of the queen's equerries carried with it the understanding that he would ultimately succeed Mary Ponsonby's Uncle Charles as the queen's private secretary.[2] When Sir Charles Phipps, keeper of the privy purse, died in 1866, Ponsonby's name was mentioned for the job, but it went to Thomas Biddulph, then serving as master of the household. John Cowell was promoted from among the equerries to take Biddulph's former place as master. Ponsonby told his brother he did not think he had had a chance at it, as there were two senior equerries before him. The mastership, which required pretty regular attendance on the queen, inviting guests, assigning bedrooms, arranging parties, was something really 'for an unmarried man' and Cowell was the foremost of those in the existing household.[3] Indeed, Ponsonby occasionally did duty as a sort of temporary master of the household when he was serving as equerry, but he did not have the knack for organising *placement*, table decorations and flowers that the most successful incumbents of the post usually have.

Equerry

From 1863 until 1870, while his friends and relations expected that something better would turn up at court, Henry Ponsonby divided his time between waitings as equerry and service as colonel in the Grenadier Guards. He was not impatient with his lot or anxious for quick advancement. He shared the sufferings of the widowed queen and her family, who were neighbours, and to a certain degree, friends. He felt genuine affection for the queen, but there was an unmistakable distance between them, as there was between her and most of the household. A little more than a month after his return from Canada, Henry Ponsonby came into waiting on the queen.[4] He attended her throughout the month of November, not writing to his brother until the end of his month with her to say 'The Queen is I think very well though much older than when I saw her last'.[5]

On the second anniversary of the prince's death Victoria asked all the royal servants and their families at Windsor, more than 200 in all, to visit the Mausoleum at Frogmore where he had been buried. The queen liked to go and sit there by herself though it depressed her more than she was already. The servants were soon to resume their red liveries, however, and that was a step in the right direction.[6] Ponsonby felt for the queen, but saw the funny side of Frogmore too. In his recollections of the period is a paragraph labelled, 'Frogmore'.

> When I first came into waiting the Duchess of Kent [the queen's mother] lived here, and frequently came up to dinner at the Castle, where the Household always received her and she full of apologies for the trouble. The grounds at Frogmore are pretty but the late additions have changed them. There is the Duchess of Kent's Mausoleum, the Prince Consort's Mausoleum, not yet finished (open once a year to the Household) and a cross in memory of Baron Stockmar. King Leopold said to me one day 'Frogmore was never a very lively place but now it is a perfect graveyard.'[7]

Probably this was one of several polished stories used when showing the queen's visitors around the castle and the Home Park. It was a light way of cutting the gloom at Windsor in the 1860s without disrespect.

Ponsonby was also attached to the Prince of Wales and worried about whether the prince was responsible enough to sustain his new marriage to Princess Alexandra of Denmark. They had married while he and Mary were in Canada. He was reassured at hearing from Lady Macclesfield, one of the princess's ladies, that there had been a tender scene between them on the birth of their first child. The birth was unexpected and Lady Macclesfield had had to act as midwife.

> She ordered the Princess of Wales after it was over to be left quite quiet, and went away but came back soon and peeped in and found the Prince and Princess of Wales crying in each other's arms. Very pretty and I liked to hear it of him as it shows that he really likes her. However Lady Macclesfield ordered the Prince out of the room and enforced quiet.[8]

Two years later Ponsonby's fears, however, began to be realised. The Prince and Princess of Wales were going to great numbers of balls in London, usually staying until five in the morning 'by which time all the guests are exhausted or gone'. Further, the prince had taken a fancy to Lady Filmer and paid special attention to her in obvious ways, so obvious that one of his friends had to write him a frank letter warning him of the consequences.[9] The prince's infidelities had become routine some years later and he became publicly embroiled in the Mordaunt divorce case in 1870; it all depressed Ponsonby very much.[10] He looked back full of relief that he had *not* been named to the Prince of Wales's household while he was in Canada. He was becoming so attached to his own wife that infidelity was almost inconceivable to him. He liked the prince, but he did not respect him.

As the queen's equerry in the 1860s he was also dismayed by her staying so long away from London. Historians have sometimes described her retirement after the death of the Prince Consort as an affront to the people, who missed big ceremonies and seeing her in public. In fact big state events were few and far between even before the prince's death. The people who minded most about her being away were, first, ministers who had the inconvenience of going to Scotland or the Isle of Wight to get papers signed. Second, members of the urban upper middle classes missed court functions and the opportunities afforded for establishing their rank and promoting marriageable daughters. These functions resumed on a limited scale in 1864, though the Prince and Princess of Wales often deputised for the queen. The impression remained, as did the reality, that the queen came to London as little as possible.

This might not have mattered at all except that those who took an active interest in the political world began to be bothered about her being away when the debate about extending the franchise was renewed in the mid-1860s. Politicians became more fretful about the queen's absence in the context of political disputes and potential disturbances attending a new reform of the constitution. Then as now uneasiness about changes in the constitution had a way of magnifying lesser concerns about the popularity of the monarchy, the visible symbol of the state. So Queen Victoria was not wholly to blame for the increased attention and displeasure focused on her as the reform debates sharpened. Still, Henry Ponsonby reported to his brother in 1866 after the Liberals under Lord John Russell had been defeated over their reform proposals that the queen had been 'forgetting her duties in the pleasant breezes of Scotland'. It was awkward for the retiring ministers who had to wait several days for her return before they could hand over their seals of office. Henry Ponsonby said he was 'surprised that the growls which were deep and numerous on Her absence have not found vent in the press although some few remarks have been made. She sent a sick certificate to say She couldn't be back till today.'[11] The 'sick certificate', which she had certainly trumped up with her doctors' connivance was Ponsonby's way of amusing his brother with a situation that nevertheless might turn serious.

He was never critical of the queen for her friendship with her Scottish servant, John Brown. In 1866 he dismissed as a libel a report about Brown in the Lausanne *Gazette*.

We do not know what the libel is and I believe The Queen is as ignorant as any of us, but I hope She will not hear it, as I believe it to be a statement that She has married John Brown. And the idea that it could be said She was marrying one of the servants would make Her angry and wretched. Brown has always been a favourite with the Royal Family and has lately been raised to be personal attendant. This is all. Messages come by him. As he is always dressed as a highlander [he] is conspicuous and so is talked of. Besides which he certainly is a favourite, but he is only a servant and nothing more. And what I suppose began as a joke about his constant attendance has been perverted into a libel that The Queen has married him.[12]

Ponsonby had chances to observe the queen on familiar terms, so his report to his brother that the marriage to Brown was a lie has to be taken seriously. On the other hand, at the very least she had an intimate and romantic friendship with him. His presence on the royal scene together with all the special privileges he enjoyed adds to the baroque ridiculousness of the queen's entourage that was one of the usual motifs of Ponsonby's letters home. The queen had Brown's picture painted leaning with a proprietary air in the open doorway of her new house, the Glassalt Shiel on Loch Muick. He supervised the extension and arrangement of the house; she never stayed there again after his death in 1883.[13] When he died she set out to memorialise him in words and statues in precisely the same way she treated the Prince Consort on his death in 1861. When she died, she left instructions for her doctor to place Brown's photograph and a case containing some of his hair in her left hand before the coffin was closed.[14] Then there is the story, perhaps apocryphal, passed down via the descendants of Lady Ely. It is said that the queen went out driving one day from Balmoral, with the most loyal, though perhaps also the most craven, of her ladies, Jane Ely. They stopped at a house belonging to one of Brown's relations. The queen and Brown disappeared inside while Lady Ely remained outside in the carriage, soaking in a gentle rain. After some time, a footman came out bearing a glass of champagne and said to her 'The Queen and Brown would like you to drink their healths'. She did so and returned the empty glass. After more waiting, the queen and Brown emerged. The queen was immensely happy. Brown got on the box as usual and they drove on without a word said.

Ponsonby noted in his diary for May 1867 that the queen had taken Brown along, as usual, for the opening of the Royal Albert Hall. He deprecated rumours that the people lining the route had received the queen with only halfhearted applause. He also wondered why so much notice was taken of Brown.

John Brown dressed in Stuart tartan and kilt followed in the procession with the servants and was much taken notice of, indeed there was an almost audible murmur of 'John Brown' when he appeared. Why he should not have been there as much as the Sergeant Footman with whom he walked there is no reason yet it certainly created a bad feeling. We drove through Rotten Row, the crowd there being respectable and smart and not given to cheering, still there was much waving of handkerchiefs. After Marlborough House we returned to Windsor as arranged at 2. But in London a story was disseminated that The Queen had been hissed and that furious and indignant she had returned to Windsor earlier than intended.[15]

Ponsonby was used to seeing Brown everywhere; the crowd, who had recently been reading the rumours about him and seeing him carica-tured in journals, was not. Hence Ponsonby's surprise that they should recognise him. There is just a hint though that Ponsonby's account grasped an element of the satirical in Brown's attendance. His mentioning 'Brown dressed in the Stuart tartan' suggests that he may have seen the irony of the queen dressing her Highland servants in the colours of the family through whose defeat her own family had come to the throne. In fact the Stuart tartan was all over Balmoral: in the curtains and carpets as well as kilts. Even George IV had worn it when he visited Scotland in 1822. The tartan played a part in royal romanti-cisation of the Scottish past and the dynasty through which the English and Scottish thrones were first united. However, for Ponsonby, Macaulay and the nineteenth-century survivors of the Whig families who served the Hanoverians, the Stuarts were despots, kings who had tried to usurp parliamentary rights. They had been forced to abdicate by parliamentary lords who established a constitutional monarchy based on Protestant rather than on strictly hereditary descent. The story is told of Macaulay's meeting with Queen Victoria. She described the Stuart who had fled in 1688, James II, as her ancestor. ' "Your Majesty's predecessor, not ancestor," cried the historian.'[16] The queen might trace her descent from the Stuarts all she liked, but in fact she reigned because Parliament allowed it. Brown in the Stuart tartan, though harmless, was still worth a smile.[17]

At this early stage, when he was only in waiting a few months of the year, Ponsonby did not yet know all of what was going on. Grey, the private secretary, did not discuss the queen's business with Ponsonby until just before he died. The queen held the household at arm's length. Only the servants really knew what happened behind closed doors. It was not until he became private secretary himself that Henry grasped the enormity of trivial affairs at court and how seemingly unimportant fancies the queen had for one or other of her personal attendants might grow into publicity that could affect the standing of the monarchy itself.

*

Of course no one thought very much then about the way in which what we call public relations today might affect the standing of a public institution. Even though there was a large newspaper press, expanding in readership among all classes, no one sought to manage the flow of information. The queen's private secretary monitored what the newspapers said, but did not try to control them. She released statements about her health through the court circular. Some of the household leaked innocuous paragraphs to the press about what the queen was doing, or whom she was seeing. None of them understood that scandal, gossip and intrigue were as much a part of the monarchy's appeal as domestic propriety. The Brown scandal, which came to be fairly common knowledge in London society, was a titillating contrast to the dull but correct story of the queen's having loved her husband and raised nine children. That story, in turn, had been an edifying contrast to the tales of George III's sons, their mistresses and their debts. The monarchy's appeal depends on this _combination_ of moral propriety and wicked lapses. As with a good _beurre blanc_, there has to be a tart undertone or the butter is too rich. Similarly, the attraction of the monarchy for a reading or a viewing public depends on the extent to which people can see their darker sides revealed as well as be provided with a moral example they might like to emulate. Striking the balance is all. Henry Ponsonby did not exactly think in these terms, but his instinct to make light of the monarchy when it was all getting too serious represents a similar understanding of its appeal.

Henry Ponsonby's sense of humour was a family trait. His cousin, Spencer Ponsonby-Fane, was appointed to be comptroller of the Lord Chamberlain's Office in the 1850s. The two men acquired a reputation for their amusing stories and prompt, if irreverent, attention to the business of the court. In March 1865 there was trouble when a foreign office official, supposedly under instructions from Ponsonby-Fane, sent out invitation cards for a diplomatic reception

to say The Queen would receive the '_Corps Diplomatique Male et Femelle_' [meaning the male and female of an animal, e.g. cock and hen]. They were furious and haven't yet got over their anger. Spencer never told Cust to issue any cards, and I don't think he ought to be blamed. The

Queen I heard said 'It would be as well if Mr Ponsonby was cautioned not to be so funny.' I am sorry she has got this idea into her head, as she will think the whole family such wags that we are liable to be misunderstood.[18]

Henry Ponsonby could be relied on to relieve the tedium of a dinner table with a few light asides, but too many jokes annoyed the queen. Her taste was for ladies whom she could dominate, or servants who could dominate her. Sometimes men like Arthur Helps, secretary of the Privy Council, could win her trust. Helps was the sort of effeminate royalist whom Ponsonby could not understand at all, but whom the queen found useful. Helps assisted her in the writing of her *Leaves from the Journal of Our Life in the Highlands*, as well as in setting up memorials to the Prince Consort. At the unveiling of a new statue to the prince in November 1865 Ponsonby noted in his diary: 'Helps [was] the chief man who managed everything. A sickly looking somewhat affected, very pleasant and agreeable man.'[19] If Henry Ponsonby was sometimes critical of courtiers like Helps whom he saw as trying too hard, he tempered his criticism with an admission that the man was a pleasure to have in company.

The equerry's duty had to do with companionship and facilitating transport. The gentlemen in waiting, though usually military men, did not discharge any function as bodyguards. Even companionship was not much wanted in the 1860s, as the queen avoided contact even with the household. There was very little security around her; one or two police officers generally sufficed. In 1867, however, the Home Office discovered plans by Irish rebels, known as Fenians, to kidnap the queen. Henry Ponsonby's account to his wife of the precautions that were taken at Balmoral shows just how exposed the queen could be.

General Grey received a telegram from Manchester to say that a detective had attended a Fenian meeting there. About 40 men were present armed with revolvers, and the subject discussed was the carrying off of The Queen. Several persons seemed to be acquainted with Her habit of taking long drives unaccompanied by any of the Household, only Brown and the servants. It probably was nonsense, but it would not do to treat it as such. An armed body of 40 men suddenly pouring down even on the Castle might effect much. So 50 highlanders 93rd were sent from Aberdeen, and I made arrangements for putting them up at Abergeldie, and police were sent from London ... The Queen didn't quite think all the fuss was necessary. She went out to tea with Lady Ely on the top of Carrop and found a London policeman there. She went up Glengelder and found another, etc. It rather bored her.[20]

If the queen was annoyed by too much attendance by policemen, she was also irritated by too little attendance by equerries who were meant to assist the royal family in and out of trains. In those days there were no loudspeakers warning 'Mind the Gap'. Princess Beatrice, as a child, fell into the space between the train and platform as the queen and her party were leaving Windsor for Osborne in May 1867. Henry Ponsonby recorded 'we lugged her out without more damage than the fright', but the queen sent a note saying it would be well if the gentlemen in waiting paid more attention.[21]

Occasional spells of hard work occurred when foreign heads of state came to Britain on official visits. Ordinarily the queen refused such visits or discouraged them, but when the sultan of Turkey, who was regarded as important to keeping the sea route to India open, came in 1867, no effort was spared. Ponsonby was on duty for eleven strenuous days in which he helped the Prince of Wales to receive the sultan at Dover; attended receptions, dinners and parties while making small talk with pashas and effendis; took the sultan's party sightseeing in London and to a naval review off the Isle of Wight; and guided the sultan's entourage through grand and badly organized parties given by the City authorities in the Guildhall. It was exhausting and after seven days Ponsonby recorded that the 'Turks [were] rather knocked up'.[22]

The queen's visits abroad also required more attention than usual on the equerry's part, although these too were fairly unusual. The first major trip she made after the death of the Prince Consort was in August 1868 to visit Switzerland. Although the going out and coming back required extensive consultations between equerry and special couriers, who acted as the queen's travel agents, once they arrived it was Brown who looked after most of the queen's needs. He forbade her from keeping hours different from those she kept at home, so she often did not drive out from her rented villa until four in the afternoon. Suggestions about excursions from the household Brown frequently vetoed as too much trouble or too risky because of his unfamiliarity with the foreign surroundings. The queen relied on what the household could tell her of their day trips at dinner and on Henry Ponsonby's light touch to relieve the gloom of Brown's diktats and decrees. The fact that he was on good terms with Brown was another recommendation to the queen when it came time to choose a new private secretary.

Ponsonby claimed to his wife that on one evening he was not trying to be funny, but sent the whole dinner table into fits. While they were all out together in Switzerland, the queen's physician, Sir William

Jenner, was telling the story of a mountain climbing expedition with Miss Bauer, the German governess.

> I do not know why my remarks are supposed always to be facetious when they are not. I simply asked what the tourists thought of their relationship. He replied 'Oh, of course they thought she was Madame,' which created some laughter. Then he added 'The guide was very decided and made us give up the horses. We rode up and came down in a chair.' 'What?' I asked. 'Both in one chair?' Well, there is nothing odd in this – but everyone laughed. I turned to Mary Bids [Lady Biddulph]. She was purple. On the other side I tried to speak to Princess Louise. She was choking. I looked across at Jenner. He was convulsed. Of course this was too much. I gave way; and we all had a *fou rire* till the tears ran down my cheeks which set off the Queen. I never saw her laugh so much. She said afterwards it was my face. At last we got a pause when Jane [Churchill] to set things straight again began with 'Did you find it comfortable?' which started us off again.[23]

A *fou rire*, or helpless laughter, was a treasured event in the Ponsonby household. It was this sense of the ridiculous that was Ponsonby's special contribution to the queen's entourage. This had serious consequences for the atmosphere and attractiveness of Queen Victoria's court. Ponsonby's manner suggested that respect be paid to royal highnesses, but that fun could be had with them, even at their own expense. Especially as private secretary, Ponsonby would come to be the contact man with civil servants, ministers, generals, clergymen, pressmen and railway officials. They were often nervous and intimidated by their first approach to a high court official, the descendant of an old family with aristocratic connections. Instead of stiffness they found that he could be a delight and a wry tease. For a wide swathe of officialdom, Ponsonby *was* the monarchy and they found him a far less starchy, much more amusing presence than they had expected.

It was his habitual approach to life to relish absurd moments. Shortly before he became private secretary he was in waiting at Balmoral. His strategy to relieve the boredom of the long separations from his wife was to write to her about episodes in the retired life of queen and household that would be bound to amuse her. Imagine his well-concealed but heightened interest then when told by one of the servants that the queen's dressers had been making excursions to view an enormously fat woman living in a cottage not far from Balmoral. When one of the dressers had gone, all the others wanted to go. Soon, Ponsonby wrote, the queen herself drove out in the general direction of the fat woman, not with the announced object of seeing her, but making a stop by her cottage possible as a slight detour. Two days later, the queen's going had made it all right for the rest of the household to go. 'In consequence of the Queen having been to see the Fat woman all the household have now been and Spor the packer who is our fattest individual has exchanged photographs with her.'[24]

Army

The duty as equerry occupied only a part of Ponsonby's time in the 1860s. He was also a colonel in the Grenadier Guards, regularly on duty in London, Windsor and occasionally in Ireland. He inspected his soldiers' kit and quarters. He conferred with the non-commissioned officers who really looked after the men, for he looked after his men in theory more than in practice. Occasionally there were field days. One day in March 1862 he took 172 soldiers from London to Eastbourne to practise drills and musketry: this came to an end after a few days because they ran out of ammunition.[25] Less than a year after their return from Canada, Ponsonby received new orders to return there. Mary was now pregnant with their second daughter, Magdalen. However, they both made plans to go abroad and pack up their house all over again. Mary went up to London to send their two-year-old, Betty, back to her mother's in Devonshire. At the last minute, though, Ponsonby learned that, through General Grey, the orders for him to go had been withdrawn. He telegraphed to stop Mary from putting Betty and her nurse on the train to Lady Elizabeth Bulteel's. He gave his brother Arthur an account of the dramatic scene on the railway platform.

> I telegraphed up to the stationmaster to stop Betty at Paddington just in time. Mary had taken leave of her when she saw the nurse and child hauled out of the carriage by two guards. Of course an excitement in the station and my second telegram to Mary herself delivered by a breathless boy. All the porters in the station crowded round and the passengers to see what it was, and the Bishop of Oxford was left struggling with 6 portmanteaux in the distance, porterless.[26]

The Ponsonbys were saved from this new posting to Canada because they had friends in high places. Mary's uncle was able to make a special case to the queen's cousin, the duke of Cambridge, about the orders causing hardship to the Ponsonbys. The duke, as commander in chief of the army, played a considerable role in Ponsonby's life. In this case he saved him from an irksome duty, but as private secretary, Ponsonby would spend much time trying to placate, mollify and persuade the duke not to resist reforms of the army proposed by responsible ministers. There may well have been a Cambridge connection with Ponsonby's mother, Lady Emily, who appears to have been in waiting on the duke of Cambridge's mother. Possibly it was this that led to Henry's appointment as a member of the committee that oversaw the Cambridge Asylum, a charitable foundation in Surbiton. One or two of the queen's maids of honour were also on the committee and Ponsonby attended these committee meetings regularly in the 1860s. Unlike his wife, who was passionately committed to her philanthropies and cared deeply about advancing educational and working opportunities for women, Henry Ponsonby merely served on this committee as a dutiful son and loyal member of the household.

Henry Ponsonby was not afraid to challenge his patrons or to oppose those who were in authority over him. He began a lifetime of patient and respectful disagreement with the duke of Cambridge on army matters at a dinner in May 1867. Ponsonby had been lobbying some MPs in the United Services Club in favour of the abolition of flogging. Clearly Henry had never forgotten the man he saw flogged in the Crimea who later killed himself in shame. An MP named Otway was bringing forward a resolution deploring the increase in numbers of offences for which flogging was a permissible punishment, and declaring that it was neither fit nor civilised to hand down corporal punishment in a time of peace.[27] Ponsonby heartily agreed, but the duke, who 'came up and caught hold of my arm' opposed him. Cambridge was of the old school who thought of soldiers as hardy thieves who could only be kept in line with repeated threats of bodily harm.

'Good heavens! [he told Ponsonby] What would you have in its place? Of course I am against it if I could discover any other swift and deterrent punishment, but what would you do with a man who knocks you down?' I answered, first, that Sir T. Pakington's proposals would prevent my flogging him if he were in the first class; second that I thought imprisonment would be the punishment for the crime. The Duke said, 'Oh all that stuff brought in by Pakington must be changed. It's all nonsense. Damnedest nonsense. But as to your imprisonment, why what do villains care about that? Why they don't care a damn for it!' He rattled on very good-humouredly and not at all indignant against those who took an opposite view to his.[28]

Cambridge would grow to be a considerably more painful thorn in Ponsonby's side when he became private secretary. Indeed, the duke was the first to raise objections when Ponsonby's name was mentioned as a possible successor to General Grey as private secretary. Ponsonby noted this in a memorandum after he was appointed, saying that the duke of Cambridge

> was foremost in expressing a regret that one who was known to have such extreme radical tendencies on military and other matters should be placed in such a position and the Duchess of Cambridge made no secret of her son's dislike to me for my political views and told my mother at the meeting of the Cambridge Asylum that although she congratulated her and considered that in many ways I would make a good Secretary, she would not disguise from her that the Duke believed the appointment a bad one from a political point of view.

Thus, early on in his career Ponsonby had the boldness to take a very different line from his superiors in military matters, aligning himself with those who wanted to treat soldiers in a more humane fashion. He was also an early advocate of Liberal plans to reform the officer class by introducing competitive examination and abolishing the system whereby men purchased their initial commissions as well as their promotions. This was as bold in the 1860s as it would be today for an officer to advocate that the armed forces should admit and acknowledge the contributions of homosexual men and women. In taking such prominent and controversial political stands, Ponsonby was taking a considerable risk of being passed over for future promotion.

Ponsonby had been fairly conventional in his views when he was on his own in Ireland. It is probable that he was converted to these liberal and progressive views in the 1860s by the greater radicalism of his wife and by the open-mindedness of his brother, his two principal loves and his two principal correspondents. As the years of his marriage passed, he became much bolder in taking a reformist attitude, especially in military matters. No critiques of the military status quo emerged from his time at the Viceregal Lodge in Dublin, and only a few after he served in the Crimea. They date mainly from the period after he was married. Further, his brother Arthur, finding the Grenadier Guards too smart or too expensive or both, had transferred back to a more workmanlike regiment of the line in 1863. Through Arthur, Henry Ponsonby learned how the other half lived. He was surprised and pleased by his younger brother's attempts to ameliorate conditions for soldiers in the ranks. In

Dublin Arthur Ponsonby had started a military exhibition, in which soldiers produced displays for the public demonstrating some of the skills and crafts necessary for a life in uniform. This had received good notices in the press both for the pride in their profession it instilled in the men and for encouraging enlistment: it was the exact opposite of managing men by threats of flogging. Two years later Arthur wrote to Henry from his new posting in India: 'The more I see of soldiers the more convinced I am that we treat them too much as children. They ought to have more liberty and different punishment.'[29]

In 1865 Henry still believed that the men under him were in fact child-like and needed to be treated as such.

> I think your men in the line must be more intelligent than ours [in the Guards]. We have fine strapping fellows who are incapable it seems to me to take care of themselves, and I don't believe they could argue questions such as your men do. However, I may libel them for it is difficult to see much of one's men. If I get to talk to them the Adjt. or Sgt. Major look sour and hurt, and the man invariably gets drunk and is brought up for absence etc. next morning which the two above named people think is entirely owing to his having been taken notice of.[30]

In his later years in the royal household, Henry Ponsonby had a reputation for being left of centre in his views on military matters. He also was known as someone who had a common touch, who could get along as easily with John Brown as with ministerial dukes. In the 1860s, however, he was still in transition. His wife and his brother both contributed to the change which made him more sensitive to the needs of ordinary soldiers and more impatient with rigid, old-regime arrangements.

Toward the end of the 1860s, service with the Guards twice took Henry Ponsonby back to Ireland. He had not done duty there since before the Crimean War. These two spells in Ireland also made a contribution to his mature character, making him readier to confront controversy and requiring him to adopt calming diplomatic skills. In the summer of 1869 he was sent to Belfast. There he was ordered to take command of troops assigned to keep order during the Orange anniversaries when, then as now, clashes were expected between Protestants and Catholics. Despite the fact that she had four young children at home between the ages of two and seven, Mary went with him. She felt that her duty, whenever possible, was to her husband. Further, she was more combative than Henry and relished the feeling of being useful in a political dispute. She helped by attending several of the rival churches with her husband on the eve of 12 July when there were to be marches and meetings commemorating the victory of the Protestant forces of William III at the Battle of the Boyne in 1690. They came across Ulstermen and their families 'covered with orange scarves intent on prayer' and the next day Catholics 'adorned with green ribbons [who] wanted to attack them'.[31] Henry conferred with both the Protestant mayor and the Catholic resident magistrate. He brokered a compromise; there were clashes but no violence.

More violent, perhaps, were the arguments he had with Tories and representatives of the Protestant landowning ascendancy in the South. His battalion was called to Dublin in case there were troubles as Gladstone's bill disestablishing the Protestant Church of Ireland passed through Parliament at Westminster. 'Bitterness' against Gladstone's bill was so general that he found it 'a relief' to get to Dublin Castle. There he found Lord and Lady Spencer, who had been sent out to discharge the viceregal function, and were, like him, warm supporters of Gladstone's bill.[32] Here too, though, Ponsonby knew how to placate his enemies by accepting a portion of their argument. Although he was in favour of Gladstone's plans to acknowledge the just grievances of the Irish,[33] he also accepted the Tories' insistence on more law and order in Ireland. This was not so much a diplomatic tactic as the natural view of someone who was a soldier as well as a Whig and a Liberal.[34]

One final element of the Irish scene that foreshadowed changes Henry would experience on a larger scale and on a more prominent stage in his service with the queen were shifts in the character of Dublin society. He found more state, more show and more formality, especially at the viceregal court, than formerly. He was surprised to find every lady, including Lady Spencer, making a low curtsey to the viceroy as they left the dining room.[35] The Spencers appeared to be fighting Tory bitterness against Gladstone with feudal manners and big parties. Ponsonby dined one night with them in St Patrick's Hall when they gave a dinner to a hundred guests. Ponsonby, who hated dressing up in uniform, and was unpleasantly 'stunned with the band', did not enjoy himself.[36] He was also surprised that even aristocratic families like the Pakenhams were going in for these big showy entertainments.[37] He thought all this dressing up and showing off was a bit middle class, characteristic of civic authorities, mayors and their wives, who delighted in wearing their chains, robes and insignia of office, earning them the sobriquet, 'the chain gang'. Henry had grown up among old governing families in which shabby was chic and ostentation vulgar. Sometime in the 1860s, perhaps with the second reform bill, which had enlarged the middle class and urban element in the British electorate, the tide had changed. This social shift was as much responsible for dissatisfaction with Queen Victoria's quiet style of living in the days following the death of the Prince Consort as her moderate retirement from London society. She had retired only a little, but both London and provincial society had begun to entertain a lot. The increasing demand for grand processions and state occasions that would come to fruition in the jubilees of 1887 and 1897 had already begun in the 1860s. It was as much a result of a new social composition in the governing classes as it was of Disraeli waving an imperial wand. Disraeli merely responded to something already in the electorate. He did not create the taste for display and grandeur: he capitalised on it. Ponsonby disliked Disraeli's sympathetic response to the new taste for show. He was nonplussed by the new style of entertaining in Ireland, but it would be his fate to preside over an era in the evolution of the monarchy in which these social changes would make themselves emphatically felt.

He never let such things embitter him, however. He turned away his slight disapproval of the social scene in Ireland with a keenly observed vignette. In May 1869 an ambitious Irish hostess, Mrs Murphy, gave a ball for the whole regiment and was walking around trying to look after her guests. She came across one of Ponsonby's fellow officers.

> She had asked the whole regiment en masse so didn't know who any of them were. Seeing Ranfurly standing alone she asked, 'Will I introduce you to a nice young partner.' 'If you please,' replied Ranfurly. 'Would you tell me your name?' 'Lord Ranfurly.' 'A rale lord! Oh my conscience! Then I'll dance with ye meeself.'[38]

These tours of duty in Ireland were Ponsonby's last active service with the Grenadier Guards. Although he approved of Edward Cardwell's plans to reform the officer class by abolishing purchase, he and many fellow officers worried that the Cardwell reforms might reduce the amount of their purchase money returned to them when they retired from active duty. General Grey and the queen had already agreed on Ponsonby as Grey's successor and he began to have a small share of Grey's work in April 1869. No doubt his wife's uncle had told Ponsonby that the office would eventually be his. Furthermore, Ponsonby and his wife both understood that the private secretariat would require constant attendance on the queen and that he would thus have to give up active service with the Grenadier Guards. It was a difficult parting for him. It was the duke of Wellington's old regiment, his father's old regiment and the only profession he had ever known. He heard in March 1870 that he could get back £8,500 of his original purchase money if he acted at once; the opportunity might vanish if Cardwell's reforms went through. After long conversations with Mary, Henry decided to retire to the reserves by going on the half pay list. The expressive entry in his diary, ordinarily a bare record of events, almost never of feelings, was 'sorry to leave'.[39] Within the month, General Grey was dead and Henry Ponsonby's new life had begun.

In the middle ages kings had been military figures who defended the borders and kept order. They only ceased leading men into battle in the eighteenth century. Although she never visited a battlefront, Queen Victoria remained deeply interested in the Army. Her father had been a soldier. Troop reviews were among the first public functions she resumed after the death of the Prince Consort.[40] Her court remained predominantly a martial one, filled with serving officers, retired officers and officers in the reserves. When Henry Ponsonby left active duty with the Guards and took up full-time work as private secretary, he was hardly entering a brand new world. It was simply a different chamber of the military edifice he had occupied since his schooldays. We have become so used to the picture of Queen Victoria as wife, mother and widow, that we sometimes forget how big a part the military element played in forming the atmosphere of her court. Henry Ponsonby's experience as a peacetime colonel in the Grenadier Guards during the 1860s put a distinctive stamp on his private secretariat. He valued plain speaking and organisation. He assumed that hierarchy and obedience to superiors was part of the natural order of things. Given these typically army attitudes, his coming development into a Liberal who bucked the military establishment is surprising indeed.

Politics and Politicians

Henry Ponsonby adored his wife, loved his younger brother Arthur, and felt affection for the Grenadier Guards. Next in line among his animating passions were politics and politicians. This naturally suited him for his job as private secretary, a happy coincidence between hobby and paid employment that makes for the best and luckiest of careers. He mixed with politicians who were in attendance while he was in waiting as equerry. He also saw leading men of the political world when he and Mary attended Lady Waldegrave's parties. In the 1860s Lady Waldegrave, whom Mary had known before she married Henry, and a prominent Whig politician, Chichester Fortescue, were installed at Horace Walpole's gothic folly near Twickenham, Strawberry Hill. She attempted to keep up the tradition of the regency *salonnière*, who had cemented alliances and furnished opportunities for political discussion to the influential men of the day. In such *salons* upper-class women asserted their rights and demonstrated the abilities that enabled them to take part in the political world. It was no wonder Mary Ponsonby had been enthralled by Lady Waldegrave as a young woman. At one of her parties in June 1865 the Ponsonbys met the future chancellor of the Exchequer under Gladstone, Robert Lowe, the editor of *The Times*, Delane, and Henry's cousins, the Bessboroughs.[41] Lady Waldegrave was among the last of these women who led political discussion from their sitting rooms. Even as the upper classes ceded ground to middle-class politicians, and aristocratic ladies withdrew to the sidelines along with their husbands, there were still considerable opportunities for such women to exercise political influence.[42]

A chance set of circumstances brought the politicians Henry knew best into office at roughly the same time as he began to have professional contact with them as private secretary. To many of the Whigs he was related either by birth or marriage. He found them friendly, but close-lipped when he tried to get them to talk informally about business. For example, Ponsonby in January 1869 met his patron, Lord Clarendon, newly appointed to the Foreign Office in Gladstone's first government. He 'has got to look old and worn but is as agreeable as ever except like all Whig Ministers upon his own Department and if you touch upon that he shuts up at once'.[43] Cardwell at the War Office and Granville at the Colonial Office were the same. However, 'Mr. Gladstone in the respect of talking freely is unlike the other Whigs'.[44] Ponsonby had an opportunity of comparing Gladstone and Granville in August 1869 when he and Mary went to Balmoral. There Gladstone succeeded Granville as the minister in waiting. When it was Gladstone's turn,

> There was no light and airy persiflage. All was earnest and deep. Not that he dislikes a joke or a good story but his common conversation is to strike at the root of the argument. He was very agreeable and talked on anything. Of course the Irish land question was uppermost in his mind and he discussed the different plans proposed with eagerness. He enjoys a drive discussing metaphysical problems sometimes with Mary and was a great walker. He was fond of talking Church matters with Duckworth.[45]

'Eager' was commonly a word the Whigs used to criticise what they thought of as Gladstone's madness, his 'enthusiasm' that savoured to them of seventeenth-century Puritanism or eighteenth-century Methodism. Although Ponsonby wryly acknowledged here the dim view taken of Gladstone by many of his cousins, still he was pleased by Gladstone's frank discussion of the leading political issue of the day, the Irish Land Bill. Moreover, Ponsonby liked Gladstone's ability to touch on philosophy with Mary and religion with the queen's chaplain, Canon Duckworth. Ponsonby was more open-minded and less horrified by Gladstone's evangelical zeal than his aristocratic connections were. In the later 1860s he and Gladstone were just beginning a society of mutual admiration that would last for nearly three decades.

One of the things Gladstone and Ponsonby had in common was friendliness to reform of the constitution. Perhaps it is more accurate to say that Ponsonby thought the reform movement unstoppable and that it could produce desirable changes in both Britain and Ireland were it seized and guided by capable hands. Of the hands available he had most confidence in Gladstone's. At the time of the second reform bill in 1867, when a second large extension of the franchise was in prospect, Ponsonby was impatient with those who wished to resist a measure that was at once just and inevitable. The Whigs, including Mary's uncle, the third Earl Grey, seemed a bit 'out of it'. Grey registered some of the upper classes' alarm 'at the prospect of admitting so large a number of new voters' and told Ponsonby that he intended 'to try and purify the bill as it passes through the Lords'. Ponsonby thought 'he might as well try to dam up the Thames at London Bridge'.[46]

Ponsonby's confidence in the strength of parliamentary democracy was so firm that he could maintain goodwill towards reform while simultaneously directing troops to curb the excesses of pro-reform meetings. In July 1866 several reform meetings took place around London with the plan of marching to Hyde Park for one big meeting. The leaders were denied admission to the park, whereupon the crowd tore down the railings and rushed in anyway. Ponsonby was in command of a battalion of Grenadier Guards stationed at Chelsea and kept in barracks on alert to help the police restore order. In the evening Ponsonby toured the destruction in the park with Lord Frederick Paulet, who was in command of the different regiments in town to keep order. Ponsonby was in plain clothes, though Paulet may well have been in uniform. Ponsonby told his brother, Arthur, 'It's all very well for you living in quiet India, while we are campaigning in warlike London.' The crowd had at first cheered both him and Paulet, but afterward 'hissed, hooted and pelted us'. The railings along Park Lane and also the Bayswater Road were all down. As it grew dark the crowds roaming through the park decreased, but one group at Marble Arch had set alight some gas made by knocking down the lamps and built an enormous fire.[47] Though this was not a revolutionary riot, it was unusual and fairly frightening in London. It kept Ponsonby and his men in a state of tension and readiness for more than a week.[48] The anticipated battle between crowd and soldiers never came.

There were more demonstrations in December 1866 when members of various trade unions came together to register the support of working men for reform. Henry and Mary Ponsonby came up to General Grey's house to watch the procession being marshalled. This time the crowd, numbering nearly 25,000, was orderly and Ponsonby felt no qualms about taking his sisters to see the procession as it marched along Knightsbridge.[49] In February 1867 Ponsonby and his men were again in readiness for another reform meeting. But by this time, the events had become spectacles, not unlike big royal ceremonies in reverse. The Prince of Wales even came to London, 'drove though the crowd with much cheering and took a place at a window in the United Services Club where also there were many ladies. The Duke of Cambridge seemed a little surprised at the Prince of Wales consenting to an ovation on this occasion.'[50] But the reactionary duke had got it wrong, and the prince, enjoying a fine day out with lady friends, had got it right. His attendance symbolised the alliance of royal family and reformers. That he cheerfully took a place in the audience to view the procession, rather than in the ceremonial cavalcade itself, was a sort of good-humoured participation in a world turned upside down, a *charivari* in which the crowd was on show and the heir to the throne applauded from the audience.

The greeting that met the queen when she opened Parliament in the same month was exactly the reverse. When she opened the carriage window she saw 'a sea of "nasty faces" screaming for Reform'.[51] The contrast between the prince who stayed in London and welcomed the reformers and his mother who stayed away produced this result. Although in private she was urging reform on the ministers, she failed to see how public gestures of her confidence in reform were equally necessary.

Two years later further troubles were expected, this time in Ireland, when Gladstone introduced legislation after 1869 to disestablish the Irish Church and answer grievances of the Irish tenantry. This was why Ponsonby was repeatedly sent to Ireland with his men on the eve of his becoming private secretary to the queen. At Osborne in January 1869 he repeated in his diary a story told by Archbishop Tait and Dean Stanley about Archbishop Howley, who had been much hated in Canterbury because of his vote against the first reform bill. He and Archdeacon Croft had to ride through the town being jeered at by a hostile crowd. The man driving the carriage

> lost his way, with the crowd bellowing after them and throwing filth at them. A dead cat judiciously thrown entered the post chaise and struck Archbishop Howley. Archdeacon Croft who was with him threw it out again. The mob hurled it in again. The Archbishop said 'Mr Archdeacon, we will show better generalship this time and keep the cat.'[52]

At the moment of his becoming private secretary, Ponsonby was well schooled in reform agitations. He had working relationships with the politicians, like Gladstone, who were leading what they conceived to be a movement towards improvement and more justice in the constitution. He knew that good generalship, whether in the Church, in Whitehall, or at the palace, meant knowing when not to throw back the dead cats.

A personal tragedy struck Henry on the eve of his becoming private secretary. His brother Arthur died of cholera while serving with his regiment in India. He was 41. This was a shock and caused Henry real sadness. Arthur had been a best friend to him as well as a brother. Before Henry's marriage, Arthur was his most regular correspondent. The two brothers shared a sense of the ridiculous, but in every other way they were different. Henry moved easily through drawing rooms and levees; meeting the queen and the lord lieutenant made Arthur nervous. Henry had a distinguished career at Sandhurst; Arthur was held back a year for beating up another boy. Henry married a formidable young woman in a society wedding; Arthur married secretly a Greek woman he had met in Corfu and only gathered courage to tell his family some time after the event. Henry concealed deep emotions underneath a polished exterior, devotion to duty and wry jokes. Now more than ever he looked to Mary for love and support. She was sympathetic about the loss of his brother, and returned his affection, but equally, she set out to establish an identity and an existence separate from his.

CHAPTER 6

An Independent Wife

c. 1863-78

Once they had come back from Canada in 1863 and a sudden alarm that they might have to return in 1864 had passed, Mary Ponsonby settled down at number six, The Cloisters, Windsor Castle, to make a home and have children. There is a nice irony in their choice of such a monkish-sounding address given Mary's girlhood dream of entering a monastic order. She also began to be known by a new name; in the family she now went simply by her initials, MEP, a brisk and abbreviated version of Mary Elizabeth Ponsonby. Although she renounced her adolescent ideals and ceased gradually to be attached to high church religion, there are still significant continuities between Mary Bulteel and MEP, the wife of an officer and equerry raising a family in Windsor. Not least of these was her determination to be different from other army wives. MEP's bravery in asserting that difference in the midst of such deeply conventional and conformist worlds – court and castle, parish and garrison – makes her an attractive character. Her success in being accepted in these places also raises questions about whether the Victorian monarchy and its surroundings were not more open to dissent and unconventionality than has usually been thought. To follow the first decade or so of MEP's life as a young mother and wife is to see how she developed her own independence in the context of her marriage to Henry, as well as how she used the court's prestige to encourage greater independence among women at large.

The Children

MEP's first two children were both girls. Alberta or Betty was born only months before her parents were obliged to go to Canada in 1862. The second daughter, Magdalen, who was called Mags or Maggie in the family, was born in June 1864, less than a year after their return. MEP loved these two girls. She longed to be reunited with Betty at the end of their year in North America. Magdalen was to become a companion and friend to her parents in their old age, closer to them than any of the others. As a young mother, however, MEP was unwilling to give up the serious reading in difficult books that had become such an important part of her identity when she was in her twenties. She returned now to her self-examination diary rarely, and then only when she was dispirited. So the following entry is not necessarily typical of how she thought about her children all the time. It does show how occasionally she resented the intrusion of childbearing into her studies. It also shows what a pessimistic and fatalistic attitude she could sometimes take towards the world – as who does not when a little depressed? 'The next three years,' she wrote several months after Magdalen's birth, interposing 'if I live' melodramatically, 'will be the last of complete control over my own time. The children will come after that.' The nurses would hand the girls over to her as she intended to take a hand in their schooling. 'So immediately the thing to try for must be to work hard at my books and all head work and now there is no question of America to get some outside work ... in the parish.' She would not let having children interfere with the disciplining of her mind, nor must it be allowed to stop her doing some good work in Windsor as she had tried to do in the parish at Holbeton where she had grown up. She rued the fact that she had 'lost' all her 'sanguine ways of looking at plans for schools or other good works but there are still some things that may be done that would make me of some use to one's fellow creatures. There must be while there is sorrow and sin in the world'.[1] This was her devout voice reasserting itself. The best we can expect in this life is some occasional relief from suffering. Good works cannot save us, but they may salve our consciences.

Still, MEP's conscience, what Freud would have called her super-ego, was a little harsh, because really she was doing a lot. She collaborated with Henry on several articles for the *Pall Mall Gazette*, a weekly newspaper that combined Liberal editorials with insider gossip about what was going on in the government.[2] She did not record whether she was resentful that she could not accompany Henry to the annual *Pall Mall* dinners. These were all-male parties where prominent writers such as Matthew Arnold, George Meredith and Anthony Trollope, whose books she had read more avidly than had Henry, assembled as guests of the editor and publisher.[3] She did get involved, however, in a published exchange with Frederic Harrison, about his having omitted to consider properly the rights of working women in an article reviewing the condition of labour in the country and his considering women working bad when they 'cut out' the men. Henry reported proudly in his diary that

Her answer to him was excellent pointing out that no objection was ever made to [women] working in coal mines etc. but very much to their working in quiet trades such as tailoring etc. Mary's letter was very comprehensive and Harrison owned himself beaten on several arguments but held to the rest.[4]

Nor would Henry allow her to be serious and studious all the time. They took their two little girls on outings around the country and kept a log of their adventures. Usually the log has satirical drawings by Henry and rather professional watercolours by Mary. On the title page of one of these, 'The Log, Our Journal of Permiscuous Travels, 1865', Henry with big shoes forms the letter 'L' while Mary shaking out a picnic blanket is the letter 'O'. The letter 'G' is Mary playing with Alberta and Magdalen (see Plates).

Light moments with Henry aside, Mary would not allow the birth of more children to stop her plans for her own education. She rebelled against the convention of the day that prevented women from being trained in anything more taxing than French, singing and needlework. She set out a plan to translate from German and teach herself algebra. She wanted to continue reading John Stuart Mill on psychology and logic. Herbert Spencer's essays, in which he tried to synthesise biological and social observations, and the historian, Lecky, were also on her reading list. She wrote all this down shortly after giving birth to her third child and first son. There is a connection between her renewed determination to get on with 'head work' and the birth of her son, John, or Johnny, who was born with a slight deformity: he had no roof to his mouth. The legend, according to his wife Mollie, was that his life was so despaired of that he was immediately 'baptized in the bathroom'.[5] MEP wrote sadly in her diary, 'A little boy born. Poor darling with no palate and a hare lip. A terrible blow and disappointment. I had dwelt so on the thought of having a little son to bring up and now a kind of pall seems to have fallen over every project ....' She then proposed to relieve her despair as a mother by restating her commitment to philosophy: 'I feel that perfect freedom of thought and intense striving after what is highest, deepest, broadest, truest in the *widest* meaning of the word, is the real object of life.'[6] She would sink her anxiety and disappointment at her little boy's misfortune in striving after oceanic conceptions of truth.

Though there are continued anxieties about his health in his parents' letters in the 1860s and 1870s, Johnny grew to be quite a strong child. His speech was always a little difficult to understand, but those who knew and loved him had no trouble following what he had to say. He cast something of a shadow over his mother's life for the next year. She was pregnant again in 1867 and desperately worried that there might be something wrong with this baby too.

In the end, she need not have worried. Her second son, Frederick, or 'Fritz', named partly for the husband of her good friend the crown princess of Prussia, Queen Victoria's eldest daughter, who was his godmother, and partly for Henry's father, was a perfectly normal baby and grew into a blonde boy with curly hair. The birth of this, her next-to-last child, however, made Mary very ill.[7] This was perhaps the reason for Henry and Mary's last child following his brothers and sisters only after a significant gap of nearly four years. Arthur was born in 1871 and named for Henry's brother who had died three years earlier. With his birth, MEP, now 39, put an end to childbearing and turned with a will to her children's education.

She was able to combine her taste for serious reading with giving the children their lessons. Staying with her mother at Pamflete in 1868, she found she could put theory into practice. She absorbed Enlightenment reading on education in the form of Rousseau's *Emile* and applied it in teaching her six-year-old, Betty. Rousseau drew a distinction between the artificial and the natural in bringing up children that appealed to MEP enormously. Parents must avoid giving their children 'artificial faults' by forbidding too much. Instead, they must listen carefully to their children and watch for their natural aptitudes. Children must be encouraged to use 'their natural faculties' and 'weigh the things taught them by experience, instead of cramming them with books'.[8] This method, with its emphasis on searching for children's inborn aptitudes, was unconventional. It was the opposite of that adopted by the queen and Prince Consort, especially in bringing up the young Prince of Wales, who had been so crammed with books as a child that after he came of age he probably never picked up another one in his life. It was also the opposite of the tactic adopted by the crown princess of Prussia, who allowed her son Wilhelm's tutor to drill him to tears.[9]

Mary took exception, however, to Rousseau's ideas about women's education and thought them very wrong. 'He does not want them to know anything, but to be the centre of a kind of *culte*.'[10] She did not want her girls to be raised as little idols suitable for worship, she wanted them given the same teaching as boys. When it came time, much later, for one of her sons to go to university, she reflected with some regret on how long it had taken to form her own views on life, which she had only worked up herself on her own with her books and no particular guidance. Young men at university learned things so quickly with their access to tutors, lectures and libraries. How she would have adored going to university is the undertone of her advice to her son, though she never explicitly expressed bitterness or resentment.[11] How feelingly she would have agreed with Virginia Woolf that women needed income, independence and a university training equal to men's if they were ever to achieve true intellectual as well as civic equality.[12]

Mary gave no indication to her children that she would rather be doing anything else than teaching them. If they expressed any interest in a topic, however obscure, she looked it up herself and entered into their enthusiasms. Fritz Ponsonby remembered that if, as a boy, he had wanted to be a boot black, his mother would have looked up some books on polish and shoes. Arthur Ponsonby recalled simply adoring time spent with his mother. He disliked having to compete with older, more vociferous brothers and sisters. When he was ill and had her all to himself was the most precious time of all. She gave quite advanced lessons and expected her children at a young age to master material that most mothers would have left to nannies, governesses or schoolmasters. 'The first thing I can remember my mother teaching me,' Arthur wrote in an unpublished essay entitled 'My Mother',

> was about triangles which I made on her bed with joined bricks. Squares, parallelograms and a rhombus followed. I particularly liked the rhombus. A little later came physical geography, mountains, rivers, rain and snow. Then drawing and the elements of perspective. This last continued for many years. When she went out sketching I sat by her side … [13]

Indeed Arthur preserved in an album a photograph of his mother sketching with him sitting next to her at Balmoral. Mary followed closely her children's natural interests and she involved them in hers. All of them grew to love books, to be adepts at word play and to enjoy serious discussions. They all knew how to shine in a debate. Mary taught her five children to enjoy and excel at the intellectual pursuits for which she had sometimes been seen by other courtiers as too serious, bookish and clever for a young maid of honour.

Schools

After Magdalen was born in 1864, MEP gloomily thought there would not be much time left for philanthropic pursuits outside her family. In fact, schools and schooling continued to be one of her passions both inside the family with her own children and outside it. The school she and her sisters had founded at Holbeton was still flourishing in 1864 and she was proud enough of it to show Henry her achievement.[14] In the 1870s she took courses in drawing and perspective herself. She even thought of taking a certificate so that she could be a better teacher to her children.[15] She was involved in several different projects to found schools at Windsor: in 1874 she attended a committee meeting to organise a local school, on which she served along with several other members of the community, including the royal librarian, Richard Holmes.[16] In 1877 she and several of her friends among the Eton masters formed a school to teach Windsor ladies.[17] In their free time and using Eton's facilities, Eton masters such as Oscar Browning gave history lectures on the French Revolution. Physical science was taught in one of the labs using the same apparatus that the boys used in hours when the boys were elsewhere. Mary herself attended these classes and reported to Henry that the queen's daughter, Princess Helena, was

> annoyed because they won't alter the hour for her, but we get the theatre and apparatus rather *en cachette* [secretly], so we must not ask to upset the Eton hours, or everything will be stopped. As it is, Hornby [head-master and afterwards provost of Eton] is against us, and had up Browning to reprimand him for giving History lectures. Browning said, as it was in his leisure moments, he must decline to make any alteration.[18]

She enjoyed twitting the authorities on the subject of women's educa-tion. She was sorry she had missed a committee to found a combined men's and women's college as she was dying to have a fight with any fool who would propound some 'nonsense about the impropriety of mixed schools'.[19] All her life MEP ranged herself against the forces of those who argued for what it was proper or improper for women to do. Instead, she sided with anyone who would argue in favour of expanding opportunities for women to work as well as cultivating their natural abilities and intellect. Here was a woman serving at the very centre of a court where propriety was all, who was prepared to damn the niceties in order for women to be more free.

The most remarkable of all MEP's efforts on behalf of schools was her involvement in the foundation of the first college for women at Cambridge, Girton. She contributed her time and her money. She persuaded friends and family members to subscribe even greater sums. She served not only on the large governing body meant to sponsor and guarantee the respectability of the college, but also on the smaller executive committee meant to supervise the college's ongoing operations. Perhaps most importantly of all, she made use of the status and prestige of the monarchy to advance what was then a truly radical measure. Girton shows Mary Ponsonby at her best: feisty, impatient, determined to resist the forces of conservatism or what she called 'stupidity', willing to play all the royal cards in her deck to trump her opponents.

In that era there was no provision for higher education for women. Oxford and Cambridge were exclusively male. A number of women set out to change things. MEP and Henry were friends with Lady Stanley of Alderley, who was one of the first sponsors of the idea of a college for women that would train them for the same exams men at the universities took. Emily Davies, who was to be the first mistress of the college, and the most active proponent of training women for professional work, had decided to put together 'a rather large general committee of distinguished people, to guarantee our SANITY and an executive [committee] to do the work'. This was after Davies and Barbara Bodichon, a prominent campaigner for wider employment opportunities for women, had had their proposal of a college for women at London University rejected.[20] In the late 1860s, when Davies and Bodichon persuaded Lady Stanley of Alderley to support their idea of a women's college, most people thought higher education for women was a preposterous idea. The idea of women sitting exams for higher degrees and preparing themselves for more professional work scandalised many Victorians because they thought it would rob women of their femininity, coarsen them, make men out of them. It would turn the world upside down.

This was precisely the sort of opposition MEP delighted in attacking. It is unclear exactly when she got involved, and whether she was introduced to Davies and Bodichon by Lady Stanley of Alderley or by another of the queen's maids of honour, Lady Augusta Bruce, who resigned from the household to marry the dean of Westminster, A.P. Stanley. Augusta Stanley was also an early member of one of Girton's committees. In 1869 MEP was already so deeply caught up in Girton affairs that Henry felt he had to caution her not to be in such a rush.[21]

Two years later while he was away at Balmoral, and without consulting him beforehand, MEP sent papers to Jane Ely requesting her to ask the queen to be patroness of Girton. Henry had to write back and say this was wrong. Jane Ely could not give such papers to the queen; a submission had to come either via him or via the keeper of the privy purse, their good friend, Thomas Biddulph. Henry also had to say that Biddulph would probably have to refuse her request, because 'the college is not yet an accomplished fact'. Henry understood that the idea was, in MEP's terms, 'to create a sounder opinion', or to put the weight of the queen's name behind a project that still needed social approval and financial backing. He had to tell her, though, that he doubted 'whether it is part of The Queen's duties to create opinions'. He advised her to write to Biddulph, and as the court looked upon political women with some suspicion, she had better refer him to some man he could consult on the topic.[22]

Although she failed to get the queen to act as patron, MEP does seem to have been connected with getting her daughter, Princess Louise, involved. Louise was the most bohemian of the queen's daughters. She had friends among artists and writers. She was a sculptor herself; her statue of her mother sits outside the east front of Kensington Palace today. Louise served as president of the National Union for the Education of Girls of All Classes above the Elementary, and was later patron of the Girls' Public Day School Company.[23] Her name came forward as a person who might lay the stone of Girton's first building. Henry had to reassure MEP, who still had doubts whether Louise's laying the stone would have as great an effect as the queen. No, he told her, 'Her laying the stone will be of great use to you' because it would stamp 'the institution with a brand of genuineness'.[24] She was still, however, a little disappointed not to have been able to use her big guns.

This did not deter her from approaching everyone else she knew to raise money for the fledgling college just north of Cambridge proper. Between 1867 and 1882 she contributed £70 of her own money, a not insignificant sum for a woman who depended on her husband's salary for most of her needs. Her much richer brother-in-law, Henry Bingham Mildmay, she persuaded to give £170. Sir James Clark, one of the queen's physicians and a regular among the social callers at Balmoral, whom Henry particularly liked for the brave way he stood up for Liberal opinions, gave £30. The earl of Airlie gave £10. Matthew Arnold gave £2 and 2 shillings. The biggest contributor was Lady Stanley of Alderley who gave £1,600.[25]

Not everyone acceded to Mary's requests. One of the most galling rejections came from her former fiancé, with whom she had preserved a friendship over the years since she had broken off their engagement. William Harcourt, though a friend to most Liberal and even radical social measures, told her he was against any proposal that would tend to make women's status at all similar to that of men. 'It seems to me,' he told her, that women's 'charm, their influence, their force depends so much on their dissimilarity – in modes of life, modes of action, modes of thought.'[26] This made MEP angry. His charm for her had always been that they seemed to be equals in discussion and conversation. How dare he suggest they were not?

College records and Henry's letters to her suggest that her involvement in the college's affairs was most intense in the early 1870s. Her attendance at meetings of the general and executive committees became more sporadic in the later 1870s. Still, when she went up to Cambridge to take her first look at the place in 1876 (all the committee meetings were held in London) she told Henry she was 'highly delighted with Girton, a much prettier building than I expected and a look of go and life and doing about it which pleased me'.[27] Even in her old age, after she had resigned from the two committees, MEP had Betty write to the mistress of the college to ask whether there was not a pamphlet history of Girton that she could read and keep.[28] The success of Girton and the feeling that she had been one of its early champions still pleased her when she was in her eighties and the battle had been handed over to others.

Women

Philippa Levine, an expert on Victorian feminism, has written that 'To be a feminist in mid- or late nineteenth-century England was to court contempt, ridicule and hostility'.[29] Mary Ponsonby never described herself as a feminist but she was publicly and passionately involved in a whole variety of feminist causes. She cared more about women's education and expanding opportunities for working women than she did about winning the vote for women. She and Henry followed Josephine Butler's campaign to repeal the contagious disease legislation, which unfairly targeted women in an effort to reduce venereal disease. MEP does not seem to have been involved in the crusade, however. There were other causes that were closer to her heart. She was deeply interested in the struggles of working women and followed sympathetically the accounts of working men who went on strike to improve their position. Her comments on a strike of engineers at Newcastle in 1871, for example, show that she favoured the men over their employers. It was such an unequal struggle, she thought, as the men had 'to contend with the accumulated capital of generations'.[30] Here she was, wife of the queen's private secretary, in the year of the Paris Commune, speaking the language of Marx and Engels. Indeed MEP kept a scrapbook filled with photos of all the prominent French Communists, whom she clearly admired.[31] She tended to be hard on herself when she reflected on her few merits and many failings, but towards the end of her life, she allowed herself one small entry in the 'credit' column. She had always been sincere in 'indignation roused by the mean, silly, conventional, cruelty of the prosperous to the strugglers for life'.[32]

Starting in 1866 and throughout the 1870s and 1880s MEP lent her efforts to another unequal struggle. She became a member of the Society for Promoting the Employment of Women; she served on both its general committee and the executive committee that managed its daily affairs.[33] Another member of the Society was her friend Lily Wellesley. One of the founders of the Society was Barbara Bodichon, whom MEP knew from Girton. Another was Jessie Boucherett. Boucherett, like Emily Davies, the mistress of Girton, who was also on the two committees, was a Conservative.[34] Both came from landed or professional families: although radical in their goals for women, few of these agitators sought to overturn the social hierarchy. Davies, Boucherett, Bodichon and Ponsonby were all out to facilitate small incremental gains in liberty and equality for Victorian women. A potential governess, for example, might profit both intellectually and financially by taking a degree at Girton. All these women believed there should also be more opportunities for women, whether educated or not, beyond the teaching of little children.

The Society for the Promotion of the Employment of Women was founded in 1859 to help middle-class women. Thoroughly educated women, or working-class women, though they might have problems finding work, were less at a disadvantage, the Society thought, than the

> daughters of professional men, merchants, and shop-keepers, whose parents, from straitened means or other causes, have not afforded them the advantages of systematic training, and who have grown up in a home of more or less comfort, and perhaps reach middle age without having learned a single thing thoroughly, and are then plunged at once into a sea of perplexities as to how to get bread to eat and clothes to wear.[35]

MEP, who regretted her own lack of systematic training all her life, and who delighted in working with her hands, threw herself into the work of the Society. A register was kept at its offices where women looking for work could advertise their skills and employers might find workers. The Society worked hard to find places for women to work in trades that then had not been ordinarily opened to women. They found jobs for women as bookkeepers, copy clerks, glass engravers, woodworkers and decorators of china. The *Report* of the Society in 1867 noted that 'nearly half the applicants at the office are wives who have lost their husbands, or who have made unhappy marriages'.[36]

The Society attracted in the later 1860s a range of Liberal supporters, for example, Mr & Mrs Gladstone as well as Mrs Tait, wife of the archbishop of Canterbury. John Stuart Mill was a subscriber. The crown princess of Prussia had encouraged a sister society in Berlin and Hamburg. By 1869 Princess Louise and the queen herself had become patrons. It is not unlikely that MEP had something to do with this. After 1869 the queen subscribed ten guineas annually. In 1878, the year Henry became privy purse as well as private secretary, the queen gave £50 as well as her annual subscription. MEP gave a pound every year and her mother-in-law, Lady Emily, subscribed a guinea annually. MEP also persuaded the husbands of her sisters to contribute £5 each in 1866.

The work of the Society increased in volume. In 1869 48 women were enabled to obtain permanent work and 46 to find temporary employment. In its annual report for 1880 the Society could record that it had helped 68 women into permanent and 238 into temporary jobs.[37] Its business was also advocacy and investigating why women were kept out of certain professions. At a meeting of the Society in 1874 MEP and Boucherett took the chair together and looked into a strike at Kidderminster where they wanted to help the working women. Male carpet weavers had gone on strike because, on a piecework basis, they were undersold by women weavers who accepted a smaller sum for their work. The result was that the employer refused to allow women their looms in order to get the men back to work – so the women were unemployed. Henry sympathised with Mary's interest in the problems of women workers and kept her up to date on proposed legislation.[38] Sometimes the Society had success as a pressure group. In 1879 MEP told Henry about a long committee meeting, in which a deputation from the City had explained that they wished to spend a substantial sum on technical classes for girls, as well as to pay the salaries of the teachers and to make a further contribution to the society for their help. 'So,' she concluded, 'we are looking up.'[39]

Another issue that attracted MEP's interest and indignation in the 1860s and 70s was the refusal of medical authorities to sanction women being trained to be doctors. Sophia Jex-Blake was one of the first women who, denied entrance to medical schools in London, was admitted to study at Edinburgh.[40] Later, the university senate refused to examine the Edinburgh women for their degrees, leading to a court case where the university won on appeal. The royal household smiled at Jex-Blake as if she were the most red and revolutionary of radical women. Henry had to confess teasingly to MEP that the household looked on her as a sort of 'medium between royalty and Jex Blake'. They expected MEP to write to Jex-Blake as a friend when in fact the two women had never met. MEP, nevertheless, was wholly on the side of the women students in the case and was so passionate on the issue that she carried her husband along with her. He reported a dinner-table conversation at Balmoral during which one of the queen's ladies in waiting, the duchess of Roxburghe, started the topic of women as doctors. One of the other guests was a Scottish clergyman, Dr Caird, who gave his view on the recent goings-on at Edinburgh University.

> At dinner I had another struggle with her [the queen]. The Duchess [of Roxburghe] condemned the women doctors and Caird did too tho' very slightly and the Duchess got The Queen to abuse the Edinburgh women. I said 'I am not going to defend the principle which may be right or wrong ... '
>
> The Queen stopped me 'Oh dear Col. Ponsonby and I never argue about this.'
>
> 'No,' I said, 'I don't want to say anything on that but I must say that when the Senate told them [the women] that they might come and study they had no right to break faith with them.'
>
> 'Is that so Dr. Caird?' asked The Queen.
>
> 'It is quite true Your Majesty. The Senate made the mistake either in allowing them to come or in refusing them after they had come.'

Henry concluded, 'The consequence was a change in the conversation.'[41]

Another pioneer in the field was Elizabeth Garrett Anderson who was one of the first women to be allowed to practise as a doctor in Britain, having been licensed as a medical practitioner by the Society of Apothecaries in 1865 and taken a degree abroad.[42] MEP took an active interest in Miss Garrett's candidacy in 1870 for the London School Board,[43] and when she needed a doctor in the 1890s, had no hesitation in approaching Mrs Garrett Anderson to be her physician.[44] MEP may well have been the prime mover behind the Prince and Princess of Wales agreeing to open the Elizabeth Garrett Anderson Hospital on the Euston Road in 1889.[45]

Many, though not all, of these women who were working to improve conditions in women's education and labour, as well as to open the professions to women, were unmarried. Some preferred friendship with other women to marriage. Lillian Faderman, who set out to contextualise these female friendships, discovered that 'it was virtually impossible to study the correspondence of any nineteenth-century woman, not only of America, but also of England, France, and Germany, and not uncover a passionate commitment to another woman at some time in her life'.[46] Victorian women who lived and worked together never aroused the sort of hostility, arched eyebrows or outrage that have sometimes met them in the latter part of the twentieth century. Perhaps because many Victorians believed women ought not to enjoy sex, there was no question of two women settling down with one another having anything other than an asexual relationship. Mary Ponsonby herself had a number of close female friends in the 1860s and 1870s. She sometimes described them in terms that sound more like romantic friends than sisterly companions. We must be careful not to read too much into this as the Victorians, like the Romantics, were inclined to give way to transports of emotion (at least in print) when describing their friends. Philippa Levine points out that 'the nineteenth-century women's movement offers so many examples of deep and unashamed love between women – who often chose to spend their lives together' that the question of sexual contact 'seems an irrelevant index of these friendships'. Still, it is a dimension of Mary Ponsonby's experience that is worth exploring because it shows the breadth of her sympathies and her brave embrace of relationships that she suspected in advance were bound to disappoint her.

After she married Henry in April 1861, Mary saw less of her friend Lily Wellesley at the Deanery. For some reason Lily pulled away from her. She had been married less than a year when she recorded in her diary that she had received 'A letter from Lily. Now a rare event.'[47] Lily came to visit her just before Betty was born and just afterwards as well, but she left a feeling of dissatisfaction behind. 'Alone most of the day,' she wrote on 28 May 1862, 'Henry in town and Lily only with me for 10 minutes.'[48] Thereafter she was in Canada and the relationship became less preoccupying. They were still near neighbours when the Ponsonbys returned to Windsor as they both lived within the precincts of the castle. They saw each other at committee meetings and had dinner at each other's houses. However, Lily seemed to shy away from her and this caused sadness that her growing attachment to Henry and occupation with the children did not alleviate.

Then in 1868 Mary met a younger woman, Lady Agnes Courtenay, daughter of the earl of Devon. She was also the niece of the Hon. C.L. Courtenay, who was a canon of St George's and a chaplain to the queen. On Good Friday, always an important confessional day in her self-examination diary, even now that her religious feelings had diminished, Mary wrote about this new friend as if it were the opening of a completely new chapter in her life.

> My friendship with Agnes Courtenay is a new phase in my life. Since my disappointment about Lily, I have always shrunk from fresh friends, but Agnes came here last year and in her grief for her mother and desire for help and sympathy day by day and hour by hour became very dear. I feel I might be of use to her for with her gifts of deep feeling, strong imagination, quick intellect and enthusiasm, she is impulsive and any one with more experience and yet with sympathy might be a strong and firm help to her.

MEP believed that, if she could help this younger, less experienced woman, Agnes could also help her. Her attachment to her religion had become less intense since her reading of Mill and Eliot. Nor did her husband share her high church asceticism and this had weakened its former hold on her. But Agnes's 'love of what is good, her belief in that which I have grown cold about, her realization of the next world seems to have freshened up my hopes and aspirations and given a purpose and interest to duties too much neglected of late'. It was as if she had rediscovered the passion and faith of her girlhood at the same time as a sympathetic soul with whom she could share it. Then come two closing lines that suggest the relationship had its potential perils as well. 'The danger will be,' MEP wrote, 'of allowing ourselves to be too much engrossed, to giving an exaggerated and morbid turn to a love which may prove the blessing of our lives.'[49] Perhaps she sensed a longing in herself that she wished to forbid or repress, hence she held it at arm's length with words like 'morbid' and 'danger'.

Exactly one year later, on Good Friday in 1869, she sat down again to write about the principal feature of the last year: 'Agnes is the principal feature, foolish perhaps that it should be so ...'. There is an eloquence and a rush to her entries about Agnes that sound like someone who has tried and failed to stop herself from falling in love.

> And when I try to remember the details of this year, it seems all to take one shape, the wish and hope and love of being with her, much too strong, much too intense because such exalted ideas of friendship are sure to go through contradictions and reactions. The first disillusionment with her was that as we became better known to each other so it seemed that sympathy upon the highest subjects, intellectual or religious, seemed to diminish and a more *personal* feeling to take its place. That has held fast

1. Henry Ponsonby self-portrait in the Crimea, 1856, aged 30.

2. Flete Saloon, a photograph of one of the reception rooms in the house where Mary Ponsonby grew up. The house had to be sold, but it was later purchased by her sister and brother-in-law.

Beautiful window at Vicenza
Some people like fine art better than tea
Some like tea better than fine art

3. Mary Ponsonby holds a teapot while Henry Ponsonby concentrates on his plate in Italy on their honeymoon in 1861. Henry's caption reads: 'Beautiful window at Vicenza. Some people like fine art better than tea. Some like tea better than fine art.'

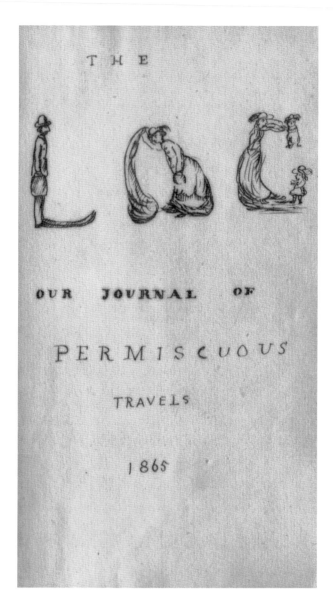

4. The Ponsonbys kept logbooks of their different holiday outings. 'The Log, Our Journal of Permiscuous [sic] Travels, 1865', is the title page of one such book.

5. Henry and Mary Ponsonby in Canada in 1862 falling out of their sleigh into the snow. The caption says 'An Upset'.

6. The Ponsonbys made a visit to the USA in 1862 and returned to Canada via a steamer up the Hudson River. Henry's caption says 'Rather windy on the Hudson'. At left a boy appears to be climbing a rail and showing his mother 'No hands!'; at right a man is holding on to his hat.

7. 'Mrs P. in her garden.' The Ponsonbys moved to a summer house at Chambly, outside Montreal, in the summer of 1863.

8. Mary Ponsonby taught schoolchildren in Montreal in 1862. Henry's caption reads 'Mrs P. at her school'.

9. & 10. Two pages from family logbooks. The first is of Henry and Mary Ponsonby captioned 'Sleighing, Canada, 1862'. The second, captioned 'The Summit of Lochnagar', is of an expedition to a peak near Balmoral in the 1860s, with, from left to right, Hermann Sahl, the German secretary, Henry Ponsonby, equerry, Mary Ponsonby, the duchess of Atholl, lady in waiting, and Miss Cathcart, maid of honour.

The Summit of Lochnagar

11. Mary Ponsonby with her first child,
Alberta Victoria, in 1862.

through all, steadily and deeply yet I felt as was natural that an impulsive eager *wilful* nature like hers must *possess* some one for good and all if she was to be happy ... it cost me much pain to think these pleasant hours devoted to each other must cease.

MEP sometimes had a taste for self-sacrifice, for nailing herself like a martyr to a cross. So she imagined a husband coming along to take Agnes away from her, while she remained behind biting her lip and hiding her pain. Sadly, her fearful fantasy came true. 'I did wish that someone could come' and propose marriage to Agnes,

> and not until he did come could I have realized how very much, *too much*, engrossed with her I have been. I won't dwell upon it. She is happy. They are both together and I begin again. This does not seem to have much to do with Good Friday and yet in any self examination truth must come first. This *is* and has been for two years a leading feature in my life. I fought against it, wished it would be taken from me and yet when it *was* taken cried my eyes out. How can I who thought I had learnt to be unmoved by every thing for the last few years talk of resolutions without owning this strong feeling.[50]

In the very years that her husband, a prominent officer in the most prestigious regiment in the Army, was being groomed for high office in the household, Mary was head-over-heels for a woman several years her junior. When she had four small children at home and a house full of nannies and nursery maids, there was no one whom she enjoyed spending time with more than Agnes Courtenay. Henry must have known this, but he loved her a great deal. There was a self-denying quality in his make-up that made him always put himself last. He was not the sort to complain. There was no question of the two women disguising themselves in jodhpurs or making a mad Vita Sackville-West and Violet Trefusis dash for the continent. Still, in many marriages, what seems a united front, actually hides complexities, strains and compromises. MEP was a more difficult woman to be married to probably than most because she held in check something inside herself that she was always a little afraid might break free. She always a little hoped that it might break free as well.

Portrait of a Marriage

From the very first moment of her marriage to Henry Mary realised that there was a gulf between them in religious feeling. He liked books quite as much as she did, but there was a less deep intellectual curiosity and restlessness on his part than on hers. When they were travelling together on the continent during their honeymoon, she would sometimes try 'to get away into a church to pray' but Henry disliked this 'so gave it up'. Henry's was a more broad church religion. He was more relaxed about doctrinal differences than she was, more intent on avoiding anything like religious passion or enthusiasm than she was. He would never have dreamed of going to the lengths Mary did in chastising herself for not keeping up a higher standard of prayer and devotion. His religion was that of the court or the broad church Whigs. The church had its place, but should never be allowed too absorbing or stimulating a role in a person's emotional life. Mary confided her disappointment to her self-examination diary. She confessed that she 'was sometimes unhappy' that she and her new husband were not in sympathy on religious topics. She felt 'more completely alone' when it came to religion 'than I ever was before, for Lily has left off being as much with me or speaking or writing as she used to ... '. Still, she had chosen to marry him partly because he seemed in some ways her moral superior. 'I can truly and I *do* truly look up to my husband for he is far better than I am in his absolute truth, fearlessness, honesty and unselfishness, but I know now that the devotional in religious as well as the imaginative in other matters must be kept to myself.'[51] These were the slightly pessimistic conclusions she reached after spending several weeks abroad with Henry following their marriage in 1861. She cannot be the first young woman whose honeymoon had its share of disappointing accommodations as well as joys.

As a young woman she had sometimes cautioned herself against the temptation of spending more time with Lady Waldegrave. Frances Waldegrave was a society hostess, the daughter of an opera singer. She married four times and became immensely rich through husbands who died before her and left her a string of stately homes.[52] She was known for acting in comic roles in private theatricals at Woburn as well as for giving parties that became a magnet for Liberals and the remnants of the Whigs. Her company was light and gossipy. She approached social improprieties with jolly unconcern, as befitted a woman who had lived in prison with one husband and married another who was 36 years her senior. William Harcourt was the nephew of Lady Waldegrave's third husband and he may have introduced MEP to her. The attraction of Lady Waldegrave was her zest for life in the present, her Disraelian love of sumptuous drawing rooms filled with handsome men and sparkling women. Mary sometimes was horrified, however, at this eat, drink and be merry philosophy. Something about Henry's lack of religious devotion repelled her in the same way. Shortly after their marriage she wrote of her 'dread' of 'the "*vivre pour vivre*" [life for life's sake] and nothing else that I sometimes think I am falling into'.[53]

Gradually, though, her attachment to Henry increased. Four years after their marriage she wrote with some tenderness, 'My husband [is] much more to me than ever.'[54] When she looked back on the decade between 1862 and 1872 in later life, she made a catalogue of all Henry's attributes that she most admired: 'strength, unselfishness, excellence, devotion, realized more fully year [after] year. Henry's qualities I see to be exactly those I am wanting in.'[55] They established an intense ability to talk over everything in conversation and in letters. She found it difficult to talk so honestly with anyone else. 'I get no talk of any sort,' she complained to him in one letter when he was away. 'Do you think we shall get into a fatuous state of thinking nobody else's conversation suits us but each other's?'[56] These conversations were sometimes arguments: the sharpness of their exchanges bothered their youngest son, Arthur, and the servants were often glad that attendance on the queen required the two to be separated more often than not, as the atmosphere in the Norman Tower then became less stormy. When in 1872 Henry had to leave her to follow the queen, MEP told him:

> I enjoyed your days here *too* much, for it seems very dull to have no one to quarrel with, no one to love, and to be without the possibility of your coming into the room at odd moments. The servants are congratulating themselves on not being on the high seas as the sudden hurricanes and *bourrasques* [squalls] are fearful. I think it is the comet![57]

Comet or no, their relations were sometimes tempestuous because MEP was capable of putting the same vigour into her marriage that she had into the religious discipline of her youth. She could also be as critical of him as she was of herself. In the later 1870s, the queen's taking the new title, empress of India, and the government's attitude toward the Ottoman Turks were both exercising all his energies. She told him bluntly that in his efforts to be fair and just to both sides on these two controversial issues, he was too slow to make up his mind. 'You never venture to condemn for fear of being unfair.' She admitted that she was inferior to him in grasping the details of political problems, but 'my first judgment' she told him, 'is as often, if not more often, [more] right than yours'.[58] So the quarrelling carried on even when they were apart. It was not the dominant mode of their relationship, but it was persistent evidence of their deep feeling for each other. Henry could be annoyed with the queen. Mary could be exercised by the attitude of male employers. It was only Henry who could make Mary truly angry, and vice versa. While she sent him brutally honest assessments of his weaknesses, he would send her indirect, if loving, barbs. He knew that she sometimes waited for him to leave before having a dinner party for her friends. He found also that even when he had been away for months in Scotland, she would not necessarily wait anxiously for the hour of his return if there were a party or a committee meeting or an opera she wanted to run up to London to attend. So he would send her the occasional wry remark on her news of what she was up to in Windsor: 'So like you,' he wrote in 1872, 'to have a dinner when I'm away'.[59] Or, when they went on holiday to Ireland in 1877, he drew a comic sketch of himself at the Viceregal Lodge pointing out to Mary and the children the window of his former room. 'That is where I lived for 6 years', he has written in the caption, while he has drawn Mary looking on with a slightly superior expression (see Plates).

The only serious challenge in the Ponsonbys' marriage came in the shape of Mary's former fiancé, William Harcourt. Harcourt had married a niece of Henry's patron, Lord Clarendon, in 1859. His wife died in 1863 and he did not marry again until 1876. In the years between, he started to come and call on Mary again in the Norman Tower. She recalled those days when Henry was often away and she could feel the pull of her old fascination with Harcourt. She asked herself a pointed question about him in her self-examination diary.

When W H[arcourt] turned up again in my life after his wife's death and I, left alone often for weeks and weeks, had many opportunities of seeing him, was it an arduous process of fighting with scruples and casuistries and debates which made me put a stop to these pleasant (and *harmless*) hours of companionship? I think not – it was much simpler. Just a dislike of tortuousness and crooked ways, a feeling it was not quite loyal *not* to mention how often he came. And so it ended – to begin again from time to time always with the same result. A matter of natural taste and not the working of an artificial conscience.[60]

She congratulated herself that it came very naturally to tell him he must stop coming to call on her. It is clear, though, that he would break off and then reappear again later.

Henry and Harcourt were obliged to have some quite fierce arguments in the 1880s. These arose mainly because Henry, like it or not, had to support the queen's right to question and object to Liberal policy when Harcourt was in office as home secretary in Gladstone's 1880-5 government; but there may also have been an undertone of lingering personal tension between the two men, who in every other respect were of the same political opinions and from the same Whig background. Among Henry's papers survives a note of Harcourt having apologised to him for some unspecified wrong against him. Evidence of such a serious disagreement is rare, if not unexampled, in the whole of Henry's correspondence.

Mary could never quite get Harcourt out of her mind or off her conscience. In a last diary, kept in the decade before she died, she mentions having come across some letters from the time when she broke off her engagement to him. 'There were few explanations. There were no recriminations but altogether it was a miserable time.'[61] It was as if she wanted mercy or forgiveness for a wrong that was more her responsibility than his.

Near the conclusion of her self-examination diary she congratulates herself for very few things. She makes an exception for Henry. She has never failed to appreciate his sterling qualities. 'The just, fearless, kind, loving, noble nature I have had ever by me for years seems to assume proportions that I cannot exaggerate and which it has been my one merit never to have been blind to.'[62] She could resent his family for taking it for granted that she was to give up society and bring up her children in the castle, when 'I might have done very differently if I chose'.[63] On the whole, though, MEP was contented with her lot and happy in the choice of the man she had married in 1861.

The Court

After her marriage, Mary was only occasionally invited as a guest to Osborne and Balmoral. For the most part the wives of equerries were expected to be content with staying behind when the court moved away from Windsor. If the wives were there, the queen could not have the gentlemen's full attention, or be sure that they would be in their rooms when she wanted them. It was unusual for MEP to be alone, but she enjoyed time spent with her books too, and valued her independence, so her husband's absences sometimes suited her very well. What was 'strange' was to go to Osborne as a guest in 1865. She told her younger sister, Emily, that 'So many waitings and lady-in-waitings come into my mind at every turn. The last waiting I had here was with Lady Macdonald! yet all my associations are disturbed by the new part of being treated like a guest.' She had also forgotten how badly decorated it was.

> You cannot think, after the pretty furniture in your house, and Georgie's [Mary and Emily's other sister], how some of the atrocities here strike one. It certainly is the oddest combination of upholstery; hideous presents they have received, and as ill-arranged rooms as I ever saw, yet sprinkled also with beautiful things ... and a certain kind of *luxe* which exists nowhere else.[64]

She did not envy Henry, who had to spend a great deal more time there than she did.

After Henry was appointed private secretary in the spring of 1870, Mary was invited along for that year's autumn move to Balmoral. This began in mid-August and could stretch until late November, the brilliant September sunshine giving way to dark days of rain and snow before the queen reluctantly decided to come south again. This invitation to Balmoral was exceptional; MEP may even have been substituting for a lady in waiting who had cancelled at the last minute. Ordinarily, the queen did not invite Mary to Scotland, perhaps sensing that she took what was, in the queen's mind, too great an interest in the political secrets that crossed her husband's desk. Mary's description of the routine at Balmoral is interesting, however, for the light it sheds on what everyone did all day while the queen lived on the Dee. Mary was put into a sitting room and bedroom that opened into the queen's room. 'Sometimes in the morning,' Mary told her sister, 'the Queen gives me things to copy and sort, which it is a push to get done before the messenger goes. Then I get reckless and go out sketching, and have to finish writing 500 miles an hour before dinner, to be able to say I have done it.'[65] She was never disrespectful to the queen, but she sometimes underrated the importance of what she thought of as clerical tasks so that she was perhaps a shade less punctual than the queen wished in doing the things she had been asked to do.

> The routine is breakfast [at] 9:30 [she continued]. Then we go to write till 12:30, when the messenger goes. If the Queen goes out for the day we make an expedition, taking luncheon with us, but that happens rarely now. If not, I generally slip out to sketch for an hour, and then we have to wait for orders till 4:30. Everybody goes out then till 7:00. Now it is getting cold to stay out later, though the Queen sometimes stays till 8. It is a comfortable moment to come in and find the post, a good fire and lots of candles – so cheerful that one is quite glad not to dine till 9.[66]

MEP found the routine appealing because she went up to Scotland with the queen so rarely. For Henry it came to be a dreadful bore, especially as Mary was from this time on almost never with him there, and he always heaved a deep sigh on his arrival. However, in 1870 he was still in the first flush of his new position as private secretary. The Franco-Prussian War had begun and he had such immense work deciphering telegrams and keeping the queen up to date with troop movements on a map that he rarely had a free moment. He was at work until 2 a.m. and got up to look at the latest telegrams at 6 a.m. Mary told her sister, 'I go to his office now and then to take a bird's-eye view of affairs.'[67]

The queen disapproved of Mary knowing about affairs, and this was why, at first, she was so seldom invited along on the court's peregrinations. The queen thought of Mary as a little too assertive when it came to books and politics and big ideas. The Ponsonbys' eldest daughter, Betty, remembered that there were other reasons in the early 1870s for her mother's unpopularity. Betty once saw a diary entry of one of the ladies in waiting who wrote, 'Mary Ponsonby is in the Queen's bad books as she refuses to go to Crathie [Presbyterian] Church'. Betty's parenthetical explanation for this was that her mother was then in the full flow of her agnostic phase. But MEP compounded her crime by never visiting the gamekeepers' wives.[68] Mary could not be controlled as easily as some of the other ladies at court and visiting the game-keepers' wives was a charade in which she wanted no part.

Occasionally Mary's contacts in the literary world were useful to the queen. She was asked in 1868 to arrange an interview with a popular novelist, Margaret Oliphant. Oliphant had written a review of the queen's Highland journals in *Fraser's Magazine* that had highly pleased the queen.[69] She did not want Mary, however, to interfere in the private secretary's affairs and Henry was cautioned about this more than once, either by hints from friends or direct letters from the queen. In fact, he consulted MEP frequently about thorny problems that came across his desk, reserving only occasional details, for example about the queen's will, when MEP passed on a request to know more about it from one of her radical friends.[70] On this subject Henry would not even share details with his wife.

On 13 July 1870 the Ponsonbys moved from the Cloisters in the lower ward of Windsor Castle into the Norman Tower.[71] Now in the upper ward of the castle, they were adjacent to the quadrangle around which the castle's state rooms and the queen's private apartments were arranged. They could see from their windows across to the doorway where the queen came in and went out for her daily drives. They could hear the crunch of the soldiers' boots on the gravel as they passed back and forth in their bearskins. They had commanding views over Eton and a sizeable garden in the dry moat of the Round Tower. They had a big dining room, sitting room and principal bedroom arranged one on top of the other, and nearly a dozen other smaller bedrooms, arranged in nooks and crannies, reached by nearly a dozen other small stairs.

Although this was a grace and favour residence, tenable only so long as Henry held his position as private secretary, Mary immediately set about making alterations as if she owned it. She began to make a garden in the moat and on the neglected slope of the Round Tower. She built a shed at the entrance to the garden where she put her lathe, blowtorch and wood files. Her most ambitious project was to expose the original walls by removing the plaster in two rooms over the gateway. They had been prisons in Plantagenet times and again during the seventeenth century, where royalists had been locked up after the defeat of Charles I. MEP had to get permission not only from the queen, but also from the Office of Works, which was in charge of the castle walls. Neither was initially happy about her plans, but she persisted. Eventually both the queen and Office of Works gave their consent. In August 1872 as the plaster came off, she made an interesting discovery. In black chalk was the name 'Thomas Piggott, Abbot of Chertsey'. The royal librarian, Richard Holmes, 'rushed to the library' and found that Piggott had been last abbot of Cherstey in the early 1400s. Holmes, Mary told Henry, 'is rather cool and conceited – might he write to the Archaelogical Society, and say he had found it, because he had deci-phered it. I said, "Yes, of course," but his whole bearing provokes me.' No doubt she would have liked to write something herself on the subject, but she conceded 'he has a knowledge of these things, so one must succumb'. She also discovered 'much of that old English scrib-bling, but difficult to make out'. To her delight she found ' "Mary" plain enough'.[72] These two rooms are in many ways the best rooms in the house. MEP called them 'The Prisons' and they were to be her sitting rooms throughout the whole of their time there. It is unclear where Henry had his worktable; it would have been like him to take a poky old corner without making a fuss about it.

To recapture how pleased and snug Mary felt in these rooms, we need to remember the Victorian rage for the medieval. Walter Scott was enjoying mass popularity. Hundreds of churches were being built on the basis of the best medieval research. William Morris was adapting designs from medieval patterns for wallpaper and furniture. Law courts, country houses and even train stations were being modelled on gothic motifs. To move into genuinely medieval rooms in the 1870s was to be exactly in accord with the temper of the times. The Victorians' ideas about interior design were as dependent on historical reconstruction as ours at the turn of the twenty-first century have been on minimalism and imagining the future.

Only one thing remained to complete Mary's happiness. She wanted a hole knocked through for a door from the Norman Tower into the Royal Library, which adjoined it. Mary loved books. The queen seldom used the library. How could she possibly object? But object she did and returned a grim negative to Mary's request, clearly thinking that in even daring to make it, she had really gone too far. Henry had to tell her patiently that there was no appeal against the queen's decision.

The next serious clash between MEP and the queen came in the later 1870s. The Ponsonbys were Gladstonians on principle as well as long family connection with Whigs and reformers. The queen so completely identified political questions with the personalities who moved them that she would not consider even the mildest dissent from Disraeli's policy, which by then she regarded as her friend's policy. Dissent from Disraeli she regarded as a personal affront. Knowing that direct opposition never worked with the queen, Henry had disagreed in the most circumspect and indirect way with a number of Disraeli's measures, but Victoria was not fooled. She sensed Ponsonby's suspicion of Disraeli and blamed Mary for it: she wrote and spoke to the dean of Windsor, asking him to tell Henry to be more sympathetic to her and to Disraeli. In November 1876 Mary and Betty went for a walk 'on the slopes' of Windsor, that is in the Home Park that was closed to the general public, but open to residents of the castle. There they met the dean who told Mary of 'his warnings to' Henry

and said H. M. had complained before now that she was sure you were influenced by my *decided* politics – he said he did not know whether she meant him to give me a hint, but he fancied she did. She really is *very* much afraid of me ... Really it is so absurd that it makes me feel inclined to put on a mysterious look as if I were in hourly communication with the opposition.[73]

These last lines were written in anger and exasperation. The queen was actually a good judge of character and it was perfectly true that Henry came to be friendlier to high church views, women's education and other positions the queen considered subversive after his marriage than before. The queen was also in a difficult position; it was, after all, her job to sustain a credible neutrality and give her unwavering support to whichever set of ministers happened to be in office. Mary was amused by Disraeli as a person, but made no secret of her view that the Tories were the 'stupid' party. She enjoyed arguments much too much for the queen's comfort. While the two women seldom disagreed with one another face to face over political questions, the queen had plenty of moles all over the castle who reported back to her what Mary said. In the first years of his private secretariat, though her counsel was often of use to Henry, Mary may have played a material role in making the queen think that perhaps she had better get a new private secretary who had a less opinionated wife.

Relations between the queen and the Ponsonbys were to be uneasy in the later 1870s. At one point Henry and Mary seriously considered the possibility of Henry's taking the post of Black Rod. This was a parliamentary position and would have taken them both out of royal service altogether. Mary consulted her friend and Gladstone's former foreign secretary, Lord Granville, who told her that he would hate to see her husband leave the queen, as he did her immense good.[74] Possibly this was the sort of reassurance they both needed from a close friend with political connections. As long as the queen did not take any direct action to remove him, and as we will see in a following chapter, she did consider doing just that, they decided to stay.

Nevertheless, in this very season, Mary expressed her deepest doubts about the direction in which Disraeli, with the queen's assent, seemed to be moving the monarchy: he had roused the queen, she thought, with all his high-blown talk of her having the power to do whatever she wanted without consulting ministers or Parliament. Mary believed that this was simply a return to the high ambitions Stockmar and the Prince Consort had had for the monarchy. The difference was that

> While they lived [Stockmar and the Prince Consort], the current of public opinion, especially among the Ministers, kept the thing between bounds, but they established the superstition in the Queen's mind about her own prerogative, and we who know her, know also perfectly how that superstition, devoid as it is of even a shadow of real political value, can be worked by an unscrupulous Minister to his advantage and the country's ruin. If there comes a real collision between the Queen and the House of Commons (say, for instance, that the country insists on Gladstone for the next Liberal Prime Minister) it is quite possible she would turn restive, *dorlotède* [spoiled] as she has been by Dizzy's high-sounding platitudes, and then her reign will end in a fiasco or she prepares one for the Prince of Wales; for I do think in a tussle of that sort, and I do hope and pray it should be so, that the People win the day.[75]

Here in the heart of the queen's household was a champion of Parliament who was stiffening her husband's resolve, not to thwart Disraeli exactly, but to put in wherever he could a charming (and possibly amusing) word for those who opposed his high-prerogative views. To hear Henry's side of this story, and to see what it was like from his point of view to manage the queen *and* his marriage, we must turn now to him, retracing our steps to his appointment as private secretary, and a brief review of the men who had held and defined the job before him. For it was he, in consultation with Mary, who largely redefined the position and made it what it is today.

CHAPTER 7

Henry Ponsonby as Private Secretary

1870-8

Following Henry Ponsonby's appointment as the queen's private secretary in April 1870, his surviving letters increase both in number and in interest. At this point the correspondence becomes most revealing about the inner workings of the monarchy. It also points directly at the Ponsonbys' peculiar attitude to the throne. A small pause to look back at the origins and history of the office will provide a useful context to understand the work Henry was now called upon to do.

History of the Private Secretariat

The office of private secretary to the sovereign originated not in the sovereign's readiness for business, but in the sovereign's incapacity for business.[1] The position dated from early in the nineteenth century when the king was no long able to correspond personally with ministers. Further, the post came to be officially recognised rather late in the nineteenth century. Ponsonby's predecessor, Charles Grey, was the first person to be gazetted officially with the title 'private secretary' to the sovereign, and it occurred only in 1867 after Grey had long been acting in an unofficial capacity as the queen's private secretary. Official recognition came not when it was realised that someone who gave wise advice could hold the post, but only when politicians felt that the sovereign's powers were so negligible that her personal advisers no longer really mattered. So Henry's appointment was not as auspicious a beginning as one might think.

Herbert Taylor was appointed to be the first unofficial private secretary to a British sovereign in 1805. He was appointed on the recommendation of the prime minister, William Pitt, the younger, to George III. By 1805 the king was effectively blind. He needed someone to read him the government's despatches abroad, for which his formal approval was required, as well as to carry on his correspondence. There had been no private secretary up to this point, as previously George III had written out his own letters, read and made his own copies of important documents, as well as kept his own files. To the extent that he had any assistance in his work as sovereign, he was assisted by his ministers, or secretaries of state, who carried out his business in parliament. The foremost of these was the first lord of the treasury, who was slowly coming to be known as his first or prime minister.

Statesmen were jealous of any intermediaries coming in between the king and his ministers. This was partly because the convention had grown up that the king gave the seals of office and his confidence to only one set of ministers at a time. They acted in the king's name, in varying degrees consulted with him, and thus constituted the government of the day. Dislike of intermediaries was partly to do also with a deep suspicion of 'favourites' that stretched back well into the Middle Ages. A favourite might be a friend or lover or confidante of the king. Such people could be dangerous as they could exploit the sovereign's affections either to line their own pockets, or to make the king forget his public duties in favour of his private comforts. A favourite was likely to prevent the sovereign's ruling with the well being of his subjects in mind and to encourage him to rule selfishly.

Herbert Taylor escaped the accusation of being a favourite. The prime minister appointed him, initially against the king's wishes, so that he could not be thought of as the king's friend. His appointment did not appear in the *Gazette*, which would have made it official and suggest that it might continue in the future. Further, Taylor did not have the stature to come in between the king and his ministers. He was the son of a vicar from a rural parish; the ministers were noblemen or the sons of grandees. Nor did Taylor try to usurp the ministers' places. His main job was to try to persuade the king to focus on signing warrants, approving despatches and acknowledging the submissions of secretaries of state at a time when George III was much distracted. Before the king's final and complete loss of his powers, Taylor won his trust. Other members of the royal family, including the Prince of Wales, also liked him, which was no small feat considering the usual Hanoverian hostility between father and son. Taylor was more like an amanuensis than an adviser: more like a governess or a librarian than a favourite intriguing on his own or the king's behalf.

George III's eldest son succeeded him as regent when his father's illness settled in after 1810. The Prince Regent, who became King George IV on his father's death in 1820, had three unofficial 'private secretaries' over the course of his regency and reign – but all three were closer to favourites or intriguers than to helpers on the Taylor model.

John MacMahon and Benjamin Bloomfield who succeeded him both fulfilled the duties of a private secretary while at the same time serving as keepers of the privy purse, a much older office dating back to the seventeenth century and involving responsibility for the management of the king's private money. Throughout the regency and reign of George IV politicians objected to the private secretary being in any way entrusted with messages that should be transmitted between king and ministers in person. The Whigs were especially vociferous against this, objecting to the presence of an irresponsible adviser who had constant access to the sovereign. By 'irresponsible' they meant that the private secretary might advise the king to do something which, unlike ministers who were answerable for their advice in Parliament, the private secretary could not be called before Parliament to defend. To defuse such criticism, the Prince Regent paid MacMahon's salary out of his own private money, the privy purse, rather than out of one of the civil list classes devoted to salaries for public servants. The criticism, however, was never entirely silenced and in 1822 George IV abolished the post of private secretary and appointed his doctor, William Knighton, to be his keeper of the privy purse. Knighton was a *de facto* private secretary as well, but he did not have the title.

George IV's most recent biographer, E.A. Smith, describes the king's relationship with Knighton as 'more than that of patient and physician; it anticipated that of a twentieth-century dependent patient to a dominant psychotherapist'.[2] George IV relied on Knighton for everything. Indeed, the position of doctors at court deserves more study. Even in Ponsonby's day, Queen Victoria relied on her doctors, Sir William Jenner and later Sir James Reid, for much more than medical advice.

Neither MacMahon nor Bloomfield appears to have interfered in political business as much as Knighton did. After 1822 ministers found that they had to figure Knighton into their calculations about how to deal with the king. But all three men engaged in shady transactions on behalf of the king; MacMahon, for example, tried to bribe some of the press who favoured the queen in the king's divorce proceedings into reversing their view and supporting the king.[3] Bloomfield bought hostile caricatures so as to prevent them from circulating, and he also paid the newspapers to keep his own name out of print.[4] It is unclear whether any of the secretaries embezzled funds entrusted to them; they were certainly bribed by George IV to keep quiet. All three men intimidated George IV, as they knew many of his secrets, and used this information to strengthen their own positions. They may also have simply benefited from his open-handed largesse.

MacMahon left at his death a huge estate of £90,000 and Knighton also died a rich man.[5]

These three men owed their jobs to the king's incapacity for business. They did things for him that were too humiliating for him to do himself. Moreover, because he was less conscientious than his father had been in his prime, they did things he could not be bothered to do for himself. The protests of politicians, both Whig and Tory, against them related to the fact that they were aiding a prince who still had real power to make mischief, for example to misappropriate public funds and to burden the Lords with legal proceedings against his wife.

The office of private secretary was revived in 1830 with the accession of William IV. Everyone seemed to trust Herbert Taylor, now reappointed to the post, to be as upright as he had been with George III. The position was also revived because the new king, not having anticipated coming to the throne, was literally incapable of carrying out all that was expected of him without help from someone who knew the ropes better than he did.

Taylor had a tough time. He had to steer a Tory king through delicate negotiations with Whig ministers in the biggest political crisis of the century, the expansion of the franchise with the passage of the first reform bill in 1832. He was also the first private secretary to the sovereign who saw his role not as someone who should help the king struggle against ministers, as William IV sometimes wanted to do in obstructing his Whig ministers' plans for parliamentary reform. Rather, he thought it his job to encourage the king to support his ministers, of whatever party they might be.[6] Even before Prince Albert and Baron Stockmar began to insist on the neutrality of the crown in political disputes, Taylor felt that the private secretary should have no particular political bias. He also saw before William IV did (if he ever did), that the sovereign must take a purely disinterested attitude toward the disputes of the political parties.[7] If he did not, the sovereign would be subject to the same fluctuations in popularity and effectiveness suffered and enjoyed by politicians. Taylor did what Ponsonby was frequently to do for Queen Victoria; he exerted a mollifying influence on his employer. He smoothed down William IV's intemperate outbursts in order to ease royal relations with men who gave the king apoplexy, but who were absolutely necessary to the conduct of government business. The difference between the two, an important one, is that Taylor did not share Ponsonby's sense of the ridiculous. Taylor's attitude toward the monarchy was one of 'feudal devotion'.[8] Ponsonby could not bear to take it all so seriously, although he hid his amusement under an open-faced mien. The consequence of Taylor's secretariat was that collisions between William IV and his ministers, though not entirely prevented, were significantly minimised. Taylor set a precedent for the private secretary acting as an emollient between the sovereign and the ministers.

*

When Queen Victoria came to the throne in 1837 she was only eighteen. She asked Taylor whether she should have a private secretary. 'Is Your Majesty afraid of the work?' he asked. She said she was not, and Taylor replied that she should not have a private secretary. He may have been trying to save her from antagonising her Whig ministers who had been so critical of George IV's secretaries. He may also have heard that her uncle, Leopold I, king of the Belgians, had been advocating the appointment of his former doctor, Stockmar, to be her secretary as a way of keeping his finger on British policy.[9] Whatever the reason, the queen accepted the advice. For thirty years, between 1837 and 1867, the office was technically in abeyance. A series of individuals, to varying degrees officially recognised, took on the duties of a private secretary, but none had the name.

To begin with, the queen's prime minister, Lord Melbourne, was in such constant attendance on her that there was no need for a secretary. He told her what she needed to sign, where she needed to go and advised her whom to appoint to her household. She had no comments to make on his policy other than to applaud it, as she was thoroughly under his spell and accepted all he said as the best of all possible worlds. When he was not there, she relied on her former governess Louise Lehzen, for secretarial help and advice. Lehzen knew little about English politics; she was German and had been employed by the queen's mother, the duchess of Kent, to look after Victoria's education. To Lehzen have been attributed two of the serious missteps of the queen's early reign.[10] Lehzen did not prevent and may have encouraged the queen's accusation of one of her ladies, Lady Flora Hastings, of being pregnant when in fact she had cancer. Nor did Lehzen – unlike Taylor – see the need to diminish the queen's partisanship. When Sir Robert Peel asked to be able to dismiss some of her Whig ladies of the bedchamber as a mark of confidence in him when he was forming her first Tory government she refused, having been taught by Melbourne that Whigs were good and Tories bad. Both incidents adversely affected the queen's popularity. One even temporarily disrupted the administration. Lehzen had acted as a favourite, acquiescing in the queen's whims without trying to foresee or estimate the likely impact of her actions either on policy or on her popularity and advising her accordingly.

Sustaining the popularity of the sovereign and eliminating her reputation for Whig partisanship were Prince Albert's two priorities when he and the queen married in 1840. He was eventually allowed to send Lehzen back to Germany, but he was only slowly permitted into the queen's confidence. During her first pregnancy, the queen began to rely on him more. Albert increasingly took on the management of all her relations with ministers, as well as the financial arrangements of the household, the two most important functions of those who served the queen in a private capacity. At the same time three men, all from powerful Whig and aristocratic families, came to help him. Two distinct approaches to the monarchy by chance coincided. The powerful advocacy of a Stockmar-and-Albert view of the monarchy coincided with a Whig insistence on ministerial and parliamentary supremacy over all significant actions of the court. This deeply affected the monarchy and the position of private secretary to the sovereign.

Albert and Stockmar believed that a change in the sovereign's public profile and manner of dealing with ministers would enhance the throne's power and stability. They believed that if the royal family lived up to high moral standards, it would provide an attractive contrast to the broken marriages, mistresses and bastards that featured prominently in the two previous reigns. This would add to the sovereign's popularity and increase royal power over ministers. They had no intention of reducing the sovereign to a political non-entity. Rather than favouring Tory ministers, however, and trying fruitlessly to thwart Whig and radical measures, as the previous two kings had done, they intended that the sovereign should be neutral. The queen should support whichever political party held the balance of power in Parliament. She should use the prestige and ultimately the popularity of her position to require information from ministers. She should be fully informed of their plans so as to form an independent judgement and to provide impartial scrutiny of ministerial policy. She might thus privately point out apparent flaws in ministerial measures while publicly giving her full support to the men for the time being who held office. Stockmar and Albert envisaged a monarchy that could provide constant critical oversight of government actions so as to insure that no steps were rashly taken, and that the country would not suffer from purely partisan measures. Their view was at odds with the view today that the Victorian monarchy was slowly withdrawing from a political role into powerless neutrality. Far from it, they saw neutrality as the new basis for a powerful and continuous review of policy.

Indeed, the controversies that dogged Albert throughout his time in England indicate how suspicious ministers were of his intentions. They began by cutting down the annuity proposed to defray his personal expenses and refusing anything like the title of 'king consort' that the queen wanted for him. (It should be remembered that this also took place against the backdrop of Chartist agitation. Ministers may have been as keen to avoid charges of over-generosity to princes as they were to clip Albert's wings.) Later, during the Crimean War, there were sharp debates in Parliament about Albert's interference at the Foreign Office. Ministers refused to grant him the title of 'Prince Consort' by an act of Parliament, so the Queen was forced to grant the title in 1857 by letters patent. In short, politicians realised that Albert was acting as the queen's private secretary and they still objected to the influence that such a person so near the sovereign – but without a ministerial obligation to appear before Parliament – might exercise.

Ironically, Stockmar and Albert were assisted by Whig secretaries whose party had been vocal in its criticism of the whole idea of a secretary to the sovereign. Lord Melbourne shifted his own private secretary, George Anson, over to help the young man who was shortly to arrive in England to marry the queen. Anson served for seven years as the prince's secretary and was succeeded by Charles Phipps. When Phipps was appointed to be keeper of the privy purse in 1849 Charles Grey succeeded him as the prince's secretary. All three came from a political tradition that regarded princes imported from Germany as at best a sad necessity. All three grew up in Whig territorial families whose time in the highest political offices had mainly passed by the 1850s, but among whom there were still active memories of power more as a family tradition than an elective office. None of them seems to have come into serious conflict with either Prince Albert or Baron Stockmar. This may have been because Albert, like most Whigs, was in favour of a mild politics of reform. Albert identified with the active commercial forces of industrial towns rather than with the conservative agricultural squirearchy. Further, the Albert-and-Stockmar view that ministers should be strengthened and supported by the sovereign was probably a relief to Whigs who were accustomed to George IV and William IV scheming behind their backs. Anson, Phipps and Grey were unaware or did not foresee the more significant consequences should a popular sovereign, armed with all government departments' reports, object to a policy proposed by ministers.

What the Whig secretaries and Stockmar-plus-Albert effected

together is more interesting. They brought about a horror of even the appearance of partisanship, which has persisted at the palace down to modern times. The Albert-and-Stockmar reason for such neutrality was to enhance the sovereign's influence. By contrast, the Whig view was that everyone would be better off if few people knew how little influence the sovereign had. The important point to remember is that after Victoria's early years everyone was a good deal more circumspect about what took place in interviews between the sovereign and her prime minister. This worked to the advantage of the monarchy in that the throne acquired a compelling reputation for benign non-interference that it had never had in the past. It also worked to the benefit of ministers in that they rarely had to deal with a sovereign confident, skilled or well-informed enough to place serious difficulties during these secret interviews in the way of their policies.

Had the Prince Consort lived the case might have been different. Disraeli's much-quoted line that Albert might have become a dictator if he had not died so young was not just a throwaway exaggeration. He worked too hard and wore himself out. Even in those days, the business of government was becoming far too complex and varied for any one person to stay on top of it all. He asked for and received too many returns from government offices. He introduced an excellent archival system for preserving documents in all the different files to which they related, but it led to more work for him. He made many of his own copies of important memoranda and did much of the filing himself. He re-organised the administration of the household, supervised the acquisition of two large estates, commissioned the building of two sizeable houses and codified procedures especially in the philanthropic work of the privy purse. It was too much for one man. He ate his food quickly and drank water rather than wine. He took too little pleasure in his dinners and too little satisfaction in all that his work was bringing to pass. Had he lived he might well have acquired in just a few more years a formidable influence from all the information he had mastered. As it was he died aged 42 in 1861, his eyes fixed on one of the Raphael drawings in the dressing room where he slept at Windsor Castle.

The queen was truly at a loss after Albert's death. The emotional loss of course came first, but Albert had organised all her dealings with the government as well as the management of her money: she had been freed up to give her energies to the birth of nine children, no small job. With her husband gone, she wished to appoint his private secretary, Grey, and to retain Phipps as privy purse, both of them to act together as her joint private secretaries. The prime minister, Lord Palmerston, refused. In some measure this was due to dislike of the power that Prince Albert had acquired. It was also due to the old Whig objection to a private secretary to the sovereign. Palmerston blamed his refusal on popular misconceptions about the private secretary's relation to the sovereign, but he wheeled out the same arguments the Whigs had used against George IV's appointment of MacMahon. He wrote to the queen four days after the death of her husband that

> The appointment of private secretary to the Sovereign has at all times in this country attracted much attention and has been viewed with some jealousy and it has indeed been the subject of discussion in Parliament. The Public exaggerate the nature of the office, and the influence which its holder can exercise, and there is a general impression against irresponsible advisers.[11]

Palmerston thought it would be fine if Grey and Phipps continued to act informally on the queen's behalf; he would even authorise their being given keys to the cabinet despatch boxes, but he positively refused to have their posts officially recognised. In a second letter he told Phipps that to make the appointments official 'would give rise to much remark and invidious observation'. It would cause people to suspect that the sovereign had privileged but unaccountable advisers whispering in her ear. This was 'a Position entirely at variance with the Principles and Practice of the British Constitution'.[12] Thus, as late as 1861 the post of private secretary to the sovereign could not be recognised because its influence over the queen was deemed to be dangerously unconstitutional.

The prince's death also re-illuminated the private secretary's relationship to the sovereign's incapacity for business. The private secretariat is most in evidence not when the sovereign is prepared to do business, but when for whatever reason this is not possible. The queen tried hard to make ministers see that her husband had truly transacted everything and that she had only a vague idea where to begin again herself. She instructed Phipps to make it clear to the government 'that the support and assistance which her Majesty has heretofore received is gone for ever, the mind that conceived it, the head that judged it is gone'.[13] She virtually denied any independent judgement on the affairs of the preceding twenty years: it had all been him. What precisely had he done? She had the impression that he worked all the time. She was annoyed with him for working as hard as he did. Her main idea of the job was that she should stay on top of the correspondence and monitor the newspapers. She had no plans for actively requiring more information from departments or encouraging intellectual and industrial enterprise as the prince had done. Her letter to Grey gives some indication of the routine she contemplated for her private office as she emerged from the first shock of her husband's death.

> General Grey do be so good as to let the Queen know *whenever* he has any letters to show to her, and if she has time She will see him, and if not he may send them up. But he should let her know daily and in this same way be so kind as to look through all the newspapers and tell her what is in them ...
>   She is so anxious that everything should go on regularly as it used to do, and her life is now merely *for work*.[14]

That last little sad emphasis on 'work' is perhaps the best indication that she suspected that what her husband had done would be uncongenial to her, but that she would embrace it as part of a fate that was as bitter to her as being alone.

In fact, she suited herself and did not work all that much: she provided the formal signatures that were required of her; she saw ministers occasionally. She did not take an active interest in politics, or require more information, or suggest alterations in the wording of diplomatic telegrams, all of which her husband had done. She appeared in public as little as possible, first because she was in mourning, later because it made her nervous and gave her headaches. It was this failure that most annoyed ministers; they were quite content that she let them get on with their own departments with little interference, in fact much less interference than they had been accustomed to under Albert. It is a mark of how little she was doing that Charles Grey, who was acting jointly with Phipps as her secretary, had the time to publish a book. At her command he wrote a biography of Prince Albert's early life, first for private circulation and then for the general public.[15] This was what Victoria considered to be her real work in the 1860s: to show the public how important to her and how important to them the prince had been.

When Charles Phipps died in 1866, the question arose again of official recognition of her private secretary. Grey was tired of doing the work without the title and without the pay. As an ordinary equerry he received considerably less than Phipps had as keeper of the privy purse. The request went forward from the palace that Grey should be officially recognised as private secretary. Once again the Whig premier, now Earl

Russell, objected. The same criticisms as those in 1812 of MacMahon might be revived. He thought it would be safer if Phipps's replacement, Thomas Biddulph, and Grey were to be appointed joint keepers of the privy purse. He deemed it a significant enough question to bring before the cabinet for official advice. The cabinet concurred with his advising against it.[16]

There are two wonderful features of a letter Russell sent to Grey on the subject. Grey had complained that it was ridiculously jumpy to fear that the objections against MacMahon should still apply more than fifty years later to his acting as private secretary to Queen Victoria. One is the fact that the Whig cousinhood, so dominant a feature of the previous century of aristocratic oligarchy, was still going strong. Russell reminded Grey how much 'George Ponsonby, your uncle' [Grey's mother's brother, hence Mary Ponsonby's great uncle and a distant cousin of Henry Ponsonby's] had dwelt on the evils of surrounding the throne with irresponsible advisers. The letter might be a reminder of what an uncle had said to a nephew at a family dinner rather than an official reply from prime minister to the sovereign's *de facto* private secretary. The other remarkable feature of the letter is an ironic remark made at the end in which Russell indicates to Grey that they both knew how little in 1866 the queen was actually doing. '[I]f she has reigned 29 years without having any person with that title [private secretary]' he asks, 'why not continue so till she becomes through age or infirmity incapable of that daily minute attention she now gives to public affairs?'[17] They both knew she was doing nothing of the sort; and it suited their political principles very well that she did not.

There the matter lay until Russell left office less than a year later, when Lord Derby and Benjamin Disraeli formed a Tory administration. Immediately the queen asked them not only to recognise officially that Grey was private secretary, but also to get a vote from the House of Commons to pay his salary. Conservatives were always more willing than Whigs or Liberals to magnify the dignity of the throne. Derby replied that there was no problem whatsoever about having Grey's title officially gazetted.[18] Disraeli, however, resisted a vote to pay for Grey's salary. Large sums were being paid over as savings from the civil list to the privy purse. To avoid protests in Parliament, Grey's salary had better be paid from the privy purse.[19] Disraeli was not always a syco-phant and where money was concerned he was prepared to take a firm line with the queen.

The new arrangements whereby Biddulph was to do the duty of keeper of the privy purse and Grey private secretary also occasioned a memorandum written by Grey setting out their different duties. It sets out precisely what the private secretary was expected to do and the nature of his relationship to the other powerful officer, the keeper of the privy purse. Grey's first point was that 'during the temporary absence of either his duties shall be discharged by the other'.[20] As a similar point is made towards the end of the memo, it appears there was overlap between the two posts. Both were to be acquainted with what was on the other man's desk so as to be able to step in when necessary. Grey, the private secretary, was to handle the queen's

> Correspondence with Her Ministers, and business connected with the Fine Arts, Ceremonies such as laying First Stones, opening Institutions, etc. etc. while Sir Thomas Biddulph shall take charge of the Privy Purse business properly so called, including everything connected with Her Majesty's pecuniary or Household concerns, the distribution of Her Majesty's patronage, dispensation of charities, etc. etc.
>
> Sir Thomas Biddulph will also be charged with all communications with the Admiralty and Duchy of Lancaster, the former involving many questions connected with Her Majesty's personal and domestic affairs and the latter consisting almost entirely of financial business.

So one job was mainly public and political. The other was more to do with private and financial affairs, though no very bold line could be drawn between them. Indeed the line between the sovereign's public and private affairs, between the king's two bodies, between his capacity to act as a crowned king on the one hand and as an ordinary person on the other, is the fault line on which the monarchy rests. It is the source of all potential disasters as well as the centre of its unique popular appeal. This was the line that the private secretary had to get to know intimately.

The job of private secretary could be very frustrating. After two years as the officially recognised secretary (though really about eight years doing the job since the death of the prince, as well as twelve years as secretary to the prince before that) Grey told the Queen he wanted to retire. In 1869 he was 65 years old and had first mentioned retirement when he was 63. He told the queen that he felt 'old age creeping on' and that he also wanted to spend more time with his family. As he was in constant attendance on the queen, he did not see as much of his family as he would have liked. He was often away at Balmoral or Osborne while his family stayed behind at Windsor. There was a good deal of busy work connected with the office. The Prince Consort's filing system required multiple copies of important documents, and though there was a clerk available to do copying in the privy purse office at Buckingham Palace as well as one at Osborne, Grey had to copy more confidential documents himself. Finally, and most importantly, Grey was from a family that enjoyed commenting on political affairs. Such talk had never been banned under the Prince Consort, but it was now taboo at Queen Victoria's dinner table. This rule was more than irksome to Grey. It was his job to keep up the sovereign's superintendence of public affairs at a time when she wished to retire more and more into private life. Grey told the queen robustly that she ought to do more in the way of public work; she complained to her daughter that he had become cranky, unpleasant and impossible.[21] No wonder then that by his mid-60s he had had enough.

There seems to have been no question in the queen's mind of anyone but Henry Ponsonby to take his place. Ponsonby had been at court since 1857. Stockmar liked him. Prince Albert had made him an equerry. Grey and Biddulph, as well as Lord Granville, the colonial secretary, and Gerald Wellesley, the dean of Windsor, had all recommended him. The queen first intimated that she had him in mind as Grey's successor when she asked Grey to have Ponsonby help him in 1869. When Grey died of a stroke in 1870, the queen appointed Ponsonby promptly to replace him.

Her only fear was that Ponsonby was a too-outspoken admirer of the Liberal party. Her cousin, George Cambridge, who was about as conservative as he could possibly be and had already crossed swords with Ponsonby on the subject of flogging, may have stirred up this suspicion; but she may also have been afraid of what she thought of as Mary Ponsonby's political radicalism. In the queen's inner circle Mary had been branded with the epithet 'clever' and the queen was always a little wary of women with genuine intellectual interests. The Prince of Wales when learning of the appointment of Ponsonby gave it only his lukewarm approval: 'I have no doubt you will have every reason to be satisfied' he wrote his mother 'tho I am not aware if he [HFP] knows much about politics, his opinions are I believe of the "advanced Liberal" kind'.[22] The Prince of Wales himself was not at that stage a distinguished judge of character or appropriate behaviour in political circumstances. He passed around confidential Foreign Office telegrams at a dinner party even after being warned to be careful and flirted with a mad woman who got him into the divorce courts.

Ponsonby took offence at the queen's repeated cautions that he should drop all political talk. He wrote to Biddulph coolly, 'I perfectly understand the value of discretion and though I am not aware that I have ever manifested any strong views on political matters, I will be careful not to express myself in such a manner as to lead others to consider me an extreme partisan.'[23] The fact was that by the late 1860s the court was already made up of people of increasingly conservative if not Conservative views. They looked with alarm on Gladstone's proposals to disestablish the Irish church and increase the rights of Irish tenants, seeing them as the first attacks on the Established Church and on property owners in England. Even a mild defence of Gladstone, which Ponsonby had from time to time proposed, would have made him into an 'extreme partisan' in the eyes of the army officers who were the queen's equerries and the Tory doctor, Sir William Jenner, on whom the queen relied.

The queen's youngest son, Prince Leopold, was also critical of Ponsonby's appointment. Grey stood up to the queen. Leopold thought Ponsonby 'obsequious', possibly because he got on well with John Brown, whom Leopold particularly detested.[24] Ponsonby's ability to get on with Brown, about whom the queen grew more defensive the more he tangled with the rest of her entourage, was probably an additional mark in favour of Ponsonby in her mind.

Ponsonby's appointment as private secretary, with Biddulph continuing to act as keeper of the privy purse, was the occasion for a new memorandum setting out precisely what the queen expected them to do. Despatches from ambassadors abroad or submissions from government departments which she sent down were to be read. Occasionally she might ask them to make an abstract of a complex document. Then they were to return the paperwork to the appropriate department in one of the red leather despatch boxes in which it had arrived. Above all, the queen wrote,

> Both Sir Thomas and Col. Ponsonby should *keep watch* on what goes on in and out of Parliament and *draw* the Queen's attention to *any* questions which affect the prerogative, or the Army, Navy, – or in short anything, – so that should the Queen *not* have been informed or asked, she can ask for explanation, or remonstrate. *This* is of the *utmost* importance for the Queen has not the *time* to watch everything and is sadly overworked and is so often unwell now as to require much help. In the same way if anything in the Despatches, private letters and Draft[s] of importance strikes Sir Thomas and Col. Ponsonby *they should call* the Queen's attention to it.
>
> In the present day when the old Traditions are being more and more lost, the Queen feels it of the *utmost importance* that the greatest watchfulness should be exercised.[25]

Here the queen was sounding the keynotes of the Prince Consort's system: keeping watch, asking for explanations, remonstrating if necessary. This, combined with unexceptionable family life, made evident to the public in appearances before them, was the Albert-and-Stockmar plan for preserving and enhancing royal influence over politicians. The trouble was that by 1870 the queen had withdrawn from the public appearance part of the formula. In those years she was also less interested in what was going on inside or outside Parliament, despite her protestations to the contrary. The line about 'old Traditions being more and more lost' was the homily of a lady beginning to feel her age. She was sticking to the line her husband had taken without investing the energy he had in making it work. She ordered her secretaries to keep things up for her because she was unequal to it herself.

Once again there was a direct relationship between the need for a private secretary and the sovereign's unwillingness or inability to do the work. Further, the job was at last officially recognised. There was no question of keeping Ponsonby's name out of the gazette. The Whigs had become submerged in their alliance with the Liberals. There was no indication from politicians of any stripe that they worried about the queen taking any more interest in politics that could somehow damage, or even affect their transaction of business. The impression is that the sovereign had declared herself incapable of business and that politicians, at last, believed her. Her private office consisted of two gentlemen, in fairly constant attendance on her, though seeing her only occasionally, living out of the spotlight, who replied to letters from ministers, kept copies, sorted papers, dispensed charity and invested her savings. The work was improvised, inconspicuous and fairly inconsequential from a political point of view. The advisers were not equipped to formulate policy, make selections among competing ministers or even to influence cabinet decisions. There were indications, however, that a new generation required a new sort of monarchy and the key problem, as it had never been under George III, George IV, William IV, or under Albert, was the queen's invisibility. It was a general complaint. It was the first and foremost problem that the new private secretary was called upon to address. It was the hallmark of a new sort of monarchy that perhaps even Ponsonby was slow to recognise, acknowledge and assimilate.

Gladstone and the Queen's Invisibility

One of Gladstone's most quoted pronouncements on the monarchy appears in a letter to Lord Granville at the beginning of his first premiership. 'To speak in rude and general terms,' he wrote, 'the Queen is invisible, and the Prince of Wales is not respected.'[26] More than any other prime minister in the nineteenth century, he insisted that the proper role of the monarchy was to be visible and to be respectable. The sovereign might still possess a smidgen of influence on policy, but a political role was not only wholly subordinate to, but also wholly dependent on, the royal family's sustaining their popularity by pleasing people and being seen. To please people, princes ought to behave with dignity. They had to find some happy compromise between their own personalities and the people the crowd expected princes to be. Gladstone believed that the Prince Consort had got the formula pretty nearly right: he had done his duty in public and enjoyed doing it because he was genuinely interested in bridge-building, sanitation and proselytising about the superiority of English industrial machinery. These were the sorts of thing on which he and the queen had set the royal stamp of approval. The Prince Consort and the queen had set a high tone in society too by espousing sobriety and hard work, rather than the 'loucheness' of the queen's uncles. Therefore they had built up tremendous popular support, particularly by this contrast with previous reigns. True to his own commercial origins, Gladstone compared this popularity to the acquisition of a large sum of money. As Ponsonby wrote to his wife from Balmoral in the autumn of 1871, Gladstone had told him that the queen had 'laid up in early years an immense fund of loyalty, but she is now living on her capital'. Gladstone was afraid that she would spend it all and that worse, her son would begin with no capital at all, and 'what is a sovereign to do who begins without any such capital? He referred much to Bagehot'[27] remarked Ponsonby. This was the depressing state of the monarchy, as Gladstone saw it. It was the 'Royalty Question' for which he wanted an answer.

*

Gladstone is so often portrayed as hopelessly wrong-headed about the monarchy – hectoring the queen in private audiences and sending her thirty-page memoranda that she found impossible to read – that it is worth pointing out some of the contemporary contexts for his concern about her unpopularity. The electoral franchise had doubled in 1867 and Gladstone's government was the first that had been elected on the new register. No one knew how loyal or orderly the new electors, many of whom were from the urban working classes, would be. Radicals on the left of Gladstone's party like the mayor of Birmingham,

Joseph Chamberlain, and Sir Charles Dilke, appeared to have a real hold on sections of this new urban electorate. Both Chamberlain and Dilke were ambitious young men, powerful speakers and in some cases quite openly anti-monarchical. What the public thought about the queen thus mattered a great deal more than it had in the pre-reform days when few of them had access to the vote. Further, in the first few years of Gladstone's ministry, France's second empire collapsed under the pressure of the Franco-Prussian War. Napoleon III and his empress went into exile. Monarchical institutions might seem grand and imposing, but they could totter and fall with startling rapidity. For a brief period, under the Commune, radicals governed Paris in the name of the working classes. There was also a rising socialist movement dominated by the Communist Internationale, which held a large meeting in The Hague in 1872. So the royalty question was really a question about whether the old social order was not eroding rather quickly. Finding an answer to it, deflecting criticism of the throne, was really about finding stability in what contemporaries perceived as dangerously shifting times.

Gladstone never got his answer. But he did acquire a willing pupil in Henry Ponsonby. In the autumn of 1871 Ponsonby had been only a little more than a year in the job. Though an alert and senior officer in the Army, he was still trying to find his way among the intricate passages of Westminster and Whitehall. Gladstone taught Ponsonby several important lessons that would affect the way he conducted his private secretariat. First, he referred him to Bagehot's *The English Constitution*. The book's reflections on the usefulness of the monarchy in adding a little theatricality and sparkle to the dull business of government had been published in 1867. Gladstone also taught Ponsonby the importance of the queen's supporting her ministers even when she disagreed with them. Under Gladstone Ponsonby learned, in addition, how to support himself in tough times, when the queen and her prime minister were coming to detest one another, by savouring a sense of the absurdity of it all.

The closest Gladstone ever came to saying publicly and in writing why he thought the queen needed to be seen, why she and her son needed to provide a moral lead to society, came in a book he wrote as a young man. He wrote *The State in Its Relation with the Church* (1838) in a Tory, high church phase of his youth and later disavowed it. Much of the book was a defence of the Anglican establishment, and appeared to contemporaries to try to turn back the clock, and to disapprove of the admission of dissenters and Catholics to the full rights of citizenship under the constitution, measures that had become law only a few years before the book's publication. In it Gladstone set out some ideas that go far towards explaining why he laid so much stress on the queen's visibility. Why do we spend so much money on public buildings? Why do we make them attractive and imposing? Gladstone asked. Why make the queen go through the elaborate ritual of the coronation? The answer, he replied, was because of the high dignity of the idea of a free people with a long history of self-government. He was referring to the outward display of the new houses of Parliament, then being rebuilt in the form we know today following a fire that had destroyed them in 1834. Another contemporary reference was to the splendour of Queen Victoria's coronation, which Gladstone had witnessed in 1838. Both of these corresponded to the inward splendour of the form of government they represented. The Palace of Westminster and the coronation order were both visible symbols of an intangible idea: a Christian people who had a tradition of independence and discussion at the core of their institutions of government. Seen in this light, the queen was no stand-in for papal despotism. She did not represent bending your neck to your betters. Rather, she was the embodiment of a peculiarly parliamentary monarchy that was medieval in its origins.[28]

Ponsonby was unlikely to have agreed with all of this. Macaulay, one of the fiercest critics of Gladstone's book, had also been his teacher. Ponsonby's whiggish sense of history would have led him to date the origin of the monarchy only as far back as 1688-9, when Parliament first frightened off one king, James II, and effectively invited a foreigner and a Dutchman, William III, to take his place. He did follow Gladstone, however, in deploring the fact that the queen did not keep up what he called her 'show duties'.[29] The queen had such a horror of being seen that she could sometimes be invisible even to members of her own household. If Ponsonby wanted to see her, he had to send in a note via a footman or Brown or one of the ladies in waiting. Often he did not see her for days at a time and they carried on their business in notes that went back and forth in the red leather despatch boxes. Queen Victoria's idea of heaven was to go off to her small granite house on the edge of Loch Muick, several miles from the castle at Balmoral, where only a dresser, Brown and perhaps a cook looked after her. After the death of Prince Albert, she had got into the habit of seeing as few people as possible. Not until 1865 did she reappear before the assembled household and allow the band to play after dinner. All the household considered this a huge step forward.[30] In the early 1870s when Ponsonby took office she was not more inclined to socialise.

In 1871 MEP suggested to Henry that it was a pity the queen did not see more people, and particularly refused to see the sort of intellectual company MEP most enjoyed. She rued the fact that the queen preferred speaking to the wife of one of the gamekeepers at Balmoral, Mrs Grant, to the wife of the historian of ancient Greece, Mrs Grote. Henry agreed, though he teased his wife by pointing out it was easier to speak to the gamekeeper's wife, who talked about scones, than to speak to Mrs Grote, who might raise the question of women training to be doctors. The queen had learned to avoid controversial topics and even among the household would start calling out the name of her dog sitting under the table – 'Tumby, Tumby' – when someone at dinner raised a subject too near the politics of the day. Still, Henry conceded that 'it is a sort of madness to hear no one speak for fear they should get on points of doubt'.[31]

Gladstone had a variety of plans to answer the royalty question. He asked the queen frequently to appear in public: to open Parliament in person and to be present at the dedication of public works. Most of these she refused, claiming she was too weak and unwell. She referred him to her doctors for support. So Gladstone turned his attention to the Prince of Wales. He consulted Ponsonby throughout the summer of 1872 on several different options for giving the prince some worthwhile public duty to perform. Ponsonby suggested the prince might sit on the India Council; Gladstone wanted him to go to Ireland.[32] Most of the options either the queen or Ponsonby or the prince's friends rejected as either ill-suited to the prince's personality or beyond his abilities. Even more, the queen disliked any question of rivalry with her heir.

The plan in which Gladstone invested the most energy was to send the Prince of Wales to Dublin for a few months in the year during which he might discharge the function of lord lieutenant. It was part of his plan to pacify Ireland by framing legislation to redress grievances as well as – equally important from his point of view – to bring the Irish back into the fold by allowing them to claim the royal family as their own. This was not so different from the political intent behind the queen's visits to Ireland with her husband in 1849 and 1853. The visits were meant first to soften the tough legislation that had been required to restore order at the time of the famine, and then to congratulate the Irish on their recovery. What she had agreed to when her husband was alive and when Lord Clarendon recommended it, however, the queen would not do for Gladstone in the 1870s. Her heart had hardened toward the Irish. Nor did she want her son saddled with the extra expense entailed in discharging the viceroyalty. She was adamantly against the idea even when the government proposed that the prince be given extra money to do the job. So, during his first government, she repeatedly thwarted Gladstone in his efforts to answer the royalty question. It was Ponsonby who had to come between them. It was Ponsonby who now learned also, this early in his job, how little real influence he had with the queen on the question of public appearances.

W.E. Forster, one of the more radical members of the cabinet, proposed to Ponsonby that he tell the queen, who was angry about not getting a reply on some matter from London, that if she came to London more often, there would not be such difficulties. Ponsonby told his wife, 'I gave a sickly smile and said "No" '.[33] He found that he must discourage ministers from approaching topics that would make her angry. This was the only way for him to help them preserve whatever influence they still had with her.

It certainly distressed Ponsonby that he could find no way of getting the queen to listen to Gladstone or his colleagues on the need for her to be a more visible sovereign. In his early years as private secretary his cardinal doctrine was that he must get her to rely on those men who for the time being held the seals of office. He and Biddulph reminded her when she wished to support her cousin, the duke of Cambridge, in a dispute with the war minister over army reform that 'Your Majesty's wish and interest is always to support the Government of the day'.[34] She must not oppose ministers fruitlessly or ask for positive measures where there was no hope of success.[35] 'I am all for asking reasons why things are done,' Henry told Mary when the queen had once again been snubbed by the war minister, 'but not in making opposition where opposition is useless.'[36] It was safer simply to use her prerogative to ask for more time or more information on measures about which she was dubious.[37] She was dubious about a whole variety of legislation put forward by Gladstone's first government, including most importantly Edward Cardwell's measures for army reform. She was put up to resisting this by the duke of Cambridge. She did not take a sustained enough interest in government business, however, to be able to oppose what she disliked effectively. In a sense this suited Ponsonby: he supported Gladstone and he thought Cardwell was bringing forward reforms of the Army he loved that were in some cases regrettable, but in most necessary. Seen from a different perspective, however, her lack of interest in what was going on bothered him. Was he properly looking after the interests of what he called ironically his 'department' if he allowed the queen's influence over ministers to slip away?

*

The queen liked to let it be known that though she was too weak to appear in public, she had incessant work to do in private. Indeed, the number of documents requiring her routine signature or approval, for example officers' commissions and acts of the Privy Council, was significant, and required some time and attention on a regular basis. It would have been easy to get bored, or to shirk it, which she did not. On the whole, though, Ponsonby did not think she worked very hard. When a Scottish clergyman wrote to him saying he knew how very hard the queen worked, Henry reported it to MEP with some added exclamation marks to indicate his arched eyebrows. He then showed the clergyman's letter to the queen's doctor, Sir William Jenner, who also laughed at it – but Ponsonby saw Jenner as part of the problem. He believed that Jenner was one of the chief conspirators in disseminating the lie about the queen's health being unequal to public duties.[38] When Disraeli made a speech in September of 1871 saying the queen was 'physically and morally' incapable of performing her duties in public, Ponsonby suspected Disraeli had received hints about what he might say from Jenner or Jane Ely. They must have told Disraeli that such a defence of the queen would win him points with her.[39]

Henry told Mary that the queen did not do nearly as much 'work' as Disraeli claimed. She saw a few despatches from the Foreign Office, perhaps one a week. The Colonial Office, once a month, forwarded a list of despatches that had been sent, though not the despatches themselves. Even these lists, Ponsonby confessed in October 1871, he had not seen for more than six months.[40] The notion that the queen was advising on these despatches was entirely fictional. Mary replied that her Uncle Charles had also found the queen 'uninterested in affairs' during his time in office.[41] Henry was not sure where it would end. He wanted ministers in constant attendance on the queen as they once had been so they could answer themselves and in person the questions raised about their policies by the Tory rumour mill at court. The queen, however, was happier if they stayed away.[42] He thought she was losing her influence and tried to hint as much to her[43] – but she took no notice, as even the ministers she liked and trusted, like Lord Granville, were unconcerned by her lack of interest in politics. It made it easier for them.

Very quickly Ponsonby came face to face with the frustrations of his position. He enjoyed the contact with Gladstone and the confidence the prime minister placed in him. He was flattered by Gladstone's invitation to come to Hawarden, which he turned down only because he longed to be back in Windsor with his wife.[44] But any illusions he may have had

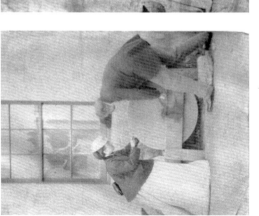

12. Three photographs of Mary Ponsonby and her uncle, General Charles Grey, with Henry Ponsonby (seated) at Balmoral in the mid-1860s. Mary Ponsonby is sharpening an instrument.

13. In 1877 the Ponsonbys visited Ireland. Henry points out his old room in the Viceregal Lodge in Dublin's Phoenix Park.

14. The Norman Tower, Windsor Castle, a photograph taken from the garden in the dry moat: 'a modern civilised house inside an entirely uncompromising feudal fortress'.

15. Mary Ponsonby with her last child, Arthur, in the mid-1870s.

16. Arthur Ponsonby and Mary Ponsonby in the workshop at the Norman Tower, probably early 1880s. 'The occupation we shared together most of all and which I enjoyed the most because I had her exclusively to myself, when my brothers were away, was metal repoussé. We even used to warm up our pitch and hammer away after everyone else had gone to bed.'

17. Mary Bulteel sits with Lady Jocelyn, '*femme du monde* to the tips of her fingers and *grande dame* of the most exclusive *ançien régime* kind'.

18. Mrs Wellesley ('Lily'), wife of the dean of Windsor, sits while Agnes Courtenay, niece of a canon of St George's, stands, c. 1870s. 'My friendship with Agnes Courtenay is a new phase in my life. Since my disappointment about Lily, I have always shrunk from fresh friends ...'

19. Mary Ponsonby, 1870s, photographed in the Norman Tower. 'She "had discovered and laid bare the stone walls of two octagonal rooms in the tower which had been prisons in the olden times for state prisoners and she had left the walls bare ... She had made these two rooms her sitting rooms."'

20. The bedroom at Osborne Cottage on the Isle of Wight where Henry Ponsonby had his last illness in 1895. 'I should always be prepared to go, but my grief and pain would be to leave my dear, dear wife and my children.'

21. Mary Ponsonby, aged between 70 and 80 at her house, Gilmuire, in South Ascot. 'I have no fear of death but to anyone within measurable distance of that awful mystery it seems incredible that it should not be more overwhelming.'

22. Henry Ponsonby in uniform, 1880s. Prince Leopold and the Prince of Wales asked him, 'who shall command the Army. They or the Government? They seem to ignore the fact that this was settled by the late Charles I'.

about taking part in political negotiations were largely shattered. Stockmar, he told MEP, had been a real adviser to the queen. Henry seldom gave advice. Even when he tried to give advice about a small matter concerning the mixing up of the privy purse and household accounts, the queen had 'civilly but firmly' told him that he knew nothing about it. There were so many difficulties in giving the queen advice, in approaching her on topics where they might possibly disagree, that sometimes it was safer not to give any advice at all.[45] If that was the case, was there really any need for a private secretary?

Henry coped with his difficulties by sending his wife amusing stories from court. On one occasion he made fun of the local population at Ballater, the Aberdeenshire town close to Balmoral. In the morning it was a fast day. The town was deserted and all the Ballater population was at church. In the afternoon, however, everyone seemed to be drunk.[46] It was the combination of unexpected opposites that amused him. Severe Presbyterianism in the morning combined with drinking oneself helpless in the afternoon was not unlike the clergyman who spoke of the queen's unceasing work while in fact she was spending months in remote locations where much work was impossible.

Had he got it wrong? Was he making too much of a fuss over the queen's lack of interest in political affairs? Was not the centre of her appeal the amusement these little preposterous vignettes of court life provided for husband and wife? It is true that neither of them would have explained the appeal of the monarchy in these terms. It is also true that when the newspapers reported on the queen, it tended to be in tones that were graver and more unctuous than anything that appeared in the letters of Henry and Mary. Still, the light-hearted descriptions of trivial events that populate Henry's letters are not far from the queen's own instinct about what was most appealing to her larger public. In 1868 she had published extracts from journals of her happier days when she and her husband had gone on holiday to Scotland. This was her *Leaves from the Journal of Our Life in the Highlands*, a book unprecedented in the history of the British monarchy and which had huge sales. It was unprecedented in that other than King James's early seventeenth-century injunctions to obedience, sovereigns have not published their views and certainly not their journals. Queen Victoria was stung by the increasing demands for her retirement to end. Perhaps she thought that homely, pedestrian details of daily life with her husband in Scotland would help to satisfy the demand for her to appear in public without her actually having to appear in person. The huge sales suggest that there was a large public willing to consume trivial information about picnics, dancing reels and pony treks. If the queen were largely invisible, at least she could be imagined: Victoria, by the grace of God queen of Great Britain and Ireland, tasting oatmeal porridge ('which I think very good'), riding her pony up a cabbage field ('very steep') and visiting the cabin of Kitty Kear ('who is eighty-six years old').[47] The juxtaposition of the grandeur of the author and the ordinariness of the journal was the book's most titillating feature. It is both the attractiveness and the absurdity of this juxtaposition that was also at the centre of all of Henry's best jokes about the monarchy. The Ponsonbys' opinion of the Victorian monarchy was this: the balance was all. Certainly the throne ought to inspire respect. It ought to inspire an unspoken ethic of service in all public servants. The Ponsonbys' private letters suggest, however, that much of the monarchy's attraction lay also in its ability to divert, to entertain and to inspire what they called *fou rires*, or helpless laughter. It was a mistake to put too much emphasis, as Bagehot had, on the queen's remaining prerogatives – to encourage, to warn and to be kept informed. If the queen chose not to appear in public, it certainly adversely affected her popularity, but with a simple book she could keep her appeal alive, ignore her prime minister's suggestions and dispense as well with the advice of her private secretary.

Disraeli and 'Affairs'

Disraeli understood viscerally what Gladstone understood intellectually. What the one had put into closely written pages about the monarchy representing self-government, the other put into flirtatious letters to the queen, calling her not only the sovereign of his body, but also the sovereign of his heart.[48] Disraeli was himself a showman. He approached questions of display with none of the Ponsonbys' aristocratic disdain: as a young man he wore his dark hair in ringlets and dressed up in waistcoats with shockingly feminine colours. Even in his old age he made an indelible impression on the young Arthur Ponsonby as he followed his father and Disraeli home across the fields from the church at Whippingham one Sunday. The prime minister was wearing white gloves with the fingers covered in rings, the rings worn outside the gloves.[49]

Disraeli's sense of showmanship and his talent for exaggeration were the secrets of his success. Anything less likely to impress a woman who had made plainness a religion and who liked nothing better than a wet picnic in the company of not very talkative gamekeepers is hard to imagine. And yet it worked. Disraeli revived in the queen a love of her office that she had not felt since her first prime minister, Lord Melbourne, had inspired in her a girlish crush and a passion for being royal.

The usual view is that Disraeli's flattery brought the queen out of retirement where Gladstone's hectoring had utterly failed. Disraeli's heaping it on with a trowel worked where Gladstone's addressing her as if she were a public meeting did not. This is wrong. Two points need to be made about what Disraeli did do. First, he spoke to her as if he really did believe in her wisdom, sagacity and power to do whatever she wanted – and it made her more interested, not in public appearances, but in politics than she had been since the prince's death. The queen wrote to one of her ladies in waiting after she first commissioned Disraeli to form a government in 1868, 'He repeatedly said whatever I wished shd. be done whatever his difficulties might be!'[50] Second, his elaborate though perhaps slightly phony deference, his building of imaginary castles in the air for her to inhabit, these figures of speech were his version of what Gladstone had put into the argument of *The State in Its Relation to the Church*. Disraeli's most recent biographer, Paul Smith, has described his approach to the queen as 'ornate deference which verged on satire'.[51] For him the monarchy was a spur to the imagination.[52] It provided the sense of history, glory and tradition that held both people and government together. Thus, when he wrote to the queen he could indulge his taste for romance, high-sounding titles and humble obedience to the full. The novelist in him could not help seeing, though, the comic effect created by the ordinary woman, inhabiting inconvenient palaces, who held these titles. Lord Blake, still the dean of Disraeli biographers, puts it this way:

> Disraeli's language should not be taken literally. It was part of an elaborate comedy of manners in which he was author, actor and spectator, with the Queen cast in the other principal role, while Whiggish figures like Derby and Ponsonby observed dryly and dubiously from the wings.[53]

In this analysis even Blake has missed something. The element of enjoyment, play and mischief in Disraeli's manner to the queen were allied to, indeed aspects of, the imaginative appeal that Disraeli sensed that the monarchy made to the people at large. Thus, absurdity and satire were not incongruous parts of Disraeli's flattery of the queen, but integral parts of it. The irony is that although Henry distrusted Disraeli, the two were both masters at sending up the queen at the same time as they served her.

Neither the queen nor Ponsonby saw this. They both misunderstood Disraeli's vision. For Disraeli, the crown's value as theatre of ye olde worlde was a necessary counterpart to his speaking to the queen as if she were an all-powerful despot. The one neutralised the other. But his flattery had unintended consequences. The queen appeared a little more often in public, but she took a great deal more interest in cabinet business, what MEP's Uncle Charles had called 'affairs'. She personally helped to originate two major pieces of legislation that alienated Disraeli from some of his own supporters and took up a good deal of parliamentary time. Further, her intimacy with Disraeli, and her increasingly Tory leanings, meant that Ponsonby was sidelined, ignored and deprived of information during the 1874-80 ministry. Thus, the theme of the private secretary's relationship to the sovereign's incapacity for business returns. When the sovereign was interested in doing business, when she was capable and willing to deal with ministers herself, the importance of the private secretary's office declined.

Two measures highlighted the queen's renewed interest in politics and required legislative attention from Disraeli's 1874-80 government.[54] The public worship regulation act of 1874 was a reflection of her dislike of the tendency among ritualist clergy to adapt Roman Catholic practices to Church of England services. The royal titles bill of 1876 added the words 'Empress of India' to Victoria's title as queen of England, effective from 1 January 1877. Both were measures that had been spoken of and desired by others; neither would have come forward, or been given parliamentary time, without her backing and insistence. It is interesting that both acts were essentially about forms and ceremonies. Both acts occurred in the period when the queen was coming to regard Disraeli, the great lover of forms and ceremonies, not only as her minister, but as her friend. Yet the queen may have misunderstood Disraeli's magic, may have heard his praises about her great powers and the importance of ceremonial without perceiving how equally important was a sense of humour or satire allied to it.

Certainly, the two bills had real consequences. Disraeli had to squander some of the good feeling that attends the formation of any new government on the public worship regulation act. It alienated high churchmen among his own supporters and stirred up an ecclesiastical hornets' nest. The bill did not eliminate the feeling of disquiet and anti-Roman Catholic prejudice that had been provoked by the wide variations in the way high, low, and broad church clergymen conducted Church of England services. Henry in a letter to Mary made fun of the queen's hatred of the ritualist clergy. She believed exaggerated stories about high churchmen turning the commemorative act of the communion into a superstitious ritual.

> I wonder who furnishes The Queen with Church stories. She told me this morning of a Bishop who went to give the Sacrament in a very high church in the west of England. All the clergy wore all sorts of dresses and the Bishop (perhaps it was only a clergyman but she got so impressed and spoke low so I couldn't catch it all) got so nervous that he accidentally dropped some of the wine on which to his horror the 3 attending clergy fell flat down and licked it up. This is a propos to the Church bill now going through Parliament.[55]

The problem was that the queen often got her political ideas from sources her private secretary could not trace. She had always known that Ponsonby and his wife identified themselves with Liberal or Whig positions. When she was really pro-Disraelian, she inclined to think them both radicals. As Disraeli increased in favour, these outside sources, whom Ponsonby would have called into question if he and the queen had not already been getting on to shaky terms, increased in number.

Ponsonby was even more surprised when Disraeli attributed the church bill entirely to the queen. They had a talk as they came across the Solent from Southampton to Cowes on their way to Osborne.

> He called the Public Worship Bill 'The Queen's Bill' and said she [had] carried it entirely. 'If I had tried to make it a Government measure it would have broken up my cabinet; it is entirely owing to The Queen that it has passed. I thought it nearly hopeless yesterday. But it is now through and I am indeed most glad of it.'[56]

Ponsonby thought Disraeli's calling it 'The Queen's Bill' an exaggeration knowing how much the archbishop of Canterbury and other leading clergy had also pressed for it. Disraeli's speaking in this way, however, was exactly what entranced the queen and encouraged her to proceed with other big plans. MEP thought the whole question was pointless. The entire Church she predicted would in the long run 'founder on the scientific and rationalist rock ahead'.[57] Yet both Mary and Henry were a long way off believing that the public worship regulation act was a good thing. Neither of them believed that it was the queen's bill. Both believed that it was dangerous for the queen to advance, and Disraeli to allow, such forceful advocacy of a politically controversial measure.

Neither of them liked the royal titles bill either. It had complex origins, dating back to an 1843 memorandum written by Prince Albert, who deplored the way the East India Company was 'sucking the riches of that country' rather than governing for the welfare of its inhabitants.[58] It came to the fore in 1876 because the Prince of Wales made an unprecedented trip to India that began in 1875. He told the queen that she was sometimes called 'Empress' there and that making this title official would tie her more closely to the Indian subcontinent, as well as please Indians by appealing to oriental notions of rank. Further, there were problems of precedence on the continent, where the queen's children were sometimes placed below the salt because they were thought to rank beneath those who were children of the German or Austrian emperors. This incensed the queen, who maintained that she was an empress as well. She asked Disraeli to enact this and he did her bidding; although it once again caused parliamentary trouble which he had not anticipated. It also annoyed the Prince of Wales as the legislation went through while he was away and without anyone first mentioning it to him. The Ponsonbys appreciated aristocratic bearing and charm, but were deeply contemptuous of anybody who insisted on the recognition of his rank. Their attitude to the titles bill may be summed up in a letter Henry wrote two years later reporting the squabbles of some of the queen's German relations about their precedence: 'Dr. Johnson was once asked a question of precedence and said you must first tell me which goes first a louse or a flea?'[59] Henry and Mary both thought questions of rank ridiculous, which sometimes placed them in an odd position at a court where questions of rank were often raised.

Disraeli believed that the royal titles bill could be got through quickly and without opposition. It was something the queen wanted. All he had to do was to make that clear and he was quite certain he could get MPs of all parties to agree to it, especially as it involved no money. To Liberals, however, the word 'emperor' smelled of despotism. It was 'foreign' and continental. They would have nothing to do with it. The queen was outraged when she heard of their objections in Parliament, and she blamed Ponsonby for not keeping what she thought of as his friends in order. He told Granville that he was 'in black books' with the queen as a result.[60] Granville, a former favourite of hers, who had objected to the bill in the Lords using the most polite language possible, she never really forgave.

Ponsonby believed that Disraeli had mismanaged the bill. He had not consulted the opposition in advance, as was customary with measures affecting the royal family and in which politicians, whether Tory or

Liberal, liked to keep a high degree of unanimity. Much as he wanted to, however, Ponsonby did not feel he could blame Disraeli for the opposition raised in both houses of Parliament and in the newspapers to the royal titles bill. His job was to make the queen rely on ministers, to advise her not to act independently of them. He tried to explain the Liberal objections to her, at the same time telling her firmly 'You must however abide by Disraeli's advice. He had introduced [the] measure in the way he thinks most judicious and he must advise Y[our] M[ajesty] how to go thro with it.'[61]

The royal titles bill represented a decisive stage in which the queen did just that. She relied more and more on personal communications with Disraeli and Tory members of her household and family. She relied less and less on Ponsonby. The latter part of Gladstone's first ministry had been the high water mark of her confidence in him. She believed that he had managed a series of delicate problems with particular success, for example Princess Louise's marriage to Lord Lorne in 1871 and the thanksgiving at St Paul's for the recovery of the Prince of Wales in 1872. As a mark of her gratitude and of recognition she wanted to make him a 'CB' or commander of the order of the Bath in 1872. He refused it and the episode is telling about the sort of gap that came between them on questions of titles, but on larger issues as well.

Ponsonby did not want the decoration first because it was a civilian order and he still considered himself a soldier. The addition of letters after one's name, or a title before it, he looked upon with distaste. His keynote was self-effacement, getting things done without demanding the credit. This was the old-fashioned gentlemanly creed: put yourself last and avoid the first person pronoun whenever possible. The number of people scheming for honours and peerages appalled him. Although he never used these terms, MEP was not afraid to. She thought such scheming the height of vulgarity, and she taught her children that to boast of one's position was equally wrong.[62] At length, the queen withdrew her offer, saying she knew that the reasons he gave for declining did him credit. Nevertheless, he had to endure an article in the newspapers, possibly written by the garter king of arms, Sir Albert Woods, who always took the turning down of honours as a sort of personal affront, arguing that it was ungentlemanly to refuse an honour from a lady.[63]

A few years later in 1879, the queen renewed the question. This time she offered to make Henry a knight commander of the Bath, or KCB, hence for the first time 'Sir' Henry and 'Lady' Ponsonby. Once again he wanted to refuse. This time she tried to get him to accept by having Jane

Ely write to the dean of Windsor in order to get him to intercede with Henry. Henry replied to the dean's letter in a rare burst of pique that accepting this honour would be like making the dean accept the title of 'Moderator of the Dissenting Chapel in Peascod Street', a commonplace street lined with shops in Windsor.[64] At length, however, Henry dropped his objections. He and Mary took the alterations in their names unwillingly, but saw that more objections would only further sour their relations with the sovereign they were both pledged to support.

The question of titles is telling. Queen Victoria was following Disraeli, and Disraeli himself only reflecting a greater social trend toward showiness and display that began between the third and fourth quarters of the nineteenth century. Conspicuous consumption was becoming more acceptable than it once had been. Ritualists moved towards more theatrical religious services. Actor-managers put on spectacular productions of Shakespeare with hundreds of people on stage. The duke of Norfolk built a big showy castle on the remains of a more modest, medieval building at Arundel. Triumphalism was in. Quietness was out. Orchids in buttonholes and furled umbrellas carried like swagger sticks were in. Shabby tailcoats and half boots with elastic sides for easy slipping on and off (what Henry usually wore to work) were out. So when the queen and Ponsonby disagreed about the royal titles bill, she was being more prescient, more in touch with the way attitudes toward titles were going, than he was.

MEP told Henry in 1878 that the love of 'glitter' by which she meant titles, social display and emphasis on rank was becoming widespread, especially among the middle class. The only people who were above it were intellectuals and the upper echelons of the aristocracy. 'The people who in England care least for the kind of show that Dizzy delights in,' she wrote to him, 'are of the Huxley or of the Duke of Somerset type. Below these, in both planes, I think there is a great love of it.'[65] She wanted to say that Disraeli's delight in show was vulgar, but she had to concede that she found him entertaining. She very much enjoyed his sense of humour. Henry too felt that there was something wry, ironical or burlesque under Disraeli's elaborate homages to the queen. He did not enjoy it as much as his wife did because he was afraid of the ideas he might give the queen if Disraeli led her to believe that her judgement was superior to that of her ministers. Nor could he bring himself to be amused by Disraeli's flattery, reporting with satisfaction one day an episode in which the flattery had failed to work. At Balmoral in 1874, Ponsonby, Disraeli and the queen's son, Prince Alfred, duke of

Edinburgh, as well as Alfred's new Russian wife, were having a discussion on toadstools, which the duchess of Edinburgh insisted were generally both edible and good.

> The Duke of Edinburgh made some remark I didn't hear about them and Dizzy replied 'His Royal Highness must with his great knowledge of men and things gained in all the countries of the world through which he has travelled know the real state of the case better than any one.' The Duchess cut in sharply 'No! he knows nothing at all about it.' Dizzy looked at her with that comic face he puts on when he finds his flattery fails and simply said 'Hum!' I couldn't help laughing at her eagerness.[66]

He thought Gladstone really believed in the queen, whereas Disraeli did not.[67] Biddulph agreed with him that Disraeli was always 'humbugging' the queen, concealing the truth beneath phrases about 'her most puissant majesty'. Fundamentally, he told Mary, Disraeli was oriental, and 'not one of us'.[68]

The phrase recalls Margaret Thatcher's famous question about the loyalty of her supporters in Parliament. 'Is he one of us?' she used to ask. Queen Victoria was the same. She had an equally stubborn sense of being either 'with us' or 'against us' as she grew fonder of Disraeli. There was little room in her mind for criticism of her 'friend's' policy. Hence, when the Eastern Question blew up again in 1876, the stage was set for the coldest period in her relationship with Ponsonby.

*

The Eastern Question of the later 1870s was a renewal of instability in the region where the Crimean War had been fought in the 1850s. This instability was partly due to religious and ethnic hatreds. It was related to and not unlike the bloodshed and 'ethnic cleansing' that took place in the former Yugoslav territories in the later 1990s. Orthodox Christians and Muslims who inhabited the Balkan borders of the Turkish empire's boundaries with Russia committed atrocities against one another. Instability in the region was also caused by the ambition of larger powers seeking either to secure or improve their positions as the Turks receded from their former position of dominance in the Balkans. In the later 1870s Disraeli pursued a pro-Turkish policy, designed to keep up a bulwark against Russian designs in the Mediterranean and the northern boundaries of India. Gladstone pointed to the atrocities committed against Christians in Turkish-dominated territory and demanded more widespread moral condemnation of the Turks under whose aegis – at least technically – these atrocities had occurred. The queen followed Disraeli in wishing to support the Turks; Ponsonby followed Gladstone in being suspicious of them.

When the Eastern Question arose the queen and Ponsonby were initially in agreement on it. The queen was as appalled by Turkish atrocities as anyone. It was a mark of how much Disraeli had renewed her interest in politics that she actively discussed this at the dinner table late in 1876. Formerly she would have coughed noticeably if anyone approached a political issue, but now she took up politics, especially foreign affairs, with relish.[69] It was one of Ponsonby's principles to manage the queen 'by speaking to her plainly from the start'.[70] Thus, he boldly struck out and supported the opposition when they attacked Disraeli for his pro-Turkish policy. Ponsonby believed that Disraeli was not speaking to her plainly and that he owed it to her to be frank. The queen, however, had long had a horror of disagreement. When she was first married to Albert, and before she trusted him entirely, she refused to have political conversations with him. She felt that it was difficult to preserve her dignity and be disagreed with at the same time, even by her husband. She had always had strong likes and dislikes of the people who served her. When they were high in her favour, Melbourne, Brown, Albert, Disraeli and the Munshi could do no wrong. Anyone who suggested otherwise must be disloyal to her. So Ponsonby's mild but frank protests about Disraeli's handling of the Eastern Question upset her deeply. She decided to work around him.

He remained her private secretary. She made sure that others did the work. She carried on her correspondence either direct with Disraeli himself, or via Lady Ely. She rarely showed him her correspondence with the prime minister so he felt he was entirely in the dark.[71] Disraeli was a willing and enthusiastic participant in this; he often instructed his secretary to write to one of the ladies in waiting instead of Henry.[72] Henry gleaned what he could from the newspapers. Even the German librarian, Herman Sahl, knew more than he did, as Sahl was employed to decipher confidential foreign office telegrams, a job that once would have been strictly the private secretary's.[73] The queen made increasing use also of her youngest son, Leopold, to help with correspondence that would have routinely gone through the private secretary's office.[74] Leopold had a key that opened the red despatch boxes, a privilege denied to his brother, the Prince of Wales.[75] He became so powerful for a time that Ponsonby went so far as to outline his views on Turkey to him, rather than to the queen. This was dangerous, as the Tory Leopold passed on Ponsonby's views that were critical of Disraeli to the queen, prompting a renewal of hostilities between them.[76] The queen would not confront Henry. Instead, she would send him a hint via someone else. One such hint came in the autumn of 1876.

> The message came by Lady Ely who went on to say that the Queen wanted me to like Beaconsfield [as Disraeli had now become]. I replied that I thought he was one of the most amusing people I knew. Lady Ely said 'No, no, that is not it. She wants you to like him.'
>
> 'Say then that I will love him.'
>
> 'No, no dear General Ponsonby that won't do. She wants you to like him politically.'
>
> 'Well if he disagrees with The Queen am I to like Her politically or to like him?'
>
> Lady Ely said she could get no answer from me.

Eventually through the dean of Windsor, the queen told him that if he could not get to *like* Disraeli, he should remain silent.[77]

Henry was rarely angry in his letters to his wife, preferring to be tickled or amused even by the humiliations in his work for the queen. But in the later 1870s he was clearly upset at being 'muzzled' by the queen on politics, and depressed at the prospect of more work for her when in fact she was doing everything possible to avoid him. When Tory courtiers made jibes at Gladstone in Henry's presence at Balmoral, he glowered at them and told them that such comments were all very well when they knew he must not speak.[78] He wrote a memorandum summarising the wish of the British ambassador to Turkey, Sir Henry Elliot, to retire at a crucial moment during negotiations with Russia. Ponsonby wrote that Elliot's ill health was undoubtedly a polite cover for irreconcilable differences with his chief, the foreign secretary, Lord Salisbury. This he conceded, hinting at his own position, was an unpleasant feeling.[79] Henry too feared that he has irreconcilable differences with his chief.

In 1878 Ponsonby's colleague, the keeper of the privy purse, Sir Thomas Biddulph, died. It indicates how out of favour Ponsonby was, and how incautious the queen was becoming under Disraeli's influence, that she considered making an openly partisan move. She approached Lord Beaconsfield's private secretary, Montague Corry, and asked him whether he would be willing to join her staff.[80] Corry was a young man who had first admired Disraeli from a distance. An introduction was arranged, and Beaconsfield took him on first as private secretary, then as friend. Later they doted on each other and used the extravagant romantic language of friendship that to a twentieth-century reader makes them sound as if they were lovers. The queen accorded privileges to Corry that were never accorded the private secretaries, or even the wives, of her other prime ministers. When Beaconsfield came to Osborne, Corry was invited to come along and even to stay in the house as well, a marked compliment to both. She thought of making Corry her private secretary now and moving Ponsonby over to Biddulph's place as privy purse. She also considered appointing Corry as master of the household, the position from which she had previously promoted Biddulph after a spell of getting used to the routine. In the end, Corry refused to leave Beaconsfield and Ponsonby hinted that he would prefer to resign rather than exchange the private secretary's place for that of privy purse. A different solution was arrived at. Ponsonby became both private secretary and privy purse with a promise from the queen that he should have assistants appointed to help him and hence have a little more leave to see his wife. The episode ended in a sort of endorsement of Ponsonby's standing and authority within the household, while on political topics he and the queen continued, at best, to agree to disagree.[81]

It may seem odd that Henry was promoted at a time when he and the queen were barely on speaking terms. This came partly from his seniority in the household. He knew too much and had become indispensable. When he refused the queen's suggestion of becoming privy purse, she could hardly get rid of him altogether. Also, to be fair to her, there was a certain method in her sidelining of Henry during the 1874-80 ministry. She frequently employed Tory members of the household to write to Tory ministers. Jenner, Jane Ely and Leopold had the best and most sympathetic contacts with Beaconsfield and his assistants. Similarly, Henry could gain a hearing from Gladstone and his secretaries, men like Edward Hamilton and Horace Seymour, who were friends as well as colleagues of Henry's, that no Tory member of the household ever could. As much as they often disagreed with her, both Henry and Mary admired the queen's shrewdness and instincts about how to manage people. Henry's promotion to a position in her private office that no one had held since the death of the Prince Consort may well have been a further sign of her knowing ultimately what was for the best.

Looked at from a different angle, however, one has the sense that Beaconsfield, the queen and Ponsonby all three were under different misapprehensions toward the end of the 1874-80 ministry. Beaconsfield did not see, or at least never admitted, how his flattery had led the queen, and even some among his own followers, to high prerogative views he did not wish to endorse.[82] Some of his cabinet colleagues did see this as a problem. As Paul Smith points out, 'Derby warned Disraeli in the form of a question in May 1874: "Nobody can have managed the lady better than you have, but is there not just a risk of encouraging her in too large ideas of her personal power, and too great indifference to what the public expects?" '[83]

The queen and many latter-day historians missed the satire or irony in Disraeli's flattery. It encouraged her to come out of her shell, but she failed to see how much of what he said about her was actually an elaborate tease. When she sent him a bunch of flowers from Windsor, he thanked her by saying 'It was a gift worthy of Queen Elizabeth, and of an age when great affairs and romance were not incompatible'.[84] He did not really mean that he was in love with her, nor that she should have a tenth the power Tudor queens possessed. She saw the exaggeration and did not plan an Elizabethan renaissance, but she did have more determined views about her right to be involved at the highest levels of policy-making from the moment of her friendship with Disraeli forward.

Ponsonby too got it wrong ever so slightly. He was distressed when the queen was too high-handed about legislation, when he felt that he had failed to make her see that she must rely on ministers rather than act on her own. He did not appreciate that his most original insight on the monarchy derived from his brilliant aptitude for a joke. His dry observations rendered the spectacle of princes faintly comic, yet comic in such a gentle way that they might themselves appreciate the joke. For example, he wrote this record of a dinner table conversation with Prince Louis of Hesse, the German husband of the queen's daughter, Princess Alice.

Sat next to Princess Alice at dinner and she talked a good deal now and then touching on political matters which make The Queen cough. Louis' English is *infime* [infinitesimal], the whole of his conversation consists in 'You have in your country a – a – what you call – Ah So! Like – a what you call – Alice! Alice! *Was heist sie ein Wohlengeblantersaber*?'

'Fog.'

'Ah so yes a fog, which makes what you call – ah. Alice, Alice – *was ist Geblantersabenwohlenshamstinkenseit*?'

'Dark.'

'Ah so yes dark' etc.

I dare say if I understood him he would prove to be full of talents.[85]

It was this family of German royalties about which Ponsonby found it was impossible to be too sentimental, much less deferential. Indeed, it was only the very young among the royal family who acted naturally, who were impervious to any nonsense 'spell' cast by the great white queen, their grandmother. One day Ponsonby observed the Prince of Wales's two little boys, Eddie and George, preparing to go out fishing on the Dee at Balmoral. At the last minute they received a command to join the queen on her afternoon drive.

> The little Princes here declare the weather is warm and that they must go out fishing ... and all was prepared yesterday when they received a summons to drive with The Queen instead; an honour that they did not appreciate, and burst into tears with some not very loyal expressions.[86]

Henry's life was filled with frustration in the later 1870s. He was in constant attendance on the queen when he would have rather been with his wife and family. He was deeply interested in the political scene but was banned from saying what he thought at court. His only real pleasure was in capturing the occasional ridiculousness of it all. This made the pill less bitter for him to swallow. Mary was the only person to whom he could confide the difficulties of his office. She received his letters and provided a sympathetic outlet. He was so often away, though, that she had no choice but to carve out a life of her own.

CHAPTER 8

Mama and Her Friends

c. 1874-94

Mary had foreseen when she was pregnant with her third child that soon there would be no longer as much time as there had been formerly for outside activities. There would be less time for schools in Windsor and colleges in Cambridge, less time for committees intended to widen spheres for working women. She intended to occupy herself with the children's schooling, although she did hire nannies and allowed them to do some basic teaching. The boys would attend schools later on; even in this comparatively progressive household, there seems to have been no question of any organised schooling for the girls. Much of her children's early education, however, MEP decided should come from her, and she gradually gave up some of her public commitments and London friends in order to spend more time in Windsor. She made very few exceptions to this rule. One was for her old friend from the household, Lady Jocelyn, whom she began to see again in the 1870s. This occurred via Lady Jocelyn's son, Lord Roden, a young man in his twenties. The three began a delicate triangular relationship which became an important feature of MEP's life. In the 1870s MEP also got to know one of the leading intellectual celebrities of the day, George Eliot. The story of their friendship sheds light on MEP's trajectory from devout young woman to a mature agnosticism. These are both important contexts not only for understanding her life in the 1870s, but also for colouring in some of the unusual tints in the background of the late Victorian monarchy that the usual pictures obscure.

Lady Jocelyn and 'Bobby' Roden

MEP started a new journal in the year of the queen's Golden Jubilee. It was a significant anniversary, fifty years since the queen's accession to the throne, a time for looking back and reassessing significant times in one's life. 'My life is behind me,' Mary wrote in 1887, indicating the faintly depressed and pessimistic mood that usually overcame her when she wrote her diary.[1] She wanted to write a narrative of her life, to move beyond the censorious self-examination diary and to give some idea of the significant friends who appeared in that narrative. There are hints here and there that she thought her children might read it. The principal friendship that she devoted herself to describing was an extension and an elaboration of her early life at court. The memory of her resumed friendship between 1874 and 1880, as well as the whisper of a new romantic friendship with Lady Jocelyn's son, quickly dispelled the gloom with which she began the new diary in 1887. She remembered keeping to her 'plan of being busy with the children in the morning', but when Lord Roden came into the household as a lord in waiting in 1874, gradually 'he and Lady J. took up all the time and thought I had to give any friends'.

She reflected that 'It was in some ways about the most curious friendship of my life'. Frances Jocelyn, the wife of an Irish peer, who was heir to a large Ulster estate, had first impressed her when she was a young woman in her twenties. She had looked up to Charlotte Canning as someone who set a high standard and spurred her to set equally lofty standards for herself. Both women were senior members of the household, elders and mentors to the young Mary Bulteel, but Frances Jocelyn was better-dressed, moved in smart circles and made Mary laugh. Indeed, laughter with Lady Jocelyn was not unlike the glue that held her to Henry, as both he and Lady Jocelyn had a keen sense of the absurd. Lady Jocelyn also had some of the polished manners that attracted Mary all her life. 'Her habits and ways, looks and dress were of a type now nearly extinct, *femme du monde* to the tips of her fingers and *grande dame* of the most exclusive *ançien régime* kind.' The rustle of her skirts coming into a drawing room was enough to set the hearts racing of men and women alike. She combined an ability to make amusingly cutting remarks with an utter religious simplicity born of contact with her husband's ultra-Protestant relations. Her husband's family was allied with bigoted Ulster Orangemen, but Lady Jocelyn somehow managed to steer clear of their prejudice and fanaticism, while taking on the lack of pretension and humility of their religion. Mary remembered what a figure Lady Jocelyn was in the Society, capital 'S', of her youth and how hugely flattered she had been that Lady Jocelyn should even notice her.

> This brilliant woman, so difficult to please, so hard to impress, seemed charmed to have me as a companion, laughed and walked and talked with apparently perfect contentment with an insignificant girl like me. No

wonder my head was turned, how I delighted in it all. How the hours and days flew when I was at Windsor or Osborne with her. My grave books were put on one side and forgotten and the bright sparkling side of life was taken up.

Lady Jocelyn was a glass of champagne after months of tap water in a chipped tumbler.

Then terrible things happened. First, Lady Jocelyn's husband died of cholera. Then her mother 'to whom she was passionately devoted' died, as well as a sister from cancer. Next she lost a son at the age of nineteen and a married daughter who was only twenty. Frances Jocelyn herself developed cancer and suffered 'an attack of facial paralysis, which disfigured her greatly' and underwent 'the most excruciating operations' in order to try and improve her condition. Lady Jocelyn gave up her post in the household, and as Mary herself had married and begun a family, they saw much less of one another in the 1860s than they had in the 1850s. Still, she was not forgotten. The queen, who knew of MEP's attachment to Lady Jocelyn, sometimes spoke to her about their friend's series of tragedies, saying ' "Of all the admired and brilliant people in society of my youth, she was the most irresistible and the most successful, and now!" '

At some point in the early 1870s MEP ran into Lady Jocelyn's son, 'Bobby' Roden, in a shop. 'In a pretty, shy, yet man of the world way, (he was about 19) he came up and said "Will you forgive me if I ask why you don't come and see Mama? It would make her so happy if you did." ' This young man, who knew how to flirt boldly with women, caught MEP's attention. She was flattered that he should approach her and moved that his mother should remember her. However, MEP was more often in Windsor than in London and Lady Jocelyn was out of society, first because of mourning and later due to ill health. It took Bobby Roden's coming into waiting at Windsor to re-establish the link.

Bobby succeeded to his grandfather's title, earl of Roden, aged 26 in 1870. Four years later Disraeli appointed him to be a lord in waiting. This was a political post, not unlike serving as a sort of whip in the House of Lords, used in this case by the Conservatives to please and secure the support of Ulstermen in Parliament. The eight lords in waiting were still expected to attend the queen several times in the year, though she often dispensed with them when she was away from Windsor.

Bobby Roden's first social interest in the castle was Lily Wellesley's drawing room at the Deanery. Lily and Mary had drifted apart. 'Such is human nature', Mary wrote, that when she saw Bobby Roden pursued 'by Lily W. and notes and messages flew thick and strong' between them, 'I became a little provoked and wondered she could be so silly, especially as he always' hinted to Mary that 'he was a little bored' with Mrs Wellesley. Mary set out to win him for herself. If Lily Wellesley talked to him of people and religion, Mary would talk to him of ideas and books. 'He was a little ashamed at first of the graveness of some [of our] conversations and then he delighted in it.' They were both able to laugh 'over some foolish little thing the absurdity of which struck us both', just as she had done with his mother. Then, he would turn a 'gentle, deep, grave look' on her and with 'sparkling blue eyes' say ' "Now let us really think aloud it is so pleasant." ' She was as smitten with the son as she had been with the mother.

He was 'cruelly sensitive' and had 'fastidious habits'. Yet he also had his mother's poise and performed well in a racy conversation with a married woman fourteen years his senior. Mary believed that he was not so young that there was not occasionally 'a little tinge of unexpressed sentiment' between them. She described him as 'versatile, quick, full of perception, very handsome, ... intensely refined and *grand seigneur*'. In 1876 he schemed to get her to come to visit him at his house in northern Ireland, Tollymore, without exactly telling his mother beforehand 'how hard he had worked' to make Mary go. Lady Jocelyn simply believed that Mary had come to visit her. Mary did in part go to see Lady Jocelyn and afterwards took up calling on her regularly at her London house in Hertford Square. There is no doubt whatever, though, that she was as pleased by this young man's attentions as she was happy to resume her friendship with this entrancing woman of her youth, who happened to be his mother.

Then in the 1880s both mother and son were suddenly taken away from her. Lady Jocelyn succumbed to cancer. Bobby, who had always been delicate, died aged 33, unmarried, at Mentone in the south of France. MEP missed them both deeply, though she must have been prepared by their long history of ill health for both of them to die prematurely. She had no crisis of conscience about her intimacy with these two. She was sometimes aware of a small twinge of jealousy on Lady Jocelyn's part, who might tease her a little by saying with a twinkling eye, ' "I think you *koutou* to Bobby a little too much." ' On the whole, though, 'Had there been any doubleness or pretense in any of our minds, the whole fabric would have given way. As it was there never was one single word during those six years said by any one to spoil or disturb the most perfect confidence that ever existed between 3 people.'

The glimmers of absurdity repeatedly being reflected by court life and the peals of laughter MEP shared with mother and son had serious undertones as well. A sense of the ridiculous is perhaps one of the deepest bonds that two human beings can share. MEP's tender assessment of Lady Jocelyn was that 'The deepest thing about her was her wit, not her feeling or her religion, it was the only profound and perfectly satisfactory part of her character. I say profound because by means of the quickness of her wit she perceived and measured depths otherwise undreamt of by her. It was through her wit that she was sympathetic and even affectionate.'

Lady Jocelyn's wit was not unlike the sense of humour MEP was drawn to in Henry. Together she and Henry could also pay unaffected respect to the monarchy at the same time as the customs of princes made them collapse with laughter. The shared jokes of the Ponsonbys and Lady Jocelyn suggest the proper balance when discussing royal questions between dignity and comedy. To laugh at princes is really to take a careful measure of our own human frailties.

George Eliot and Religion

After the many pages of MEP's 1887 journal in which she describes Frances Jocelyn and Bobby Roden, there is a much briefer passage that sets out what was nonetheless an equally significant relationship. 'The only person besides I saw much of then,' MEP wrote, 'was George Eliot.' Her personal encounter with the celebrated author was a high point of the spiritual and intellectual journey she had begun much earlier.

In the later 1850s MEP had attributed dissatisfaction with religious rigidity and a new enthusiasm for the widest possible liberty to her reading in John Stuart Mill and George Eliot. Marriage to Henry, who was less high church than she was, as well as wider reading in what she called 'the scientific school', which challenged the account of human creation set out in the Bible, began to awaken religious doubt.[2] Geologists and proponents of Darwinian theories of evolution had provided new evidence to undermine the Biblical narrative of creation. Controversies raged in densely-packed reviews between clergymen and supporters of the new theories. Gradually, over the decade of the 1860s, Mary moved towards a reluctant agnosticism. She embraced the new scientific knowledge without ever quite escaping nostalgia for the religious certainty that had animated her girlhood. Nor did she ever relinquish an appreciation for some of the aesthetic qualities of religion, especially the music and the sense of awe inspired by high church worship. Throughout the 1860s, when they were apart, she and Henry often discussed religious questions in their letters.[3] Though she had begun to have doubts, MEP's fundamental sympathies were still with the Anglican high church. She often defended the ritualists, who had been inspired by the Oxford Movement in the first half of the century. These clergymen wanted to highlight the historical authenticity of Anglican services, and their continuities with those of the pre-Reformation church, by employing practices then more usual in Roman Catholic churches than in Protestant ones, such as wearing colourful dress, making the sign of the cross and burning incense.

Along with most Whigs and almost all courtiers, Henry was inclined to make fun of this in his letters to Mary. On the other hand, he would use some of Mary's arguments to defend the ritualists when what she called some of the greater 'philistines' in the household protested against them. He twitted her by returning to one of her favourite distinctions between natural and artificial manners. He told her in July 1868 when he was away doing duty with his regiment in Aldershot that he had read in an old copy of one of the high-brow weekly periodicals, *The Spectator*, that 'The taste for plain dress ... is artificial, a result of culture; the taste for finery is natural else why do savages wear feathers or why are the Guards fretting because someone wants to make their uniform more economical?'[4] This, he said triumphantly, was in favour of his argument that curates should wear plain dress, as it was a product of learning rather than instinct. He was safe in quoting the passage to her because it included a criticism of his own regiment's insistence on finery, as well as *her* queerly dressed curates, as *both* being a bit savage.

Defend high churchmen as she would, MEP's reading still told her increasingly that man was merely the result of a chance combination of molecules rather than a miraculous birth. The hope that George Eliot held out to her was that one might still reach some sort of satisfactory synthesis between religion and science. She hoped to retain the moral greatness of religion, the sense of duty, honour and self-sacrifice inspired by religious teaching, while jettisoning religious teaching about the origins of man. Added to this was the attraction of George Eliot's intellectual celebrity. MEP savoured and stored up recollections of brief encounters with great authors and learned men. Men like John Henry Newman and John Stuart Mill fascinated her. She met the French author, Ernest Renan, who had written a controversial biography of Jesus Christ.[5] She also was pleased to meet the historian of the Tudors, James Anthony Froude.[6] She had got to know the novelist, Margaret

Oliphant, well enough to introduce her to the queen. These were acquaintances more than friends. It does give some indication, nevertheless, of her profound admiration for writers and intellectuals.

By far the greatest of the people she knew was the author of *Middlemarch*. 'Like everyone else,' she wrote in her 1887 diary, 'I had read everything by George Eliot twice and three times.'[7] When a friend of hers offered to take her to St John's Wood to introduce her to the author, she jumped at the chance. She explained 'the involuntary deep curtsey I greeted her with' by the fact that she had never approached any emperor or king in her court days with anything like the respect she had for George Eliot, or Mrs Lewes, as she was referred to by friends and acquaintances. Perhaps MEP also felt a glint of satisfaction knowing that, in those puritanical days, the majority of respectable society would not call on Mrs Lewes and her husband, the critic G.H. Lewes, because the two had lived together unmarried before the death of his first wife. MEP would have enjoyed the unconventionality of calling on the ostracised Mrs Lewes.

At first MEP was disappointed. She thought Mrs Lewes mannered and stilted, artificial rather than natural. She disliked attending at the Lewes's house an event that was successful as neither a salon nor a seminar; but this did not prevent her pouring out her heart in a letter to Mrs Lewes that autumn. She wrote 24 confessional pages in October 1874 charting her religious journey since the age of sixteen. She explained her religious difficulties to Mrs Lewes because she believed from having read her novels that she possessed 'some secret' which made it possible for her 'to combine sympathy for modern scientific thought with "approval for moral greatness and beauty and purity in the high ideals you would set before us." '[8] Mrs Lewes replied in December, acknowledging what MEP had 'confided' in her and feeling 'the confidence to be a strong link between us'.[9]

An intense correspondence began between the two that lasted for a number of years. They also saw one another frequently. 'When I was allowed to see her alone, which happened at last pretty often, I thought that to speak to her of all that was lying deepest in one's heart and mind without reserve, and to be received in the kindest and most sympathetic way, was a rare delight.'[10] There is never quite the warmth of feeling in her diary entries about George Eliot, or her letters to her, that MEP had for Lily Wellesley or Agnes Courtenay, or even for Frances Jocelyn or Bobby Roden. She did feel an intellectual communion with her that she felt with few others. She was also flattered that George Eliot should take her seriously. George Eliot tried to talk MEP out of the religious position she had arrived at by the 1870s. George Eliot characterised this position as a sort of fatalism, a feeling of resignation that chance or arbitrary laws of molecular physics were more powerful and more determinative of human life than human love or moral aspiration.[11]

For her part, MEP feared George Eliot was equally wrong in erecting a new dogma to replace the old dogma of religion.[12] She disliked what she saw as George Eliot's putting human beings at the centre of a new 'religion of humanity' when the latest scientific research, in her mind, had the effect of showing how subordinate human beings were to long-term physical processes. MEP preferred a combination of scientific facts verifiably established with a large, mysterious, spiritual sphere about which no facts could be established.[13] She would continue to read molecular physics in her sitting room in the Norman Tower and then walk three minutes steeply downhill to hear the choral evensong at St George's Chapel. She was interested in hearing Arthur Balfour talk about how one might dispassionately and scientifically investigate the strange happenings at a séance.[14] At the same time she 'invested in a silver gilt rosary' as a gift to herself on a trip to Germany where she was chaperoning Gladstone's daughter, Mary.[15] They were in a party travelling to hear musical concerts in Düsseldorf that included Balfour and one of Mary Gladstone's Lyttelton relations.[16] Of a communion service at St George's, which she had enjoyed in spite of herself, she wrote to Henry, 'I see the beauty of the chain binding mysteriously those in Communion with each other and with Christ ... but the supernatural is always difficult for me to accept'.[17] MEP was in an awkward position. She had lost her faith in religion, but was not entirely satisfied with scientific explanations of how the world turned. In George Eliot she sought and failed to find the solution to her longing for intellectual consistency. In this she was entirely typical of late Victorian intellectuals, but it is still surprising to find this striving after higher truth in the wife of the queen's private secretary, because the queen's circle has always had a reputation for being unintellectual.

Husband and Children

The most powerful motif of the hundreds of letters Henry wrote to Mary in his regular absences from home is his love for her. Few of her letters to him have survived so it is impossible to say whether her sentiment for him was the same. The sense of what does survive is that she certainly loved him, though perhaps with more restraint than he loved her. She sometimes appears to love him as a result of a just assessment of his very admirable traits; she seldom appears as powerless before her love as he does before his feeling for her. Certainly she expressed her feelings less than he did. Nothing survives in her papers that indicates quite the strength of her love for him as this letter, written to her by Henry in 1878.

> The question is, was it my luck, my good fortune, my principles, my moral character, my superior intelligence, my leg or my whisker which secured for me the priceless treasure.
>
> Am I joking? No I am not for you are a priceless treasure and those words very feebly represent what I think of you. I never can be sufficiently thankful for your having been given to me, for what you have done for me and for what you are to me, Everything. Every moment I am with you is a joy and a pleasure, every moment I am away from you is a lapse in my life my own dearest darling wife.

He closed the letter as he always did, 'God bless you'.[18] Nevertheless, MEP was clearly much attached to her husband, as a rare surviving letter from her in 1882 shows. He had been in Windsor a short while and then gone off again to follow the queen. 'I do miss you so dreadfully' she wrote to him. 'It is tantalising to have a bit and then always to be saying goodbye.'[19]

Inevitably, as the years passed, the frequency of his letters to her diminished. In the 1870s he wrote to her every day he was away. As he got older, he wrote less, but loved her more. Writing from the royal train in the summer of 1890 as he accompanied the queen to Scotland he told her, 'As I get older I hate leaving you more than ever and I feel low at being away from you.' This lament was the feature of dozens of his letters to her and the melancholy grew deeper, the separations less tolerable, as the years passed.[20]

*

Mary had congratulated herself at the end of the epitome made in the 1880s of her early self-examination diary that she had never been blind to Henry's excellence. With nearly the last words in a diary in which she has often been excessively hard on herself, she seems at last to warm up and to expand. One of the last entries is: 'And the children. They make me happy every day. I am not afraid of the platitude of saying it.'[21]

They were indeed a happy family, perhaps happiest at the dinner table where they would seize on a topic, make it into a joke and toss it around the table.[22] The children all had separate tables, called 'offices', for their 'occupations'. They also had a museum-for-fun called the 'Bod-leum' after they had all made a visit to Oxford. They filled it with various exhibitions, such as the one commemorating Admiral Nelson's dying words to the officer kneeling beside him at the battle of Trafalgar, 'Kiss me, Hardy'. This was a scrap of grey paper with a wet kiss imprinted on it. The Bodleum also gave medals to members. Arthur Ponsonby remembered that 'Papa wore his with great solemnity and preferred it I think to his real medals and orders'.[23]

The sad thing for Henry was that he was often away not only from his wife, but also from the family circle. He did not share as regularly as he wished in the upbringing of their children. His most poignant letters home were written on occasions when he could not be with them for Christmas. He once tried to cheer himself up by telling the story of how when the German secretary, Herman Sahl, climbed on top of one of the tables to reach a treat tied to one of the upper branches of the Christmas tree, the table collapsed with a crash. But it was no use.[24] He was miserable without them. How he would have been desolate had he lived to read Arthur's memoir of his childhood in which he wrote, 'Papa we saw very little of. He was always away at his office. He very seldom seemed to have any holiday. He never played with us.'[25]

Mary had the greater share in raising the children. Although this was a conventional Victorian division of labour, all the children acquired both their parents' bookish and satirical unconventionality. The eldest, Betty, went through a high church phase, just as her mother had, and decided she wanted to become a Roman Catholic. MEP talked her out of it. Betty was also interested in political action to alleviate working conditions in factories and was friends with Charles Dilke's niece and biographer, Gertrude Tuckwell.[26] Betty wrote poetry and was friends in the last decade of the nineteenth century with members of the Souls, young society people who had intellectual aspirations. She was the only one of the children for whom MEP seems to have had hopes of making a brilliant marriage. Henry was instructed to take her on a tour of some of the great Liberal country houses after she came of age and was presented at court. The man she chose, William Montgomery, was an officer in the Grenadier Guards, like her father, who was interested in manners, like her mother. Montgomery once told Ethel Smyth in a drawl. ' "I always think it a mistake ... to say a man's not a gentleman, because" – (a pause) – "you so often find out he is." '[27] Betty and Montgomery were married in 1891, with the queen present in the congregation. They lived principally at Grey Abbey, a country house in

Ireland with connections to Mary's Grey side of the family. They had no children.

Maggie was Henry's favourite of the children and the child who remained at home unmarried to become her parents' companion. She had a talent for mimicry and Arthur remembered her as one of the most 'amusingly loquacious' of his brothers and sisters. According to her niece, Loelia Lindsay, whose words have to be weighed as she enjoyed satirising her relations, Maggie 'went in for religion and joined the elderly ladies who were in love with Dick Shepard, the vicar of St Martin in the Field'.[28] Magdalen was also a great friend of her mother's writer friends. Arthur Benson and Edmund Gosse both liked her and saw her on their own. For a time she acted as her cousin, Maurice Baring's, manager and literary agent. Among playwrights, she knew Laurence Housman. A letter survives in which she responds to Housman's questions about court life for a play he was writing, possibly *Victoria Regina*. She punctures all his reverent pomposities about the court with typical Ponsonby light-heartedness. Housman asked her whether the Prince Consort, when angry with his eldest son, would address him as 'Sir' or 'Wales' or 'Boy' or 'Bertie'. Magdalen's reply was that 'Consort was in Paradise when I was born, so I never heard much about his temper. I imagine Bertie or Sir'.

'How would the Queen address a Bishop in private audience?' Housman asked. Magadalen answered, 'Never having been at that audience I don't know but I imagine a judicious mixture of My Lord Bishop and "but my dear Bishop of Timbuctoo I hope your wife is well." '

Housman wanted to know if the queen wished to speak to someone among her guests after dinner, 'is there a Lady in Waiting who goes and fetches them?' Yes, Magdalen said, 'Lady in Waiting fetched the victim. Q.V. dismissed with a little bow and smile.'[29]

The eldest boy was the subject of anguish on the part of both mother and father. Although Johnny later grew a moustache that concealed his slight disfigurement, those outside his family and friends always found it difficult to understand him. He went, like all three of the boys, first to a prep school and then to Eton. Perhaps he had fewer chances to be homesick than most as he could look up at the castle and see the windows of the Norman Tower with little difficulty from a dozen vantage points in Eton. Although all the boys were interested in reading books and all three of them published books in later life none distinguished himself academically. Johnny and Fritz wanted to follow in their father's footsteps into the Army and a Guards regiment, but they kept failing the crucial exams. Henry had to caution MEP that there were only very limited things he could do for them. He could not give them large allowances, for one, which in those days were necessary for a career in the Guards.[30] Nor was he in favour of nepotism. He did eventually write to the duke of Cambridge's private secretary to assess Fritz's chances of entering quickly into a Guards regiment.[31] Henry repeatedly refused suggestions that he should use his contacts to advance his brother, Fred's career in the church.[32] Nevertheless, the Ponsonby name was a recommendation in itself. Eventually, Johnny made his way into the Coldstream Guards and Fritz into the Grenadiers. Johnny served in South Africa during the Boer War and then in France during World War I.

Fritz, the middle son, was the best looking of the boys, the most attached to society, and the one of the children least like his parents. He started a career in the Grenadiers and collected gambling debts, which Henry had to pay off. Then he got into greater debt a second time, so that it looked as if he might have to be turned out of the regiment.[33] Henry learned about this from Arthur, to whom he replied sadly thanking him for the news. He asked Arthur to keep Fritz's money troubles a secret from MEP. He was unusually ruffled by the incident, as he was already struggling to pay Fritz's earlier debts. Fritz had given his father a promise that he would not get into any fresh trouble when he asked if he might go to Ascot. The news via Arthur that Fritz had broken his word deeply shocked Henry.[34]

MEP did eventually find out about Fritz. She devised various schemes to save him, which would have made Henry blanch, since they all involved pulling strings, and imposing on the kindness of officers Henry had to work with in his capacity as private secretary.[35] At last they decided that Fritz might go out to India, where he could at least save money. Before very long the queen recalled him from India to fill a vacant equerryship in 1894. This was a mark of honour to his father, but Fritz quickly showed that he had not his father's tact or knack for indulging the queen's susceptibilities. He almost immediately outraged her by questioning the social status of her Indian favourite, Abdul Karim. She did not speak to him for weeks afterwards. In fact, he found her household, like his father, old and grey; he much preferred the people around the Prince of Wales, with whom he shared an un-Ponsonby-like love of medals, uniforms and ceremonials.[36] He had ambitions to be private secretary himself one day, and although he rose to be keeper of the privy purse under George V, he did not have the diplomatic skills necessary for the bigger job.

It is clear from the tone of her letters to him that Arthur was MEP's favourite child – the youngest boy who followed the others by such an interval that he was perhaps an afterthought. He was allowed privileges that may have been denied the others. When he was a little boy and away at prep school, she let him address her with the same diminutive she used with him. 'My dear Mamma' Arthur wrote, 'I have got something rather nasty to tell you. I was caned the other day with [the] rest of my room for making a noise ... I am very sorry darling. I hope you will forgive me.'[37] She believed that later his taking up a radical and socialist line in politics came from her, as did his love of drawing, painting in water-colours, reading and writing. Of all her children, he was the most prolific author. Having grown up in a house where both mother and father inter-mittently kept diaries, he came to be an authority on British diarists.[38] His mother wrote long and sympathetic letters to him when he began to have religious doubts.[39] One of his most vivid memories of her was an occasion when they were both sitting in the stalls at St George's Chapel. He had shown 'not only inattention but irreverence during the service. A very cutting reprimand came from her because although by that time she was completely agnostic the idea of irreverence made her furious.' You might respect the forms and enjoy the music of a church service without believing the creed, she taught him.

We know from Arthur that when MEP was angry she was a formi-dable figure indeed. One day he was having lunch with his mother and Maggie. 'With the zeal of the newly converted ... I was laying down the law about Socialism. My sister ... argued with some violence and at last exasperated me and I told her with warmth she was talking "pure bunkum".' A mild insult, surely? No. MEP was as angered by disrespect paid to a sister as irreverence during a church service. Arthur's story continues, 'The words were no sooner out of my mouth than I saw my mother's eyes flash and with her grey gloved hand she pointed at the door and told me to leave the house then and there.'[40] He obeyed and was only reconciled to mother and sister after a few days.

Most of Arthur's memories of his mother and the family circle were happy ones. 'With all their faults,' Arthur wrote in his retrospect of the first twenty years of his life, 'my family were as a whole the most amusing people I ever met. No one outside made me laugh or realised amusing situations as they did.'[41] They all loved and had a special apti-tude for acting. As Queen Victoria grew older and took up again her love of amateur theatricals, members of the Ponsonby family were sometimes commanded to Balmoral or Osborne to take a part in the latest romp. As their father also had a reputation as a wit, the impres-sion given is that they were sometimes jesters as well as advisers.

The queen named Arthur to serve as a page of honour when he was a young boy. This was a further mark of confidence in his father, about which she was punctilious, even when they were having political disagreements, or perhaps especially because they were having disagreements. He served from 1882 to 1887, from the age of eleven to sixteen. The duties were few. He had to help carry the queen's train on the relatively few occasions during the year when she held court functions in London.

On the occasion of a drawing room I put on my red coat and white breeches and was called for in a royal carriage. At Buckingham Palace joined by my colleague we went to the Queen's bedroom door and were handed the train by the dressers. She rolled along the passages fairly fast with [the lord chamberlain] walking backwards in front ... We first went to a room where the rest of the royal family were assembled and the guttural gurglings of conversation stopped short when we came in and everyone bowed to the little woman in black with the garter and a small diamond crown. Then we went into the throne room[,] the band played God save the Queen and the function began. It was very tiring standing still for an hour and a half. At first she stood all the time but towards the end of my time she sat most of the time or went away before the end and the Princess of Wales finished it for her.[42]

He later said that his boyhood was the right time for enjoying ceremony.[43] 'Uniforms, functions, bands, guards of honour, liveries' were all exciting when he was growing up, but a bore, if not positively distasteful to him as a Labour MP.[44] When he was a page, however

It was fun getting a day off school and court functions were quite amusing at that age. I was never impressed by them nor was I the least proud of being a page. I took it quite naturally because my family with all their faults were never proud of their position and if anything looked down on rank and grandeur. Mama taught us that to boast of such things or even to talk of such things with a view to impressing people was vulgar and vulgarity was a greater sin than any other. I have often been guilty of vulgarity since because I have found unfailingly that I obtain silence and rapt attention when I begin 'When I was page to Queen Victoria ... '[45]

Arthur Ponsonby's charming self-indictment at the end of this passage adds one more interesting shade to the portrait of his mother. To teach one's children to avoid vulgarity, whatever they do, may be essentially a form of heightened awareness of rank. It may be true that MEP did not care whether you were duke of Bedford or a bootblack, and that she admired the work of expert carpenters more than the conversation of countesses. But she did know the difference between the two. Her repeated appreciation of manners befitting a *grande dame* or *grand seigneur*, the cardinal feature of which was a sort of natural artifice that rank did not really matter, suggests that she did enjoy observing social customs. Certainly young men who liked aristocratic manners were attracted to her because she was quite willing to have a conversation in which she made quite clear who behaved well and who did not.

The Empress Frederick and Everard Primrose

Two of MEP's good friends show different features of her relationship to people with titles. The queen's eldest daughter, Victoria, Princess Royal of Great Britain, married Frederick William of Prussia in 1858, and became crown princess of Prussia in 1861. She was for a brief time empress of Germany during her husband's short reign in 1888, for a much longer time dowager empress during the reign of her son, Kaiser Wilhelm II. The crown princess and MEP were similar in age and had got to know each other when Mary had been maid of honour in the 1850s. Arthur Ponsonby describes her as 'a friend' of his mother's, 'full of ideas and originality, but with royal limitations'.[46] The crown princess was 'Vicky' to her mother, but 'Ma'am' to MEP. To the crown princess MEP was 'dearest Mary'. MEP genuinely liked and respected her. She sympathised with her love of English customs and her inability to get on in the Prussian court, with its 'terrible amount of etiquette'.[47] According to MEP the crown princess 'had a keen analytical mind like her father, and divided everything into three heads, turning them about so much that she often came to a wrong conclusion'.[48] She and her husband were Liberals, hence distrusted by the emperor's chancellor, Prince Bismarck, and by their own son, who mistreated his mother after the death of his father and throughout her long widowhood. Espionage surrounded her. This spying made the crown princess a little paranoid and sometimes inclined to use overly-secretive methods herself, 'But all her life,' MEP wrote, 'she remained one of the most undeceitful women I have ever known. I cannot say that she had the same charm as the Queen: in her great seriousness there was too much of the professor about her; all the same she was an exceptionally clever woman and wonderfully loyal to her friends.'[49] MEP could discuss politics with the crown princess much more uninhibitedly than she could with the queen, as they both had firm Liberal instincts. Betty remembered that her mother had also talked politics with the crown prince. He was a tall man; Mary was relatively short. Betty recalled him 'at Osborne. MEP putting in his big, extended hand some little socialistic paper book on St Simonism, co-operation, the "familisterre" etc. and his bending down, with a kind smile, to look at it.'[50] Here then was the wife of the queen's private secretary trying to convert the future German emperor to socialism. It was a bravura performance typical of her.

MEP returned the crown princess's loyalty by assisting her in the great crisis of her life. In 1887 the crown prince developed cancer of the throat. The doctors disagreed in their diagnosis: the German doctors diagnosed a malignancy, but an English doctor, to whom the crown prince and his wife naturally clung, said the growth was benign. In the south of France, where the prince and his wife went at Christmas to try and regain strength, a public controversy between the two medical camps stirred up nationalist sensitivities in Germany. The crown princess was assailed by press and courtiers on the one hand, harassed by her husband's poor health on the other. MEP gave up Christmas with her own family to go out with Maggie to France and be with her friend. From there she was able to write letters to Queen Victoria about her daughter's state of mind and her son-in-law's health. This was a service to both sides of the family as the crown princess could only write guardedly to her mother in the atmosphere of controversy and suspicion that surrounded her. She had reason to believe that her letters were intercepted and opened.

Henry was genuinely distressed to learn in Scotland in the autumn of 1887 that MEP was contemplating a trip to the Riviera at Christmas. He and the children did the best they could without her, though he tried to make light of it. He wrote to say that he and Johnny both protested at the way MEP had described Windsor and East Cowes from her hotel room in the south of France. 'We are both indignant,' he teased her, 'especially Johnny at your having called Windsor a dull cathedral town and Cowes a little fishing village. Johnny observed with vehemence that Windsor was a Royal Borough.'[51]

Betty remembered that when her mother went to France in 1887 her father 'had visited it hard on me and John and Fritz at Osborne and would hardly forgive her when she returned. So that she said to me: "What *is* the matter with your father?" '[52] When he had to accompany the queen to France the following spring there is a note of genuine asperity in his reply to an offhand remark in her letter. She had teased him in turn about going on a pleasure trip. 'I was miserable when you left last November' to stay with the crown princess in San Remo. 'I did not come away this time of my own accord at all.'[53]

The crown princess sometimes abused her friendship with Mary to put forward suggestions to her mother, through Henry, that she did not want to raise directly. In this she was no different from the rest of the queen's children, who trusted Henry to choose the right moment to propose something to their mother that they had not the courage to put to her themselves. In the case of the crown princess, however, the message-carrying via Mary was more serious, as she was a prominent figure in the government of one of Britain's rival powers. Still, MEP kept her sense of humour about this. On the eve of the crown princess becoming empress in 1888 Mary wrote to Henry imitating the crown princess's style of writing to her.

'There dear Mary you will look after the governesses for me, you will try and get Layard [politician and diplomat] made a peer and then dearest there is the English fleet which in the case of a quarrel with Russia *must* go to the Baltic.'
   'Very well, ma'am.' I only thought that I rather dreaded the day when she becomes powerful.[54]

For all this gentle ridicule, MEP was attached to the crown princess and was happy to see her when she made trips, often with her daughters, to England. For her part, both as crown princess and as widowed empress, Victoria relied on and trusted Mary. The relationship is evidence that Mary could be a friend to princes as well as a critic. She could share in this woman's joys and sorrows, as both wife and mother, forgetting except for the occasional 'Ma'am' the rank of the person she addressed.

Very different, though equally characteristic, was her friendship with Everard Primrose. He was the younger brother of the fifth earl of Rosebery, who would succeed Gladstone as prime minister and Liberal leader in March 1894. There have always been rumours about Rosebery's sexuality. Rosebery's brother Everard certainly had the camp style of the confirmed bachelor. He was a friend of Bobby Roden's and shared MEP's anguish when Roden fell ill.[55] In fact Primrose was himself to die quite young at the age of 37 in 1885. Like Roden he never married. In the meantime, he was just the sort of brilliant, flighty young man to whom MEP was frequently attracted.

Primrose was in the Grenadier Guards and went as military attaché to Vienna in the 1870s. Probably the authorities recognised his flair for the dramatic and sent him as well to help represent Britain at major ceremonies in Madrid and St Petersburg. He wrote MEP from Vienna in 1879: 'Here I am surrounded by gaunt Roman-nosed Princesses, but no friends, and I miss all those I used to meet in England very sadly'. He liked describing parties, people and ritual. He wanted to give her his impression of the Viennese social whirl and could not help poking fun.

> The first spectacle that presents itself to the intruder on entering Viennese Society is a bench of long, bony, bleak Majestic ladies – each with a goitre girthed with jewels – which ladies represent the august family of Liechtenstein. These are types of all the rest. They lift their aristocratic muzzles in the air, and like hounds sniff the coming stranger – they nod at him from their Olympus, but of conversation they have not a spark.[56]

Three years later he had to report that the parties at Vienna were all much the same.

> Imagine, for example, a long table spread with oranges, cigarettes, barley sugar and a samovar. On one side are two or three elderly ladies with a decorous general. On the other a few septuagenarians ... Conversation is languid, for the same party met yesterday, the day before that, and the day before that, and will meet again an hour hence at a similar coterie.[57]

He knew she would recognise the boredom of it.

Primrose went to assist Britain's special ambassador to the wedding of King Alphonso XII at Madrid in November 1879. In describing the processions and ceremonies he managed to send up Spanish magnificence, British dowdiness and French hopelessness all at the same time.

> ... [T]here have been coaches and six – and *panaches* and liveries and gay cavaliers and bands and diamonds and gold lace enough to content any public mind and to astonish that of the Britons generally accustomed to the wicker-work landau and dingy kilts of their own Imperial equipages. The French Ambassador's coachman between fat and emotion fainted away on his hammercloth and had to be ministered to by attachés before his Excellency could advance.[58]

This was also the Ponsonby view of ceremonial. The more grandiose it was, the more ridiculous. They might too have questioned whether the plain old wickerwork carriages and fake kilts were adequate to represent the quiet superiority of British constitutional forms to chaotic continental arrangements. Where Primrose was different from them was in the sharper edge to his humour. In his next letter on the Spanish wedding, he reported that Queen Isabella had 'asked with much effusion after the Empress at Windsor'. This was a dig at the queen having become empress of India in 1877, of which Rosebery and his brother disapproved as much as the Ponsonbys had. Queen Isabella had also asked Primrose about Napoleon III's widow, Eugénie, 'at Chislehurst "*qui a toujours eu les mêmes goûts que moi* [who has always had the same tastes as me]", by which her most Christian Majesty merely meant an attachment to country life, but it sounded startling'.[59]

These lampoons of excessive splendour and politeness have a serious side. Primrose and the Ponsonbys agreed in thinking that too much display of rank and grandeur was barbaric, childlike, oriental. Primrose went to stay at his brother's house in Buckinghamshire, Mentmore, which he had acquired through his marriage to Hannah Rothschild. He conceded that this rich family had stuffed their house with genuine treasures 'of perfect taste'. However,

> Amid Venetian furniture, brocades and gilded thrones, tables of tarsia and tortoiseshell, Gobelins hangings and the spoils of Fontainebleau and the Trianon, one sighs for an old armchair, a drugget one need not hesitate to tread on, and a table which will conveniently hold something.[60]

The letter gives the impression that the Rothschilds were guilty of trying too hard to impress. MEP preferred quiet to loud, natural to artificial, absolute confidence in self to worrying about what others might think as the keys to conduct in social life.

Primrose attended the coronation of a new tsar and tsarina in Moscow in June 1883. He found there the same conspicuous consumption he had both admired and lampooned at Mentmore. 'The blaze of jewels is astonishing,' he wrote, sounding a little like Disraeli tempting the queen to show him her emeralds. The 'Grandduchess Constantine could scarcely support the weight of countless precious stones, while Princess Kotzoubey wore a wig of pearls.'[61] He returned to the contrast between Russian royalty and the British variety, finding the one too grand and the other not grand enough. 'For the first time one realises the picture[s] of toy books and playing cards and saw Royalty crowned, robed, sceptred and orbed. The gracious Victoria, alas! is generally seen in a somewhat unattractive bonnet.'[62] Primrose delighted in the coronation, but he also considered it savage and the stuff of children's books. Yet, Queen Victoria's court – dull, Scottish, black – was not exactly a flawless alternative.

As for Henry, he confessed in the same year as the Russian coronation that he was tired of hearing accounts of the Orthodox fêtes.
Although he had enjoyed it when young, he was also now too old for a
long afternoon of 'racing and smart ladies' at Ascot.[63] MEP had a knack,
like many women who seem to age more slowly than their husbands,
for staying young by receiving highly-coloured letters from young men
like Everard Primrose. She still went to Ascot in her 50s and 60s. She
would renew herself in her 60s and 70s by forming friendships with
younger women whose backgrounds were very different from hers, but
whose interests and inclinations she found sympathetic. She furnishes
several hints for growing old gracefully through the reviving possibilities of love and friendship.

Lady Macdonald's 'Character' of Mary Bulteel

In 1858, shortly after she broke off her engagement to William
Harcourt, Mary confided in Lady Macdonald and confessed how miserable she was. Lady Macdonald was one of those mother substitutes,
admired elder women among whom Mary Bulteel found support, stim-
ulation and an example to which she might aspire. Lady Macdonald
sought to comfort her by writing a 'character' of Mary, aged 26.[64] This
was a sort of country house game. It combined ruthless truth telling
with pretty compliments. It is interesting to read Lady Macdonald's
character in the light of how far MEP had come by 1894. She was now
62 and on the eve of both a great personal tragedy and a significant new
chapter in her life. What had changed since she was 26 and what
remained the same? Lady Macdonald's character was prescient; it has a
way of recapturing significant themes in the thirty or so years of MEP's
middle age as well as hinting at some of the highlights of the years to
come.

'Impulsive, energetic. Feverish longing for a wider sphere of action
than has been allotted by circumstances,' Lady Macdonald had written
in 1858. MEP had grown out of those adolescent fevers. She had made
significant contributions in the world of higher education and wider
working opportunities for women. She had nothing to be ashamed of in
the work she had done there.

Lady Macdonald went on to suggest that Mary Bulteel was somewhat
hampered by an overly-active conscience, a feeling that there were deep
passions somewhere in her that had to be repressed. She had 'An overwhelming belief in the possibility of subduing all natural feeling by
repression'. She had a 'longing for sympathy (none [had it] more so)

and for affection, a cold indifference to all and to everything is put on, and may, to a certain extent, have become reality'. She was 'Aware of a depth and force of feeling and of passion, ill suited to some professions, both must be carefully concealed, or vent themselves only in religious fervour'. Lady Macdonald goes on to describe these deep and concealed passions as 'morbid', the same word MEP had used when she described how hopelessly she loved Agnes Courtenay. Although Lady Macdonald attributed this morbidity to the 'wreck of earthly trust and hope' that had followed the failed relationship with Harcourt, what she described might equally refer to future disappointments over Lily Wellesley and Agnes.

The 'religious fervour' had by 1894 long since been replaced by a keen enthusiasm for molecular physics and evolutionary biology. MEP never lost her love of a good choir in a beautiful church. She developed a passionate interest in Marie Curie's research on radium, and a passionate hatred of Friedrich Nietzsche's critique of Christian morality. Lady Macdonald had foreseen all this. Anyone who could recover from the Harcourt heartbreak as determinedly as Mary had must be possessed of some special nerve. Lady Macdonald believed there was 'something sublime in that trust which could bridge over the shattered causeway of every earthly aspiration'. She went on to ask, at the close of her analysis, a question that was as pertinent to MEP's special problems and opportunities in the 1890s as it had been in the 1850s. 'Yet is the professed peace and calmness in this heart? Pride there is … the pride of sensitive mind and imagination, shrinking from the possibility of encountering indifference, where, on its part, genuine warmth might be at hand, the pride of intelligence, conscious of superiority, but disdaining all too much to assert it.' The crisis of her relationship with Henry would shortly arrive, in which his teasing her about her supposed indifference would suddenly take on a terrible poignancy. The question of whether she would continue to shrink from the possibility of indifference in others, to conceal the warmth of her own feelings for others, to disdain to assert her intelligence, would remain sensitive and alive for her in the 1890s and beyond. What Lady Macdonald had not foreseen in her character of Mary Bulteel was her alliance and partnership with Henry. For Henry's story at the summit of his office at court was intimately bound up with hers.

CHAPTER 9

A Serious Position and A Ludicrous One, Henry Ponsonby's Private Secretariat

c. 1878-95

When Sir Thomas Biddulph died in 1878, Henry Ponsonby became the head of the queen's private office. The queen distrusted his political instincts at this point more than at any other time during his tenure. At the moment he became chief, Ponsonby had also pretty recently been receiving hints, rebukes and what he called 'stingers' or 'stinkers' from the queen that his political opinions and political advice were unwelcome to her. A look at the post-Biddulph arrangement of the office will give an idea of the effects of all this on Henry, on his official position and on the monarchy itself.

Joint Private Secretary and Privy Purse

After the queen failed to persuade Henry to move over to take the less political position of privy purse, she consulted the dean of Windsor, Gerald Wellesley, her son Leopold as well as Beaconsfield. From among them emerged the advice that Henry should be joint private secretary and keeper of the privy purse, but have in addition at least one assistant to help him in the work. Henry did not relish this proposal. The financial work of the privy purse interested him less than the political work of the private secretary. Further, the new arrangement meant that he was going to have to do two jobs rather than one, as well as train someone new to help him. Lord Bridport, an old friend of Henry's from the household, told him, 'Now they'll try and put more work on you. Don't do it. You will break down and then there will be worse trouble than now.' Henry could not easily refuse the queen's suggestion, however, as it was a mark of favour at a time when they were barely on speaking terms. His only requirement was that whoever was to assist him should be permitted 'to work fully', that is to see the queen, to be allowed to know all the confidential business, both political and personal to the royal family, that passed across his desk.[1]

The queen agreed. She also raised his salary from £1,500 to £1,700 a year. Another perquisite of the privy purse position was that an apartment at St James's Palace went with it, so that he and Mary now acquired a small pied à terre in the capital. From their perspective, this was the best part of the new job, though in fact Henry was able to enjoy it much less than Mary could. He remained tied to the queen, who came to London rarely. They also inherited the Biddulphs' housekeeper at St James's, which Henry thought would take up a good bit of his extra salary.[2] Henry also learned that he was not to have a free hand in choosing the assistants to help him. Lady Ely came to his room acting as the queen's agent to have a discussion about who might 'do' as Ponsonby's assistant. He was told that the person had to come from among those already serving in the household. The first man Henry proposed, one of the equerries, Lady Ely rejected. 'Oh no no. The Queen won't hear of him ... [H]e is so fussy, so unfit for it in every way. She doesn't like him!' Henry mentioned another of the equerries as a possibility. Lady Ely replied 'No you mustn't suggest him. She [the queen] says he is so rough, he is so rude and would never do.' Henry tried suggesting a third equerry for the job to Sir William Jenner, who said the queen 'wouldn't hear' of him, because he was 'so tutorial and always pushing forward himself'.[3] Although the queen had said Henry was to have a free choice of his assistants, his choice was in fact pretty limited.

Eventually the choice fell on two young men with little or no previous experience of the household. Henry had nothing to do with suggesting either one. Arthur Pickard was an officer in the Royal Artillery who had served as equerry to Prince Arthur, duke of Connaught. Fleetwood Edwards was an officer in the Royal Engineers, who had been aide-de-camp to one of the generals attending Beaconsfield at the Berlin Congress of 1878. Connaught was the queen's favourite son and Beaconsfield's triumph at Berlin, where he appeared to settle the Eastern Question in Britain's favour, had earned the queen's congratulations and a bouquet personally delivered by Henry. These were probably the avenues by which Pickard and Edwards came to the queen's attention. All feared that Pickard's health was not good, and in fact he died before he had completed two years in the job. To replace him the queen appointed another officer in the Royal Artillery, Arthur Bigge. He had come to her notice when he arrived in Scotland to give the Empress Eugénie an account of her son's death in the Zulu War of 1878-9. The queen and Eugénie were friends, and the queen was deeply interested in the accounts of deaths of people she knew. Added to this, she thought Bigge handsome. On 9 August 1880 she appointed him assistant private secretary and assistant keeper of the privy purse, the same title she gave to Edwards. In practice, however, Bigge assisted with the political or private secretary's work and Edwards assisted with the financial or privy purse work.

None of these three new men came from the Whig aristocratic background that Anson, Phipps, Grey and Ponsonby had. None of them had long service at court or came up via the mastership of the household, as Biddulph had. Thus, none of them had social stature or long experience or seniority. Probably the queen thought they would be easier to control that way. Ponsonby assumed that he was on the way out, that Edwards and Bigge were probably Tories and meant ultimately to replace him. He was surprised to find that he got on well with both of them. Edwards was gradually allowed to do more and more of the privy purse work with a minimum of supervision from Ponsonby.[4] He was never a friend. Henry's youngest son Arthur's harsh verdict on Edwards was that 'we never cared about' him, but he certainly relieved Henry of much of the work he found uncongenial. Bigge on the other hand did become a friend whose company Henry enjoyed. Arthur said of him that he 'was kind and good natured but not very intellectual – no one in the court was'.[5] The real mark of Henry's confidence in him was that they could share a joke. A sample of the sort of thing they both found funny occurs in a letter of 1889. When Henry was away from Balmoral in the autumn, Bigge wrote him to give an account of the amateur theatricals going on in his absence. Bigge and Princess Louise were acting together in an English translation of a French play called *L'Homme Blasé*. The queen had watched them together in rehearsal and later written Bigge a dry note telling him that whether the script called for it or no, he was *not* to call her daughter 'a degraded woman'.[6]

It took a while though before these assistants could help Henry as fully as he needed. There were still subjects, especially having to do with her family, which the queen expected Ponsonby to keep secret from Bigge and Edwards. She 'blew up' Ponsonby twice in the later 1880s for allowing his assistants to open letters that should have been seen by him alone.[7] This was after Bigge had been working for her for more than five years, Edwards more than seven. These letters suggest that Ponsonby was still shouldering the confidential work himself.

Prince Albert had codified the routine of the privy purse office in the 1850s.[8] There is no evidence that Ponsonby initiated any great changes or reforms of the office. At the queen's accession in 1837 Parliament had voted the annual sum of £385,000 as her civil list to support the household. Of this sum she received £60,000 a year as her privy purse. The Treasury paid it quarterly into her account at Coutt's Bank. Most of the civil list was spent on salaries and pensions of officials and servants under one of the three great officers of the court, the lord chamberlain, the lord steward or the master of the horse. A significant sum was set aside in the queen's civil list for charities and state pensions. These were actually distributed by the prime minister or his wife. The privy purse, however, was the queen's, to do with entirely as she pleased. It paid the salaries of her personal attendants, among whom were the Highlanders, including John Brown, and later the Indians, among whom her favourite was Abdul Karim. It paid Ponsonby, Bigge and Edwards, as well as the clerks at Buckingham Palace. The largest outgoings from the privy purse were for the upkeep of Balmoral and Osborne, both large and expensive houses to run. The privy purse also paid allowances annually to the queen's younger children.

The privy purse also received payments from the duchy of Lancaster, one of the two hereditary estates of the Crown retained by the sovereign at the beginning of the reign. The other was the duchy of Cornwall, income from which went to the Prince of Wales. The duchy of Lancaster was made up partly of agricultural property, partly of valuable urban property, especially in London and Harrogate. Its value increased over the course of the century and payments from the duchy to the privy purse rose from £12,000 in 1840 to £50,000 in 1890.[9]

Lastly the privy purse benefited from savings transferred to it from other departments of the civil list. These savings were generated by reforms of the household carried out by Prince Albert. The savings transferred were highest in the period just after the prince initiated the reforms. The average amount transferred in the 1840s was just over £27,000 annually. Many people in the 1860s thought that these savings had increased by the queen's retirement, which fuelled republican sentiment. In fact the savings tended to diminish after the prince's death, perhaps because the household was not as tight a ship after his death as it had been before. If anything, the privy purse charges were higher after the prince's death, as the queen undertook to pay for the members of his household and his servants. The average amount transferred annually in the 1860s was about £17,000; between 1878 and 1882, it was just over £15,000. In the late 1880s, the savings came to an end altogether. From about the year of the Golden Jubilee in 1887 the expenses of the three great officers' departments exceeded the amount set aside for them in the civil list act of 1838. In 1887 the queen agreed to pay a huge sum, nearly £50,000, for the entertainment and housing

of guests who came to Britain for the jubilee. From then on the
expenses of the great officers' departments were pretty much always in
the red. Rather than apply to Parliament to reduce the excess, it was
decided that in view of the savings that had been transferred to the
privy purse since the 1850s, the queen should pay off the departments'
debts from her personal money.[10]

Henry Ponsonby was not very interested in any of this. Then as now
there were periodic excitements in the press about the queen having
amassed a huge fortune from her savings in the civil list. At least once,
Ponsonby denied this publicly, though his general policy was to take no
notice. Indeed, he may have underrated the way in which rumours spread
by the newspapers, and met simply by silence from him, could later tie the
hands of household officials. He even had to deny to his own wife that
the queen was super-rich. She had acquired a 'moderate' fortune and that
was all. It was a mark of his discretion that he would not say, even to
Mary, what the precise value of that fortune was. He did tell her, almost
as if she were a radical reporter who needed to be reminded of the useful
purposes to which the queen's fortune was put, that he annually paid
more than £10,000 a year to charities out of the privy purse.[11] At about
10 per cent of her annual income, that was not an insignificant sum.

Where he could Ponsonby left the management of the queen's property to others. When the Prince of Wales's comptroller, Dighton
Probyn, took Ponsonby around Sandringham, Probyn seemed to know
all about the tenants, their wives and their farms. 'Quite different from
me' was Henry's self-deprecating remark.[12] His own management of
the queen's property was more offhand. He left Balmoral, from which
there could occasionally be profit from the sale of timber or rearing of
livestock, to the factor to manage. 'I only superintend the financial
parts', he told Mary, 'fortunately having nothing to do with beasts and
crops' although he conceded that he sometimes regretted knowing so
little.[13] Some idea of the typical expenses Henry paid from the privy
purse may be had from an 1887 document summarising the annual
outgoings of the privy purse. The queen gave £2,000 to the duchess of
Albany, the widow of her son, Prince Leopold. She spent £1,700 on
telegrams and £1,037 on the band. The upkeep of Balmoral cost
£16,739 and that of Osborne £9,087. The cost of her annual donations
to charities and similar institutions was £9,217.[14] In the last years of her
reign other typical annual expenses met from the privy purse included
£11,000 in pensions to retired servants, £5,120 for her private secretaries, £1,500 for her personal physician as well as £1,200 for the
librarian and purchase of books at Windsor.[15]

The political business of his office interested Ponsonby a good deal more. Over the course of his private secretariat he evolved a series of principles, meant to preserve some influence for the sovereign as well as to protect the monarchy's public reputation. The first of these was that the queen should do as little as possible on her own. She must be made to rely on the advice of ministers. When the Eastern Question arose in 1877 and Beaconsfield's policy of protecting Turkey – even to the extent of threatening war – was distasteful to Ponsonby, he told MEP that he must try to get the queen to stick to Beaconsfield's advice, not to second-guess him. Nor should she try to thwart policy on which the cabinet was decided. Although he disliked Beaconsfield's attitude to Turkey, he saw that his main interest was to get the queen to listen to whoever was in office. His instinct was that the Liberal objections to Beaconsfield were correct. He knew, however, that it was his job as private secretary not to undermine the queen's confidence in those who held the seals of office. After he had been given hints that he was not to raise any points critical of Beaconsfield with the queen, he confided to Mary that

> ... it is hard that The Queen should not know there is another side to the question and that those who do not agree with Beaconsfield do so because they think he is leading the country astray, and because they wish for another path to lead to the honour and glory of the country, and not because of disappointed ambition ... All I would have wished is that she should know this and talk it over. But she must take his advice and act with him as long as he is Prime Minister.[16]

Her occasional tendency to remember that she was queen and that she might do as she liked – an idea that some members of her family encouraged – Ponsonby wished to discourage.

Ponsonby did want to keep up the queen's influence over appointments in the Church and in the armed forces. In order to do this he tried to limit direct defeats. Ministers were less likely to accede to a direct suggestion from the queen when a vacancy occurred. They were more likely to allow her to veto a name when several were submitted to her for a proposed place. For example, when there was a question in 1885 of a bishopric that the queen wanted to fill, Ponsonby reminded her

> Dean Wellesley always advised that Your Majesty should not propose names for vacant sees as this would weaken Your Majesty's power of

vetoing those suggested by the Prime Minister; and he believes Dean Davidson [Wellesley's successor] is of the same opinion. It might therefore be as well to await Lord Salisbury's proposals before entering into the subject.[17]

It was also Ponsonby's cardinal principle to get important advice from ministers in writing. That way there was less chance of misunderstanding as well as a precedent that might serve as a guide to future action. It was particularly important to get ministers' advice in the change of a government. In 1885 Gladstone left office and Salisbury came in for a few months before the appearance in the next session of the first Irish home rule bill. Before Salisbury would agree to take office, the two men bickered about the terms under which Salisbury would agree to serve. They sent messages to each other via the queen.[18] Ponsonby told MEP after a busy day of this 'I always advise The Queen, make them write down what they say. So we can go by something.'[19]

Sometimes he would receive some advice, or expression of policy in writing that he knew would be deeply unwelcome to the queen. This was one of the awkward bits of his job. He often had to convey to Gladstone the queen's enthusiastic dissent from his policy without actually insulting Gladstone or seeming to withdraw her confidence from him. In 1884 when the queen and Gladstone were in the middle of a hot disagreement on a whole range of personal and policy issues, Ponsonby simply withdrew from the contest. He told Mary that after conveying one of the queen's most marked rebukes to the prime minister, he had told Gladstone that he might reply direct to the queen rather than, as was the convention, to Ponsonby as her private secretary. He had no desire to put his 'finger in between two iron clads colliding'.[20]

Another method of retaining influence for the monarchy, which had been much used in the Prince Consort's day, was to ask for more information. Few ministers disputed the queen's right of access to confidential information from their departments, though they might dispute the conclusions she drew from it. Sometimes, when the Tories were in office and the queen was pleased with their policy, she would reject Ponsonby's suggestion that she ask for more information. 'I cannot suggest her asking for information,' he told Mary, 'as I used to do, for I am snubbed and told Lord Beaconsfield had written to her upon it.'[21] Gladstone's letters were routinely channelled through him so he knew what was going on. Beaconsfield often wrote to the queen direct; Henry only saw the letters if she chose.

Above all Ponsonby tried to keep the queen's name out of any dispute likely to attract notice. This was his principle in 1873 when Disraeli and Gladstone were manoeuvring around each other after Gladstone's defeat over the Irish university bill. Ponsonby thought Disraeli in particular was given to public hints that the queen had refused him a dissolution, which she had not, as an excuse for not taking office. He had to hold the line against this and refuse to allow the queen's name to be brought into the parliamentary rivalry between the two politicians.[22] It was the same case when the queen bought some property at Claremont and a dispute seemed about to blow up about long-term tenants' right of way over her land. Henry had to concede the queen's rights over her property, rather than go to law or allow local residents to accuse her publicly of abridging their rights.[23]

His most important principle, if never explicitly stated, was to know the mind of the sovereign. Never to attempt to browbeat, or to press unwelcome advice, where there was no chance of success. He learned that he could give disagreeable advice only once, and that afterwards the queen would stay silent on the topic. All chances of discussion on that topic would be at an end. In 1878, for example, the queen wanted to go to war over an Afghan insult, while Henry urged peace. 'People constantly say "Why don't you advise The Queen?" One can do so once, but she takes care you shan't press unwelcome advice upon her by preserving strict silence on the subject.'[24]

He did develop clever dodges to get around this. He would write the draft of a letter to a minister both with what the queen wanted to see and with his own views on what ought to be said lightly crossed out. Then he would submit the draft to her for approval. Sometimes she would decide the crossed-out language was better than what she had originally wanted. Or he would find a seemingly offhand way of returning in conversation to a first refusal from the queen. For example, when the queen asked who might represent her at the funeral of the empress of Russia in 1880,

I said, the Duke of Edinburgh [her son, Prince Alfred]. The Queen said, 'No, of course he couldn't.' I said, 'Of course he couldn't.' But as I did not know why, I got back to him in the course of the conversation and said it was a pity he couldn't. So she telegraphed to ask him if he could and he said he would.[25]

Thus Ponsonby often got his way with the queen through a combination of system and indirection.

His attitude to the role of the sovereign in the constitution remained that of a Whig of a hundred years earlier. He spent all his time serving the queen, yet he enjoyed deprecating the importance of the monarchy. Possibly this was a joke at his own expense. His days were filled with passing the queen's comments on policy to ministers and interpreting their replies to her. Yet, aside from her useful interventions when there was a serious clash between the parties, or if there was a change of government, he thought it was better if her influence were limited. Especially after 1874 he spent more time trying to hold her back than encouraging her to get more involved in cabinet affairs. He was delighted to come across a letter from one of his Bathurst uncles who, though a Tory, had written in the reign of George IV that English kings were inconsequential. Henry's uncle was concerned that the death of George IV's daughter, Princess Charlotte in 1817, might bring the crown to the duke of Kent, the father of the as yet unborn Queen Victoria. ' "Not that it matters much to us Englishmen what sort of men our Kings are, but I should be sorry if the Crown went to that odious and pompous Duke of Kent." His handwriting and style,' Henry told Mary, 'are so like mine that I have had to look at the signature sometimes to see whether it was one of my letters or not.'[26]

Henry had a conversation on a similar topic at Osborne with Lord Bridport. Bridport was a Conservative, but he bridled when Ponsonby proposed this. Should Parliament refuse to grant the Prince of Wales an adequate financial settlement on his becoming king, he could retain the Crown Estate. This was the property usually relinquished to the Exchequer at the beginning of a reign in exchange for the civil list. Bridport retorted, ' "You forget that if Parliament did not choose, the prince could not ascend the throne at all".' Britain's monarchy owed its existence to parliamentary consent. 'True,' wrote Henry with some amusement 'but there are things we do not speak of here.'[27] He doubted that the queen would find this funny.

Much of Ponsonby's time was spent on the Army. Throughout the discussion of Cardwell's army reform measures of the 1870s, Ponsonby tried to get both the queen and her cousin, the duke of Cambridge, to rely on Cardwell's advice. He advised dissenting only where they could provide constructive criticism, rather than obstructing wherever possible, which is what both were inclined to do. One historian has called the successful negotiation of the Cardwell reforms around court obstacles Ponsonby's 'greatest achievement'.[28] He adopted a similar attitude in subsequent discussions of the Army. Significant changes in the Army had to originate with responsible ministers.[29] Even under

Conservative governments he frequently encountered resistance, if not from Cambridge, then from one or more of the queen's sons. Who rules the army, they would write to him, is it the queen or the minister for war? Ponsonby told his wife wearily that this question had been 'settled by the late Charles I', who was beheaded after he raised an Army against parliament and lost.[30] He believed it was foolish to pretend that anybody other than the minister who was answerable to Parliament ruled the Army.

Mary was an acute judge of character. Her assessment of members of the queen's family was that they were lacking in real determination or willpower. They sometimes had good ideas, but failed to follow them through. Henry agreed, but he was less inclined to deplore what she thought a weakness in royal character. 'If they had real determination and strong convictions they would be a danger to the State. As it is they are what they should be.'[31] If they really went into political or philosophical questions as deeply as Mary did, they might acquire knowledge and confidence. This might move them to disrupt the constitutional practices where their real role was advisory and ornamental.

Still, Ponsonby did see that on more than one occasion the queen had certainly been more than this in her interventions with ministers. There was a protracted negotiation between the queen and the two political parties when the Liberals brought in their franchise extension bill, essentially a third reform bill, in 1884. The Conservatives and the House of Lords threatened to make a stand against the bill if a redistribution bill were not passed at the same time. The redistribution was to ensure that the Tories would not be wiped out in a wave of new working class and presumably Liberal voters coming for the first time to the polls. Ponsonby's role in this crisis has been described by Elizabeth Longford as the 'zenith' of his effectiveness in the office of private secretary.[32] He chose to give all credit to the queen. He told Mary that the collision between Lords and Commons would never have been averted if she had not kept up her 'incessant hammering at both sides to be moderate and insisting on their meeting' to effect a compromise.[33] He conceded that the queen could occasionally intervene with effectiveness in the political process, especially in an apparent deadlock between the parties.

Queen Victoria rebelled at the notion that her job stopped at the 'criticism of detail'. She thought that this reduced version of his proper role was what Bismarck had taught the German emperor. She was sure Gladstone was trying to do the same to her in the early 1880s, and was not above threatening abdication to counteract his attempts to reduce her influence.[34] Indeed, during his time in office Ponsonby watched her choose at least one prime minister (Rosebery) without taking or even asking for the outgoing premier's (Gladstone's) advice. He was sometimes appalled at the attention that could be got from the press and politicians for particular causes that interested her, such as safety on the railways, or cruelty to animals in medical research. There was some ambiguity in Ponsonby's position. On the one hand, he believed that Parliament was supreme and that the sovereign ought not to be regarded as too serious a player in the political game. On the other hand, his experience as well as the time he spent in his office poring over the newspapers and despatches to keep abreast of what was going on suggest the opposite. The queen was indeed a force, sometimes for good and sometimes for ill, to be reckoned with.

The Queen's Ultra Partisanship

Sir Herbert Taylor, Baron Stockmar and Prince Albert had all impressed on the queen the importance of the sovereign's taking a decidedly impartial attitude toward competing political parties. They believed the monarchy could only possess prestige if the sovereign took no side in party political battles, but instead acquired a reputation for non-partisanship so as to be able to mediate any dispute between the parties that became intractable. This was a point that the queen had impressed more than once on Ponsonby when he became private secretary. She knew he was a Liberal, but hoped he would repress his opinions in the greater interest of preserving her reputation for non-partisanship. From Disraeli onward, however, Victoria was in fact a Tory queen. She did whatever she could to help the Conservatives and undermine the Liberals. This distressed Ponsonby, who did what he could to soften or hide the queen's abandonment of neutrality. Everyone paid lip service to her impartiality, but no in-the-know politician on either side was deceived about the reality.

At some points during Beaconsfield's government, the queen and the prime minister were so entirely in each other's confidence that they kept the private secretary and the keeper of the privy purse in the dark. When Biddulph was alive, he and Henry were both surprised to learn of a major cabinet development, the resignation of Lord Derby in protest at Beaconsfield's policy, from the French governess, Miss Norèle. Biddulph was hurt and angry, but Henry consoled him by saying that 'one Tory more or less was of such minor consequence that it was a fitting matter for the French Governess'.[35] Mary also remarked in some of her dealings with her friend, the crown princess of Prussia, how like the family it was to find some out of the way and low-ranking official to do their secret business for them. Still, in 1879 Henry reached the end of his tether when not only did the queen keep him in the dark, but also denied him leave to go and see his family. She refused to lend him the house near Balmoral where the Biddulphs had always stayed, which would have at least brought his family nearer while he was on duty. She also refused to promise a long leave in the autumn so that he could go and see them then. In addition, she employed Lady Ely and a prospective maid of honour, Ethel Cadogan, to do much of the work Henry had once handled as private secretary.[36]

When the Liberals won a clear majority at the election in 1880, Ponsonby told the queen repeatedly that she had no choice but to ask Gladstone to form a government. Instead, she insisted on days of consultation with other Liberals before she was convinced that she had to employ – for that was how Beaconsfield had encouraged her to see it – the man she hated. Ponsonby saw the humour in this and cut from the newspaper a little sketch of Hartington and Granville leaving Windsor looking like schoolboys after having faced her fury and told her Gladstone must be the man. He was less amused when he learned through Lady Ely that the queen intended to carry on the unconstitutional practice of corresponding with the opposition after they had left office. Could, Jane Ely had asked, Lord Rowton write to the queen via Henry? '[M]ost certainly not' was Henry's reply.[37] He would not condone a practice that, if discovered, would show the people that the queen had no confidence in a ministry that had just been returned by a considerable majority at a recent election. Such a revelation would be disastrous for the monarchy. Whether Jane Ely actually passed these reasons along to the queen with Ponsonby's refusal to be in touch with Rowton is doubtful.

One of the marks of the queen's Toryism was her emphasis on maintaining the 'honour', 'dignity' and 'prestige' of Britain's international reputation. In this she was reflecting a larger conservatism or an imperial drift in public opinion. She came to see European or imperial questions in a hazy, romantic light, where Britain alone heroically struggled to sustain principles of justice and right. The Liberals were more worried about how much it all cost and were generally unsmitten, as yet, by the imperial idea. The queen required Ponsonby to demand of the Liberals all sorts of information which as far as he knew she had never required of the Tories.[38] She asked Ponsonby to write a critique of their Irish policy. This he had to supply by reading a speech of Lord

Salisbury's and putting his arguments into a form that she could send as a remonstrance to Gladstone.[39]

Her most famous intervention against the government could well have been made public if the men operating the telegraph had not kept it a secret. She wrote Gladstone, not in code, as was the custom, but in plain English, a sharply-worded rebuke after the death of General Gordon at Khartoum. Gordon had been sent out to put down a rebellion against English rule on the border between Egypt and the Sudan. He died partly because the government had dithered a long time before deciding to send out reinforcements to support him. This telegram not only nearly drove Gladstone to resign, but was also the subject of a fierce quarrel between Henry and Mary. Henry regarded Gordon as a sort of religious lunatic. He believed that it had been a mistake to send Gordon out in the first place to defend an unimportant garrison at such a great distance, and he could well understand the slowness of the War Office in deciding to reply to his fevered requests for more support. Mary, on the other hand, agreed with the queen for once. Gordon's death was a national humiliation. It was all about injured pride and the needless sacrifice of a hero. Henry and Mary's youngest son Arthur remembered his parents' argument becoming warm at the dinner table and seeing the seriousness of it, he only wished for them to stop.[40] So the fact that 'his friends' were in office, as the queen called the Liberal ministers in the 1880s, did not make Ponsonby's life at home or at the office any easier.

Gladstone left office in 1885 and Salisbury replaced him for a brief interval. The queen well knew that Gladstone's proposed bill giving Ireland a measure of independence in writing its own legislation might divide the Liberals and perhaps keep them out of office for a good long time. She bided her time and awaited an opportunity to help this dream of a long Tory administration come true. When she asked Ponsonby in the autumn of 1885 who Gladstone might appoint as foreign secretary in the next government, which would bring forward the Irish home rule measure, Ponsonby said he thought it might be the former colonial secretary, Lord Kimberley. At their interviews she was usually seated, while Ponsonby stood. At Kimberley's name she jumped up from her seat and cried 'Oh for God's sake save me from that!'[41] Ponsonby could barely keep a straight face.

Her political interventions in the following year, 1886, when Gladstone's home rule bill was actually under discussion, were quite serious. She intended to bolster the anti-home-rule Tories or 'Unionists' as they came to be known. She tried to weaken the Liberals by encouraging waverers or dissidents on the home rule policy, like George Goschen and Joseph Chamberlain, to join in an alliance with the Tories. Ponsonby, on the other hand, wanted some agreement between the chiefs of the two parties to reconcile their differences. The queen was in touch with Goschen in January 1886[42] as well as with Chamberlain and Goschen a few months later.[43] To a certain extent this was natural, as the sovereign was always at her most powerful when political parties were weak or fluctuating, rather than strong and united. In her view, she was merely trying to get together a strong party composed of disparate elements who would at least be united in keeping the empire together. The queen and other imperialists regarded Irish home rule as an attempt to dismember the empire at its very heart. In fact, what Gladstone proposed for Ireland in the later 1880s was a much weaker version of the devolution Labour granted Scotland in the late 1990s. But it caused a great deal more fuss, and with the queen's connivance, it meant that the Liberals did not come back into power for six years.

Seen from Ponsonby's perspective, the queen's writing to Gladstone's most prominent critics on his own side, such as Goschen and Chamberlain, at a time when he held the seals of office as her first minister, was at best unwise. At worst it might lead a prominent politician like Gladstone, himself no stranger to self-interested manoeuvre, to remove his gloves and denounce her partisan interference. Ponsonby believed that Gladstone was the only person who could keep republican radicals in order; to work behind his back in this way was to lead him into the hands of the extremists on his own side, hence a dangerous strategy.

Ponsonby did what he could to compensate for the queen's partisanship. Just as her Toryism was well known among politicians, his preference for the Liberals was also a commonplace. The difference was that he tried to be scrupulously fair to the Tories, a fact Beaconsfield acknowledged on his retirement from office in 1880. On submitting Ponsonby's name for a Privy Councillorship in the honours list, Beaconsfield wrote: 'We have passed five years in the conduct of great affairs without a cloud between us.'[44] Gladstone was alternately angered and injured by the queen's dislike of his party and him personally.[45] Ponsonby tried to soften Gladstone's hard feelings by inviting him and his wife to have dinner at the Norman Tower. Admittedly this was on an occasion when the queen contemplated an extra incivility to him. She wanted to invite him to the castle for a Saturday to Monday stay, as was the form, but refused to entertain him on a Sunday night. Her excuse was that she had a busy week ahead of her. Ponsonby rushed to say he and his wife would take the Gladstones for dinner on the Sunday night, rather than give the queen an excuse not to invite him at all.[46] On another occasion Mary went to stay with the Gladstones at Hawarden in North Wales. While she agreed with the need to show Gladstone some of the courtesy that was lacking in his relations with the queen, there was something in his earnestness that annoyed her – it may have reminded her of a like quality of her own. Gladstone and MEP both had had serious, scholarly impulses that had led them to excesses of religious enthusiasm in their youth. Nevertheless, she went to Hawarden and found it all a bit sad. In the library Gladstone had a bad portrait of the queen on the wall in the middle of the room and Mrs Gladstone had a bust of the queen on her worktable.[47]

Henry was genuinely angry to find on his return to Osborne after a short absence in April 1886 that all the ladies were wearing primroses. The Primrose League had been started after Beaconsfield's death to remember him by taking as its symbol his favourite flower. It was meant by the organisers to whip up popular Conservatism, especially among middle-class women in the constituencies. The queen was not an acknowledged supporter but she hinted to all her ladies that she would like it if they wore primroses. Ponsonby found that even Lady Ampthill, from an old Whig house, was wearing them. It was close enough to the election that wearing primroses was the equivalent of wearing a Tory blue ribbon. Henry told Mary that Osborne 'was crammed with them' and he persuaded Lady Ampthill to take hers off.[48]

Henry took his eldest daughter, Betty, who was of a marriageable age, on a tour that took them to some of the great Liberal houses in 1886. This annoyed the queen who warned him that his neutrality would be compromised if he visited Rosebery at Dalmeny and the Tennants at Glen, where Margot Tennant, soon to be Margot Asquith, was the reigning beauty.[49] However her own neutrality had been so repeatedly compromised in recent years that Ponsonby's going to Dalmeny and Glen had the effect of restoring balance in the known political preferences of the court.

Lord Salisbury caused Ponsonby fewer troubles in that his respect for the queen was not tinged with Disraelian excess. Ponsonby, however, was surprised to find that Salisbury's advice on the publication of some controversial letters tended to the same 'high prerogative' views of the queen's role that Disraeli had also professed to possess. General Gordon's sister wanted the queen's permission to publish letters that reprised the queen's denunciation of Gladstone and his responsibility for Gordon's death. The queen's reply was that certainly Miss Gordon could publish the letters. Ponsonby, however, cautiously advised consulting Salisbury. To his surprise, Salisbury advised publication of all the letters except a passage in one where the queen averred her powerlessness to do anything to help Gordon.[50] Even Salisbury wanted an image of the queen's strong influence over policy to be kept up, and approved a publication that showed her to be particularly annoyed with the century's most popular Liberal leader.

The controversy over Irish home rule that began in the late 1880s was the turning point in Ponsonby's political disagreements with the queen. From that point on, though Ponsonby was never a Tory or a Unionist, their political positions tended to converge. Mary was enraged by Gladstone's different home rule plans. Her language, like the queen's, was of the 'disgrace' and 'dismemberment' of the empire that home rule would entail.[51] Henry had to caution Mary when she told him that she planned to take a royal carriage, a perquisite of his position as private secretary, to a public anti-home-rule meeting when Gladstone was in office in April 1886. Mary had been encouraged to do this by the queen, who wanted a firsthand report of the anti-home-rule speeches from Mary.[52] Henry merely wrote to MEP advising that it would be unwise to leave a royal carriage in too prominent a place outside a hall where there was to be a meeting against the government.[53] Even Henry, though, was unable to see how Gladstone's various home rule proposals did not amount really to a dissolution of the 1800 act of union between Britain and Ireland.

Slowly he too began to use the term 'Imperial Parliament' to distinguish Westminster from a devolved parliament in Dublin. As he got older Henry joined many of the aristocratic Liberals who were sceptical about Gladstone's plans for Ireland. In their old age he and the queen were less often at odds on political topics. For significant portions of his time with her, however, his services were not wanted because the queen disliked his politics. Nor is it less clear that royal neutrality was abandoned in the decades after Disraeli became the queen's friend. The consequences of this for the monarchy were that ruses, deceptions and rebuke-softening measures had to be employed when Ponsonby as the queen's private secretary would have preferred a more honest and straightforward approach.

'Bothers'

One of the regular features of Ponsonby's work for the queen was what he called a 'bother'. These started as seemingly unimportant incidents, but rapidly escalated to involve time and energy disproportionate to their significance. Bothers often resulted from the queen's habit of doing all her business by mail or via messages that were sometimes misinterpreted by the messengers. Her refusal to confront members of her family or entourage who caused trouble also led to Henry's having to sort out the problem. Often, too, bothers involved questions of rank, as many people at court were prickly about having their proper standing recognised. To look at several of them over the course of Henry's time at court is to gain some idea of the triviality of the issues that could cause considerable heartburn. A sense of the absurd was the only remedy that gave relief.

Henry and Mary's second son, Fritz, shared his father's sense of the ridiculous. Mary's comment on Fritz also provides an interesting light on his father's character. She observed that Fritz had a 'certain indifference to success which he inherits from his father'.[54] After his parents had both died, Fritz made one of the first attempts at arranging and publishing his father's papers. Two of the most preposterous bothers, 'two storms in Royal tea-cups', occur as the first two chapters of his *Sidelights on Queen Victoria*, published in 1930.[55] He entitled them 'The Pony Row, Balmoral, 1869', and 'The Fatal Gun, 1872'. His having placed them first, long before more serious chapters on, for example, his father's involvement in negotiation of the third reform bill in 1884-5, suggests that Fritz Ponsonby also shared his father's sense that it was in the monarchy's nature to combine low comedy and high politics.

The pony dispute arose because the queen did not want her Highland ponies abused by those who did not ride them properly. Her ban fell on three men who held marginal positions in the household: the German librarian, Herman Sahl, a clergyman who acted as tutor to Prince Leopold, Canon Duckworth, and the sculptor Edgar Boehm. She instructed Ponsonby as equerry to prevent their riding very often, but also not to hurt their feelings by letting them know that the ban came from her. He did as he was told, but all three took offence and correspondence about pony riding occupied weeks in the autumn of 1869. The problem was that the three were all gentlemen who felt that their rank was being questioned because they were not also army officers. The queen wished to pay no disrespect; it was only that she did not want the animals hurt by inexperienced riders.

'The Fatal Gun' was also a question of rank. The royal yacht, present at some navy manoeuvres with the Prince of Wales on board, fired an evening gun. This surprised the commanding officer on board a neighbouring vessel. Such guns were customarily fired from the vessel with the highest-ranking official on board in order to synchronise clocks and let everyone know where the commanding officer was. The Prince of Wales, as representative of the queen, was the highest-ranking officer, but he was not in command of the manoeuvres. A furious dispute ensued that ended up in cabinet discussions. No one questioned that the sovereign was the titular head of all the armed forces or that the Prince of Wales representing his mother ranked high. The issue was where the title ended and effective control began. The Ponsonbys were always on the side of sacrificing dignity to improve efficiency. Henry's job, however, was often to mediate disputes between dignity and efficiency. His private thought was that such disputes were a waste of time and only worthwhile, as Fritz understood, to amuse a circle of trusted intimates afterwards. Henry, however, could and would never have published such anecdotes.

The celebration of the fiftieth anniversary of the queen's accession to the throne in 1887 caused dozens of bothers. The Golden Jubilee has often been seen as a turning point in the history of the reign. The ensuing popular acclaim put the period of the queen's widowed withdrawal finally to an end. Ponsonby saw all the added ceremonials, the reception of official addresses, gifts and foreign visitors, as a lot of unnecessary fuss. Everyone wanted to be involved and though the queen was more yielding than usual in 1887, she drew the line at having to go out to dinner. He had to think of a way of softening her rejection of an invitation from the Corporation of the City of London to come to the Mansion House. He suggested members of the Corporation coming to the palace instead and, as he could assure her that it would take no extra time or trouble, he also said that they should come in full state, wearing robes, chains and emblems of office. He knew it would please them. He wrote about this to his cousin, Spencer Ponsonby-Fane, the comptroller of the Lord Chamberlain's Office, hence a kind of permanent secretary there. The two cousins always enjoyed chuckling over those who cared too much for coming to court, especially as they were both always trying to get away. The queen, Henry told Spencer, 'agreed to do everything in their honour on condition she herself was not called upon to do more. This entitles me,' Henry continued with tongue in cheek, 'to say that the London Corporation may be received in full ancient state with Gentlemen at Arms etc.'[56]

Both men were critical of what they saw as an increasing demand for decorations, honours and orders. In January 1888 Henry was indignant about the cost of orders conferred by ministers on foreign princes falling on the queen's civil list. 'I confess I think excess of decorations absurd, but as you say those ordered by ministers must be paid without comment.' In this there was old-money disdain for new-money display. But they also both deplored any exaggerated mystique set up around the royal family. Queen Victoria received a host of jubilee gifts in 1887 ranging from an Indian ivory throne to caps – samples of local industry – from Stockport. The gifts were displayed for the public at St James's in the autumn of 1887. A rumour started that some roughs intended to break in to the exhibition and cause trouble. The queen instructed Ponsonby to enquire about this with the proper authorities. He told Spencer that more police had better be called in to protect the exhibition. 'H.M. feared there was intended a raid on the [Jubilee] presents and asked whether it would not be better to close it. I strongly urged not and assured her that Hertslet [clerk in the Lord Chamberlain's Office], the Queen's Guard and the Police would preserve the Stockport Caps and other articles from profanation.'[57]

There was something faintly tragic in the bothers of his office as well. When the Prince of Wales was involved in a gambling scandal in 1892, rebukes and replies flew fast and furious: not between the queen and her son, but between their private secretaries.[58] The prince's private secretary, Francis Knollys, pointed out the tiresomeness of this to Ponsonby when another dispute arose over new titles proposed for Prince George, the future George V, in 1892. 'What a curious way of doing business,' Knollys wrote. 'The Queen and Prince are close to each other, and yet the latter transmits his wishes on, what is after all a family matter, through me who am hundreds of miles off to you who are equally distant from me.'[59] Ponsonby was on much less close terms with Knollys than he was with Ponsonby-Fane, or Gladstone's secretaries like Horace Seymour and Edward Hamilton. The problem was not their politics: Knollys was also a Liberal. Rather Ponsonby saw Knollys as a slightly disreputable character who mismanaged the prince. Instead of warning him about mistresses and gaming, he believed that Knollys had joined in the fun. Henry laughed when Mary's sister, Emily, and her daughter, Elizabeth, saw Knollys at the yacht club in Cowes one summer and asked Henry, 'who that old *roué* was! Poor Francis Knollys who still thinks himself the youth of fashion'.[60] This reflected the usual rivalry and antagonism that had existed since the eighteenth century between Hanoverian kings and their heirs. But it was also Henry's feeling that if Knollys had been a respectable man, with a sense of humour, the two private secretaries might have easily solved some of the bothers together. As it was, and as the queen's family grew older and larger in the third generation, the bothers multiplied. As he got older, Ponsonby became more crotchety and sometimes failed to see the humour in them. Worse, as the queen's reign lengthened, and she became a legendary figure simply by virtue of her having been queen for so long, greater notice was taken of the bothers by the outside world.

The Press

Both Henry and Mary had written for newspapers in the 1860s. Indeed, one of the reasons the queen had selected Ponsonby to be her private secretary was for his facility as a writer. Henry had attended the annual dinners of the *Pall Mall Gazette* where he had met prominent writers and MEP also enjoyed meeting intellectuals in the drawing rooms of some of her friends. There was always a line separating the writers for the daily papers and contributors to the weekly or monthly papers, what was then called the 'higher journalism'. The Ponsonbys were much more familiar with the writers for the latter. After Henry began work as private secretary, however, he lost touch with this world of 'higher' journalists. Of course he read the papers daily; but references to meeting journalists are few. A certain dismissiveness and condescension towards the press grew up during his time in office, an attitude that persisted at the palace long after Ponsonby was gone.

The origins of Ponsonby's faint contempt for the press are difficult to understand. Not only had he begun his career by writing for some of the weekly and special-interest papers, but also he later relied heavily on the newspapers to tell him what was going on in London when he was away. Sequestered in the Highlands, or on the Isle of Wight, cut off from everyday intercourse with politicians, he absolutely depended on what was in the papers to help him make sense of the despatches and correspondence that arrived in the red boxes. He had early on been instructed to clip and send in to the queen any articles he thought she ought to see. In 1873 he was looking through at least ten daily or weekly newspapers to see whether there was anything to be sent in to the queen.[61] He believed that she was not all that interested in the political stories he sent her and often did not read them. One of the ladies in waiting occasionally read out the newspapers to the queen while she was engaged in needlework.[62] In the later 1870s, when her interest in politics revived, she read Conservative weeklies like the *St James's Gazette*, a rival of the Liberal *Pall Mall Gazette*, from which, only partly in jest, Henry told Mary he often took his political views. He himself read the London daily papers of all political stripes. When he was in Scotland he read the Scottish dailies too. During the republican crisis of the 1870s, he read working class newspapers such as the *Bee Hive*. Mary read and occasionally sent him news from French newspapers and journals. In addition, a file was kept of any newspaper story that had to do with the monarchy or the royal family. On the basis of this careful monitoring of different sorts of newspapers it would seem that Ponsonby put a sort of trust or even faith in the reliability of the press. Or perhaps it might be more accurate to say that he tried to keep abreast of the unreliable things the newspapers printed about the court.

British newspapers took themselves more seriously then. Long verbatim accounts of parliamentary debates and densely packed editorials on Britain's responsibility as a rich, industrial power to the rest of the world filled their pages. There were no photographs and few illustrations. Ponsonby occasionally wrote in his official capacity to the newspapers, either, for example, to defend the reputation of a British diplomat in Germany, or to deny that the queen had acquired a fortune of countless millions. Usually he was not personally in touch with any of them, though he sometimes met the editor of *The Times*, John Delane, when he was in London, which was less often than he would have liked, perhaps at one of Lady Waldegrave's parties during the 1870s.

He deplored the more active contacts that the Prince of Wales and his staff had with the press. He found a 'eulogistic' article on the Prince of Wales's house in Norfolk, Sandringham, in *The World*. After enquiring dryly of Knollys 'who he *hired* to write it', he found that Knollys and the prince had indeed commissioned a correspondent from the *Daily News* to write the article.[63] Arthur Helps, clerk of the Privy Council, who had helped the queen edit her Highland journals for publication in the 1860s and who had contacts among editors, gave Ponsonby some advice on the press. Articles could be got into the *Telegraph* by releasing bits of news to them; articles could be got into *The Times* by inviting the editor to 'social entertainment'. But, Henry told Mary, both of these were impossible. The queen was living a retired life. 'We never have any news to give and as no one is ever invited here except officially I don't see what we could do for Delane. On the other hand Marlborough House does both and therefore they will always be able to nobble the press. I don't mean offensively, but the press will be more friendly to them than to us.'[64] In his heart, though, Henry thought of this 'nobbling' as self-interested scheming on the part of Marlborough House. It was a variety of self-promotion that was the antithesis of his own personal ethic.

Nevertheless, he was certainly amused by articles on the court, for which reporters had been furnished no official information. *The Echo* reported on an annual ceremony in memory of the Prince Consort held privately at Balmoral. The article 'described in unflattering terms what they supposed to be the ceremony of drinking to the memory of the Prince – not very accurately. But Bridport and Jenner and I are delighted at being alluded to as "half a dozen languid London dandies" that being the Echo's conception of the Gentlemen of the Court.'[65] He was also ready to concede that the household was as fascinated as anyone by what the papers had to say about them. One journal called *Modern Society* acquired some information about the private theatricals and *tableaux* being performed by the household and members of the royal family in January 1888 at Osborne. 'Everybody here,' Henry told Spencer Ponsonby-Fane, 'declared that from what they were told it was too scandalous and 5 minutes later every one was seen slipping down the hill to the newspaper shop with a penny in their hands.'[66]

As the queen grew older, popular interest in her increased. This was reflected in and also stimulated by increased press reports about her. The origins of the first jubilee lay not in an official attempt to drum up enthusiasm for the throne, but in popular demand. The Liberals who were in office in March 1886 explicitly refused a request for government sponsorship of a celebration until there was a more marked expression of popular interest in the event.[67] People did in fact begin to write to the palace later in 1886 that there had been celebrations to mark George III's jubilee and there should again be something to mark the queen's fifty years on the throne. Papers took up the request until it was necessary for the palace to reply to what had become a popular movement. After the 1887 jubilee, this popular interest, rather than abating, increased. One of its marks was that the queen became a legendary figure in Europe, the empire and the USA as well as in Britain. When Henry travelled with the queen on the continent, for example to Aix les Bains in 1890, he found the reporters markedly less willing to leave the queen alone on her holiday than they had been earlier in the reign, and markedly less deferential than they were in Britain.[68]

The next year, when she went for her spring holiday to Grasse, she had Ponsonby insert a paragraph in the newspapers saying that there were many reports of her activities there 'not to be believed'. This in turn provoked the editor of the *Daily Telegraph* to ask for more information about the queen than was being provided in the Court Circular. Ponsonby and the queen turned him down flat, treating his request as a further invasion of her privacy.[69]

In 1892 he entered into a conversation with a reporter from *The Times* on what the reporter called the 'impending marriage' of the future George V to Princess May of Teck. This was not a topic on which Henry could give any definite information.

> I assumed a stern expression at his [the reporter's] treating such holy subjects with levity and he said 'Oh yes I know you can't say anything but we know the Prince of Wales is all for it and The Queen dead against it.'
> I said 'That's not true' and immediately afterwards felt that he had drawn me, as of course he had intended to do.[70]

He found he had neither the skills nor the patience nor the time to deal with the pressmen. His own office, which had been run by himself and Biddulph without too much trouble in the 1870s, now required three full-time men. Even they were sometimes overwhelmed, especially from the time of the first jubilee and beyond. Henry had to recommend to the queen in 1887 that they hire an extra clerk to work at Buckingham Palace in the privy purse office.[71] Ponsonby's negative attitude to the press came as a result of his having little time to deal with editors or reporters and his ranking them low on his list of priorities. He was alternately exasperated and amused by their inventing stories or pestering him for information he could not give. Their treating 'holy subjects with levity', however, was a variety of his own attitude to the monarchy.

Queen Victoria had a slightly different attitude. She was not in favour of encouraging the reporters who followed her on the continent. Nor was she ever inclined to approve the applications that flowed in at the time of the jubilee, for example, to sketch the gardens at Buckingham Palace or to describe the interior. She had an instinct, however, beginning in the 1860s, that print publicity might save her the effort and the nervous strain of actually appearing in public. The publication of *Leaves from a Journal of Our Life in the Highlands* must have arisen from her sense that a series of holiday snapshots might fulfill a public demand for her presence that days of riding down Rotten Row in Hyde Park would not.

Her success as an author disposed her in turn to use the newspapers as a way of replying to the wave of public sympathy that swelled up when the Prince of Wales grew ill and nearly died of typhoid in the autumn of 1871. Special editions of the newspapers reporting on his illness – and on crowds gathering outside to hear the news – sold out as fast as they were printed. The queen knew this, and after the prince appeared to be out of danger, she told Ponsonby to enquire of Gladstone how best to meet and respond to this public sympathy. What she had in mind was a few heartfelt lines she might write to the public and have published in all the newspapers. What Gladstone had in mind was a solemn service of thanksgiving at St Paul's modelled on eighteenth-century precedents. Much as she detested the idea of a big state pageant, she had opened herself up to it and had to give in. Gladstone also welcomed her other idea of publishing lines in the newspapers. He had his ceremony at St Paul's; she had her personal thanks printed in the newspapers. Thereafter, at the next big ceremonies of the reign, the jubilees of 1887 and 1897, she continued the precedent of putting lines of thanks direct from her to the public in the newspapers. Her idea became fixed that print publicity was a good thing, and particularly appropriate to extraordinary ceremonials in the capital.

The queen also believed that publications could serve as a fitting memorials to the dead. Hence, in addition to commissioning paintings and sculptures of the Prince Consort in 1861, she also commissioned books. She had Arthur Helps edit the Prince Consort's speeches and Charles Grey write an account of his early life.[72] *Leaves from a Journal of Our Life in the Highlands* was also in a way a memorial to happy days with her husband. She meant it to serve as a stark contrast with her grieving widowhood. Interestingly, the first widespread rumours about John Brown began to date from the publication of the *Leaves* volume. He had undoubtedly been a favoured servant of the prince and the queen before the prince died, and perhaps unselfconsciously she brought his name forward unusually often in the context of a book where her late husband reigned supreme.

She commissioned a Scottish man of letters, Theodore Martin, to write a full-scale biography of the Prince Consort, and Martin became her expert on everything to do with the London newspapers. It is not a coincidence that the same process of memorialising a much-loved friend began all over again when John Brown died in 1883.[73] She decided to bring out a new version of her Highland journal, to be entitled *More Leaves from the Journal of Our Life in the Highlands*. The 'our' in the title referred not only to the royal 'we' but also to her friendship with Brown. In addition to what she called the second volume of *Leaves*, she wanted a memoir of Brown written. Initially this was to be written for private circulation as a sort of appendix to *More Leaves*, and then as she told Henry, '(probably in a curtailed shape) published'. The queen thought the published version of the memoir might appear in a women's journal like *Good Words*. 'Her wish is that it should be *for the*

people at large.' She wanted Henry to find out whether *Good Words*
would be best for that purpose: it was to be popular, not merely for
high society.[74] Eventually, Martin was consulted[75] and the *Good Words*
idea was abandoned. Martin himself got out of writing the Brown
memoir by using an excuse about his wife's health. The queen employed
a Miss Macgregor instead.

Meanwhile, plans for the publication of *More Leaves* went ahead.
There was an idea that some of the papers might be allowed an advance
copy of the book when it was nearly ready to be published in January
1884. Martin counselled against this: 'One must give no *preferences* to
any of the Press. If this were done, there is no calculating the consequences of the fury it would provoke in the others. They are a strange
people. What I have to do is to make them all as friendly as possible ...'[76]
Francis Knollys disagreed. At Marlborough House they were more
accustomed to seeing the press as friends and allies. Knollys told
Ponsonby 'it would be politic to allow them' to review the queen's book
before it was published. 'I understand that Sir T. Martin says it will
appear in 3 weeks and that then it can be reviewed, which is rather
"thank you for nothing," whereas if they are permitted to review it now,
the Queen will be granting them a favour which they will not lose sight
of in carrying out their work.'[77] It is not clear exactly what was decided,
but Henry was more inclined to trust Martin, to distrust Knollys and to
give the press no special favours. The queen, though, thought of the
papers, *Good Words* for example, as a direct, trustworthy and unmedi-
ated way of communicating with the public, just as she had done at the
time of the prince's illness in 1871. She was confident that this was a
way of establishing sympathetic links between herself and the people,
who would be able to understand her grief as a widow, her anxiety for
a sick child as a mother, her close friendship as a sovereign with a
Scottish gamekeeper.

Ponsonby doubted the last of these three. When the queen renewed
her hints to him that she would like to have a memoir or biography of
Brown written, just as she had for the Prince Consort after his death, he
asked her permission to make more enquiries. He did not return a
direct negative, but counselled caution. He must have been alarmed
when she clipped a review of *More Leaves* in one of the newspapers in
order to make her point that a memoir of Brown would be required to
set the record straight. She singled out a line in which the reviewer had
clearly, taking her side, tried to dispel the rumour that she and Brown
were secretly husband and wife. 'There was a paragraph' in one of the
newspapers, she pointed out to Henry. It read, 'We do not gather from

these memorials [*More Leaves*] that he [Brown] was more than a kind-hearted and devoted servant whose devotion and faithfulness were rewarded by gratitude and friendship'. 'Now,' the queen continued, Brown 'was much more than that, and it is this which The Queen would wish to show.'[78] Ponsonby, together with Randall Davidson, the new dean of Windsor, were able to get the Brown memoir dropped. She was undoubtedly angry with them both and for some while would not speak to Davidson, who had told her that her relations with Brown might be misunderstood.[79] Ponsonby thought that her eccentric relations with Brown, like the similarly odd ones with Gladstone and the Prince of Wales, had better not be publicised if the monarchy were to retain public favour. A round was thus won for secrecy, discretion and keeping things out of the papers. If the whole odd business – her regarding Brown as essentially the man of the house, his alcoholism and his remarkable non-interference in the political or financial business that might have tempted a more ambitious man – had reached the papers, editors would probably have either disbelieved it, or deferentially censored the majority of it themselves.

Pure Fun

The subjects that amused Henry most were those that spoofed the ultra morality, the ultra Scottishness, or the ultra politeness of the court, all of which he felt to be exaggerated sometimes. For example, he often thought the morality of the queen's refusing to meet divorced women or those who were rumoured to have had lovers preposterous. Lady Ely whispered to him one day at luncheon that she suspected the Greek governess of one of the queen's grandchildren had an immoral past. Ponsonby told his wife that he believed the governess' lover had been either Lycurgus or Solon.

The ultra Scottishness of the court also had something harmlessly fake about it. In Ponsonby's mind the royal family were more German than Scottish. Nevertheless, they all liked to wear Scottish clothes and Prince Leopold collected Stuart memorabilia. Ponsonby saw the Stuarts as despots, banished long ago for trying to abridge English liberties. When the queen told him she would like to visit some of the places connected with Bonnie Prince Charlie and the Jacobite rising against the Hanoverians in 1745, he could not help but chuckle inwardly. He told Mary that he managed to 'unearth' a descendant of one of the Jacobite rebels who had helped Bonnie Prince Charlie, as if he were a rat, a fox, or some other pest with a burrow in the ground. He had introduced this man to the queen. He showed her some relics of the Stuart era. 'Your ancestors were indeed true to him,' said the queen to this man. He replied, ' "Yes Your Majesty my ancestor was true to your ancestor, for such was Prince Charles, as I shall always be true to you." The Queen [was] delighted and said to me "You know he was my ancestor." "Yes'M," I said, "collaterally he was." '[80] He could not help slipping in a reminder that Parliament had really decided who should occupy the throne: the collateral descendants of James II, or the Protestant Hanoverians, rather than the direct Catholic descendants of the Stuarts.

Henry also thought absurd the cult of translating from the Gaelic all the place-names of the Scottish towns they visited. For example, Aberdeen could be translated as the mouth of the river Dee. He visited a village within driving distance of Balmoral called Tornahaish, where there was nothing but a small inn. 'Did you get as far the public house?' asked one of the men of the household.

> I replied that there was only one house, so that must have been the public house.
>
>   'What is the meaning of Tornahaish?' asked Lady Errol [lady in waiting].
>
>   'I suppose it must mean public house,' I said.
>
>   Driving with the Queen she alluded to Tornahaish and told H.M. it meant public house. The Queen [was] most indignant as it is supposed to mean the cliff of the broken pledge or some such fancy word. But Lady Errol giving me as an authority stuck to her point which aggravated The Queen. Miss Pitt [maid of honour] said both were so determined that she could not at first speak for laughing but at last observed, 'Of course General Ponsonby was joking.'
>
>   Both then relapsed into an angry silence wondering how so great a man as the Privy Purse could joke, and precious hard on me who didn't mean any joke.[81]

Even Henry, however, could get tired of what he thought of as Scottish 'larks'. There is weariness in the tone of a letter he wrote in 1890 telling Mary that the royal train had arrived on schedule in the north. 'The Royalties have now put on their kilts and Scotch garments and we are now Highlanders again.'[82]

The most subversive of his satires he saved for what might be called the ultra politeness of the court, the courtesies of bowing and curtseying to princes, calling them 'Your Royal Highness', 'Ma'am', and 'Sir'. Sometimes he thought of all this as oriental, and not English, hence to bow or to curtsey was in his phrase to 'kou tou' to someone, what we would call a Chinese kow tow. An even more emphatic way of showing that he thought it uncivilised or foreign to make too much of royal rank was his jokey reference to princes as blacks or 'niggers'. This may have been general among the household of the second half of the century, and according to the *OED*, typical of the period, when the word need not refer to skin colour, but could denote a socially inferior person. For example, the queen went abroad in the spring of 1880 to Darmstadt and Baden. Lord John Manners accompanied her as the minister in attendance. His wife also travelled with the party as well as Ponsonby and other members of the household. Manners's wife wrote a satirical verse about ladies and gentlemen attending 'niggers' travelling abroad, in which she clearly means royalties travelling abroad.[83] Henry returned to the joke when his younger brother, Fred, who was a clergyman, was proposed as a candidate to fill a South African bishopric, but turned it down. In his letter telling Mary about this he made fun of his own seeming authority over princes as well. 'Fred is quite unfit to preach among the niggers and Boers. Quite as much as I should be to govern them.'[84] He meant that his brother could not preach to black men or Boers just as he, Henry, could not hope to govern princes. The word may have originated from the royal family's always mourning someone, wearing black. Arthur Ponsonby refers in his diary to playing tennis with some 'black princesses' when he was staying in Germany to learn German after Eton. He meant that the daughters of the Empress Frederick were wearing black, rather than that they were black: 'they were in mourning for somebody and the royal family like domestic servants always revel in crape.'[85] Theirs was an era less self-conscious about race prejudice than ours. The superiority of white men to blacks, among whom were counted not only Africans, but also Indians, and even sometimes the Irish, Henry believed in as a fact that went without saying. It was ironic that the queen began to employ Indian attendants from 1887 onwards and, much to the rage of the household, took a fancy to one of them, Abdul Karim. She did what rich and elderly men have been doing for centuries when she appointed Abdul her 'secretary' or 'Munshi'. This was not to displace Henry. It was merely to give her an excuse to keep him always nearby and pay him a small salary. She reproved Lord Salisbury for calling her Indian attendants 'niggers' and demanded an apology from him.

*

Henry Ponsonby's position was the fulcrum of the court in the 1890s. He and the queen had put their political differences behind them. She relied on him for advice about writing to ministers, managing her money, settling disputes among the household and taking care of all the worries of a large family in the second and third generation. Her family, generals, politicians, ambassadors and servants all depended on his advice and took their problems to his door. He had grown old with the queen and with the household. When his son Fritz arrived as equerry in 1894, he could not help noticing how grey and elderly they had all become.[86] Henry's position was a serious one that had become more distinguished the longer he occupied it and the more the queen moved toward what Lytton Strachey called her 'apotheosis'. Yet, one can imagine Henry Ponsonby's snort of derision at the notion that the queen was divine. One can imagine him conjuring up a joke to show that it really was ludicrous to treat the queen and royal family with anything other than ordinary respect. To read through his letters to his wife is to be impressed with the fact that they did not really have a conscious justification or rationale for the monarchy to exist. It just was. It went without saying, which is why he had been so speechless in the republican crisis of the 1870s when he first became private secretary. One could describe what the monarchy was on the basis of these letters, but it is more difficult to elicit a rationale or a defence of the monarchy from them. It is the fun of it all, the absurdity, its entertainment value that emerges most clearly from what these two court insiders chose to see and describe in the court circle.

Henry Ponsonby's attitude to the throne has an astonishingly contemporary cast to it. How he would have loved the captioned photographs of members of the royal family saying ridiculous things on the cover of *Private Eye* and the rubberised puppets of princes on *Spitting Image*. The Victorian era was much more serious about national symbols than that. But Ponsonby's point of view, if not dramatically ahead of its time, perhaps recalled the caricatures of the royal family by Gillray and Cruickshanks and Rowlandson that had so entertained his parents' and his grandparents' generations. Indeed several albums of these caricatures survive among the Ponsonby papers at Shulbrede.

Henry made his own album of autographs of historical figures, which he claims to have collected. In fact he invented all the autographs himself, using different handwriting to imitate, for example, Julius Caesar, and the Man in the Iron Mask. One autograph, claiming to date from the Tudor era reads, 'Do as I bidde or proude prelate I will unfrocke you. Elizabeth R'. Another autograph appears to be that of Fanny Burney, the late eighteenth-century novelist who served at the court of George III and who was known for her extravagant loyalty to the king.[87] Henry's printed note underneath the autograph says that she was 'a writer on the manners and customs of Royalty' and the autograph reads:

> The King and The Queen with the old Duchess of Mecklenburg all walked in the Great Garden. A pleasing incident occurred. The King sneezed in the Chamberlain's face quite by accident, but begged his pardon most graciously. We were all charmed with the grace of his Majesty, but the conduct of the Chamberlain in wiping off his face the Royal spray was much censured. The Duke of Mecklenburg cut himself shaving this morning but fortunately had some sticking plaister at hand. Affectionately yours, F. Burney.

The king's sneeze and the duke's sticking plaster were his lively antidotes to a career spent heading his letters 'Sir Henry Ponsonby presents his humble duty to Your Majesty and begs leave to ...'

The most sensible thing Ponsonby had to teach a subsequent generation about the monarchy was about the balance between sincere respect and the throne's comic potential. The sovereign deserves respect both as a human being and as the representative of a free people who decide in Parliament whether she is to reign or not. At the same time, it was important not to mistake all the medieval mumbo jumbo and appearing in Lord Mayor style fancy dress as anything other than theatre meant to amuse as the same time as to dignify. There was no necessary contradiction between those dramatic ends. He himself had been willing to die for the queen in the Crimea. He sent his eldest son off to a South African war. He devoted more than half his life to her service. But when one of his daughters at the dinner table referred to the queen's German sons-in-law wearing kilts, his face turned red, his eyes welled up and his shoulders began to shake.

A Marriage and a Partnership

Henry Ponsonby loved his wife intensely. In her own undemonstrative way, she loved him too, though she was more likely to convey her passion in a fierce argument with him than in a love letter. The older Henry grew, the more he loved her and needed to be with her. After he accepted the two offices of private secretary and privy purse together, the queen regularly gave them a house at Osborne, so that he might have his wife and family there in the January interval after Christmas and again in the summer when the court was in residence. He still had to separate from them for several months in the autumn and again in the spring when the queen went to Scotland or abroad, however, and he felt these separations keenly.

On the whole, though, their relationship survived and was perhaps stronger for these regular separations. They learned to enjoy their reunions and time spent together all the more. Further, their partnership and work together received repeated recognition from the queen. Not only did she commission reports from Mary on anti-home-rule speeches and her son-in-law's illness, but she also gave repeated marks of favour to the family. She made their youngest son, Arthur, a page of honour and their middle son, Fritz, an equerry. She attended the wedding of their eldest daughter, Betty, and through the intercession of her daughter, Princess Louise, she changed the warrant for their apartment at St James's so that Mary could keep the rooms for her lifetime if Henry should die before her.[88] Henry was genuinely touched by the queen's interest in his wife. The queen asked him to understand that her sending an honour to Mary on the occasion of the marriage of Princess Beatrice was also a mark of gratitude to him.[89]

The queen was distressed when Henry's mother, Lady Emily Ponsonby, died in 1877. She broke out of her usual way of writing to him to express this. 'I cannot write formally in the 3rd person to you at this moment of *overwhelming grief* ... let me say how *very very* deeply and truly I feel for you.'[90] This was a rare departure for her. She used the first person with her children and certain favourites, such as Beaconsfield, but almost never with Ponsonby. It was a more formal era. Although they had been working together and living under the same roof for nearly a decade, and had known each other for nearly thirty years, there remained a respectful if affectionate distance between Ponsonby and the other most important woman in his life.

In the year before he died, Henry became more and more reliant on Mary. He thanked her for her help in the recent crisis surrounding Gladstone's final resignation from office in early 1894. 'I feel very low at being away from you. Whatever my work has been for the last month it has been pleasant with you who have helped me in every step and I don't know [more] pleasant company anywhere than to be with you and Mags.'[91] It was a trying year. The deaths of two people who were close to him surprised him very much. His younger brother, Fred, rector of St Mary Magdalen, Munster Square in London, died quite unexpectedly. In addition, Henry's longtime colleague as master of the household, Sir John Cowell, died suddenly in August 1894. 'Poor Cowell's death,' he told Mary, 'is one of the most sad and melancholy events and most shocking for he was in such good spirits and I thought looked so well when we left him.'[92] Both of these losses unnerved him. In the autumn of 1894 he wrote a poignant note to his wife and family. He enclosed it in a small envelope with the instructions that it should only be opened after his death. 'After the terrible events of this year of Fred and Cowell [dying]' he wrote to them, 'I should always be prepared to go, but my grief and pain would be to leave my dear dear wife and my children. Bless and protect my dear dear wife and my children and may they be happy. And my dear Magdalen how [happy] I have always been with you all. But I hope a long time before I go away yet. God bless you all. Henry F. Ponsonby.'[93]

CHAPTER 10

MEP Holds Court

c. 1893-1916

In the last two decades of her life the flame of Mary Ponsonby's passions burnt very high. In her sixties she began a triangular friendship with two women who broke down her barriers of reserve and reciprocated her affection with an intensity she had not expected. At about the same time Henry became suddenly and unexpectedly ill. She spent nearly a year at his bedside and tortured herself with doubts. Had she ever properly returned or deserved his great love for her? After he died she made herself anew. She gave up the house she had made her own for twenty-five years without looking back and acquired a new one in the country. She had undreamt of success as a writer; but it was as a writer that she broke court protocol and jeopardised the career of her son, Fritz, who was serving as assistant private secretary and assistant keeper of the privy purse to King Edward VII. Her old age was bold and fiery. She became if anything more formidable than she had been in her prime. This is the story of a diminutive lady holding court amongst family, friends and admirers, all of whom loved her devotedly, but who were also a little afraid of her.

Ethel Smyth and Vernon Lee

In the 1890s Ethel Smyth was a young composer, frustrated with her lack of success in a musical world dominated by men. The daughter of an officer in the artillery, she was a fighter herself and had fought with her father to be allowed to study music in Leipzig.[1] Once there she forced her way into the circle around Brahms. On her return to England she tried to press an acquaintance with the Empress Eugénie into opportunities to have her works performed in prominent places and before royal audiences. She had an affair with an American poet, Henry Brewster, but she also loved women. She had intense friendships with Brewster's German sister-in-law, Liesl, with the Archbishop Benson's wife, Mary, with the militant suffragist leader, Emmeline Pankhurst, and with the novelist, Virginia Woolf. These may or may not have been sexual liaisons. Certainly they involved huge romantic energies on Ethel Smyth's part, and varying reciprocations on the part of the others.[2] She achieved fame as a composer and a campaigner for women's suffrage in the early decades of the twentieth century, long after her passion for MEP had passed its peak. She surprised the audience at a formal concert by mounting the podium to conduct one of her works in tweeds and a three-cornered hat. After being jailed for her part in a suffragist protest she conducted her own 'March of the Women' from a window of Holloway Prison using a toothbrush as a baton.

All that was in the future when Ethel's sister-in-law and the wife of the dean of Windsor, Edith Davidson, brought her to tea in the Norman Tower in about 1890. Afternoon tea was not a ceremony MEP set much store by, nor was she impressed that Ethel combined her devotion to music with a 'passion for hunting'. Ethel recalled that therefore 'as soon as politeness allowed' MEP 'pleaded urgent letters and vanished' from the drawing room, leaving her daughters in charge. They persuaded Ethel to sing an Irish song. She remembered that

> no sooner was it over than Betty jumped up saying, 'Mama *must* hear that,' ran out of the room, and presently came back leading in her reluctant and deeply sceptical mother. The song was repeated and after that there were no further difficulties; in fact it became my habit to bribe her with music and then settle down to the interminable talks that were to be my joy for the next twenty six years.[3]

Arthur Ponsonby thought that Ethel's sketch of his mother, from which the foregoing recollection is drawn, was a better description of Ethel's own personality than of his mother's. He conceded that Ethel's chapter on his mother 'has very good bits in it', but he went on to object that it was 'so coloured by her own dominant egotism that it reflects the irritations and even exasperations which no doubt my mother showed in her relations with Ethel but which were by no means generally characteristic of herself'.[4] Nevertheless, Ethel made a deep impression on MEP, even if the friendship was not as immediate as Ethel made it out to be.

MEP replied to a letter of Arthur's in the summer of 1891 by saying 'I have had so many Ethel-ians (i.e. interruptions without either profit or pleasure) that I have left your capital letter unanswered'.[5] Nevertheless, Ethel laid siege to MEP and was eventually successful in forcing her to read the novels of Anatole France.[6] Ethel had been partly educated in Paris so she was able to exploit their shared love of French literature as a way through MEP's defences. Maggie was her mother and father's unmarried companion throughout this period. She was suspicious of Ethel's assaults on her mother in the name of friendship because, according to Ethel,

> some years ago another woman a good deal younger than her mother, who had contrived to get through the usual defenses, turned out to be an unreliable, treacherous friend, and little as Lady Ponsonby dwelt on that or any other emotional experience, I knew it had hurt her a great deal.[7]

Little by little, however, MEP succumbed. She allowed Ethel to come more often to the Norman Tower. This was a privilege that MEP would have had no compunction about withdrawing if Ethel were indeed as great a bore as she had suggested to her son in 1891. It was Henry who must have found Ethel a bore, coming up the stairs in the evening after a long day unravelling court conundrums and finding his wife installed with this emphatic young woman in the sitting room. Ethel noticed Henry's great attachment to Mary.

> From the way he looked at and spoke to her I guessed that his chief joy, relaxation and refreshment was, whenever it was possible, to steal half an hour with his wife. Hence a slight sense of guilt on my part, and a suspicion that in his heart he must often be saying as he opened the door: 'There's that damned Smyth woman again.' If so, it couldn't be helped; as long as she liked me to be there, there I should be.[8]

So MEP allowed Ethel to come, whether Henry liked it or not. It was one of MEP's small insensitivities to Henry that he simply endured. It was not in his nature to dwell on his grievance or to exact revenge.

The relationship grew more complex when Mary accompanied her husband and the queen on a trip to Florence in the spring of 1893. They were all getting older and perhaps the queen decided that Henry ought to have Mary along in order to help keep him going. Exceptionally then, Mary was invited to come on the queen's annual excursion to warmer weather and the continent. Mary wrote to Johnny about enjoying the galleries and churches, adding 'the Q. has been very dear always managing to take me to places I couldn't see easily without her'.[9]

In Florence MEP met another independent-minded and unmarried younger woman by the name of Violet Paget. She went by a man's name, Vernon Lee, which she used as the *nom de plume* for her books.

She was a prolific author and over the course of her life produced thirty or more volumes of work on Italian history, literature and travel, as well as novels and plays. Vernon Lee lived off and on in Florence with occasional trips back to England. MEP liked Vernon Lee's books and found her charming in person. In the autumn of 1893 MEP sat down to draft a letter to Vernon Lee, much of which is actually a character sketch and a description of how she felt about Ethel Smyth. This was after MEP had brought the two of them together to meet in the Norman Tower in the summer of 1893. It also followed MEP's invitation to Ethel to come and stay at Abergeldie Mains, the farmhouse near Balmoral where, exceptionally, the queen had invited MEP to accompany Henry that autumn.

This is an unusual letter. MEP seldom wrote drafts of letters and rarely kept them among her papers when she did. Those that survive are telling. There exist drafts of letters to John Morley, when the queen had asked for Mary's help in thwarting one of Gladstone's home rule bills. There exist drafts of letters to the queen, thanking her for her sympathy at a moment of great grief when one of MEP's grandchildren died in infancy. MEP was usually so sure of herself that she seldom felt the need to draft a letter and these drafts to Morley and the queen show her deliberation at exceptional moments. Similarly, when she wrote to Vernon Lee, she was choosing her words carefully. She was too impressed by Vernon Lee herself, and too intent on getting exactly right the nuances of her relationship with Ethel, to put a foot wrong by choosing a word or phrase that was not apt. MEP began by saying she was glad Vernon had found 'the kind gentle vein' in Ethel. She went on to say 'that the gentle tenderness E. S. shows in her relations with me is the thing I like best in her'. MEP also liked Ethel's singing. 'Her singing is very beautiful and there is a vibration in it which does not suggest the cling clang of engines and the hammering out of metal on an anvil, but something much more intense and tender.' MEP was moved by Ethel 'in spite of her hectoring manner' and these were her attempts to say why to a writer whose work MEP also found stirring.[10]

For their part these two women, both in their mid-thirties, were inspired to depths of feeling for MEP that she sometimes found overwhelming. Ethel's attraction to her was in part physical. If MEP liked her singing, Ethel remembered 'the strange, half physical pleasure' she got from MEP's clear and bell-like speaking voice. She was also much drawn to MEP's 'small extremely strong hands' and the way she 'tackled ordinary little tasks, such as sharpening a pencil, sealing a letter, adjusting a lamp, finding her place in a book ... Later on I grasped the fascination these things had for me; it was the suggestion of force combined with restraint – the swift controlled energy of the violent'.[11] In Ethel's mind MEP was like a panther, graceful, poised and ready to strike. She wrote to Henry Brewster in February 1893 about MEP, who was 60, 'I should judge that in most respects her sensuous life is as strong as that of most women in their prime; as my own for instance.'[12] Ethel captured well some of the paradoxes in MEP's character, that she was 'A mixture of passionate impulse and passionate reticence; ascetic and a sybarite'.[13] What she failed to understand was why MEP repelled her physical advances. One of Ethel Smyth's biographers, Louise Collis, quotes what has to be described as a love letter from Ethel to MEP. 'You want to know what hurts me?' Ethel wrote. 'Well, just that you won't kiss me. Love and longing to see you accumulates in me in these long absences and when I see you ... I want to say nothing but hold you close to me. This you won't have and I can't resign myself.'[14] Although MEP seems to have resisted Ethel's advances, Collis believes that Ethel's music for her opera, 'Fantasio', reflected 'two of the most profound and successful love affairs Ethel ever had: Mary Ponsonby on the one hand; Harry Brewster on the other'.[15]

Vernon Lee, although a friend of MEP's,[16] was equally disappointed when her affections were not returned in exactly the way she wanted. Burdett Gardner, who wrote a Harvard PhD thesis on Vernon Lee, later published as *The Lesbian Imagination*, claims that Vernon Lee had an enormous crush on MEP. Vernon told Ethel that she had 'no charm for her [MEP]' and sighing said that MEP would 'always condemn me to pine on a perch'.[17] Ethel began to feel sorry for Vernon as she had been through the same experience with MEP and knew well her 'sensitiveness' to the 'physical aspect of her friends and acquaintances'.[18]

One dimension of MEP's having discouraged the ardours of these two women might simply have been dislike of displays of affection. Did she ever reflect herself on the series of emotional bonds that she formed with other women over a long life? It is not that she did not love men, for in different ways she did love William Harcourt, Bobby Roden and, above all, Henry. It is just that she experienced her relationships with female friends either on an elevated plane, or tortured by misgivings. She was moved to keep a written record of these relationships in a way she seldom did with men: Charlotte Canning, Frances Jocelyn, Lily Wellesley, Agnes Courtenay, Ethel Smyth and Vernon Lee are all important figures in her diaries.

Arthur Ponsonby also thought his mother's female friends important enough to make a list of them. He included this list in a manuscript entitled 'My Mother' that looks as if it might have been intended for later publication as autobiographical reflections. He remembered some women that MEP had left out of her diaries. For example, Pauline Craven, 'the wife of a diplomat, a French orthodox Catholic and an authoress (*Le Récit d'une Soeur*). My mother was fascinated by her intellect, her Frenchness but was quite out of harmony with her religion'.

Another was Eugenia Sellars, who 'came to coach my sisters. I was about 9 and at home and she was asked to give an occasional hour to me. She thought intellectually I was past praying for and she showed it. I loathed her.'

A third was Marcia Dalrymple, wife of a younger son of the earl of Stair who was also a colonel in the Scots Guards. 'She had beauty and I suppose charm. In one way or another she occupied an immense amount of time. She was kind enough to me, quite unbalanced and untrustworthy and the whole thing collapsed unfortunately and so far as she was concerned in the end tragically.' He does not say what the tragedy was but this may be the unreliable friend Ethel Smyth had been told about.

Feo Gleichen, granddaughter of the queen's half-sister Feodore, was a sculptor, a neighbour, a friend of MEP's, and indeed a friend to the whole family. 'But a certain cantankerous element in her family led to constant altercations which took up too much time.' In later life she sculpted a relief of Henry for a memorial in St Mildred's, Whippingham. She never married and died in 1922.

Connie Lytton, daughter of a late nineteenth-century viceroy of India, was Maggie's friend before she became a friend of MEP. Arthur remembered that 'she came into our family and delighted us. She stayed with us and wrote us voluminous letters which we called "Bulwers".' Connie visited when they were living near Balmoral in November 1893. She described the Ponsonbys as 'delightfully untainted by their neighbourhood' and noticed that they 'made fun of all the comicalities with as keen an appreciation as if they had seen all with the eyes of strangers'.[19] Connie was at first a little in awe of Maggie's mother. She described Lady Ponsonby to her aunt as 'an unusually clever and cultivated woman, very original' with

> an intensity of appreciation and interest in others rather than in anything of her own creation ... I never knew her at all till this visit, and looked upon her as impossibly out of reach for me, and rather alarming even from such a distance; but she was so wonderfully charming to me that I

found my jaws unlocking and my teeth ceasing to chatter in her presence, and I believe a week more of her company would have launched me forth in a sea of brazen ease ... [20]

In fact, Connie Lytton and MEP did become good friends. Connie and Johnny were nearly married, but financial difficulties kept them apart. [21] In later years, like Ethel Smyth, Connie became a militant suffragist and nearly died after being force-fed by the prison authorities while she was on hunger strike. She drifted away from MEP and the rest of the children.

Arthur's account of his mother's friends continues with a paragraph on Vernon Lee.

> She occupied a good deal of my mother's attention, because of her books. Her eccentric over-analysis of thoughts and sensations amused rather than impressed us and Maggie burlesqued them to perfection ...
>
> But it was Ethel Smyth of whom I was most jealous, as I have told her since. I found her occupying so much time and attention when I was launched in a profession and wanted in spare moments really to see my mother properly. But Ethel's singing, Ethel's arguments, Ethel's complicated and intriguing affairs held the field too often. My mother while fascinated by her was as often as not exasperated by her. But one way or the other [she was] a personality and her presence occupied an inordinate amount of time. I liked her myself but resented although I never expressed it her frequent incursions and disturbing visits.

When he was having these recollections put into a typescript, Arthur changed his mind. Possibly he decided that his account of his mother's friends emphasised his own resentment of their intrusions on time he would rather his mother had spent with him. He crossed them out. [22]

Ethel Smyth, however, refused to hold back any of her recollections of MEP and was even willing to include this account of a stormy scene with her. One evening, Ethel had bicycled over to stay with MEP at Gilmuire, the house she bought near Ascot in 1896. Maggie went out to see friends so that MEP and Ethel could have dinner alone. After dinner the two women went to sit in the drawing room and had an argument. Ethel remembered MEP saying in the midst of this:

> 'Will you kindly shut that door unless you wish every word you say to be overheard by the servants you are so fond of imitating.' At this I jumped up, ran into the porch, and began lighting my bicycle lamp. It was 9:30, a wild, wet, blustering, King-Lear night, and the long Bagshot Hill

and seven miles of pedal work against the wind lay between me and my cottage. The drawing room door opened and Lady Ponsonby advanced into the hall. 'What on earth are you doing?' she asked ... 'Don't be absurd – put out that lamp.' I uttered one word only 'Goodnight,' and shot out into the storm. Next day Maggie wrote to Betty: 'When I got back Ethel had been gone half an hour and the house was still rocking.'[23]

MEP's insult about Ethel's aping the servants is typical of her. There is a parallel between her condemning Ethel for being afflicted with 'royal *culte*',[24] that is being guilty of a degrading fascination with princes, and MEP's own use of the word to denote a kind of semi-romantic, irrational and idolatrous passion.[25] For example, in the first flush of her fascination with the books and personality of Vernon Lee, MEP confessed that she had a new '*culte*' for Vernon Lee.[26]

Of course the word '*culte*' also had a jokey quality. Henry Ponsonby was said by his daughter, Betty, to have had a *culte* for Gladstone's secretary, Eddy Hamilton, and Fritz to have had one for Lord Rosebery.[27] So the word had less to do with embarrassment than enjoyment.

MEP could also be amusing on the subject of unmarried ladies and forbidden passions. Maggie never married; like many Victorian spinsters, she looked after her parents as they grew older. Maggie was also a friend of Ethel's though more detached about her and seeing her ludicrous side more than her mother did. In the spring of 1899 Ethel and Magdalen had, according to Ethel, 'conceived simultaneously a passion for Swinburne'. The two of them sat 'at either corner of the sofa in the empty drawing room excitedly going through' one of Swinburne's poems they had both learned by heart and declaiming alternate verses aloud. They were so absorbed that they did not notice MEP coming into the room behind them. ' "I should think," said the well-known voice, "there could be no more ridiculous sight than two old maids shouting erotic verses at each other first thing in the morning." '[28]

Mother and daughter could be jointly sceptical of Ethel's machine-like energies, but Maggie also knew well when her mother enjoyed being alone with Ethel. It is likely that Ethel too understood that MEP's rages were as often due to the goads and stimulus of her own company. Philosophical calm was much more characteristic of MEP on her own, but it certainly was a mark of special intimacy with her that the people she loved could provoke her fiercest arguments. The three women understood each other well and enjoyed long conversations on literature, France and music. It is a tribute to them all that the difficulty of categorising the variety of their relationships to one another did not trouble them in the slightest.

The Death of Henry Ponsonby

In 1894 Henry Ponsonby had a difficult year. At long last Gladstone retired from the premiership while his party was still in office. Ponsonby had to manage Gladstone's leave-taking of the sovereign, which he was sure would be awkwardly, if not insultingly cool on the queen's part. He had also to worry about the queen's choosing a new prime minister, an unprecedented situation that she intended to handle without consulting Gladstone. There was some risk that this would expose her to justifiable criticism. In the end, her choice of Lord Rosebery proved uncontroversial, though he was not particularly good for the Liberal party. He resigned the following year. Nor was Gladstone's going as embarrassing as Ponsonby feared. Although he was hurt at the queen's treating him like a pack mule after he had given so many years of service, to Ponsonby he wrote a letter full of warmth and gratitude.

> But forgive me for saying you are 'to the manner born' and such a combination of tact and temper with Loyalty, intelligence and truth, I cannot expect to see again. Pray remember these are words which can only pass from an old man to one much younger, though trained in a long experience.[29]

Ponsonby was younger than Gladstone but he may well have felt his own career achieving a limit. Gladstone had been his first prime minister when he became the queen's private secretary in 1870. Now Gladstone had gone, could his own time be far off?

The cruel answer came within a matter of months. On 7 January 1895, at Osborne Cottage, where he and Mary and Magdalen had gone for their usual post-Christmas month with the queen, Henry suffered a paralytic stroke. At first he was completely unconscious. Later he came to, his right arm and leg paralysed, his speech incoherent and indistinct.[30] He was confined to his bed. MEP and Magdalen were deeply surprised and distressed, but the queen told her eldest daughter that she had long been expecting something to happen.

> I don't know whether you thought him aged him changed [sic] at Coburg? At Florence Liko [Prince Henry of Battenberg, the queen's son-

in-law] was struck by his apathy and I observed a change in his handwriting which quite gave me a shock … Added to that during the last few
weeks he had seemed very forgetful and indifferent and the last few days
confused, and looking heavy and talked rather badly.[31]

As the queen says, the change in Henry's handwriting is distinctly
noticeable during the later months of 1894, indicating that he may have
had minor seizures earlier without their having been diagnosed.

Owen Morshead, the librarian at Windsor in the 1940s, told Arthur
Ponsonby a story he had heard of Henry's last interview with the queen
in 1895. Morshead had it from the writer, Shane Leslie, whom he
thought 'well-versed in Court history' but he was not sure the story was
true. '[O]n the last morning Sir Henry attended his Royal Mistress …
he observed slowly: "what a funny little old woman you are." He had
doubtless thought it many years. The Queen answered: "Sir Henry you
cannot be well" , and rang the bell.'[32]

All the family were called to Osborne as soon as Henry fell ill. Betty
came from Ireland. Arthur came from his diplomatic post in Turkey.
Johnny came from South Africa where he was serving in the Army. Fritz
had just come into waiting as equerry, so he and Maggie were both
already on the spot. There were ups and downs in Henry's condition.
Sometimes he recovered some ability to move, at other times he would
become agitated and throw off the blankets. He recognised and smiled
at his wife and family, though he could not speak to them. It was a
comfort to be looked after by his old friend from the household, the
queen's doctor, Sir James Reid, but when a new nurse was taken on who
'fluttered about him, chirping and flirting' he said quite clearly to her,
'Will you go?' She cried, 'But I thought you never spoke!'[33] Slowly it
dawned on everyone that he might hang on in this condition for some
time. The family, who had enjoyed one another's company, and even
had themselves photographed at the dining room table with one of the
doctors, reluctantly broke up again and returned to their separate occupations. Henry understood what was happening and bid his son Arthur
a very distinct 'goodbye'.

The queen told MEP and Magdalen that they should remain at
Osborne Cottage as long as they liked. While she was in residence in
January and February she would drive over from the big house with
Princess Beatrice. Mary or Magdalen would come out and speak to them
on the lawn. The reports from the sickbed continued promising, though
the queen thought Mary in February looking 'very ill' and saw in her
friend's face the strain of looking after Henry.[34] MEP tried to remain

optimistic and in August, seven months after Henry's stroke, she wrote to Johnny who had rejoined his regiment: 'Your father is being made right by Hof[meister] and Reid every day but still unaccountable wildness and irritation comes on for no rhyme or reason.'[35] In those months of taking care of Henry MEP felt and expressed more tenderness for him than had been her rule when he was well. She began to doubt whether she had been a good wife to him. More than once she asked Ethel Smyth, 'Have I ever done enough in return for what was given me?'[36]

She had at least one additional heartache to come. In May, Reid, who had informally replaced Ponsonby as the one person in the household the queen trusted most, told MEP she would have to resign her husband's offices for him. 'It did give me a pang,' she wrote her eldest son, 'to sign away as it were all your father's career.'[37] The excuse was that ministers were pressing the queen to confirm new appointments. In fact the queen had quickly given up hope and it was inconvenient for her to linger on with Bigge as acting private secretary and Edwards as acting privy purse. She was willing to have the Ponsonbys stay on at Osborne Cottage for the duration of Henry's illness. She had agreed long ago that Mary should keep the rooms they occupied at St James's as long as she lived. She wanted the Norman Tower back in order to give it either to Bigge or Edwards. She had already stopped paying Henry's £1,700 salary and reduced it to a pension of £1,000 as soon as he became ill.[38] None of this was, perhaps, out of the ordinary, but it does seem callous in light of his 38 years of service to her and the possibility that he might recover.[39] MEP saw no choice but to send Magdalen to Windsor, for Henry could not be left alone, to begin breaking up their old home and packing away their belongings.

The release finally came late that autumn. Henry Ponsonby died in his bed at Osborne Cottage, aged 69, on 21 November 1895. He was buried in the churchyard of St Mildred's, Whippingham, the local church that had been rebuilt by the queen and Prince Consort after their purchase of the Osborne estate. Randall Davidson, now bishop of Winchester, conducted the service and signed the burial register. The queen sent a representative and attended a service of her own in the private chapel at Windsor. There is no doubt that she felt his illness and death. She had reported in March to a former maid of honour who came to visit her, 'it is too terrible for us all' and her eyes had filled with tears.[40] The queen's eldest daughter knew how much her mother would miss him. She said to her own daughter that Henry had been 'Grandmama's right hand in so many things, and I do not know *how* she can replace him.'[41]

The queen insisted that those who followed him should take him as their example. Neither Bigge nor Edwards was senior or trusted enough to hold Henry's two offices together, so they were divided again, as they had been before the death of Biddulph in 1878. She told Bigge, 'The Queen is sure that they [Bigge and Edwards] will follow in his footsteps and be as kind to all, of all ranks, as he always was.'[42] To Sir Henry Ewart, who was crown equerry, or the senior official in the master of the horse's department, she wrote, 'Dear Sir Henry was so kind and friendly to all, such a peace maker and so beloved by those under him that he will be terribly missed'.[43] She remembered him as a friend to Brown, and someone who was kind to Abdul Karim when the rest of the household thought him beneath contempt. It is just possible that MEP and her children had a bit of a wry smile at the funeral when they noticed in amongst all the big and showy wreaths from the royal family, which they would have thought excessive in any case, an equally expensive wreath from Karim.[44]

Henry was not a rich man. There had been repeated worries about finding enough money to launch the boys in their careers. But his family was not exactly destitute after Henry's death. His colleagues in the privy purse office were 'astonished' when his will was sworn at the relatively large sum of just over £71,000.[45] Several of his Bathurst relations had died leaving him significant sums and it seems as though these had been tucked away to accumulate. The principal provisions of his will were £3,000 for Mary, and after her death, lump sums of £6,000 for each of the five children. Later codicils reduced Betty's £6,000 to £3,000, as she had been advanced £3,000 on her marriage to William Montgomery. Similarly, Johnny was to have £4,000 and Fritz £3,500, as they had been advanced money to cover their initial expenses on entering the Army, as well as an additional sum to help defray debts in Fritz's case. During her lifetime, Mary was to have the interest from the trust that was to provide these sums for the children.[46] In addition the queen gave Mary a pension of £800 a year, a reduction of £200 from the £1,000 the couple had received as Henry's pension during his illness. She did, however, make Mary a separate cash gift of £500.[47] The queen also appointed her an extra woman of the bedchamber, with the prospect of some small pay if MEP stood in and did a few days' waiting when occasion arose. MEP's plan was to go abroad to Florence for four months as soon as their things from Osborne Cottage could be packed up and either brought to St James's or put in storage.

She saw the queen before going. The queen's account of their meeting is that she went after noon 'to Osborne Cottage to see poor

Mary Ponsonby, who was a little upset at first but was quiet and natural. She looks much worn and aged. She talked a great deal about her dear Husband and his illness, and was full of gratitude for my kindness'.[48] Soon MEP and Maggie had left the Isle of Wight and were on their way to Italy. She anticipated to Ethel going 'out of the world' with her husband's death.[49] She even looked forward to this. She hoped to see only a few good friends and to resume more serious work with her books. Little did she know that, rather than leaving the world, in taking up pen and paper she was about to enter it again more dramatically than ever.

Publication

MEP wrote to Johnny from Italy in January 1896 that she was considering living regularly in Florence for a part of the year, like her cousin, Katie Carmarthen. 'Of course,' she added, 'I have the blacks sometimes with the feeling the real reason of my existence is gone and there is a kind of shifting sand under my feet so that I shall never be at anchor again, but this is morbid and by degrees I shall feel brighter.'[50] What she did to cheer herself up was to take up serious and regular reading again. It was to have surprising results.

In the mid-1860s she and Henry had both written successfully for the *Pall Mall Gazette*. 'Then,' she recorded in her journal for March 1866, 'one article not being put in lost heart about it. Must try again.'[51] She also had children to bring up and it was a long while before she could return to writing. From the year following her husband's death, however, a steady stream of articles flowed from her pen. Although some of them were turned down for publication, a good many of them were accepted, especially in *The Nineteenth Century*, a highbrow Liberal monthly. All of them are interesting not only for the way they sum up the enduring concerns of her life, but also for the way they reflect the experience of widowhood and old age.

There is a real poignancy in the first of her articles, 'An Attempt at Optimism', which appeared less than a year after Henry's death. In it she made use of her personal experience in order to reach a broader, more general conclusion. She was still understandably depressed by the loss of her husband. She found, though, that in taking up reading about scientific discoveries, and in exploring the uproar caused in philosophy by Friedrich Nietzsche's anti-Christian thought, she found a workable alternative to giving in to depression or 'the blacks'. She discovered a way to counteract pessimism, feelings of uselessness and a fatalistic acceptance of her own eventual death. Resist, she told her readers, the pull of the unknowable beyond. 'In everyday life we must needs adopt the ways of science and stand courageously by our relative knowledge and, in homely language, "do our best" according to the light that is within us.'[52]

She felt that there were two poles: on the one hand, she strove toward optimism, scientific knowledge, free thought and Liberal or radical politics; on the other, she was sometimes drawn to pessimism, a fatalistic point of view, a semi-religious love of mystery and Conservative or traditionalist politics. At the turn of the century she brought a ripe experience to these old concerns that she had not possessed before. She was fascinated all over again. She was also surprised to find her optimism revived as she noticed in herself continuing powers of appreciating beauty. She believed this was common among old people.[53]

In this late flowering of MEP's career as a writer she refused to make simple choices between the apparently opposed ideals of science and religion. She returned to the favourite writer of her high church youth, Blaise Pascal. In an article published in 1903 she argued that Pascal was brilliant because his was a mind that embraced opposites. If she liked the tendency of expanded scientific knowledge to encourage optimism about the knowable world, in the Pascal article she was clearly distressed that a sort of crude scientific determinism might narrow the sphere for 'spontaneous action' based on religion, culture, morality and faith.[54]

It was the same in politics. MEP was willing to consider dispassionately, even to welcome enthusiastically, the most radical new alternatives proposed. At the same time, she could not help a sort of conservative feeling reasserting itself with some indignation when young radicals appeared to undervalue the knowledge and experience of their elders. One article not published was entitled simply 'Socialism'. For most of her generation this was a godless creed that spelled revolution. Her ideas are incomplete, but it is clear that she was not afraid of it. The manuscript shows that she took the ideas of the early French socialists, Fourier and St Simon, seriously as blueprints for future action. She also entered into a provocative published exchange in *The Westminster Gazette* with H.G. Wells. He was a popular novelist and prominent in the Fabian Society, a group of intellectuals who believed that socialism was the way forward in Britain. MEP deplored Wells's tendency to exaggerate the defects of the current system of British education, which often preserved unfair privilege. More strikingly, she agreed with Wells that 'The majority in English society must be taught that in future it will be impossible to dwell contentedly on the easy and stupid achievements of regiment, college, and school without becoming the laughing stock of the world'.[55] She was friendly to Fabian ideals and ready to strengthen their position in Britain by reminding her readers of a few older French socialists, perhaps too quickly rejected after Marx and Engels had derided them as utopians.

However, it made her angry when left-wing politicians scorned the efforts of British soldiers abroad. In another unpublished manuscript, entitled 'Depreciation', she lashed out at British critics of the Boer War, whose words were being interpreted by newspapers abroad as signs of British division and irresolution. Both Fritz and Johnny were fighting in South Africa and she was understandably incensed that her boys should be risking their lives while critics of the war carped and complained at home.[56] She never forgot that she was the wife of a soldier, and one of her other voices was that of a flag-waving Tory lady. 'In England,' she wrote in a patriotic tone, 'we prefer the men found dead with the colours of their regiment wrapped around them to the reformers who cynically advise the disuse of the flag as a useless coloured rag.'[57]

Two articles with her reflections on the status of French and English women are the most interesting of her pieces published in this period. The first of these, 'The Role of Women in Society, I. In Eighteenth-Century France', appeared in *The Nineteenth Century* for December 1900. In the same issue were articles by Leslie Stephen on Darwin's defender, T.H. Huxley, and by Prince Kropotkin, a prominent Russian intellectual and anarchist, on 'Recent Science'. She was in distinguished company. In many ways these articles represented the fulfilment of her dreams. Here she was in conversation with the best minds of the century and writing about a topic that had occupied her since she was a girl, the position and status of women in civilised society. The emphasis was on 'civilised' society, for only England and France counted with her. America and Germany were out of the question. She was also more concerned with drawing rooms, manners and influence over politicians than questions of civil rights or the vote. She was not moved by the agitations of Emmeline Pankhurst and others for female suffrage. When Ethel Smyth became involved in the suffragist marches and militancy before the First World War, MEP criticised the movement as being full of 'publicity-seeking hysterics'.[58] Rather, what interested her most was the way in which upper-class women might captivate a salon and use a social setting to promote political or aesthetic ideas. More than this she was interested in the question of charm, the art of pleasing people. Part of the fascination of these articles is that they set out her ideas not only on women, but also by extension about how the art of pleasing was central to the monarchy, as the Ponsonbys and the queen understood it.

She began by remarking that noble women who held salons in eighteenth-century France were nearly always more powerful than eighteenth-century English women. She was speaking of a small minority, mainly of the court nobility and their wives. She was critical of their artifice and extravagance, sometimes of their 'frantic struggle against ennui', sometimes of their uncritical 'ardour for knowledge' when under the influence of the Enlightenment. What she most admired in these *salonnières*, an attribute that they shared with English women of the same period, was their good manners.

Sometimes MEP sounds a little insufferable in these articles. She details the strengths and weaknesses of *la vie en château* to a middle-class readership as if they were as familiar as she was with country house life. Still, when it comes to describing the manners of these women, MEP comes near to recommending an aristocratic style that can, should and ought to be accessible to a reader of any class, or gender.

> The acquirement of a perfect manner may seem but a trivial aim; but when we find the code of rules to be observed to include delicacy of touch in dealing with the feelings of others, a readiness of perception as to what would cause offence, the avoidance of all unnecessary friction, the art of praising without flattery, of showing off the merits of others without appearing to protect them; and if you add to these characteristics the charm of ease and naturalness, and the feeling that air, manner and speech combine to convey graceful and intelligent kindness, you feel inclined to agree with the author quoted by the De Goncourts who compared the spirit of society at that time with the spirit of charity, a bold comparison, a little in the way of a very modern saying that defines 'tact as inspiration in small things'.[59]

Interestingly, the one word that occurs over and over again in those who have described the requirements of a private secretary to the sovereign is 'tact'. While apparently setting out to describe the manners of courts in the age of absolutism, she ended by emphasising the art involved in tactful dealing with others. It was an art Henry had perfected, which she admired and thought anyone could acquire.

The next article, 'The Role of Women in Society, II. In Nineteenth-Century England', is principally a comparison between the English salon hostesses of her mother's generation in the 1850s and the 'new'

women of the 1890s. She confessed that the women produced by
colleges for women, Newnham and Girton, were a disappointment in
the 1890s. They were dull and pedantic, while society at large
continued to love dress and beauty. No educating of a few future
schoolmistresses at the ancient universities could improve the position
of women in society, she argued, as the power of worship had in the
middle ages. 'The cult of the Virgin Mary in the Middle Ages did far
more to raise the status of women than any other cause at work since
the age of chivalry, and the efforts towards intellectual discipline in our
day are futile in comparison.'[60] As for the great Whig hostesses who
were giving parties when her mother first brought her and her sisters to
London, they too had died out and ceased to exercise their former sway.
These ladies' own enthusiasm for Enlightenment egalitarianism had
sapped their aristocratic self-confidence: 'manners became democra-
tized, *salons* lost their prestige because the entertainer no longer
believed in herself.'[61] Lady Palmerston, Lady Granville and Lady
Holland had been the last of the self-confident Whig *salonnières*. MEP's
old friend, Frances, Lady Waldegrave, who had so scandalised the
serious young Mary Bulteel with her eat-drink-and-be-merry philosophy in the 1850s, had tried but not quite succeeded in imitating them
at Strawberry Hill. What she found lacking in the women of her own
day, which all the women who formerly ran *salons* had in abundance,
was charm. Charm she wrote was a 'mystery' composed on the one
hand of physical, sensual beauty and on the other of 'wit', 'intellectual
fire', and 'quickness of apprehension'. In the peroration of the article
there is a romantic tremolo in her voice as she imagines what the ideal
English woman of the new century might be. 'I dream of a possible
woman having something of the frank, fearless grace, the self-reliant
daring, the open-air freedom of the Englishwoman of the past. Give her
also charm and sympathy and capability of deep passion ... '[62] Then she
breaks off, almost as if she has revealed too much and ends the article
with a refusal to predict what Englishwomen might become in the new
century.

This article was noticed in at least one of the daily newspapers, which
recommended MEP's articles to the attention of its readers.[63] Although
there were other articles she published in those years,[64] these two on
women were among her best. She loved singing the praises of aristocratic women, she loved imagining powerful and independent women
having the confidence to conquer the social heights some of their ancestors had done. She loved entering into a debate about the new woman,
in which all the contributors had so far been intent on reconstructing

social institutions so as to give women more civil rights and liberties. She argued that in fact noblewomen at Versailles, or in mid-Victorian Mayfair, had more power, position and place than modern women did in the year 1900.

Her son, Arthur, and her friend, A.C. Benson, both agreed that her writing was a little too dense, not really like her and not nearly as good as her conversation.[65] Of everything she wrote for publication, however, the most successful, and undoubtedly the most important, was a collaborative article she wrote with Edmund Gosse on Queen Victoria for *The Quarterly Review* in 1901. It has none of the faults of the other pieces because it was actually written by Gosse, a critic who had given his life to writing, from notes supplied by MEP, who had spent a lifetime at the court of the queen. It has both immediacy and authenticity: and it caused a sensation.

The Death of Queen Victoria

It is hard now to recapture the sense of shock created by the death of Queen Victoria in January 1901. She had been on the throne for more than half a century and very few people could remember the time before her accession in 1837. Even MEP, who was certainly a friend of the queen's, but who liked to pride herself on being above sentimentality about the royal family, confessed to Ethel Smyth that she had a 'dazed feeling' far more profound than she had expected. Ethel remembered MEP telling her after the queen's death that 'apart from the grief, which is one of the greatest sorrows of my life, everything being changed makes me at times doubt my own individuality'.[66] Her sense of her self was shaken.

Members of her family felt the same shock. Arthur Ponsonby, then a young diplomat at the Foreign Office, recalled what the queen had meant to him as well as to his mother and father.

The Queen. The word, the name, the idea the person seem so extraordinarily familiar as I cannot remember any time when I was not very conscious of her existence. The excitement of her presents on Xmas Eve, the Xmas tree at Osborne and being taught to make a bow. Searching for Easter eggs in the corridor at Windsor. The Queen's carriage with the well-known outrider, watching it coming in and out from the nursery window at Norman Tower. Her visits to Kent House or Osborne Cottage when we all made our bow and she smiled and said something to us. Papa and Mama dining with her and coming home and telling us about it. In fact she was connected with every day of our lives. And then as page I saw her in an official light, the same kind smiling old lady but in diamonds and crown and orders surrounded by courtiers and princes and I in uncomfortable picturesque clothes – 10 or 12 drawing rooms ... [S]he was an institution. One could not imagine it otherwise. Windsor and Osborne were all hers, every path, every room. It seemed impossible that they can belong to any one else. Before I went out to Constantinople she had me to dinner and spoke to me of my profession and her interest in the Armenian Question and again when I came home and again when I was married – she saw us both privately – never forgetting she knew what Papa was to her, what he had been to her and she was not reminded but remembered herself to keep an eye on all of us in the middle of the hundreds who were dependent on her. She gave England distinction there is no other word for it.

Nevertheless, bearing in mind how much she and the whole family admired, even loved the departed queen, MEP was annoyed by the popular hysteria about her. The newspapers represented the queen as a saint, a divinity, an impossibly good, impossibly wise woman. It was not unlike the Diana hysteria of the late 1990s. MEP thought that it was all nonsense. When it was proposed that she should contribute a more realistic assessment of the queen, she felt inclined to agree.

How MEP had come to know Edmund Gosse is unclear. He was a well-known poet, critic and man of letters at the turn of the century, who had some success writing literary biographies. It might have been through A.C. Benson, or her nephew, Maurice Baring, or her daughter, Magdalen, all of whom also knew and liked Gosse. Gosse approached her on behalf of John Murray, the publisher of *The Quarterly Review*, a few weeks after the queen's death in January 1901.[67] Would she write an appreciation of the queen? Murray was the head of an eminent publishing dynasty. *The Quarterly*, though past its early nineteenth-century prime when it had provided a conservative forum for reply to the liberal *Edinburgh Review*, was still dully respectable. MEP was flattered by the approach of these literary and publishing luminaries. She had also assembled some notes on the queen for an article James Knowles, the editor of *The Nineteenth Century*, had commissioned at the time of the Diamond Jubilee in 1897. Significantly, the queen had refused when she applied for permission to write the earlier article: perhaps there was some *pique* in her determination to go ahead with the new article. Still, she had her doubts and suggested to Gosse that he write the article and make use of her notes.

She immediately had second thoughts about even that arrangement, withdrawing her offer the next day, but later giving in to persuasion from Gosse that they should work together on the article. He would write it, using her notes, and they would meet to consult about it, though he would also consult other sources. The correspondence that has survived shows that she was delighted, though occasionally worried, by their collaboration. She liked Gosse himself, was pleased that he should be incorporating large sections of her notes with little revision and also concerned that her contribution should be concealed. The new king had not given her permission to go ahead and she wanted to preserve her son Fritz's place at court. Fritz was assistant private secretary and assistant privy purse, and hoped one day to succeed to his father's old offices. He was not popular with the new private secretary, Francis Knollys, who had demoted him and reduced his pay by hiring a second assistant when the new king came to the throne. MEP certainly did not want to endanger Fritz's career further. On the other hand, few people were as well placed as she was to describe the queen; few people had grown old with the queen as she had.

The article begins with MEP's love of contradiction and her contempt for exaggerated worship of princes. No one really knew what the queen was like. Most of the recent outpourings in the press were based on guesswork and the 'semi-religious admiration' of the queen was, the article hinted, more than a little hysterical. It was time to settle down and ask, how far was the late queen 'worthy of the idolatry' she had 'awakened? How much of the worship was paid to a woman, and how much to a fetish?'[68] The answer to these questions comes quickly. Though still paying tribute to the queen, the article intends to cut her down to size. 'The time has come,' the article continues,

> to abandon the note of purely indiscriminate praise, to put even this revered personage into the crucible of criticism – to endeavour, in other words, to note, without any blind or sycophantic laudation, what were the elements, and what the evolution of her character.[69]

The article retains a high Victorian belief in 'character' as a sort of moral chemistry that heroes have and others do not. At the same time, it has a post-Victorian, pre-Bloomsbury emphasis on wishing to see the queen as 'a rather ordinary mortal'.[70] For example, one of the principal, truth-telling criticisms of the queen's character is that the queen was an obstinate woman.

Criticism, however, does not dominate in the article. Indeed, MEP shows how much she admired the queen's 'exquisite manner' and 'human genuineness' by making her into an eighteenth-century *salon-nière*. Rather than the bourgeois *hausfrau* that had been indicated by the press and royal hagiographers, the article insists that Queen Victoria's special charm

> was made up of spontaneous kindliness and freedom from all embarrass-ment, built upon this eighteenth-century style or manner which she had inherited or adopted. She acted as a great lady of 1790 might have acted, not because she felt herself to have good 'manners,' but because that was how great ladies, trained as she had been trained, naturally behaved, with a perfect grace based upon unsuspecting simplicity.[71]

MEP had had enough of the queen being compared to a middle-class wife: 'the Queen was trammelled by no *bourgeois* fear of not doing the right thing.'[72] Rather, she had the unselfconscious appeal of a Whig hostess. This description appears to be as much a projection of Mary Ponsonby's ideals and preoccupations as the 'middle-class wife' was of the typical turn of the century journalist.

Another interesting feature of the *Quarterly Review* article is the way it returns to theatrical concerns. The article contends that much of the queen's brilliance came from her instinct as an actor and a stage manager. The queen knew how to move like an actor and 'she was never flurried by a space in front of her'.[73] Further, in later years when there was a revival of amateur theatricals at court along with new invitations to West End companies to perform at court,

> she was always an acute observer, and, when she consented to advise, a superlatively practical stage-manager; while, when professional compa-nies came down to act before her – an event to which she looked forward eagerly, and which she enjoyed like a child – it was always the effective theatrical movement which interested her the most.[74]

On the whole it was light comedy that pleased the queen most. 'She enjoyed a good farce, and laughed heartily at the jokes.'[75] She also liked Italian opera, particularly 'Norma' and 'Carmen … And the pieces of Gilbert and Sullivan were an endless delight to her; she would even take a part in these, very drolly and prettily'.[76]

The amusements of the queen's court, as MEP remembered them, were punctuated by operetta as often as by arias from grand opera. The article itself makes the queen the centrepiece of a mildly comical piece of theatre, rather than the she-god of a great empire. For example, MEP tells the story of how, after some eastern ambassadors had bowed out of the room with 'exquisite salaams' and squeezing their hands between their knees 'as men struggling with acute internal pain', the door finally closed. The queen and the household standing around her all broke into helpless laughter, the queen saying through her sobs, 'But I went through it, I did go right through it.'[77] This was hardly the imperial queen the press and others had made her out to be. Rather, she emerges from the article a jolly – although sometimes difficult – woman who could laugh at herself, sing a silly song and tap her feet along with everyone else to 'I'm the head of the queen's na-vy'.

An element of autobiography is in the article as well. Lady Canning, MEP's first mentor and *culte*, makes two appearances. MEP describes Lady Canning doing precisely the sort of things she aimed to do as maid of honour, that is attempting, without success, to convert the queen to high church views, as well as developing the queen's taste in art by encouraging her to admire the Pre-Raphaelite painters.[78] Whether MEP thus attributed to Charlotte Canning efforts that were really more in her line than Lady Canning's is difficult to say. The article goes on to make clear that though the queen and MEP knew one another well, Mary was perhaps always a little suspect in the queen's eyes. The queen

> was always a little afraid of 'clever' women; and a reputation for superior intelligence was no recommendation in her eyes. She liked the ladies about her to have extremely good manners and a pretty presence, but she shrank away from any woman who, she feared, was 'going to be clever.' It had been very early instilled into her that it was man's province to be clever, and that it was best for woman not to intrude into it.[79]

MEP remembered that Lady Canning had warned her that the queen did not make friends among her ladies. 'You will be delighted with your waiting at Balmoral or Osborne,' Charlotte Canning had told her in the 1850s.

> 'You will see the Queen intimately, riding, dancing, playing, dining. You will think she cannot get on without you. And then you will come back one day to Windsor, and somebody else will take your place, and you will have become a number on the list.'[80]

The queen's 'engrained professional habit made her free of all her ladies'.[81] Though Mary had been told this from the very start, it is also possible to see in these passages the resentment of a wife who was frequently left behind when the court moved. There is a tinge of frustration for having been suspected of motivating her husband's radical views, a hint of revenge for having been denied the privilege of writing what would have been a loyal article at the time of the 1897 jubilee.

Remarkable too in the *Quarterly Review* article is its attempt to memorialise Henry. Everyone described Henry's genius as a complete effacement of self. She wanted him to have some recognition. 'The secret of the power' Queen Victoria's private secretaries 'exercised was faithfully kept from the public, and will always be kept'.[82] By highlighting this MEP was emphasising that there were secrets to be kept and that her own husband, as the principal of the queen's private secretaries, exercised an influence exactly in proportion to his ability to take himself out of the limelight. The less people knew about him the more they should realise what a powerful presence behind the throne he had been.

That issue of *The Quarterly* had a significant sale. In the lobby of the House of Commons the Liberal leaders of the opposition – Harcourt, Spencer, Asquith and Morley – all speculated about who might have written it. Randall Davidson, bishop of Winchester and former dean of Windsor, had his ideas. The new king, Edward VII, was incensed. He thought it was much too personal as well as too critical of his mother. Gosse and MEP both dissimulated when asked by their friends whether or not they had written the article. Through Fritz, the king sent to ask MEP directly whether she had written it. She answered that she had *not* written it, which was technically true. She added that she thought it very good. She even kept up the secret with her own children, warning Gosse not to tell Betty, who was suspicious. Fritz, who was charged with carrying messages to the king, never knew the whole story either. In his *Recollections of Three Reigns* he remembered that the *Quarterly Review* article had given 'great offense'.[83] MEP realised that she had got into hot water; though she at first thought of accepting Gosse's proposal that she share half the fee for the article, she later thought better of it, even though she needed the money. After leaving the Norman Tower, she had bought a house in South Ascot, but she was compelled to let it for several summers in order to raise some cash. In order to maintain the deception that she had had no part in the piece, however, she later wondered whether any money owing to her could come via Magdalen. Later still, she thought the fee ought to go simply from *The Quarterly* to a charity she would name, for example to a fund meant to support nurses established at the time of the first jubilee. It is unclear whether, in the end, she took any money at all for her share in the work.

It was the convention during the queen's long reign that her inner circle did not speak to the press or publish memoirs about their time with her. The queen herself had been very angry about the publication of the Greville diaries, which she thought too frank about the weaknesses of her uncles, George IV and William IV. She was angrier still when Baron Stockmar's son published a life of his father with some anodyne recollections about the court. Lady Ely and Sir William Jenner sometimes spoke to *The Times*, probably by command, about the queen's health preventing her coming more to London. One of the political lords in waiting, Lord Torrington, also supplied some gossip about the court to the newspapers in the 1860s, almost certainly without the queen's consent. There was also an anonymous account of the queen's daily life, based on authentic information, published in 1897. The unsold copies were withdrawn from sale by command as soon as the queen learned about it.[84]

The MEP and Gosse collaboration was the first critical piece on the queen to be based on privileged, inside information. As a genre, insider gossip about the court was a recognised and long-established form of story telling. Horace Walpole had published his waspish recollections of the court of George II. Diarists such as Creevey and Greville had included scandalmongering detail from the courts of George IV and William IV in their books. It was simply that Queen Victoria as moral, 'middle-class' mother and widow, rising above her Hanoverian ancestors, had never been subjected to the same treatment. This was an attitude that was not disloyal, but certainly not solemn either. It was what courtiers had thought for ages. The sovereign was a necessary figure at the apex of the state who was owed respect, but the human being who occupied that position need not be regarded as sacred. It was as if this attitude, much more characteristic of the Augustan age than of the Victorian, had left the Ponsonby dinner table and found its way for the first time, after a long pause, back into print.

This is also the general tenor of Fritz Ponsonby's books on the royal family, published after the First World War. There were three and he showed his mother's bold disregard for royal disapproval in publishing them. The first and most controversial of them was *Letters of the Empress Frederick*.[85] The empress, his godmother, had given him several boxes of her papers to remove from Germany when she was dying of cancer in 1901. The letters, which he decided to publish after the First World War, made abundantly clear how ill-treated she had been by her son, Kaiser Willhelm II. The book portrayed the empress as a misunderstood mother and her son as a blackguard. Both the former kaiser, then exiled in Holland, and King George V tried to stop Fritz from publishing, but he pressed ahead and the book sold well. There was more than one English edition and a German one as well. Certainly Fritz, like his mother, needed the money, for unlike the private secretaries and keepers of the privy purse in George IV's time, none of the Ponsonbys made a fortune in royal service.

The next two of Fritz's books were more satirical. *Sidelights on Queen Victoria*, published in 1930, tells a series of stories culled from Henry's memoranda on court controversies. *Recollections of Three Reigns*, which he was preparing at the time of his death in 1935 and which was put into shape by Colin Welch for publication in 1951, was a book that delighted two connoisseurs of the absurd. Nancy Mitford described it to Evelyn Waugh as having 'a shriek on every page'.[86] Both books give grave accounts of ridiculous events. Fritz describes band members who were late for a dinner during which they were meant to play at Windsor creeping in via the windows. Queen Alexandra, on the royal train going to Berlin for a state visit, has quails dumped into her hair by a jolted waiter. Fritz tells of visiting royalties during an official visit being taken by equerries after dark, disguised in tweed jackets, to Islington for an off-colour music-hall review. In another story Queen Victoria is incandescent with rage because one of the doctors has dined with the ladies in waiting rather than with the upper servants where he belongs. The effect of these stories is to bring the monarchy alive, not by describing the virtues of princes, but by making the whole edifice rock with singsongs and farcical *faux pas*. Fritz Ponsonby took after his parents and his books are the Ponsonbys' twentieth-century legacy. They are evidence of the family's continuing influence on the public face of the throne. By all means, they seem to be saying, bow and bend the knee to the living representatives of Britain's parliamentary monarchy, but don't miss the dogs under the dinner table which bring it down to human scale.

Gentle Descent

After this flurry of literary activity lasting from about 1896 to 1903, Mary Ponsonby gradually slowed down. She went out less, ceased to go abroad and divided her time between her house in South Ascot, Gilmuire, and St James's. Occasionally her bachelor friends, who idolised her, came to call. A.C. Benson recorded one such occasion in 1904.

> So we had tea, or as much as Lady P. would give us; for she drank none herself and paid no attention, with a kind of lordly indifference to the tea

tray. She is a very impressive and interesting woman. She set out to be as happy as possible; but she has a great interest in others and a very tender heart, in spite of her keen and fastidious mind. But she would never give in to any idealizing stuff about love and self-sacrifice being the only things worth having. No: food and drink and occupation and books and talk, all the furniture of life ...

were what she recommended to Benson as a recipe for happiness.[87]

Gosse also came to see her regularly. One day in 1906, when she had been ill, she had an odd experience with him. Her doctor had prescribed her taking Indian hemp, or marijuana. This made her see two Gosses at once, 'a shadowy one in front and a real one behind'. High on the hemp, she told Gosse some false stories about Madame Benkendorff, the wife of the Austrian ambassador. She later told Benson that the stories were 'not *quite* untrue' but she had stated to Gosse as 'fact what were vague possibilities in Mme B.'s mind'. Later she heard Gosse pass these stories on to her daughter Betty and she was obliged to contradict him in front of the whole party: 'Mr. Gosse, how dare you tell Betty as *true*, what I told you were only my fancies as to what might happen'. Gosse sat and palely accepted this rebuke, but MEP was later in agonies about whether she had forfeited his friendship. She had not; he only told Benson when he saw him later in a club, 'Ah! You will find poor Lady P. much broken and aged!'[88]

The next year, in 1907, Benson found MEP at St James's 'in that pretty, dark room with its big bow window looking out on Stafford House'. She was 'pale and frail and old, but *full* of go'.[89] And in 1912 he lunched with her at St James's when she was 'nearing 80' and described her to be 'full of courage, interest and lively malice'.[90] She also continued to make short trips to see her children nearby. She went to stay with Arthur and his wife at the medieval priory near Haslemere they had moved to in 1902. Her one requirement from her hosts was that there should be a sort of low table in every room so that she could make notes on books as she sat in a comfortable chair. Until the very end she lost none of her fight and could still be a formidable personality. Fritz's daughter, Loelia, remembered being deeply impressed as a child with the curt way her grandmother dismissed one of her nannies who tried to stop her from playing at cutting up coloured papers on MEP's bed. 'That will be all' MEP said coldly and the vanquished nanny retired in confusion.[91]

In the last years of her life she wrote in her journal some calm reflections on old age. She was grateful to her children and especially to Maggie.

I can't write here what she is to me. Never making me feel for a moment the inevitable truth that every year must make me more and more of a burden to myself and necessarily to others. But they are all so wonderfully patient and kind and it makes me perfectly indifferent as to what the outside world would say or do.[92]

In about 1908 she was trying to write an article on mystery and mysticism:

which I shall never finish, but I am all of a sudden stopped by the realisation of how little time I have before me.

I have no fear of death but to any one within measurable distance of that awful mystery it seems incredible it should not be more overwhelming. I cannot say I am afraid but occasionally there is a feeling of hushed silence which I feel might be prolonged for ever. If it is suggested in a book or by a friend that it is surprising I should not be curious about what we call the next world, I must own that it is owing to my conviction that it is impossible that any one should know what the absolute and positive abstract truth is about any thing, that I am content to try and adapt my life, my thoughts, my ideals to a relative standard which is all I can realize. I do not think this diminishes the sense of mystery which must come and its accompanying terror, loneliness. *Je mourrai seul* [I will die alone] said Pascal and that is very awful.

She still had the impulse to list her faults, among which she counted 'inefficiency' and 'ineptitude', but she was now willing to speak honestly too about the good side of her personality.

Two or three redeeming points make my inner self find now and then a firm resting place where I can pause and almost take heart again. Sincerity in admiration and a passionate desire to give full credit to others for success in their work and especially where I have failed. Sincerity in indignation roused by the mean silly conventional cruelty of the prosperous to the strugglers for life. Indignation fierce and deep for cruelty to children, to the helpless and *les déclassés*. Sincerity of expression in speaking of books and authors, dreading to speak of them as if I knew more that I would allow. Having made this confession of merit (!) to myself, I will not bore myself with alluding to it again.[93]

When the war came in 1914, Mary Ponsonby was 82. Two of her boys, Johnny and Fritz, went to fight in France. Arthur, who had been elected to Parliament and was a committed pacifist, stood up and denounced the war in the House of Commons. 'Never for a moment did she blame me; never for a moment did she even show displeasure,' he remembered. 'On the contrary after an unusually virulent attack on me from many quarters I received the most loving letter of sympathy with an amusingly violent denunciation of my opponents.'[94]

At length, in 1916, MEP was confined to her bed at Gilmuire. It was clearly the end, but she charmed her worried children at the bedside by pretending not to know how ill she was. She could still get in a comment on a favourite author. When she noticed Betty sitting by the bedside reading Mill, she said 'He is so clear, isn't he?'[95] Ethel Smyth, whom she had seen less often of late, came in for a moment and pressed her hand.

Mary Ponsonby died on 16 October 1916. Though it must have been apparent that it had been coming for a long time Arthur was so distressed that he broke off writing his regular diary for months. His wife, Dorothea, wrote in her diary

> [O]ld though she was she played such an immense part in all our lives – there was no question of anybody finding her a bore and a trouble – she contributed so much. And the close of her life seemed to me the most wonderful part of it. She grew gentler and more loving – and her humility was so touching – one could not bear it when she thanked one for being kind – when it was such a great privilege to be allowed to see her and talk to her. To the end she remained extraordinarily shrewd and detached – and with her affections as strong as ever. She was vital to a degree and this has kept her alive – A[rthur] says her eyes have been so wonderfully bright ... I am so thankful they were all with her at the End including Johnny. She thanked them for being there – it must have been a comfort to her – she didn't suffer and Arthur held her hand as she died.

A.C. Benson wrote an appreciation for *The Times* and confided to his diary: 'She was very good and kind to me and I had a great affection for her. She never fussed about her friends, and I am ashamed to have seen her too seldom of late.'[96]

The roughly £70,000 left behind in 1895 after Henry's death had diminished to between £12,000 and £17,000 in 1916.[97] Gilmuire went to Johnny, who sold it. Given the young Mary Bulteel's yearning to join a religious order, it seems appropriate that Gilmuire was eventually to become a residence for nuns connected with a Catholic girls' school.[98] MEP's effects were divided up among her other children, with her will specifying which jewellery, furniture and pictures were to go to whom. Johnny was to have 'the silver canteen service for six people' given by the duke of Wellington to Henry's father. To Fritz she left 'my Ponsonby whatnot' and a 'silver cornered Cabinet made by myself'. To Betty she left a 'silver Cabinet which formerly belonged to Mary Stuart'. She left Maggie 'six silver cups with coins which were given to me by her late Majesty Queen Victoria'. To Arthur went a small Louis XVI marquetry table.[99]

There were two memorial services for her, one at St Paul's, Knightsbridge, where she had been married in 1861, which was attended by the prime minister, H.H. Asquith, and Arthur Bigge, now Lord Stamfordham, on behalf of the king. Her family attended a service at All Souls near Gilmuire in South Ascot. Sadly, the first line of her will, in which she asked to be buried next to Henry in the churchyard at Whippingham on the Isle of Wight, had to be disobeyed. The First World War was raging across the channel, shipping was strictly regulated and many steamers requisitioned for use by the armed forces. It was thought impossible to take her coffin across the Solent and bury her next to her husband. Instead, a small line was engraved at the bottom of the stone marking Henry's grave saying she *should* have been buried with him, but that her body had to be interred in South Ascot. Grass and lichens now obscure this last tribute to Mary, engraved on Henry's simple gravestone. His grave is difficult to find in the churchyard, so humble and unremarkable is it among the more elaborate and towering memorials to Victorian royalties. It is behind a tall yew hedge and ornate stone dedicated to one of the Battenberg princes. If Henry and Mary could look from beyond the grave at that big Battenberg stone, how they might glance at one another with twinkling eyes and smile with delight.

Epilogue

Nearly half a century after the death of his father, and twenty-six years after the death of his mother, Arthur Ponsonby prepared to publish a volume of biography entitled *Henry Ponsonby, Queen Victoria's Private Secretary: His Life from His Letters*. He submitted his text to the palace for approval and ran into serious difficulties. The letters he exchanged with King George VI's librarian and private secretaries about the book make fascinating reading. Not only do these letters show the spirit of the Ponsonbys still alive well into the twentieth century, they also show something that has been missing from recent accounts of how the Victorian monarchy worked and what its function was. The current literature on the monarchy lacks a dimension that Arthur Ponsonby's book throws into high relief. Above all looking through these letters helps to resolve what appears a curious contradiction in the lives of Henry and Mary Ponsonby. How to understand a lifetime of service to the crown that was the subject of so many suppertime *fou rires*?

*

In 1927 Magdalen Ponsonby published *Mary Ponsonby, A Memoir, Some Letters and A Journal*. The family considered this a success, but all the children were daunted by the much larger collection of their father's papers that survived. Johnny had inherited the papers from his mother and started to put them in order. Fritz also made some attempts at organisation, but he died in 1935, aged 68, before he could complete the task. Then Arthur took over all the boxes and began to read through them with the object of writing an account of his father's life.[1] In 1938, before he began writing, he decided to consult the king's librarian, Owen Morshead. Morshead was also assistant keeper of the Royal Archives. It was his job to advise the royal family about what they should allow to be published from among the collections of their papers. Arthur Ponsonby sent Morshead a private letter asking whether there would be any official bar to the publication of his father's papers.

    Morshead returned an unofficial reply. He told Arthur that his letter would 'be regarded as strictly private. I typewrite this reply myself, and shall file the correspondence separately from official matters.'[2]

Morshead's letter mixed warning and caution with encouragement. He enclosed an article from *The Times* of 20 July 1933 pointing out that royal copyright was so framed that the

> correspondence of a Private Secretary is reckoned in the eyes of the Law as that of his august employer. No doubt your father's papers do comprise documents which may legitimately be regarded as his own property; but equally there will be others the copyright of which is vested (not for a term of years but for ever) in the Sovereign.[3]

Morshead also told Arthur that 'the King has in the past been (rightly as I am sure you will agree) jealous of his important right to control so far as he is able any revelations of the inner working of the Monarchy'.

The letter was sympathetic in tone, however, and indicated obliquely that it would be fine for Arthur to proceed with his biography. Morshead said that 'During the 12 years in which I have been interested in such things the King has adopted a generous policy' with regard to those who sought to publish documents of which he controlled the copyright. He added, 'and after all your father's period is becoming remote now'. Although Morshead was nominally junior to the keeper of the Archives, Lord Wigram, a retired private secretary still living in the Norman Tower and sometimes advising the king, he told Arthur that it would be best not to consult the higher-ups at that point. He offered instead 'unofficial assistance in the elucidating of specific points, and you can rely on a friendly reception to any request'.[4] Arthur concluded that although there were risks, he might go ahead.

By January 1942, four years later, he had written the book, had it typed and Macmillan, his publisher, had produced proofs for him to correct. Everything promised well. His sister, Betty, and Morshead had looked at the typescript and made suggestions. Arthur now submitted the proofs officially for the king's sanction, as the book contained not only letters written by his father, but also a number of letters from Queen Victoria which her great grandson, George VI, would have to approve before he could publish them.

Three men looked at the proofs before the king saw them. Wigram had spent most of his career in the service of George V and had relinquished his official connection with the king's private office, but he was still consulted. The other two were Alexander Hardinge, George VI's principal private secretary, and Alan Lascelles, Hardinge's deputy. Hardinge's health had suffered with the strain of serving Edward VIII in the months leading up to the abdication in 1936, and he too was on the verge of retirement. Lascelles was the coming man, who would serve as the king's private secretary for the rest of the reign and in the first year of the new reign of Elizabeth II that began in 1952. All three liked Arthur's book after having read the proofs. Lascelles told Morshead that he thought the book 'a triumph' and he was 'reporting warmly on it' to Hardinge. The only cut he was proposing, Morshead wrote Arthur, 'concerns your perfectly true debunking of King Edward VII; the passage in which *you* (not your father, be it noted) say that he was all façade. So he was; and had the revelation been made by H.F.P. it might have passed.' Lascelles thought this might be needlessly insulting to the king, who could recall his grandfather perfectly, while 'Queen Victoria he regards as ancient history'.[5]

Lascelles confirmed what Morshead had already told him when he wrote Arthur in the middle of January 1942 to say:

> As who should know better than yourself, the literature through which the Sovereign's private secretaries have to wade usually brings them more grief than pleasure.
>
> So, having been privileged in my official capacity to read through the proofs of your forthcoming book, I must tell you how immensely I enjoyed it. Apart from the professional interest it must have for any of us who try humbly to follow in Sir Henry's footsteps, it is a really good biography; and there are many passages in it which made me laugh out loud …
>
> I wish I had known your father; but the reading of his letters makes one feel that there are, after all, compensations in a private secretary's life … [6]

All three of those who read the proofs recognised the work of Henry Ponsonby as having established the principles for their own. Wigram, who was living in the rooms where Arthur had grown up as a boy, told him that 'I only wish I had seen the book before I was a Private Secretary, as I think I could have taken some tips from him. His portrait hangs on the wall of the Prison Room together with all the other Private Secretaries who lived in Norman Tower'.[7] Hardinge also wrote Arthur a warm letter saying, 'I need not tell you that, as one of Sir Henry's humble successors, I read the proofs with the utmost interest. I hope it is not presumptuous on my part to say that I think we must have had a good deal in common!'[8]

The king now had the proofs submitted to him and he passed them on to his mother, Queen Mary. After looking at them, she wrote Morshead an indignant letter. She objected strongly to the book, indeed to the whole principle of the book. She said that 'she was shocked and horrified that the private affairs of the Royal Family should be put into print for the benefit of the public: how anyone in Sir Henry's position could write to his wife about such matter passed her comprehension ... '[9] Queen Mary was of the old school. Born in 1867, she was accustomed to the more rigid decorum of the Victorian era. Henry's wry letters to Mary, sending up much of what was meant to be solemn, she regarded as an example of disloyalty at the very heart of the household where one ought to have been able to count on unquestioning devotion.

Her opposition surprised Morshead. He had been writing her letters preparing her to like the book since the previous summer. He had also told her of Arthur's generosity in giving all of his father's official papers to the Royal Archives now that the book was finished. When he learned of her opposition he wrote her putting the case for openness and allowing Arthur wide latitude in publishing his book. He believed that 'this kind of book, written by somebody who is (in Disraeli's phrase) on the side of the angels, is a healthy and wise concession to modern opinion, its kindly frankness making imaginary and unhealthy books by second-rate writers not worth while'.

He went on to make a larger point about the freedom of information in Britain. One of the features of Britain in wartime was that, relative to Nazi propaganda on the continent, the news was still reliable; bad news was conveyed to the public along with the good. He had heard from a Belgian minister that everyone in Belgium 'listens to the B.B.C. news because it gives the rough with the smooth; they felt it was not faked news'. Similarly, it was in the monarchy's interest to allow the publication of criticism. He told Queen Mary that

> we must carry the public with us; and the best way to do this is to take the initiative from time to time and release a book like this. I feel that an enlightened policy of this sort strengthens the Monarchy, by demonstrating beyond the need for argument that it is strong enough to be able to act so.

The monarchy benefited from frank revelations, rather than the reverse.

However, the opposition of the king's mother made the older secretaries hedge. Wigram and Hardinge now began to have their doubts about the book and wondered whether the king should not forbid it. Lascelles, the younger man, was a modernist and still in favour. He told Morshead 'it should certainly be published'.[10] Lascelles understood Henry's resentment at being taken so often away from his wife; he also understood Henry's perverse enjoyment of some of the absurdities of royal service and the way his sense of humour helped him to cope with the sacrifices involved.

Morshead had by now so thoroughly identified himself with the project that he was the book's strongest supporter in the household. He went out of his way to keep Arthur informed at every step of the way. He even relayed a telephone conversation he had with the king to show that there was still hope. 'The King rang me up on the telephone at 7 o'clock' Morshead told Arthur

> and said, in what I judged to be a tone of appreciative amusement, 'Have you heard any more about THAT BOOK?' To which I replied, 'Not a word, Sir. I wrote to Queen Mary ... ' ('Yes, I know; Alec [Hardinge] shewed me a copy of what you said') ... 'since when I have had two letters from Her Majesty concerning normal Library affairs, but making no reference to the matter of the book.'

According to Morshead, the king had been 'reading the book with great enjoyment' and he had only one suggestion about deleting a phrase so as to improve rather than to censor one of Arthur's anecdotes. Morshead believed that the king

> was taking quite the modernist view of the book; and it dovetailed in with what Tommy [Lascelles] has been telling me lately, namely that he thinks we shall find that the (present) Queen favours its publication.

The king would now have to persuade his mother that the book should go ahead. Morshead thought there was reasonable hope that the king would succeed in mollifying her.

Morshead added that 'Our strong point, as it seems to me, is this: that Queen Mary's objection is not to any particular incidents so much as to the appearance of the book as a whole. Now clearly we cannot demand the suppression of the entire work'; nor would 'omission of all direct quotations' that the king could legally enforce satisfy Queen Mary's objection. Morshead conceded that the copyright act gave them extraordinary powers, but 'I can hardly think we should ever deem it wise to employ' these powers 'in their full amplitude'.[11] In other words, full enforcement of the provisions of the law that allowed the king to forbid certain passages would only forfeit Arthur's and perhaps the public's goodwill. This would be a significant loss for the monarchy's popularity. At the same time, if they were to enforce deletion of passages over which the king controlled the copyright, they could not stop the book as a whole because Arthur had many documents in it that were legitimately his own. Requiring many passages to be deleted would fail to meet the older generation's demand that the book be suppressed.

Faced with the possibility that his book might be altered, or even banned, Arthur looked for other allies to put his case to the king's mother. He wrote to Lady Cynthia Colville, one of Queen Mary's ladies in waiting, whose father, the marquess of Crewe, had been prominent in Liberal politics at the turn of the century. Arthur first began to move in Liberal circles after 1902 when he left the Foreign Office. He was first elected as a Liberal to the House of Commons in 1908 after having served as private secretary to the Liberal premier, Henry Campbell-Bannerman. Lady Cynthia was sympathetic to Arthur's request that she intercede, but she also explained why she imagined Queen Mary disliked the book.

> The real difficulty in this matter is, I think, that members of the Royal Family are exposed to so much unwelcome publicity, their trivial comments given ludicrous advertisement, chance remarks twisted to suit particular causes or just used to provide a public (supposedly avid for private personal details of everyday Royal life) with the twaddle it is expected to relish, that from the King onwards they have rather a 'complex' about 'revelations' of life at Windsor or Buckingham Palace, and a sense that they are not allowed the ordinary privacy accorded to every citizen of saying what he likes at home without any fear of its being one day put under a microscope for popular entertainment.

Moreover, the royal family was still upset at what had happened to Queen Victoria's reputation after her death, especially the published attempts to make her a more human and less regal figure that had begun with the article by Edmund Gosse and Mary Ponsonby. 'I think the whole family is specially sensitive about Queen Victoria!' Lady Cynthia continued in her letter to Arthur.

> Brought up to consider her as placed on an unique pedestal, the 'debunking' process has been rather painful to them, clever and not wholly unsympathetic though it has often been. Lytton Strachey, Laurence Housman and others, though they may have made her a lovable figure in some ways, have certainly made her a slightly comic one, which perhaps is a more congenial process when applied to other people's grandmothers and great grandmothers than to one's own!

Here she put her finger on the comic quality that the Ponsonby family loved in the royal family. She also touched on the irreverence that the royal family most distrusted in the Ponsonbys.

Lady Cynthia also pointed to the fault line that Henry Ponsonby had spent much of his career trying to negotiate. It was hard to decide, she said, 'between undue probing into private life' on the one hand, and on the other 'reasonable information about' the royal family's 'personal views and the part they have actually played in history'. In this case she was sure it was a matter of historical interest rather than undue probing. She believed that Arthur's father 'was, behind the scenes, a figure of such national importance that one can hardly suppose that Queen Victoria's letters or notes to him could have been purely trivial or lacking in real interest'. She hoped the issue would be decided in Arthur's favour, but said there was little she could do. She might write to Queen Mary, but that would only be successful if Arthur would write another letter to her making his case which she could then enclose in her letter to the queen.[12]

Arthur probably wrote no such letter, as he was already hearing news from Morshead. Part of the trouble was Wigram, who believed that it was a mistake to have presented the book to the king at the proof stage. Wigram was proposing to go through the proofs again to decide 'which writings of Q.V. might be deleted'. He thought it would have been better if the two of them, Wigram and Morshead, had passed it chapter by chapter in typescript. This was awkward for Morshead who had seen the book in typescript without notifying Wigram. Indeed, he had known about it from an earlier stage than anyone else. He thought in retrospect that he had done the right thing. There were too many people in the household by whom it would have had to be passed on a chapter by chapter basis. Further, the letters over which the king had direct control did not represent the majority of the book. Even if those letters were omitted, there was still much material, mainly the letters between Arthur's father and mother, that they could not prevent being published, or even demand the right to review.

The more serious difficulty, Morshead told Arthur, was still between the king and his mother. She was planning to come to Windsor for the weekend to attend the christening of one of her grandchildren, and Morshead, who had a touch of the Ponsonby sense of humour himself, predicted that there would 'be a grand Family blow-up, with dense clouds of black smoke'.

Before he could finish this letter, the king sent for Morshead to have a talk about the book. 'You know,' Morshead told Arthur in a long post-script, 'I find H. M. perfectly reasonable.'

Naturally he [the king] demurs to the principle of the thing, finding it distasteful that if he should talk disparagingly to me about X behind his back, I should go away and commit it to paper; and some years later it should all appear in print. That's not unnatural. But at the same time he enjoys it all immensely, and laughed and laughed at the strokes with which the old lady plied her numerous antagonists.

The king did have a difficult question for Morshead.

'Don't you think [said the king] that when people read this book they will go away with the idea that there was once an extraordinarily tiresome and ill-tempered old woman whose name was Queen Victoria, who would have made things very difficult for everybody if it had not been for the superlative tact of her Secretary?'

Morshead conceded that this might be the case, but it was not the

'point upon which the proofs are submitted to Your Majesty. Lytton Strachey wrote a far more exceptionable book, and never submitted proofs at all: he had no need to – and nor would Lord Ponsonby had he not desired to include certain actual notes written by Q.V. [...]

'You cannot, in fact, control what a writer chooses to say about Queen Victoria, so long as it is not libellous. We could drill holes in this book wherever Q.V.'s own letters occur; but it would only damage the book without meeting the root-&-branch objections of Queen Mary. ... I think we ought to have a policy ready before Queen Mary comes; and I hope it will not involve too many excisions.'

Morshead's policy was to maintain friendly relations with writers who, whatever unpleasant stories they chose to include in their work, were basically responsible and fair-minded. Even writers who had access to materials whose copyright the king controlled must have freedom to arrive at their own conclusions. He hoped that the king would not insist on significant omissions from the book. 'What remains to be seen is the show which he is prepared to put up against his Mother and Wig[ram]. I have great sympathy with him; left alone he would say Go Ahead. He is bothered to death by the opposition of the elder generation.'[13]

It was an anxious time at the palace. British forces were suffering setbacks in the war against Nazi Germany and the king found it difficult to worry about a book on the Victorian monarchy. Also, the abdication was still fresh in everyone's mind. The king had only been six years on the throne. His family was still sensitive about his having been thrust unprepared into the job by the unprecedented departure of his elder brother, Edward VIII, to marry Wallis Simpson, and understandably wary about Arthur's book rocking the boat. What if Arthur's parents' irreverent remarks about the queen – who was still considered one of the founders of the modern monarchy – were to destabilise it further? They could not have known that it would have the same sort of success as the BBC had had broadcasting readings from Trollope during the bleakest moments of the Second World War. Just as the BBC broadcasts rehabilitated Trollope's critical reputation, Arthur's book, which had large sales and won a prize for biography, introduced a new generation of readers to Queen Victoria.

Morshead now asked to meet Arthur at Windsor on the weekend in late February 1942 when Queen Mary would be having her talk with the king. Morshead promised to tell Arthur as soon as he possibly could about their decision, but he must not actually be seen in Morshead's office. Arthur would stay with Betty, who was living in Castle Hill House, opposite the gate into the lower ward of the castle. 'When you arrive,' Morshead wrote Arthur, 'you had better please ring me up from Betty's ... Then I will slip down to Betty's if I am free, and we will talk there; because if Wig[ram] walked into my office while you were there it would not ease matters.'[14] A second letter went out to Arthur on the same day saying that 'I'm sure the offense [taken by Queen Mary] lies in the flippant tone of the letters to your Mother; and this I think They've got to stummick [sic], like it or not.'[15]

That weekend after receiving Arthur's telephone call, Morshead walked down the hill and met him conspiratorially at Betty's gates, to which he had a key. There Arthur learned, with some relief, that the king had approved the book. Arthur was asked only to make a few small cuts where it was decided that the queen had used too intemperate language, as well as a passage that was unflattering to one of the king's great aunts who was still alive. What the king said to his mother and why she dropped her objections remains a mystery.

The book went ahead and appeared in the autumn of 1942. Morshead wrote to Roger Fulford about it. Fulford had joined the editorial department of *The Times* in 1933 and was known as both a royal biographer and one of the editors, with Lytton Strachey, of the complete *Greville Diaries*. Morshead hoped Fulford would reserve the leading article in *The Times Literary Supplement* for Arthur's book.[16]

Alan Lascelles wrote Arthur a letter of congratulations just after the book's appearance. The book had made those working in the king's private office feel prouder of their chosen profession, especially at a time of war when they sometimes wondered whether they should not be off fighting. 'You have done us professional courtiers an enduring service' he told Arthur.

> The story of your father's life disposes for ever of the myth that those who stand around the Throne nowadays are port-drinking, time-serving parasites (as they may have been in XVII and XVIII centuries), and proves them to be honest men and women who have to work hard for their livings at a job which demands a considerable deal of domestic sacrifice. More important still, it helps to lay doubts in on one's mind (doubts which must inevitably be stronger in time of war) as to whether the courtier's trade is really an honourable and worth-while one.

The book also made abundantly clear that Arthur's father had made contributions to public life. 'Henry Ponsonby was an asset to his country ... Queen Victoria, like Queen Elizabeth kept no cats that did not kill mice.'

Lascelles recapitulated his argument to the king about why the book should be published. On the one hand, it was honest and no one should 'resent the truth being told about a famous ancestor, even if some fraction of it shows that ancestor to have shared the common failings of humankind'. Honesty and the truth would improve Queen Victoria's reputation, not harm it. On the other hand, it would discourage those who wanted to make money from inventing stories about the queen. He saw that 'Posterity is going to take more interest in Q.V. probably, than in any of her predecessors. Here is a definitive and authentic portrait of her, from many angles, which will never be surpassed.'

Lascelles wrote this letter on stationery belonging to Queen Victoria which he found in a cupboard at Windsor Castle. Someone had cut out all the 'VRI' monograms, but he still enjoyed using it. He put in a postscript, 'I like to think that the next sheet above it may perhaps have been sent upstairs with Lt. Gen. Sir H.P's. humble duty'. If Queen Victoria continued to cast her spell well into the twentieth century, it is clear that for courtiers in the 1940s, Henry Ponsonby was also a friendly ghost living among them.[17]

The publication of Arthur's book is interesting not only because it shows how those working in the office his father founded felt themselves indebted to Henry even in the 1940s, but also because it suggests one solution to a puzzle that remains in the history of the modern monarchy. In recent years that history has been told less often in biography than in works that attempt to explain how the monarchy has survived and functioned in the two centuries following the French Revolution. The three most important books of the last decade have shown how, contrary to expectations, the monarchy contributed both to democratic politics and a republican civic culture during the nineteenth and twentieth centuries.

Vernon Bogdanor's *The Monarchy and the Constitution* describes the occasions on which political interventions by the sovereign have actually strengthened rather than weakened democratic politics in Britain.[18] Two books by Frank Prochaska make a similar point.[19] *Royal Bounty* examines the way the monarchy during and after the Victorian period lost political power, but gained influence in the philanthropic world. By encouraging local and self-governing charities at the expense of the central government, the monarchy contributed to the culture in which democracy thrives. Prochaska's *Republic of Britain* extends the argument of the first book by suggesting that recent debate, which assumes republicans to be in opposition to monarchists, has been misconceived. Classical republicanism was never necessarily anti-monarchical, because it was always possible to combine representative institutions with monarchical ones under the same constitution. Further, Britain's constitutional monarchy enshrined the principles of representation and self-government at the expense of royal authority. British kings, queens and princes have themselves been republican workers for parliamentary democracy by assisting the work of local committees and provincial charities – hospitals, old people's homes, libraries and universities – that were themselves representative, self-governing institutions in miniature. The royal family encouraged a kind of financial altruism that is also one of the foundations of a democratic society.

The Ponsonbys tend to lend force to these arguments. At the same time they show how current books on the topic have overlooked one dimension of the modern monarchy's appeal and staying power. What was at stake in the discussion at the palace about Arthur's book was whether the monarchy was a democratic institution or not. Could its role in history be open, honest and transparent, or ought it to be shrouded in secrecy? The latter would certainly afford greater privacy to members of the royal family, but members of the royal family depended on popular goodwill for their survival. In sacrificing his own, his mother's and his great grandmother's privacy, the king gave up something that few British citizens would be expected to do. At the same time, he demonstrated an openness and tolerance of criticism that strengthened the wartime monarchy as one of Britain's democratic institutions.

Henry Ponsonby had similar questions before him on a daily basis when he advised the queen at the end of the nineteenth century. Although democracy was not so far advanced then, and was indeed considered to be a dangerous development by many, Ponsonby and his family saw themselves as champions of parliamentary power. Henry wished to preserve a modicum of influence for the queen in political discussion, but the ministers who had responsibility for affairs in Parliament must have the final say. They must settle all argument. He was their voice to her as much as he was her voice to them.

Mary Ponsonby was on the side of those who had little or no voice in Parliament as opposed to those whose raised voices came from wealth or hereditary privilege. Her instinct was to fight on behalf of trade unionists, women who needed work and women who wanted higher education. This was to the left of Henry's usual politics, but MEP's presence in his decision-making is unmistakable. Their participation in the counsels of Queen Victoria meant that her court was never militarist or anti-democratic, in contrast to the courts of the major powers on the continent. What influence Queen Victoria did have was often moderated or controlled or softened by the Ponsonbys in a way it might not have been had she been served by a more conventional secretary. Mary Ponsonby's connection to the court also lent an official sanction to unconventional institutions such as Girton College, Cambridge and the Society for Promoting the Employment of Women that might not have prospered without it.

All this evidence so far supports the assessment of Bogdanor and Prochaska that the monarchy has survived as long as it has because it has been a help rather than a hindrance to Britain's democratic constitution. It suggests that there were good reasons why the monarchy has survived in Britain beyond the era when it ceased to frame policy or guide administration. There is much to admire in the way it fulfilled its diminished role as head of state. Of course there remains the problem of a rationale for the modern monarchy. Are leadership in philanthropy, and a historical tendency to side with progressive or democratic forces in the constitution enough to justify it?

One suggestion has been that there has been a symbolic, or a non-rational rationale for the monarchy in its expanding ceremonial role over the last two centuries. Ceremonies like coronations, weddings and jubilees conveyed historical and spiritual messages about the age of Britain's constitutional monarchy. Such occasions also provided moments for reflection about both national and individual purpose. As Ferdinand Mount has argued they provided 'historical re-enactments'[20] of significant moments in Britain's past; and, it might be added, of events in the individual lives of citizens and families. For example, a jubilee re-enacts the sovereign's accession to the throne; this is not only an event that is significant in the reign, but also a date that often makes people remember what was happening at the same time in their own lives. These ceremonies, and the popularity for the monarchy they have generated, have continued to underwrite its 'presence' in the upper reaches of governmental decision-making. This 'pervasive' presence may not always be the same as tangible influence, but so long as there is popular approval, one former editor of *The Times* concluded, sovereigns will continue to be privy to information about what key decisions are being made.[21]

Something in the way Henry wrote his letters to Mary, though, suggests that this search for a rationale for the monarchy is itself misguided. Possibly a rationale is the wrong thing to seek for the monarchy, just as one should not try to look too hard for a rationale that defends, or a function that explains the pleasure we derive from art, theatre, dressing up, acting out, or laughter. All these things have value, but their value does not depend on there being a closely reasoned argument for their existence. Similarly, what comes across most powerfully from the lives of the Ponsonbys is their enjoyment of the monarchy, their light-hearted amusement at the absurdity of it all. This enjoyment was certainly an ingredient in the happy recipe of their marriage. They may have even come together over shared laughter when they were both in waiting on the trip to Coburg in 1860. Occasional amusement at what the royal family said or did was not a reason for serving the queen, which they both devoted their lives to doing, but it certainly animated, coloured and made their lives vivid. Their real reason for serving the monarchy was this: they both believed that to serve the queen was an honour. In serving her, however, they were really serving the representative principles that made Britain's constitution admirable. They bowed not to the monarch alone, but to the constitutional or parliamentary monarchy for which their ancestors and the British people had fought.

Their legacy to the monarchy was also in the principles of Henry's private secretariat. His successors learned these principles and acknowledged their debt to him. Probably, those who came after him also believed in the same unwritten code that Henry and Mary observed. For what they believed in seriously they seldom spoke about and this was also key to the value they saw in the Victorian monarchy. They both believed in service as an honourable profession, whether military service to the sovereign, political service to the state, or public-spirited service to committees devoted to ameliorating conditions for specific groups. They were both also instinctive believers in the heredi-tary principle. It was both right and natural that families should inherit property and personality traits as well as the influence in the wider world that property and personality conveyed. Those who had inher-ited much, however, had also a greater duty to serve.

Against service, hereditary right and duty, however, has to be placed the Ponsonbys' equal conviction that too much deference was absurd in an egalitarian society; and that people should be promoted on the basis of merit rather than by the purchasing power of their property. Their best stories were saved for when these principles came into conflict. Their keen sense of the comedy of it all reflected some of the pressure points in a constitution that was outwardly hierarchical, medieval and authoritarian, but inwardly egalitarian, modern and representative. What they have to say about the Victorian monarchy was that it certainly had moments of usefulness in the political process. Through the queen's civil list, through her activities as well as those of members of her family and her household, the monarchy aided philanthropic institutions. It dignified, solemnised and made visible the unifying forces in an unwritten constitution. But it also entertained, amused and was capable of making people laugh, as King George VI and Alan Lascelles recognised when they read Arthur's proofs. This too is a dimension of its appeal and a reason why in the modern era it has continued to survive.

Laughter need not be a way of diminishing or making mockery. It can also be a way of loving or showing affection. Henry understood this well when he wrote to Mary in June 1874 about a letter the queen had received from Persia. 'The Shah writes to The Queen on business. A boundary question. He calls her "my auspicious sister of sublime nature to whose wishes events correspond." If events corresponded with my wishes I should be with you now. God bless you. HP'[22]

Notes

Preface

1. HFP to SPF, 31 Aug 1889, RA, Add A/12.
2. A. Ponsonby, 'My Mother,' TS, pp. 4-5, SHL.
3. MP.
4. JP.
5. AP.
6. AP, xii-xiii.
7. RA, Add. A/36.
8. RA, Add. A/12; the story of this gift and more on Arthur Ponsonby's biography is in the Epilogue.
9. Longford.
10. *Letters of the Empress Frederick*, ed. Sir F. Ponsonby (1929).

1. Starting in the Middle, *c.* 1870-73

1. A.C. Benson, *Memories and Friends* (1924), pp. 54-5.
2. *Ibid.*
3. Maj. Gen. Sir John Ponsonby, *The Bulteel Family* (privately printed 1942), Haile.
4. Benson, *Memories*, p. 55.
5. Quoted in P. Horgan, *Maurice Baring Restored* (1970), p. 109.
6. E. Smyth, *As Time Went On …* (1936), pp. 85-6.
7. AP, pp. 394-5.
8. Arthur Ponsonby, 'My Mother', TS, SHL, p. 2.
9. *Ibid.*, p. 3.
10. *Ibid.*, pp. 3-4.
11. *Ibid.*, p. 3.
12. MP, p.xiv.
13. Benson, *Memories*, p. 62.
14. These letters are at Windsor in the RA, Add. A/36 series.
15. HFP to MEP, 14 Aug 1873, RA, Add. A/36/600.
16. HFP to MEP, 10 Oct 1870, RA, Add. A/36/223.
17. 3 Aug 1870, HFP 1861-71 diary, SHL; HFP to MEP, 13 Jun 1872, RA, Add. A/36/433.
18. Quoted in B. Pimlott, *The Queen: A Biography of Elizabeth II* (1996), p. 221.
19. Quoted in V. Bogdanor, *The Monarchy and the Constitution* (Oxford, 1995), p. 211.
20. HFP to MEP, 3 May 1867, RA, Add. A/36/8.
21. HFP to MEP, 14 Apr 1873, RA, Add. A/36/532.
22. Quoted in AP, p. 76.
23. HFP to AVP, 27 Oct 1863, nine volumes of letters to/from Henry and Arthur Ponsonby, SHL.
24. HFP to MEP, 9, 10 Oct 1870, RA, Add. A/36/222-4.
25. HFP to MEP, 27 Oct 1870, RA, Add. A/36/240.
26. HFP to MEP, 3, 8 Jun 1871, RA, Add. A/36/290, 296. See 'English

Republicanism [Signed A Working Man]', *Fraser's Magazine*, vol. 83 o.s., vol. 3 n.s. (Jun 1871), pp. 751-61.

27. HFP to MEP, 30 Jun 1871,RA, Add. A/36/304.

28. HFP to MEP, 21 Aug 1871, RA, Add. A/36/324.

29. HFP to Lady Emily Ponsonby, 30 Jun 1873, RA, Add. A/36/577.

30. HFP to MEP, 14 Jun 1871, RA, Add. A/36/300.

31. HFP to MEP, 5 Nov 1870, RA, Add. A/36/251.

32. HFP to MEP, 15 Nov 1870, RA, Add. A/36/261.

33. HFP to MEP, 25 Apr 1869, RA, Add. A/36/55.

34. HFP to MEP, 13 Jan 1870, RA, Add. A/36/97.

35. HFP to MEP, 12 Jan 1870, RA, Add. A/36/96.

36. MP, p. xiv.

37. AP, pp. 244-5.

38. HFP to MEP, 19 Jul 1871, RA, Add. A/36/312, 313.

39. Biddulph to HFP, 19 Jul 1871, RA, E18/158.

40. AP, p. 370.

41. *Ibid.*, p. 372.

42. QV to Princess Frederick William of Prussia, 2 Apr 1870 (copy), RA, C78/130.

43. MP, p. 190.

44. *Ibid.*, pp. 191-2.

45. P. Matthieson, 'An Account of Queen Victoria', *The Journal of the Rutgers University Library*, vol. 21, no. 1 (Dec 1957), pp. 8-32.

46. On Queen Victoria's worry that she might meddle, MP, pp. 190-1.

47. MP, p. xv.

48. HFP to MEP, 7 Sep 1871, RA, Add. A/36/340.

49. HFP to MEP, 22, 23, 25, 27 Sep 1871, RA, Add. A/36/355, 357-8, 360.

50. MP, p. xiv.

51. HFP to MEP, 5 Jan 1870, RA, Add. A/36/86.

52. HFP to MEP, 23 Jan 1870, RA, Add. A/36/107.

53. 5 Jul 1904, A. C. Benson diary, vol. 55, Magdalene College, Cambridge.

54. D. de Ros to HFP, 30 Dec 1871, volume of letters to/from HFP with cuttings 1871-94, SHL.

55. Benson, *Memories*, p. 60; A. Ponsonby, 'My Mother', p. 4.

2. Henry Ponsonby from Birth to Marriage, 1825-61

1. AP, p. 4.

2. JP, p. 117.

3. JP, p. 123; AP, p. 12.

4. E.g. John Ponsonby wrote a family history [JP] from notes collected by his father, Henry Ponsonby; Arthur Ponsonby put a good deal of family history in his biography of his father [AP]; see also their brother, Fritz Ponsonby's *Recollections of Three Reigns*, prepared for the press and with an introductory memoir by C. Welch (1951); and Fritz's daughter, Loelia Lindsay, published *Grace and Favour, The Memoirs of Loelia, Duchess of Westminster* (1961).

5. AVP diary, 1827-49, written in retrospect, 1849, SHL.

6. JP, chs. 1-4.

7. Quoted in R. Jones, *Arthur Ponsonby, The Politics of Life* (Bromley, 1989), p. 1.

8. Lindsay, *Grace and Favour*, p. 17; JP, p. 15.

9. P. Mandler, *Aristocratic Government in the Age of Reform* (Oxford, 1990), p. 16, 45, 55 ff, 276.

10. AVP 1827-49 diary, SHL.

11. JP, p. 124; recipient of letter, date and punctuation corrected to match *Benjamin Disraeli Letters: 1815-1834*, ed. J.A.W. Gunn, J. Matthews, D.M. Schurman, M.G. Wiebe (Toronto, 1982).

12. 2-3 Aug 1855, HFP 1852-7 diary, SHL.

13. AP, p. 14.

14. AVP 1827-49 diary, SHL.

15. Lady Emily occupied the Housekeeper's Lodgings, listed as Suite I in E. Law, *History of Hampton Court*, 3 vols. (1888-91), III, p. 445. I am grateful to Sarah Parker for her help in identifying where Lady Emily lived.

16. AVP 1827-49 diary, SHL.

17. *Ibid.*

18. Undated letter [1839], Lady Emily Ponsonby to HFP, vol. 1 of 9 vol. H. & A. letters, SHL; see also AP, p. 19 on AVP's recollection of his brother receiving the letter.

19. S. David, *The Homicidal Earl, The Life of Lord Cardigan* (1997), pp. 54-5.

20. Undated letter, Lady Emily Ponsonby to HFP, vol. 1 of 9 vol. H. & A. letters, SHL.

21. AP, p. 19.

22. Undated letter [1842], Lady Emily Ponsonby to HFP, vol. 1 of 9 vol. H. & A. letters, SHL.

23. Undated recollection stuck in vol. 1 of 9 vol. H. & A. letters, SHL.

24. J.C. Beckett, *A Short History of Ireland* (rev. edn.; 1966), pp. 144-5.

25. Sir H. Maxwell, Bt., *The Life and Letters of the Fourth Earl of Clarendon*, 2 vols. (1913), I, p. 323.

26. Dr Helen Watanabe-O'Kelly, 'The Fabrication of the Image of Johann Georg, Elector of Saxony', paper delivered at Society for Court Studies, 15 Mar 2000.

27. R.B. McDowell, *The Irish Administration, 1801-1914* (London and Toronto, 1964), p. 66.

28. *Ibid.*, p. 66, 67.

29. Undated letter [1854?], HFP to AVP, vol. 2 (1851-4) of 9 vol. H. & A. letters, SHL.

30. 2 Feb and 6 Mar 1856, HFP 1852-7 diary, SHL.

31. Beckett, p. 147.

32. 1848, AVP 1827-49 diary, SHL.

33. *Ibid.*

34. Undated letter [1848], AVP to HFP, vol. 1 (1830-50) of 9 vol. H. & A. letters, SHL.

35. 1848, AVP 1827-49 diary, SHL.

36. 27-8 Sep 1849, AVP 1827-49 diary, SHL.

37. 28 Feb 1849, AVP 1827-49 diary, SHL.

38. 8 Aug 1849, AVP 1827-49 diary, SHL.

39. 7-8 Feb, 10 Mar 1853, HFP 1852-7 diary, SHL.

40. 31 Dec 1849, narrative of year's events, HFP 1849 diary, SHL.

41. Undated HFP memorandum in vol. 1 (1830-50) of 9 vol. H. & A. letters, SHL.

42. Unknown correspondent [Annesley?] to HFP, [undated letter] in vol. 2 (1851-4) of 9 vol. H. & A. letters, SHL.

43. Undated entry [1864?] in HFP 1864-80 diary [loose-leaf pages in green box marked 'Letters and writings Henry Ponsonby and letters received'], SHL.

44. Sir W. Russell to HFP, 31 May 1854; Sir C. Yorke to HFP, 2 Jun 1854; G. Bagot to HFP 3 June 1854; and following letters in vol. 2 of 9 vol. H & A. letters, SHL.

45. 3, 8 June 1854, AVP diary, vol. 6 (1854-55), SHL.

46. 22-3 Nov 1854, HFP 1852-7 diary, SHL.

47. HFP to AVP, 21 Jun 1855, vol. 3 of 9 vol. H. & A. letters, SHL.

48. See 21 Jul 1855 and following dates, HFP 1852-7 diary, SHL.

49. C. Barnett, *Britain and Her Army* (1970), p. 290, 285.

50. 14 Aug 1855, HFP 1852-7 diary, SHL.

51. 16 & 17 Aug 1855, HFP 1852-7 diary, SHL.

52. The full memorandum is in vol. 3 of 9 vol. H. & A. letters, SHL; a slightly shorter version is in AP, pp. 22-3.

53. Barnett, p. 282, 280.

54. 29 Aug 1855, HFP 1852-7 diary, SHL.

55. 8 Sep 1855, HFP 1852-7 diary, SHL.

56. AP, p. 24.

57. AP, pp. 24-5.

58. 12 Sep 1855, HFP 1852-7 diary, SHL.

59. 13 Sep 1855, HFP 1852-7 diary; and Lady Emily Ponsonby to HFP, 31 Aug, 8, 17 Sep 1855 in vol. 3 of 9 vol. H. & A. letters, SHL.

60. 5-27 Feb 1856, HFP 1852-7 diary, SHL.

61. Lady Georgiana Bathurst to HFP, undated [1855], vol. 3 of 9 vol. H. & A. letters, SHL.

62. David, p. 137.

63. 29 Apr 1856, HFP 1852-7 diary, SHL.

64. 29 May 1856, HFP 1852-7 diary, SHL.

65. Carlisle to HFP, 9 Feb 1856, vol. 3 of 9 vol. H. & A. letters, SHL.

66. See letters of Lady Clarendon, Lord St Germans and F. Seymour to HFP, 11-13 Jan 1857, vol. 4 of 9 vol. H & A letters; 6, 10 Jan, HFP 1852-7 diary, SHL.

67. HFP to MEP, 10 Feb 1873, RA, Add. A/36/502.

68. On his reading of the recollections of Karoline Bauer see HFP to MEP, 13-14 Oct 1884, RA, Add. A/36.

69. Quoted in AP, p. 28.

70. 9, 13, 17, 27 Feb 1857, HFP 1852-7 diary; 23 Jun 1857, HFP 1857-61 diary, SHL.

71. 22, 29 Nov 1858, HFP 1857-61 diary, SHL.

72. HFP to AVP, 6, 13 Aug 1857, vol. 4 of 9 vol. H. & A. letters, SHL.

73. B. Pimlott, *The Queen: A Biography of Elizabeth II* (1996), p. 200, 201.

74. HFP to AVP, 22 Jan 1858, vol. 4 of 9 vol. H. & A. letters, SHL.

75. Undated recollection in HFP 1864-80 diary, SHL.

76. Undated recollection of Windsor in the 1850s, vol. 4 of 9 vol. H. & A. letters, SHL.

77. HFP to AVP, 9 Sep 1858, vol. 4 of 9 vol. H. & A. letters, SHL.

78. S. Orgel, 'Familiar Greatness', in *The Power of Forms in the English Renaissance*, ed. S. Greenblatt (Norman, OK, 1982); and *idem*, *The Illusion of Power: Political Theatre in the English Renaissance* (Berkeley and London, 1975).

79. See diary entry for 1 Sep 1853, HFP 1852-7 diary, SHL: 'After dinner we had the honor of acting two charades before The Queen. 'Cornwallis' written by Cust and 'Khan-eye-ball' [cannibal] written by me both of which went off successfully.'

80. R.D. Altick, *Punch, The Lively Youth of a British Institution, 1841-51* (Columbus, 1997), p. 432; Thackeray quotation, p. 448.

3. Mary Bulteel from Birth to Marriage, 1832-61

1. Quoted in R.A. Jones, *Arthur Ponsonby: The Politics of a Life* (Bromley, Kent, 1989), p. 2.

2. See E. Smyth, *Maurice Baring* (1938), p. 1.

3. Quoted in Jones, p. 2.

4. B. Cherry and N. Pevsner, *Devon*, 2nd edn (1989), p. 553.

5. Quoted in D. Watt-Carter, *Flete: A Historical Review*, 2nd edn (published by the Country Homes Association, Aynhoe Park, Oxfordshire, 1997), p. 14.

6. *Ibid.*, p. 11.

7. *Ibid.*, pp. 15-16.

8. Maj.-Gen. Sir J. Ponsonby, *The Bulteel Family* (privately printed), p. 49.

9. Watt-Carter, p. 16.

10. Watt-Carter, p. 24; Sir J. Ponsonby, pp. 22-3.

11. MEP, 'The Role of Women in Society, I. In Eighteenth-Century France, II. In Nineteenth-Century England', *The Nineteenth Century*, no. 286 (Dec 1900), pp. 941-54 and no. 287 (Jan 1901), pp. 64-76.

12. '... In Nineteenth Century England', (Jan 1901), p. 65.

13. A.V. Montgomery, 'Phases of Thought and Favourite Writers', TS, SHL.

14. See M. Vicinus, *Independent Women, Work and Community for Single Women 1850-1920* (1985), ch. 2.

15. P. Jalland, *Women, Marriage and Politics 1860-1914* (Oxford, 1986), p. 12.

16. 12 Mar 1852, MEP self-examination diary, SHL.

17. 24 Mar 1852 in *ibid*.

18. 30 Mar 1852 in *ibid*.

19. 1 Apr 1852 in *ibid*.

20. A.G. Gardiner, *The Life of Sir William Harcourt*, 2 vols. (New York, 1923), I, p. 61.

21. 2 Oct 1854, MEP self-examination diary, SHL.

22. Gardiner, *Harcourt*, I, p. 84.

23. A. Ponsonby, diary 1871-93 written in retrospect [May 1911], TS, p. 13, SHL.

24. '1853', notes made in 1884 and afterwards after re-reading the early years of the diary, MEP self-examination diary, SHL.

25. 18 Aug 1852 in *ibid*.

26. 18 Mar 1852 in *ibid*.

27. 13 Jul 1852 in *ibid*.

28. See the chapter on court ladies in K.D. Reynolds, *Aristocratic Women and Political Society in Victorian Britain* (Oxford, 1998).

29. 6 Apr 1853, MEP self-examination diary, SHL.

30. See the chapter on Gladstone in W.M. Kuhn, *Democratic Royalism: The Transformation of the British Monarchy, 1861-1914* (Basingstoke and New York, 1996).

31. 17 Mar 1853, RA, QVJ; details of her appointment are also in W.A. Lindsay, *The Royal Household* (1898), p. 158.

32. E. Smyth, *As Time Went on ...* (1936), p. 88, 311.

33. Longford, p. 347.

34. G. Wills, *St Augustine* (New York, 1999), p. 13.

35. I owe this point to Ian Russell.

36. MP, p. 6.

37. MP, p. 7. The queen referred to Mary's 'acting at Woburn' as more formidable than singing at Windsor when she was first invited to Windsor to be inspected as a potential maid of honour; see MP, p. 10.

38. *Ibid*.

39. MP, p. 8.

40. MP, p. xiv.

41. E. Smyth, *What Happened Next* (1940), p. 140.

42. *Ibid*.

43. *Ibid*.

44. *Ibid*.

45. MP, p. 19.

46. 5 Jul 1904, A.C. Benson diary, vol. 55, pp. 17-24, Magdalene College, Cambridge.

47. MP, p. 1.

48. MP, p. 3.

49. MP, p. 6.

50. Jones, p. 64.

51. '[18]62-72', notes made in 1884 and following years, MEP self-examination diary, SHL.

52. MP, pp. 27-33.

53. '1858', recalled in 1884 and afterwards, MEP self-examination diary, SHL.

54. *Ibid.*

55. MEP, 'George Eliot and George Sand', *The Nineteenth Century*, no. 296 (Oct 1901), pp. 610-11.

56. Longford, p. 287.

57. HFP to Lady Emily Ponsonby, 2 Oct 1860, RA, Add A/36/2.

58. HFP to AVP, 4 Feb 1861, vol. 5 of 9 vol. H & A letters, SHL.

59. See Jan to Apr 1861 *passim*, HFP 1857-61diary, SHL.

60. Lady Emily Ponsonby to AVP, 18 Feb 1861, vol. 5 of 9 vol. H & A letters, SHL.

61. HFP to AVP, 17 Feb 1861, vol. 5 of 9 vol. H & A letters, SHL.

4. A Married Couple, 1861-63

1. 16 Jun 1861, HFP 1861-71 diary, SHL.

2. 29 Jun 1861, HFP 1861-71 diary, SHL.

3. 1 Jul 1861, AVP diary, SHL.

4. Lady Emily Ponsonby to AVP, 18 Feb 1861, vol. 5 of 9 vol. H & A letters, SHL.

5. See C. Barnett, *Britain and Her Army 1509-1970* (1970), p. 344.

6. D. Duman, *The Judicial Bench in England 1727-1875* (1982), p. 110. I am grateful to Mark Studer for this reference.

7. Lady Emily Ponsonby to AVP, 18 Feb 1861, vol. 5 of 9 vol. H & A letters, SHL.

8. 19, 24, 27 Apr 1861, HFP 1857-61 diary, SHL.

9. AP, pp. 29-30.

10. 7 Dec 1861, HFP 1861-71 diary, SHL; AP, p. 30.

11. HFP to Lady Emily Ponsonby, 12 Dec 1861, RA, Add. A/36/4.

12. *Ibid.*

13. HFP to AVP, 13 Dec 1861, vol. 5 of 9 vol. H & A letters, SHL.

14. HFP to Lady Emily Ponsonby, 14 Dec 1861, RA, Add. A/36/5.

15. HFP to Lady Emily Ponsonby, 16 Dec 1861, RA, Add. A/36/6.

16. D. de Ros to HFP, 16 Dec 1861, vol. 5 of 9 vol. H & A letters, SHL.

17. Quoted in D. de Ros to HFP, 19 Dec 1861, vol. 5 of 9 vol. H & A letters, SHL; Phipps's emphasis.

18. 18 Dec 1861, AVP diary, SHL.

19. He did not exactly refuse the earlier offer from Lord Canning; the offer was withdrawn. See above chapter 2.

20. 23 Dec 1861, AVP diary, SHL.

21. 31 Dec 1861, HFP 1861-71 diary, SHL.

22. See 1, 4, 23 Jan 1862, MEP 1862 diary, SHL; J.B.A. Charras, *Histoire de la Campagne de 1815: Waterloo* (1857); A.P. Stanley, *Lectures on the History of the Eastern Church, with an Introduction on the Study of Ecclesiastical History* (1861).

23. 3 Apr 1862, MEP 1862 diary, SHL.

24. 5, 6, 9 May 1862, MEP 1862 diary, SHL.

25. 6 May and 7 Jun 1862, HFP 1861-71 diary, SHL.

26. 12-14 Jul 1862, MEP 1862 diary, SHL; A. Trollope, *North America*, 2 vols. (1862).

27. 15 Jul 1862, HFP 1861-71 diary, SHL.

28. MP, p. 48.

29. 18 Jul 1862, HFP 1861-71 diary, SHL.

30. HFP to AVP, 1 Aug 1862, vol. 6 of 9 vol. H & A letters, SHL.

31. 31 Jul 1862, MEP 1862 diary, SHL.
32. 15 Oct 1862, MEP 1862 diary, SHL.
33. 18 Sep, 1, 14 Oct 1862, MEP 1862 diary, SHL.
34. 14-28 Aug 1862, HFP 1861-71 diary, SHL; HFP to AVP, 22 (-25?) Aug 1862, vol. 6 of 9 vol. H & A letters, SHL.
35. HFP to AVP, 22 (-25?) Aug 1862, vol. 6 of 9 vol. H & A letters, SHL.
36. HFP to Lady Emily Ponsonby, 30 Apr 1863, vol. 6 of 9 vol. H & A letters, SHL.
37. 2 May 1863, HFP 1861-71 diary, SHL.
38. Looseleaf page from HFP 1864-80 diary, SHL.
39. HFP to Lady Emily Ponsonby, 12 May 1863, vol. 6 of 9 vol. H & A letters, SHL.
40. HFP to Lady Emily Ponsonby, 15 May 1863, vol. 6 of 9 vol. H & A letters, SHL.
41. MP, pp. 50-1.
42. 16, 19 Aug 1862, MEP 1862 diary, SHL.
43. 18 Jun, 17 Aug 1863, HFP 1861-71 diary, SHL.
44. HFP to AVP, 2 Jul 1863, vol. 6 of 9 vol. H & A letters, SHL.
45. HFP to AVP, 17 Aug 1863, vol. 6 of 9 vol. H & A letters, SHL.
46. Aug to Dec 1862 *passim*, MEP 1862 diary, SHL.
47. HFP to Lady Emily Ponsonby, 5 Jun 1863, quoted in AP, pp. 31-2.
48. AP, pp. 30-1.
49. AP, pp. 37-8.
50. HFP to AVP, 2 Oct 1863 (also see 29 Sep 1863), vol. 6 of 9 vol. H & A letters, SHL.

5. Henry Ponsonby in Waiting, 1863-70

1. AVP to HFP, 26 Oct 1862; HFP to AVP, 31 Oct 1862, vol. 6 of 9 vol. H & A letters, SHL.
2. Maj. Gen. Sir John Ponsonby, *The Bulteel Family* (privately printed 1942), Haile, p. 50.
3. HFP to AVP, undated [1866], vol. 7 of 9 vol. H & A letters, SHL.
4. 1 Nov 1863, HFP 1861-71 diary, SHL.
5. HFP to AVP, 1 Dec 1863, vol. 6 of 9 vol. H & A letters, SHL.
6. HFP to AVP, 16 Dec 1863, vol. 6 of 9 vol. H & A letters, SHL.
7. Undated looseleaf page of recollections, vol. 4 of 9 vol. H & A letters, SHL.
8. HFP to AVP, 11 Jan 1864, vol. 7 of 9 vol. H & A letters, SHL.
9. HFP to AVP, 26 Jun 1866, vol. 7 of 9 vol. H & A letters, SHL.
10. HFP to MEP, 23 Feb 1870, RA, Add. A/36/130.
11. HFP to AVP, 26 Jun 1866, vol. 7 of 9 vol. H & A letters, SHL.
12. HFP to AVP, 30 Oct 1866, vol. 7 of 9 vol. H & A letters, SHL.
13. D. Millar, *The Victorian Watercolours and Drawings in the Collection of H. M. The Queen*, 2 vols. (1995), II, p. 810.
14. M. Reid, *Ask Sir James* (1987), p. 216.
15. 20 May 1867, HFP 1864-80 diary, SHL.
16. *The Private Life of the Queen by One of Her Majesty's Servants*, reprint intro. E. Sheffield (1897; Old Woking, 1979), p. 121.
17. On tartans see D. Millar, *Queen Victoria's Life in the Scottish Highlands* (1985), ch. 4.
18. HFP to AVP, 15 Mar 1865, vol. 7 of 9 vol. H & A letters, SHL.
19. 7 Nov 1865, HFP 1861-71 diary, SHL.
20. Oct 1867, HFP 1864-80 diary, SHL.
21. 2 May 1867, HFP 1864-80 diary, SHL.
22. 11-23 Jul 1867, HFP 1861-71 diary, SHL.
23. Quoted in AP, p. 393.

24. HFP to MEP, 5, 6 Sep 1869, RA, Add. A/36/77, 79.

25. 18-21 Mar 1862, HFP 1861-71 diary, SHL.

26. HFP to AVP, 29 Apr 1864, vol. 7 of 9 vol. H & A letters, SHL.

27. *Annual Register 1867* (1868), p. [127].

28. 30 Mar 1867, HFP 1864-80 diary, SHL.

29. AVP to HFP, 26 Mar 1865, vol. 7 of 9 vol. H & A letters, SHL.

30. HFP to AVP, 10 May 1865, vol. 7 of 9 vol. H & A letters, SHL.

31. Jul 1869, HFP 1864-80 diary, SHL.

32. Mar 1869, Feb 1870, HFP 1864-80 diary, SHL.

33. HFP to MEP, 18 Sep 1869, RA, Add. A/36/63.

34. HFP to MEP, 10 Feb 1870, RA, Add. A/36/121.

35. Mar 1869, HFP 1864-80 diary, SHL.

36. Feb 1870, HFP 1864-80 diary, SHL.

37. HFP to MEP, 27 Feb 1870, RA, Add. A/36/134.

38. HFP to MEP, 10 May 1869, RA, Add. A/36/60.

39. 16 Mar 1870, HFP 1861-71 diary; longer explanation at Mar 1870, HFP 1864-70 diary, both SHL.

40. W.L. Arnstein, 'The Warrior Queen: Reflections on Victoria and Her World', *Albion*, 30 (Spring 1998), pp. 1-28.

41. 24 Jun 1865, HFP 1861-71 diary, SHL.

42. See K.D. Reynolds, *Aristocratic Women and Political Society in Victorian Britain* (Oxford, 1998).

43. Jan 1869, HFP 1864-80 diary, SHL.

44. Apr 1869, HFP 1864-80 diary, SHL.

45. Aug 1869, HFP 1864-80 diary, SHL.

46. Jun 1867, HFP 1864-80 diary, SHL.

47. HFP to AVP, 26 Jul 1866, vol. 7 of 9 vol. H & A letters, SHL.

48. See 21-30 Jul, HFP 1861-71 diary, SHL.

49. 3 Dec 1866, HFP 1861-71 diary, SHL.

50. 11 Feb 1867, HFP 1864-80 diary, SHL.

51. Longford, p. 351.

52. Jan 1869, HFP 1864-80 diary, SHL.

6. An Independent Wife, *c.* 1863-78

1. 'Pamflete Oct 1864', MEP self-examination diary, SHL.

2. AP, p. 37; Mar 1866, MEP self-examination diary, SHL.

3. Henry attended the dinners in 1866 and 1867. See 14 Jul 1866, HFP 1861-71 diary; 10 Jul [1867], HFP 1864-80 diary, SHL.

4. See Jun 1867, HFP 1864-80 diary, SHL. I have not been able to trace the articles.

5. Lady Ponsonby to the author.

6. 25 Mar 1866, MEP self-examination diary, SHL.

7. 'Good Friday', 10 Mar 1868, MEP self-examination diary, SHL.

8. MP, p. 61. Some of this passage has been incorrectly transcribed from a vol. of typed letters 'left over' from notes prepared for the publication of MP, SHL. See in particular notes written by MEP, 5 Jan to 2 Feb 1868, Pamflete, SHL.

9. J.C.G. Röhl, *Young Wilhelm: The Kaiser's Early Life, 1859-1888*, trans. J. Gaines and R. Wallach (Cambridge, 1998), ch. 7.

10. Notes written by MEP, 5 Jan to 2 Feb 1868, Pamflete, SHL.

11. MP, p. 228.

12. V. Woolf, *A Room of One's Own* (1929).

13. A. Ponsonby, 'My Mother', TS, p. 2, SHL.

14. Sep 1864, HFP 1861-71 diary, SHL.

15. MP, pp. 82-3.

16. MP, pp. 77-8.

17. MP, p. 101.

18. MP, p. 176.

19. MP, p. 78.

20. R. Strachey, *'The Cause': A Short History of the Women's Movement in Great Britain* (1928), p. 145; see also M.C. Bradbrook, *'That Infidel Place': A Short History of Girton College, 1869-1969* (1969).

21. HFP to MEP, 28 Jan 1869, RA, Add. A/36/50.

22. HFP to MEP, 21-22 Nov 1871, RA, Add. A/36/391-2.

23. G. Sutherland, 'The Movement for the Higher Education of Women: its social and intellectual context in England, c. 1840-80', in P.J. Waller, ed., *Politics and Social Change in Modern Britain* (Brighton, 1987), p. 94.

24. HFP to MEP, 29 May 1872, RA, Add. A/36/418E.

25. Printed appeal literature. Contributions from Feb 1867 to 30 Jun 1882. Girton College Archive, Cambridge.

26. Quoted in A.G. Gardiner, *The Life of Sir William Harcourt*, 2 vols. (New York, 1923), I, p. 229.

27. MP, p. 123.

28. A.V. Montgomery to mistress of Girton, 23 May 1913 [?], Girton College Archive, Cambridge.

29. P. Levine, *Feminist Lives in Victorian England, Private Roles and Public Commitment* (Oxford, 1990), p. 60.

30. MP, p. 67.

31. Undated notes by A.V. Montgomery on draft MS of AP, SHL.

32. Undated reflections [after 1908?], small blue book, writings of MEP 1907, 1908, 1910, SHL.

33. 25 Mar 1866, MEP self-examination diary, SHL; see for example, *Eighth Annual Report of the Society for Promoting the Employment of Women in Connexion with the National Association for the Promotion of Social Science* (July 1867) and following years from which it appears MEP was continuously on the two committees from 1867 until 1896; her financial subscription ended in 1897.

34. 'Boucherett, Emilia Jessie' (1825-1905), *DNB*; on the Society for Promoting the Employment of Women see also B. Caine, *English Feminism 1780-1980* (Oxford, 1997), p. 94; and *idem*, *Victorian Feminists* (Oxford, 1992), p. 242.

35. *Report of the Society for Promoting the Employment of Women* (1867), pp. 4-5.

36. *Ibid.*, p. 15.

37. See the *Tenth Annual Report* (1869) and the *Twenty-First Annual Report* (1880) of the Society for Promoting the Employment of Women.

38. MP, p. 79. See also HFP to MEP, 16 May 1873, RA, Add. A/36/543 in which he refers to sending her a draft of proposed legislation where working women would be given 4 whole days' paid holiday.

39. MP, p. 150.

40. 'Jex-Blake, Sophia' (1840-1912), *DNB*.

41. HFP to MEP, 26 May 1873, RA, Add. A/36/553.

42. 'Anderson, Elizabeth' (1836-1917), *DNB*.

43. HFP to MEP, 10 Oct 1870, RA, Add. A/36/223.

44. E. Smyth, *What Happened Next* (1940), pp. 146-7.

45. F. Prochaska, *Royal Bounty: The Making of a Welfare Monarchy* (New Haven and London, 1995), pp. 147-8.

46. L. Faderman, *Surpassing the Love of Men: Romantic Friendship and Love Between Women from the Renaissance to the Present* (New York, 1981), pp. 15-16.

47. 23 Jan 1862, MEP 1862 diary, SHL.

48. 22 Apr, 28 May 1862, in *ibid*.

49. Good Friday, 10 Mar 1868, MEP self-examination diary, SHL.

50. Good Friday, 1869, MEP self-examination diary, SHL.

51. 14 May to 29 Jun 1861, MEP self-examination diary, SHL.

52. 'Waldegrave, Frances Elizabeth Anne, Countess Waldegrave' (1821-1879), *DNB*.

53. 14 May to 29 Jun 1861, MEP self-examination diary, SHL.

54. Windsor, Feb 1865 in *ibid*.

55. [18]62-72, notes made in 1884 and afterwards, in *ibid*.

56. MP, p. 70.

57. MP, p. 72.

58. MP, pp. 128-9.

59. HFP to MEP, 21 May 1872, RA, Add. A/36/417K.

60. [18]62-72, notes made in 1884 and afterwards, MEP self-examination diary, SHL.

61. Undated reflections [after 1908?], small blue book, writings of MEP 1907, 1908, 1910, SHL.

62. [18]62-72, notes made in 1884 and afterwards, MEP self-examination diary, SHL.

63. *Ibid*.

64. MP, p. 59.

65. MP, p. 65.

66. MP, p. 65.

67. MP, p. 66.

68. A.V. Montgomery on draft MS of AP, SHL.

69. Feb 1868, HFP 1864-80 diary, SHL.

70. HFP to MEP [re Lyulph Stanley's wanting to know about the queen's will], 16 Jul 1873, RA, Add. A/36/586.

71. 13 July 1870, HFP 1861-71 diary, SHL.

72. MP, pp. 73-4.

73. MP, p. 131.

74. MP, pp. 133-4.

75. MP, p. 145.

7. Henry Ponsonby as Private Secretary, 1870-78

1. H. Van Norden, 'The Origin and Early Development of the Office of Private Secretary to the Sovereign', unpublished PhD dissertation (Columbia Univ., 1952) informs much of what follows. See also G. Curry, 'The Sovereign's Private Secretary', *History Today*, 9 (1959), pp. 122-31; R. Mackworth-Young, 'The Royal Archives, Windsor Castle', *Archives*, 8 (1978), pp. 115-30; *Office Holders in Modern Britain*, XI, *Officials of the Royal Household 1660-1837*, *Part I: Department of the Lord Chamberlain and Associated Offices*, compiled by J.C. Sainty and R.O. Bucholz (1997), pp. 5-6; and P. Emden, *Behind the Throne* (1934).

2. E.A. Smith, *George IV* (New Haven and London, 1999), p. 220.

3. Van Norden, p. 58.

4. E.A. Smith, p. 217.

5. Van Norden, p. 55, 74. See also Lord Colville to HFP, as well as HFP mem. 17 Jan 1880, RA, Add. A/12/508-9, where George IV appears to have *given* large sums to Bloomfield and Knighton as gifts in addition to their salaries.

6. P. Ziegler, *King William IV* (1971), p. 165; see V. Bogdanor, *The Monarchy and the Constitution* (Oxford, 1995) on the trend toward political neutrality.

7. Van Norden, p. 110, 120.

8. *Ibid.*, p. 119.

9. *Ibid.*, pp. 124-5; the story is also in Emden, p. 14.

10. Van Norden, pp. 126-8.

11. Palmerston to QV, 18 Dec 1861, RA, M 58/2.

12. Palmerston to Phipps, 20 Dec [?] 1861, RA, M 58/6.

13. Phipps to Palmerston, 18 Dec 1861, RA, M 58/5.

14. QV to Grey [copy], 15 Feb 1862, RA, M 58/26.

15. *The Early Years of His Royal Highness the Prince Consort*, comp. by C. Grey under the direction of H. M., the Queen (1867).

16. Russell to QV, 1 Mar 1866, RA, C 78/34.

17. Russell to Grey, 5 Mar 1866, RA, C 78/61.

18. Derby to Grey, 25 Apr 1867, RA, A 35/59-60.

19. On savings in the civil list, see W.M. Kuhn, 'Queen Victoria's Civil List: What Did She Do with It?', *Historical Journal*, vol. 36, no. 3 (1993), pp. 645-55; Disraeli to QV, 10 Dec 1866, RA, C 78/79.

20. Grey memorandum, 4 Mar 1866, RA, C 78/60.

21. QV to Victoria, crown princess of Prussia [later Empress Frederick] [copy], 2 Apr 1870, RA, C 78/130; also correspondence between QV and Grey in late Jan and 2 Feb 1869, RA, C 78/80-2.

22. Prince of Wales to QV, 3 Apr 1870, RA, C 78/136.

23. HFP to Biddulph, Apr [?] 1870, RA, C 78/129.

24. Leopold to G. Stirling, 3 Apr 1870, RA, Add. A 30/349; on Leopold and the Browns, see C. Zeepvat, *Prince Leopold: The Untold Story of Queen Victoria's Youngest Son* (Stroud, 1998), *passim*.

25. QV to Biddulph, 1 Apr 1870, printed in P.F. Mattheisen, 'An Account of Queen Victoria', *The Journal of the Rutgers University Library*, vol. 21, no. 1 (Dec 1957), pp. 30-31; also in RA, C 78/126.

26. *The Political Correspondence of Mr. Gladstone and Lord Granville 1868-1876*, A. Ramm, ed., Royal Historical Society, Camden Third Series, vols 81-2 (1952), vol. 81, p. 170.

27. HFP to MEP, 30 Sep 1871, RA, Add. A/36/364.

28. See the chapter on Gladstone in W.M. Kuhn, *Democratic Royalism: The Transformation of the British Monarchy, 1861-1914* (Basingstoke and New York, 1996).

29. HFP to MEP, 1 Oct 1871, RA, Add. A/36/365.

30. See 21 Nov 1865, Lady Waterpark's diary, BL, Add. 60750, fol. 4; and 21 Nov 1865 in HFP 1864-80 diary, SHL.

31. HFP to MEP, 9 Oct 1871, RA, Add. A/36/373.

32. See HFP to MEP, 15 Jun, 1 Jul, 1 Aug 1872, RA, Add. A/36/435, 437, 447.

33. AP, p. 242.

34. HFP to QV, 13 Jul 1871, RA, E 18/57.

35. See for example his letter asking her to wait before writing more letters or asking for an increase in troop strength at the time of the Franco-Prussian War. He was clearly afraid that a snub from the government would disincline ministers to listen to her. HFP to QV, 27 Jul 1870, RA, E 17/108.

36. HFP to MEP, 24 Sep 1873, RA, Add. A/36/648.

37. See the undated draft of his letter to the Chancellor of the Exchequer, Robert Lowe, deploring that the queen should be asked to approve moving the army barracks away from Knightsbridge too quickly and without time to ask for proper explanations. 'The Queen would have wished to have been fully informed on the subject from the first.' HFP to R. Lowe, RA, E 17/147.

38. HFP to MEP, 11, 13 Sep 1871, RA, Add. A/36/344-5.

39. HFP to MEP, 28 Sep 1871, RA, Add. A/36/362. On his suspicions about Lady Ely see HFP to MEP, 9 Oct 1871, RA, Add. A/36/375.

40. HFP to MEP, 1 Oct 1871, RA, Add. A/36/365.

41. HFP to MEP, 5 Oct 1871, RA, Add. A/36/369.

42. HFP to MEP, 31 May 1872, RA, Add. A/36/418G.

43. HFP to MEP, 21 Nov 1873, RA, Add. A/36/693.

44. HFP to MEP, 2 Oct 1871, RA, Add. A/36/366.

45. HFP to MEP, 23 Dec 1872, RA, Add. A/36/477.

46. HFP to MEP, 3 Nov 1870, RA, Add. A/36/248.

47. Queen Victoria, *Leaves from the Journal of Our Life in the Highlands*, ed. A. Helps (1868), p. 9, 54, 161. For two different analyses of the book by cultural critics see M. Homans, *Royal Representations: Queen Victoria and British Culture, 1837-76* (Chicago and London, 1998); and G. Turley Houston, *Royalties: The Queen and Victorian Writers* (Charlottesville and London, 1999).

48. Emden, p. 265.

49. AP, p. 246.

50. Quoted in P. Smith, *Disraeli: A Brief Life* (Cambridge, 1996), p. 172.

51. *Ibid.*, p. 173.

52. *Ibid.*, p. 160.

53. R. Blake, *Disraeli* (1966), pp. 548-9.

54. *Ibid.*, p. 547.

55. HFP to MEP, 5 Jun 1874, RA, Add. A/36/756.

56. HFP to MEP, 6 Aug 1874, RA, Add. A/36/773.

57. MP, p. 86.

58. Prince Albert mem., April 1843, RA, Z 273/24.

59. HFP to MEP, 28 Feb 1878, RA, Add. A/36.

60. AP, p. 140.

61. *Ibid.*

62. A. Ponsonby diary 1871-93, written in retrospect (May 1911), SHL, TS, p. 8.

63. There is a file on the refusal of the CB at SHL; see also AP, pp. 66-7.

64. AP, p. 67.

65. MP, p. 146.

66. HFP to MEP, 8 Sep 1874, RA, Add. A/36/808.

67. HFP to MEP, 2 Jun 1875, RA, Add. A/36/918.

68. HFP to MEP, 13 Aug 1876, RA, Add. A/36/1091.

69. See for example, HFP to MEP, 16 Jul 1876, RA, Add. A/36/1082.

70. HFP to MEP, 9 Apr 1876, RA, Add. A/36/1040.

71. Draft mem. of HFP, undated, RA, A/12/316.

72. P. Smith, p. 174.

73. HFP to MEP, 22 Feb 1878, RA, Add. A/36/1396.

74. S. Heffer, *Power and Place: The Political Consequences of King Edward VII* (London, 1998), p. 33.

75. When Leopold died, the Foreign Office asked to have the key returned; see RA, A/12/923-4.

76. Zeepvat, pp. 128-9.

77. HFP to MEP, 27, 28 May 1877, RA, Add. A/36/1233-4.

78. HFP to MEP, 29 May 1877, RA, Add. A/36/1237.

79. HFP mem., undated, RA, A/12/354.

80. Emden, p. 269.

81. HFP to MEP, 29, 30 Sep, 1, 2 (and enclosed draft of HFP to Jenner), 3 Oct 1878, RA, Add. A/36.

82. R. Williams, *The Contentious Crown: Public Discussion of the British Monarchy in the Reign of Queen Victoria* (Aldershot, 1997), p. 123 ff shows how in the period between 1876 and 1879 there was increased debate on the royal prerogative in the press.

83. P. Smith, p. 174; see also R. Blake, *Gladstone, Disraeli, and Queen Victoria* (Oxford, 1993), p. 17.

84. Quoted in T. Aronson, *Victoria and Disraeli: The Making of a Romantic Friendship* (1977), p. 151.

85. HFP to MEP, 17 Apr 1875, RA, Add. A/36/894.

86. HFP to MEP, 23 May 1874, RA, Add. A/36/744.

8. Mama and her Friends, *c.* 1874-94

1. All following quotes from MEP 1887 diary [dark blue book], SHL.

2. See MEP to A. Ponsonby, 12 Jul 1890, vol. 1 of 3 vols. of MEP and A. Ponsonby letters, SHL.

3. See for example, HFP to MEP, 3 May 1867, 5 Jan 1869, RA, Add. A/36/8, 34.

4. HFP to MEP, 7 Jul 1868, RA, Add. A/36/20.

5. MP, p. 142.

6. HFP to MEP, 2 Jun 1877, RA, Add. A/36/1246.

7. MEP 1887 diary, SHL.

8. *The George Eliot Letters*, ed. G.S. Haight, (1956), vol. 6, p. 97, no. 3.

9. MP, p. 93.

10. MP, p. 91.

11. MP, p. 94.

12. MP, p. 92.

13. MP, p. 98.

14. MP, pp. 111-12.

15. MP, p. 113.

16. MP, p. 105 ff.

17. MP, p. 175.

18. HFP to MEP, 24 Apr 1878, RA, Add. A/36/1429; also in AP, p. 385.

19. MEP to HFP, 5 Jun 1882, SHL.

20. HFP to MEP, 26 Aug 1890, RA, Add. A/36.

21. Notes made in 1884 and afterwards, MEP self-examination diary, SHL.

22. E. Smyth, *As Time Went on ...* (1936), p. 188.

23. 1871-93, A. Ponsonby diary written in retrospect (May 1911), TS, p. 5, SHL.

24. HFP to MEP, 24 Dec 1874, RA, Add. A/36/868.

25. 1871-93, A. Ponsonby diary written in retrospect (May 1911), TS, p. 5, SHL.

26. A.V. Montgomery notes on draft of AP, SHL.

27. Smyth, *As Time Went on ...* , p. 87.

28. L. Lindsay, 'Preface' to F. Ponsonby, *Recollections of Three Reigns*, selected and with an intro. by A. Lambton (1988), p. vii.

29. L. Housman queries and M. Ponsonby replies, [undated], Bryn Mawr MSS.

30. On the impossibility of large allowances see HFP to MEP, 1, 2 Jul, 3 Nov 1888, RA, Add. A/36.

31. HFP to MEP, 3, 15, 18 Nov 1887, RA, Add. A/36.

32. HFP to MEP, 7 Dec 1887, RA, Add. A/36.

33. F. Ponsonby, *Recollections of Three Reigns*, prepared for press and with intro. by C. Welch (1951), p. 8.

34. HFP to A. Ponsonby, 12 Sep 1892, SHL.

35. MEP to J. Ponsonby, 27 Jul 1892, Haile.

36. L. Lindsay, *Grace and Favour: The Memoirs of Loelia, Duchess of Westminster* (New York, 1961), p. 32.

37. AP to MEP, undated, SHL.

38. See for example, A. Ponsonby, *English Diaries: A Review of English Diaries*

from the Sixteenth to the Twentieth Century with an Introduction on Diary Writing (1923).

39. MEP to A. Ponsonby, 12 Jul 1890, vol. 1 of 3 vol. MEP & A. Ponsonby correspondence, SHL.

40. A. Ponsonby, 'My Mother', TS, p. 5, SHL.

41. 1871-93, A. Ponsonby diary written in retrospect (May 1911), TS, p. 12, SHL.

42. *Ibid.*, p. 8.

43. A. Ponsonby, *Casual Observations* (1930), p. 55.

44. 1871-93, A. Ponsonby diary written in retrospect (May 1911), TS, p. 4, SHL.

45. *Ibid.*, p. 8.

46. *Ibid.*, p. 15.

47. MP, p. 241.

48. MP, p. 242.

49. MP, p. 243.

50. A.V. Montgomery notes on draft of AP, SHL.

51. HFP to MEP, 6 Dec 1887, RA, Add. A/36.

52. A.V. Montgomery notes on draft of AP, SHL.

53. HFP to MEP, 26 Mar 1888, RA, Add. A/36.

54. MEP to HFP, 10 Apr 1888, in vol. 1 of MEP letters to A. Ponsonby, SHL.

55. MP, pp. 150-1.

56. MP, p. 147.

57. MP, p. 159.

58. MP, p. 151.

59. MP, p. 153.

60. MP, p. 154.

61. MP, p. 166.

62. MP, p. 167.

63. HFP to MEP, 10 Jun 1883, RA, Add. A/36.

64. Lady Macdonald, 'A character', [copy] Nov 1858, box of letters (not typed) to MEP, SHL.

9. Henry Ponsonby's Private Secretariat, 1878-95

1. See HFP to MEP, 29, 30 [two letters] Sep 2 [two letters], 3 Oct 1878, RA, Add. A/36.

2. HFP to MEP, 10 Oct 1878, RA, Add. A/36.

3. HFP to MEP, 1 Oct 1878, RA, Add. A/36.

4. HFP to MEP, 13 Nov 1878, RA, Add. A/36.

5. A. Ponsonby 1871-93 diary, written in retrospect (May 1911), TS, p. 7, SHL.

6. AP, pp. 83-4.

7. QV to HFP, 4 Sep 1885, 22 Dec 1886, RA, Add. A/12/1183, 1320.

8. 'General Rules and Principles Observed in the Offices of Privy Purse, and Private Secretary to the Prince', 10 June 1858, RA, MRH/VIC/HH 1/24.

9. W.M. Kuhn, 'Queen Victoria's Civil List: What Did She Do with It?', *The Historical Journal*, 36 (1993), p. 653.

10. *Ibid.*, p. 655; 657-8.

11. HFP to MEP, 24 Mar 1882, RA, Add. A/36.

12. HFP to MEP, 25 Apr 1889, RA, Add. A/36.

13. HFP to MEP, 5 Sep 1881, RA, Add. A/36.

14. HFP notes on privy purse accounts for 1886-87, RA, Add. A/12/1520.

15. Kuhn, 'Queen Victoria's Civil List', p. 649.

16. HFP to MEP, 28 May 1877, RA, Add. A/36

17. HFP to QV, 1 Nov 1885, RA, Add. A/12/1198.

18. *LQV*, ser. 2, vol. 3, pp. 671-8.

19. HFP to MEP, 18 Jun 1885, RA, Add. A/36.

20. HFP to MEP, 22 Jul 1884, RA, Add. A/36.

21. HFP to MEP, 13 Nov 1878, RA, Add. A/36

22. HFP to Lady Emily Ponsonby, 15 Mar 1873, RA, Add. A/36/515. For a similar case in 1885 see *LQV*, ser. 2, vol. 3, p. 675, n. 1.

23. HFP to MEP, 30 Jan 1884, RA, Add. A/36.

24. HFP to MEP, 30 Oct 1878, RA, Add. A/36.

25. AP, p. 146.

26. HFP to MEP, 23 Mar 1877, RA, Add. A/36/1202.

27. HFP to MEP, 30 Mar 1877, RA, Add. A/36/1205.

28. P. Emden, *Behind the Throne* (1934), p. 182.

29. See for example his reply to Lord Wolseley on the proposal that the queen's son, the duke of Connaught, should replace the duke of Cambridge as commander in chief, *LQV*, ser. 3, vol. 1, p. 679.

30. HFP to MEP, 4 Nov 1881, RA, Add. A/36.

31. HFP to MEP, 26 Apr 1884, RA, Add. A/36.

32. E. Longford, *Queen Victoria: Born to Succeed* , US paperback edn (1964; N.Y., 1965), p. 469.

33. HFP to MEP, 10 Nov 1884, RA, Add. A/36.

34. 23 Jan 1882, HFP mem., RA, Add. A/12/696.

35. HFP to MEP, 1 Sep 1894, RA, Add. A/36.

36. HFP to MEP, 13, 14, 16, 18 Jun 1879, RA, Add. A/36.

37. HFP to MEP, 1 Jun 1880, RA, Add. A/36.

38. *Ibid*.

39. HFP to MEP, 21 May 1881, RA, Add. A/36.

40. A. Ponsonby diary, 1871-93, written in retrospect [May 1911], TS, pp. 14, 5, SHL.

41. HFP to MEP, 14 Oct 1885, RA, Add. A/36.

42. HFP to MEP, 5 Jan 1886, RA, Add. A/36.

43. HFP to MEP, 19 Apr 1886, RA, Add. A/36.

44. AP, p. 248.

45. See HFP to MEP, 28 Mar 1881, RA, Add. A/36, in which Henry reported Gladstone had spoken to him in an 'agitated' and 'mournful way' about the way he held back the younger anti-monarchical members of his party.

46. HFP to MEP, 19 Nov 1883, RA, Add. A/36.

47. MP, p. 178.

48. HFP to MEP, 20 Apr 1886, RA, Add. A/36.

49. See H. Stopford to HFP, 4 Sep 1886, RA, Add. A/12/1296; AP, p. 398.

50. See Lord Salisbury to HFP, 31 Aug 1887, RA, Add. A/12/1498.

51. See MEP to HFP, 5 Jan 1886, and her draft letter to John Morley, 6 Jan 1886, RA, Add. A/36.

52. The unsigned telegram addressed to HFP and reporting the events at this home rule meeting, misattributed to Lord Rowton, is almost certainly from MEP; see 15 Apr 1886, *LQV*, p. 105.

53. HFP to MEP, 13 Apr 1886, RA, Add. A/36.

54. Undated [1908?], MEP Writings 1907, 1908, 1910, small blue book, SHL.

55. F.E.G. Ponsonby, *Sidelights on Queen Victoria* (1930), chs. 1-2.

56. HFP to SPF, 29 Apr 1887, RA, Add. A/12.

57. HFP to SPF, 30 Oct 1887, RA, Add. A/12.

58. See for example, F. Knollys to HFP, 17 Apr 1891, RA, Add. A/12/1773.

59. F. Knollys to HFP, 14 Apr 1892, RA, Add. A/12/1854.

60. HFP to MEP, 6 Aug 1884, RA, Add. A/36.

61. HFP to MEP, 16 Jun 1873, RA, Add. A/36/575.

62. Diary of Elizabeth Jane Waterpark, BL, Add. 60750, *passim*.

63. HFP to MEP, 29 Jan 1877, RA, Add. A/36/1181.

64. HFP to MEP, 22 Oct 1874, RA, Add. A/36/829.

65. HFP to MEP, 2 Sep 1878, RA, Add. A/36.

66. HFP to SPF, 30 Jan 1888, RA, Add. A/12.

67. W.M. Kuhn, 'Queen Victoria's Jubilees and the Invention of Tradition', *Victorian Poetry*, 25, nos. 3-4 (1987), p. 108.

68. HFP to MEP, 1 Apr 1890, RA, Add. A/36.

69. *LQV*, ser. 3, vol. 2, p. 70, 72.

70. HFP to MEP, 13 Apr 1892, RA, Add. A/36.

71. HFP to QV, 13 Feb 1887, RA, Add. A/12/1393.

72. *The Principal Speeches and Addressees of His Royal Highness the Prince Consort* (1862); *The Early Years of His Royal Highness the Prince Consort*, comp. under the direction of H. M. the Queen by C. Grey (1867).

73. M. Reid, *Ask Sir James: The Life of Sir James Reid, Personal Physician to Queen Victoria* (1987), pp. 54-5.

74. QV to HFP, 17 Jul 1883, RA, Add. A/12/842; the whole story is summarised in AP, pp. 146-7.

75. HFP to QV, [no date, but clearly a reply to no. 842], RA, Add. A/12/843.

76. T. Martin to HFP, 5 Jan 1884, RA, Add. A/12/889.

77. F. Knollys to HFP, 13 Jan 1884, RA, Add. A/12/890.

78. QV to HFP, 23 Feb 1884, RA, Add. A/12/899.

79. G.K.A. Bell, *Randall Davidson: Archbishop of Canterbury*, 3rd edn (1952), pp. 92-5.

80. HFP to MEP, 15 Sep 1873, RA, Add. A/36/637.

81. HFP to MEP, 3 Nov 1878, RA, Add. A/36.

82. HFP to MEP, 26 Aug 1890, RA, Add. A/36.

83. The verse, apparently by Lady John Manners, has a note that 'niggers' was a word used for royalties; it is in the box of HFP to MEP letters for the first half of 1880, RA, Add. A/36.

84. HFP to MEP, 21 Oct 1885, RA, Add. A/36.

85. A. Ponsonby diary, 1871-93, written in retrospect [May 1911], TS, p. 19, SHL.

86. F. Ponsonby, *Recollections of Three Reigns*, prepared for press with note and introductory memoir by C. Welch (1951), p. 13.

87. Burney, Frances (Fanny) later Mme d'Arblay (1752-1840), *DNB*.

88. HFP to MEP, 15 Nov 1890, RA, Add. A/36.

89. QV to HFP, 22 Jul 1886, RA, Add. A/12/1279.

90. QV to HFP, 2 Feb 1877, RA, Add. A/12/370.

91. HFP to MEP, 14 Mar 1894, RA, Add. A/36.

92. HFP to MEP, 30 Aug 1894, RA, Add. A/36.

93. HFP to MEP and children, 19 Sep 1894, SHL.

10. MEP Holds Court, *c.* 1893-1916

1. 'Smyth, Dame Ethel Mary (1858-1944)', *DNB*.

2. *The Memoirs of Ethel Smyth*, abridged and introduced by R. Crichton (Harmondsworth, 1987), p. 8.

3. E. Smyth, *As Time Went on ...* (1936), pp. 84-5.

4. Ponsonby, 'My Mother', TS, p. 1, SHL.

5. MEP to A. Ponsonby, 12 Aug 1891, vol. 1 of 3 vol. Arthur/MEP letters, SHL.

6. E. Smyth, *Impressions That Remained: Memoirs*, 2 vols. (1919), vol. 2, pp. 249-50.

7. Smyth, *As Time Went on ...* , p. 133.

8. *Ibid.*, p. 104.

9. MEP to JP, undated [1893], Haile.

10. MP, pp. 183-6.

11. Smyth, *As Time Went on ...* , p. 86.

12. *Ibid.*, pp. 233-4.

13. *Ibid.*

14. L. Collis, *Impetuous Heart: The Story of Ethel Smyth* (1984), p. 68.

15. *Ibid.*, p. 76.

16. Smyth, *As Time Went on ...* , p. 214.

17. B. Gardner, *The Lesbian Imagination (Victorian Style)* (New York and London, 1978), pp. 78-9, 81.

18. *Ibid.*, p. 71.

19. C. Lytton to A. Villiers, 8 Aug 1893, *Letters of Constance Lytton*, selected and arranged by B. Balfour (1925), p. 47.

20. *Ibid.*, p. 48.

21. P. Miles and J. Williams, *Uncommon Criminal, The Life of Lady Constance Lytton, Militant Suffragette* (Knebworth, 1999), p. 8.

22. See A. Ponsonby, 'My Mother', MS, SHL. One woman who, unlike the others, made it into Arthur's TS was Edith Sichel, who met MEP about the time of the First World War. She settled down with a female friend in the country at Chiddingford and established a home for girls from the East End of London. Sichel had fond memories of MEP; see E. Sichel, *New and Old* (1917), p. 56.

23. Smyth, *As Time Went on*, pp. 98-9.

24. *Ibid.*, p. 309.

25. MEP's use of the word may derive from her reading of J.-J. Rousseau: see *Emile*, intro., trans. and notes by A. Bloom (N.Y., 1979), p. 425. When she was first giving Betty her lessons, she objected to Rousseau's making women the centre of an idolatrous '*culte*' not unlike the way a lover places his female lover on a pedestal. So for her the word had both religious and romantic overtones.

26. P. Gunn, *Vernon Lee: Violet Paget, 1856-1935* (1964), p. 131.

27. A.V. Montgomery comments on draft of AP, SHL.

28. E. Smyth, *What Happened Next* (1940), pp. 125-6.

29. AP, p. 264.

30. M. Reid, *Ask Sir James: The Life of Sir James Reid, Personal Physician to Queen Victoria* (1987), pp. 162-3.

31. QV to the Empress Frederick, 7 Jan 1895, TS, RA, Add. U32/733.

32. O. Morshead to A. Ponsonby of Shulbrede, 16 Mar 1943, SHL.

33. Smyth, *What Happened Next*, p. 19.

34. 23 Jan, 14 Feb 1895, RA, QVJ.

35. MEP to J. Ponsonby, 1 Aug 1895, Haile.

36. Smyth, *What Happened Next*, p. 19.

37. MEP to J. Ponsonby, 6 May 1895, Haile.

38. See F. Edwards to QV for her approval, 2-3 Dec 1895, RA, PP Vic 13724.

39. By modern standards, the queen was stingy with pensions to the wives of her former secretaries. Charles Grey had a salary of £1,500 a year. After his death in 1870 the queen granted Caroline Grey an annuity worth only £500 a year according to the 'List of the Papers of General Charles Grey', Dept. of Palaeography and Diplomatic, University of Durham, p. 9. There is a mention of Mary Biddulph being in financial distress after the death of her husband in the letters from Henry to Mary Ponsonby, 1878, RA, Add. A/36.

40. *Life with Queen Victoria: Marie Mallet's Letters from Court 1887-1901*, ed. V. Mallet (Boston, 1968), p. 57.

41. *The Empress Frederick Writes to Sophia, Her Daughter, Crown Princess and Later Queen of the Hellenes*, ed. A. Gould Lee (1955), p. 187.

42. QV to Bigge, 8 May 1895 [copy], RA, C76/19.

43. QV to Ewart, 26 Nov 1895, RA, Add. A26/7.

44. Papers connected with the death of Henry Ponsonby, SHL.

45. W. Gibson to F. Edwards and Edwards's reply, 27 Dec 1895, RA, PP Vic 13477.

46. Will and codicils of Henry Frederick Ponsonby, Probate Registry, York.

47. F. Edwards to QV, 2-3 Dec 1895, RA, PP Vic 13724.

48. 19 Dec 1895, RA, QVJ.

49. Smyth, *What Happened Next*, p. 136.

50. MEP to J. Ponsonby, 12 Jan 1896, Haile.

51. Mar 1866, MEP self-examination diary, SHL.

52. MEP, 'An Attempt at Optimism', *The Nineteenth Century*, no. 235 (Sep 1896), p. 476.

53. *Ibid*.

54. MEP, 'Port Royal and Pascal', *The Nineteenth Century*, no. 312 (Feb 1903), p. 228, 239.

55. H.G. Wells and MEP reply, 'Science and Character' [letters to the editor], *The Westminster Gazette*, undated cuttings and TS, SHL.

56. MEP, 'Depreciation', MS, SHL.

57. MEP, 'The Role of Women in Society, I. In Eighteenth Century France', *The Nineteenth Century*, no. 286 (Dec 1900), p. 946.

58. Collis, p. 102.

59. 'Role of Women in Society, I', pp.945-6.

60. MEP, 'The Role of Women in Society, II, In Nineteenth-Century England', no. 287 (Jan 1901), p. 69.

61. *Ibid*., p. 66.

62. *Ibid*., p. 76.

63. See 3 Jan 1900 newspaper cutting, SHL.

64. MEP, 'George Eliot and George Sand', *The Nineteenth Century*, no. 296 (Oct 1901), pp. 607-16; 'Behind the Veil and Beyond' [on Vernon Lee], and 'The Simple Life', cuttings from unidentified journals, signed 'M.E.P.', SHL.

65. A.C. Benson, *Memories and Friends* (N.Y. and London, 1929), p. 73; A. Ponsonby, 'My Mother', TS, pp. 6, 8, SHL.

66. Smyth, *What Happened Next*, p. 170.

67. What follows is based mainly on P. Mattheisen, 'An Account of Queen Victoria', *The Journal of the Rutgers University Library*, 21 (Dec 1957), pp. 8-32; and 'The Character of Queen Victoria', *The Quarterly Review*, 193 (Apr 1901), pp. 301-37.

68. 'Queen Victoria', *Quarterly*, p. 302.

69. *Ibid*.

70. *Ibid*., p. 303.

71. *Ibid*., p. 311.

72. *Ibid*., p. 313.

73. *Ibid*., p. 312.

74. *Ibid*., p. 315.

75. *Ibid*., p. 324.

76. *Ibid*.

77. *Ibid*., p. 317.

78. *Ibid*., p. 320, 323.

79. *Ibid*., p. 327.

80. *Ibid*., p. 330.

81. *Ibid*.

82. *Ibid*., p. 331.

83. Quoted in Mattheisen, p. 10.

84. Anon. ['by one of Her Majesty's servants'], *The Private Life of the Queen*, intro. by Emily Sheffield (1897; reprint with new intro. 1979).

85. *Letters of the Empress Frederick*, ed. F. Ponsonby (1929).

86. N. Mitford to E. Waugh, 1 Dec 1951, *The Letters of Nancy Mitford & Evelyn Waugh*, ed. C. Mosley (1996), p. 253.

87. 5 Jul 1904, A.C. Benson diary, vol. 55, Magdalene College, Cambridge.

88. 24 May 1906, A.C. Benson diary, vol. 82, Magdalene College, Cambridge.

89. 2 May 1907, A.C. Benson diary, vol. 92, Magdalene College, Cambridge.

90. Apr-Jun 1912, A.C. Benson diary, vol. 132, Magdalene College, Cambridge.

91. L. Lindsay, *Grace & Favour: The Memoirs of Loelia, Duchess of Westminster* (1961), p. 25.

92. Undated [1908?], MEP journal, small blue book, 'Writings 1907, 1908, 1910', SHL.

93. *Ibid*.

94. A. Ponsonby, 'My Mother', TS, p. 6, SHL.

95. A.V. Montgomery, 'Phases of Thought and Favourite Writers', TS, p. 14, SHL.

96. *The Times* appreciation is reprinted in Benson, *Memories and Friends*; see also Oct-Dec 1916, A.C. Benson diary, vol. 162, Magdalene College, Cambridge.

97. 26 Dec 1916, *The Times*, p. 9.

98. Thanks to Veronica Hodges for this information.

99. Last will and testament of MEP, 18 Dec 1906 and codicil, 11 Jan 1911.

Epilogue

1. AP, p. xi; A. Ponsonby, 'My Mother', TS, p. 2, SHL; R. A. Jones, *Arthur Ponsonby: The Politics of a Life* (Bromley 1989), pp. 231-3.

2. O.F. Morshead to A. Ponsonby, 15 Mar 1938, SHL.

3. *Ibid*.

4. *Ibid*.

5. O.F. Morshead to A. Ponsonby, 14 Jan 1942, SHL.

6. A. Lascelles to A. Ponsonby, 15 Jan 1942, SHL.

7. C. Wigram to A. Ponsonby, 15 Jan 1942, SHL.

8. A. Hardinge to A. Ponsonby, 28 Jan 1942, SHL.

9. O.F. Morshead to A. Ponsonby, 31 Jan 1942, SHL.

10. *Ibid*.

11. O.F. Morshead to A. Ponsonby, 7 Feb 1942, SHL.

12. C. Colville to A. Ponsonby, 18 Feb 1942, SHL.

13. O.F. Morshead to A. Ponsonby, 16 Feb 1942, SHL.

14. O.F. Morshead to A. Ponsonby, 18 Feb 1942 [first letter], SHL.

15. O.F. Morshead to A. Ponsonby, 18 Feb 1942 [second letter], SHL.

16. O.F. Morshead to A. Ponsonby, 17 Sep 1942, SHL.

17. A. Lascelles to A. Ponsonby, 1 Nov 1942, SHL.

18. V. Bogdanor, *The Monarchy and the Constitution* (Oxford, 1995).

19. F. Prochaska, *Royal Bounty: The Making of a Welfare Monarchy* (New Haven and London, 1995); *The Republic of Britain 1760-2000* (2000).

20. F. Mount, *The British Constitution Now: Recovery or Decline?* (1992), p. 96.

21. C. Douglas-Home, *Dignified and Efficient: The British Monarchy in the Twentieth Century*, completed by S. Kelly (Brinkworth, Wiltshire, 2000), p. 214.

22. HFP to MEP, 6 Jun 1874, RA, Add. A/36/757.

Select Bibliography

Manuscript Sources

The British Library. Diaries of Elizabeth Jane, Lady Waterpark [*née* Anson], Add. 60750.

Bryn Mawr College, Bryn Mawr, Pennsylvania. Letters of Laurence Housman and Magdalen Ponsonby.

Girton College, Cambridge. Letters of Mary Ponsonby and A.V. Montgomery as well as Printed Appeal Literature.

Haile Hall. Letters and albums of Major General Sir John Ponsonby.

Magdalene College, Cambridge. Diaries of A.C. Benson.

The Royal Archives, Windsor. Henry Ponsonby's correspondence with Mary Ponsonby (Add. A/36), as well as a collection of his office papers, including letters to Spencer Ponsonby-Fane and Horace Seymour (Add. A/12).

Shulbrede Priory. Diaries, letters, logbooks, photograph albums and miscellaneous papers belonging to Henry and Mary Ponsonby, as well as to their parents, brothers, sisters and five children.

Published Sources
[The place of publication is London unless noted otherwise.]

Albert, HRH Prince [The Prince Consort]. *The Principal Speeches and Addresses of His Royal Highness the Prince Consort*. 1862.

Altick, R.D. *Punch: The Lively Youth of a British Institution, 1841-51*. Columbus, 1997.

Arnstein, W.L. 'The Warrior Queen: Reflections on Victoria and Her World'. *Albion* 30 (1998): pp. 1-28.

Aronson, T. *Victoria and Disraeli: The Making of a Romantic Friendship*. 1997.

Barnett, C. *Britain and Her Army 1509-1970*. 1970.

Beckett, J.C. *A Short History of Ireland*. Rev. edn 1966.

Bell, G.K.A. *Randall Davidson: Archbishop of Canterbury*. 3rd edn 1952.

Benson, A.C. *Memories and Friends*. New York, 1927.

Blake, R. [Lord Blake] *Disraeli*. 1966.

——— *Gladstone, Disraeli, and Queen Victoria*. Oxford, 1993.

Bogdanor, V. *The Monarchy and the Constitution*. Oxford, 1995.

Bradbrook, M.C. 'That Infidel Place': A Short History of Girton College, 1869-1969. 1969.

Caine, B. *English Feminism 1780-1980*. Oxford, 1997.

——— *Victorian Feminists*. Oxford, 1992.

Cherry, B. and N. Pevsner. *Devon*. 2nd edn 1989.

Collis, L. *Impetuous Heart: The Story of Ethel Smyth*. 1984.

Curry, B. 'The Sovereign's Private Secretary'. *History Today* 9 (1959): pp. 122-31.

David, S. *The Homicidal Earl: The Life of Lord Cardigan*. 1997.

Douglas-Home, C. *Dignified and Efficient: The British Monarchy in the Twentieth Century*. Completed by S. Kelly. Brinkworth, 2000.

Duman, D. *The Judicial Bench in England 1727-1875*. 1982.

Emden, P. *Behind the Throne*. 1934.

'English Republicanism [Signed A Working Man]'. *Fraser's Magazine* 83 old series, 3 new series (1871): pp. 751-61.

Faderman, L. *Surpassing the Love of Men: Romantic Friendship and Love Between Women from the Renaissance to the Present*. New York, 1981.

Gardiner, A.G. *The Life of Sir William Harcourt*. 2 vols. New York, 1923.

Gardner, B. *The Lesbian Imagination (Victorian Style)*. New York and London, 1978.

[Gosse, E. and Mary Elizabeth Ponsonby.] 'The Character of Queen Victoria'. *The Quarterly Review* 193 (1901): pp. 301-37

Gould Lee, A., ed. *The Empress Frederick Writes to Sophia, Her Daughter, Crown Princess and Later Queen of the Hellenes*. 1955.

Graham, L.J. *If the King Only Knew: Seditious Speech in the Reign of Louis XV*. Charlottesville and London, 2000.

Grey, General C., comp., under the direction of H. M. the Queen. *The Early Years of His Royal Highness the Prince Consort*. 1867.

Gunn, P. *Vernon Lee: Violet Paget, 1856-1935*. 1964.

Haight, G.S., ed. *The George Eliot Letters*. 9 vols. 1954-78.

Heffer, S. *Power and Place: The Political Consequences of King Edward VII*. 1998.

Homans, M. *Royal Representations: Queen Victoria and British Culture, 1837-76*. Chicago and London, 1998.

Horgan, P. *Maurice Baring Restored*. 1970.

Houston, G. Turley. *Royalties: The Queen and Victorian Writers*. Charlottesville and London, 1999.

Jalland, P. *Women, Marriage, and Politics 1860-1914*. Oxford, 1986.

Jones, R.A. *Arthur Ponsonby: The Politics of Life*. Bromley, 1989.

Kuhn, W.M. *Democratic Royalism: The Transformation of the British Monarchy, 1861-1914*. Basingstoke and New York, 1996.

—— 'Queen Victoria's Civil List: What Did She Do with It?' *Historical Journal* 36 (1993): pp. 645-65.

—— 'Queen Victoria's Jubilees and the Invention of Tradition'. *Victorian Poetry* 25 (1987): pp. 107-14.

Law, E. *History of Hampton Court*. 3 vols. 1888-91.

Levine, P. *Feminist Lives in Victorian England: Private Roles and Public Commitment*. Oxford, 1990.

Lindsay, L. *Grace and Favour: The Memoirs of Loelia, Duchess of Westminster*. New York, 1961.

Lindsay, W.A. *The Royal Household*. 1898.

Longford, E. *Queen Victoria: Born to Succeed*. 1964.

—— *Wellington: The Years of the Sword*. 1969.

Lytton, Constance. *Letters of Constance Lytton*. Selected and arranged by B. Balfour. 1925.

McDowell, R.B. *The Irish Administration, 1801-1914*. London and Toronto, 1964.

Mackworth-Young, R. 'The Royal Archives, Windsor Castle'. *Archives* 8 (1978): pp. 115-30.

Mallet, V., ed. *Life with Queen Victoria: Marie Mallet's Letters from Court 1887-1901*. Boston, 1968.

Mandler, P. *Aristocratic Government in the Age of Reform*. Oxford, 1990.

Matthieson, P. 'An Account of Queen Victoria'. *The Journal of the Rutgers University Library* 21 (1957): pp. 8-32.

Maxwell, Sir H., Bt. *The Life and Letters of the Fourth Earl of Clarendon*. 2 vols. 1913.

Miles, P. and J. Williams. *Uncommon Criminal: The Life of Lady Constance Lytton, Militant Suffragette*. Knebworth, 1999.

Millar, D. *Queen Victoria's Life in the Scottish Highlands*. 1985.
────── *The Victorian Watercolours and Drawings in the Collection of H.M. The Queen*. 2 vols. 1995.
Morris, M. *The British Monarchy and the French Revolution*. New Haven and London, 1998.
Mount, F. *The British Constitution Now: Recovery or Decline?* 1992.
Munich, A. *Queen Victoria's Secrets*. New York, 1996.
Orgel, S. 'Familiar Greatness'. In *The Power of Forms in the English Renaissance*, edited by S. Greenblatt. Norman, 1982.
────── *The Illusion of Power: Political Theatre in the English Renaissance*. Berkeley and London, 1975.
Pimlott, B. *The Queen: A Biography of Elizabeth II*. 1996.
Ponsonby, A. [Lord Ponsonby of Shulbrede] *Casual Observations*. 1930.
────── *English Diaries: A Review of English Diaries from the Sixteenth to the Twentieth Century with an Introduction on Diary Writing*. 1923.
────── *Henry Ponsonby, Queen Victoria's Private Secretary: His Life from His Letters*. 1942.
────── *Queen Victoria*. 1933.
Ponsonby, F. [Lord Sysonby], ed. *Letters of the Empress Frederick*. 1929.
────── *Recollections of Three Reigns*. Prepared for press and introduction by C. Welch. 1951. With introduction by A. Lambton and preface by L. Lindsay. 1988.
────── *Sidelights on Queen Victoria*. 1930.
Ponsonby, Major General Sir J. *The Bulteel Family*. Privately printed, 1942.
────── *The Ponsonby Family*. 1929.
Ponsonby, Magdalen, ed. *Mary Ponsonby, A Memoir, Some Letters and A Journal*. 1927.
Ponsonby, Mary Elizabeth. 'An Attempt at Optimism'. *The Nineteenth Century*, no. 235 (1896): pp. 474-7.
────── 'George Eliot and George Sand'. *The Nineteenth Century*, no. 296 (1901): pp. 610-11.
────── 'Port Royal and Pascal'. *The Nineteenth Century*, no. 312 (1903): pp. 225-40.
────── 'The Role of Women in Society, I. In Eighteenth-Century France'. *The Nineteenth Century*, no. 286 (1900): pp. 941-54.
────── 'The Role of Women in Society, II. In Nineteenth-Century England'. *The Nineteenth Century*, no. 287 (1901): pp. 64-76.
The Private Life of the Queen. 1897. Reprint, 1979.
Prochaska, F. *The Republic of Britain*. 2000.
────── *Royal Bounty: The Making of a Welfare Monarchy*. London and New Haven, 1995.
Ramm, A., ed. *The Political Correspondence of Mr. Gladstone and Lord Granville 1868-76*. Royal Historical Society, Camden Third Series, vols. 81-2. 1952.
Reid, M. *Ask Sir James: The Life of Sir James Reid, Personal Physician to Queen Victoria*. 1987.
Reynolds, K.D. *Aristocratic Women and Political Society in Victorian Britain*. Oxford, 1998.
Röhl, J.C.G. *Young Wilhelm: The Kaiser's Early Life, 1859-88*. Translated by J. Gaines and R. Wallach. Cambridge, 1998.
Sainty, J.C. and R.O. Bucholz, eds. *Office Holders in Modern Britain, XI, Officials of the Royal Household 1660-1837, Part I: Department of the Lord Chamberlain and Associated Offices*. 1997.
Sichel, E. *New and Old*. 1917.
Smith, E.A. *George IV*. New Haven and London, 1999.
Smith, P. *Disraeli: A Brief Life*. Cambridge, 1996.
Smyth, E. *As Time Went On … .* 1936.

—— *Impressions That Remained*: Memoirs. 2 vols. 1919.

—— *Maurice Baring*. 1938.

—— *The Memoirs of Ethyl Smyth*. Abridged and introduced by R. Crichton. Harmondsworth, 1987.

—— *What Happened Next*. 1940.

The Society for Promoting the Employment of Women. *Annual Reports*. 1859-.

Strachey, R. *'The Cause': A Short History of the Women's Movement in Great Britain*. 1928.

Sutherland, G. 'The Movement for the Higher Education of Women: Its Social and Intellectual Context in England, c. 1840-80'. In *Politics and Social Change in Modern Britain*, edited by P.J. Waller. Brighton, 1987.

Vallone, Lynne. *Becoming Victoria*. New Haven and London, 2001.

Van Norden, H. 'The Origin and Early Development of the Office of Private Secretary to the Sovereign'. PhD diss., Columbia University, 1952.

Vicinus, Martha. *Independent Women: Work and Community for Single Women 1850-1920*. 1985.

Victoria, Queen. *Leaves from the Journal of Our Life in the Highlands*. Edited by A. Helps. 1868.

—— *More Leaves from the Journal of a Life in the Highlands, 1862-82*. 1884.

—— *The Letters of Queen Victoria*. First series, 1837-61. Edited by A.C. Benson and Viscount Esher. 3 vols. 1907. Second series, 1862-78. Edited by G.E. Buckle. 3 vols. 1926-28. Third series, 1879-1901. Edited by G.E. Buckle. 1930-2.

Wantanabe-O'Kelly, H. 'The Fabrication of the Image of Johann Georg, Elector of Saxony'. Paper delivered at the Society for Court Studies, London, March 2000.

Watt-Carter, D. *Flete: A Historical Review*. 2nd edn Aynhoe Park, 1997.

Williams, R. *The Contentious Crown: Public Discussion of the British Monarchy in the Reign of Queen Victoria*. Aldershot, 1997.

Wills, G. *St Augustine*. New York, 1999.

Woolf, V. *A Room of One's Own*. 1929.

Zeepvat, C. *Prince Leopold: The Untold Story of Queen Victoria's Youngest Son*. Stroud, 1998.

Ziegler, P. *King William IV*. 1971.

Index

DUCKBACKS

The Life of Walter de la Mare
Theresa Whistler   £9.99 Paperback   0 7156 3216 7

Walter de la Mare is the writer of his age most in need of reappraisal. Well-known in his lifetime, with a wide circle of literary friends, including Edward Thomas, Rupert Brooke, Katherine Mansfield and Thomas Hardy, he has been largely ignored by recent critics. Few know of his personal life, of his loving but difficult marriage, and his passionate, platonic affair with Naomi Ryde-Smith which was so crucial to his poetry. *The Life of Walter de la Mare* provides us with a remarkable reassessment of the man and his work.

'Impeccably researched and written, it is difficult to see how this biography could be bettered, much less replaced.'   *London Evening Standard*

Siegfried Sassoon: The Making of a War Poet
Jean Moorcroft Wilson   £9.99 Paperback   0 7156 3121 7

The first volume of Jean Moorcroft Wilson's magnificent biography of one of the twentieth century's finest poets, published in conjunction with the eagerly awaited second volume. Wilson traces the origins both of Sassoon's patriotism and of his anti-war stance that culminated in a statement that was read out in Parliament and a spell in a convalescent home, covering his life up until the end of the Great War.

'A story in which the roots are as interesting as the core ... invaluable to historians of the period.'   Andrew Motion, *The Times*

'Thorough and perceptive'   Jeremy Lewis, *Observer*

ORDER FORM (BLOCK CAPITALS PLEASE)

SURNAME_____ FIRST NAME_____

ADDRESS_____

_____ POSTCODE_____

METHOD OF PAYMENT (PLEASE TICK AS APPROPRIATE)

☐ Invoice to my Grantham Book Services account
☐ By cheque (payable to Duckworth Publishers)
☐ Please send account opening details (trade customers only)
☐ By credit card (Access/ Visa / Mastercard / Amex)

Card no: ☐☐☐☐ ☐☐☐☐ ☐☐☐☐ ☐☐☐☐

Expiry date: / / Authorising Signature: _____

POSTAGE (Private customers) Please note that the following postage and packing charges should be added to your order:

UK deliveries: £4 on orders up to £20; £5 on orders over £20
Export surface: £5 for first book + £1 for each additional book
Export airmail: £9 for the first book + £2 for each additional book

QTY	ISBN	TITLE	PRICE	TOTAL
__	_____	_____	£_____	£_____
__	_____	_____	£_____	£_____
__	_____	_____	£_____	£_____
__	_____	_____	£_____	£_____
__	_____	_____	£_____	£_____

POSTAGE £_____

TOTAL £_____

To: Sales Dept, Duckworth, 90-93 Cowcross Street, London EC1M 6BF
Tel: 020 7490 7300 Fax: 020 7490 0080
Heidi@duckworth-publishers.co.uk